A Nobel Fellow
on Every Floor

A Nobel Fellow on Every Floor

A History of the Medical Research
Council Laboratory
of Molecular Biology

John Finch

Published in the UK in 2008 by
The Medical Research Council
Laboratory of Molecular Biology
Hills Road
Cambridge CB2 0QH

ISBN: 978-1840469-40-0

Typeset in 11/13 Classical Garamond by Marie Doherty

Book production by Icon Books, Cambridge

Printed and bound by 1010 Printing

Contents

Origin of the Book   xi
Author's Introduction   xiii

1   **How molecular biology came to the Cavendish**   1
     Lawrence Bragg   1
     J.D. Bernal   3
     Max Perutz   5
     John Kendrew   9

2   **The MRC Unit**   11
     Medical Research Council Unit for the Study of the Molecular
     Structure of Biological Systems   11
     Hugh Huxley   12
     The phase problem   14
     The phase problem solved   16
     The structure of myoglobin   17
     Haemoglobin   20
     David Blow   21
     Michael Rossmann   23

3   **Watson and Crick and DNA**   27
     Francis Crick   27
     Jim Watson   30
     Maurice Wilkins   32
     Rosalind Franklin   33
     DNA model 1   35
     DNA model 2   36

4   **Post DNA**   53
     Virus structure – Don Caspar   53
     Vernon Ingram   55
     Sydney Brenner   56
     The genetic code   58
     Transfer and messenger RNAs   59

5	**Accommodation – The new LMB**	**61**
	The Austin Wing	61
	The hut	62
	Fred Sanger	64
	Moves for a new building	66
	The Birkbeck group	68
	The new LMB	71
	Michael Fuller	73
	The move	74
	Four Nobel Prizes	76
6	**Structural Studies**	**79**
	Max Perutz and the haemoglobin group	80
	After retirement	82
	'The new Marxism' – defending the MRC	84
	John Kendrew and the myoglobin group	87
	The myoglobin group	87
	Hugh Huxley and the muscle group	88
	Electron microscopy	88
	X-ray work – more powerful sources	90
	Electron microscopes	95
	Uli Arndt	96
	David Blow	100
	Rossmann and Blow	100
	α-Chymotrypsin	101
	Brian Matthews and Paul Sigler	101
	Flying Spot densitometer	104
	Richard Henderson and Tom Steitz	105
	tRNA synthetase	106
	Alan Wonacott	107
	Tony Jack	107
	Move to Imperial	109
	Alan Fersht	110
	Gerard Bricogne	110
	Jude Smith	111
	Aaron Klug	113
	Ken Holmes	115
	Reuben Leberman	115
	Caspar and Klug – quasi-equivalence	117
	Optical diffraction and filtering	117
	Towards 3D reconstruction	120
	Tobacco mosaic virus	121
	tRNA	123

Other nucleic acid work   126
Chromatin and the nucleosome   127
Zinc finger   131
Alzheimer's disease   133
Uli Laemmli and Jake Maizel – 'SDS gels'   133
Linda Amos   138
Anne Bloomer   139
Jo Butler   140
Tony Crowther   141
Daniela Rhodes   142
Later groups and people   143
Brad Amos   143
Joyce Baldwin   144
Chris Calladine   145
Cyrus Chothia   147
Bob Diamond   147
Phil Evans   148
Wasi Faruqi   149
Judd Fermi   150
Richard Henderson   151
Terry Horsnell   152
John (Jake) Kendrick-Jones   153
Andrew Leslie   154
Michael Levitt   155
Jade Li   155
Andrew McLachlan   156
Hilary Muirhead   157
Kiyoshi Nagai   158
David Neuhaus – NMR   158
Venki Ramakrishnan   159
Clarence Schutt   160
Murray Stewart   160
Nigel Unwin   161
Alan Weeds   162

7   Molecular Genetics (became Cell Biology in 1970)   167
Francis Crick   168
Sydney Brenner   170
Sidney Altman   171
Joan Steitz   172
Mark Bretscher   172
John Smith   175
Tony Stretton   177

Rita Fishpool, Eileen Southgate, Leslie Barnett, Muriel Wigby   177
   Rita Fishpool   177
   Eileen Southgate   177
   Leslie Barnett   179
   Muriel Wigby   180
Andrew Travers   180
Brian Clark   182
Division of Cell Biology   182
   Nichol Thomson   184
   John White   185
John Sulston   187
Genetic engineering   189
Sydney – Director   190
Genomes – The Sanger Centre   191
New groups and people   194
   Peter Lawrence   194
   Michael Wilcox   195
   John Gurdon and Ron Laskey   196
   Mariann Bienz   197
   Matthew Freeman   198
   Jonathan Hodgkin   198
   Jon Karn   199
   Rob Kay   199
   John Kilmartin   201
   Ed Lennox   202
   Graeme Mitchison   202
   Sean Munro   203
   Kim Nasmyth   203
   Barbara Pearse   204
   Hugh Pelham   204
   Karol Sikora   205

8 **Protein Chemistry (became Protein and Nucleic Acid Chemistry in 1965)** 209
Fred Sanger   210
   RNA   210
   DNA   214
Brian Hartley   222
Ieuan Harris   224
John Walker   225
César Milstein   230
   Monoclonal antibodies   233
Patent problems and later developments – technology transfer   238
   Greg Winter and CAT   240

CONTENTS

Terry Rabbitts   245
Michael Neuberger   247

9   **Other Sections**   **253**
    The Mechanical Workshop   253
        X-ray generators   256
        The confocal microscope   257
        Other work   260
    The Techniques Laboratory – Electronics   260
    The Library   262
    Archives   264
    Photography – Visual Aids   265
    Peptide and nucleic acid chemistry and synthesis   267
    Director's Section   269
    Computers and computing   270
        Main computers   270
        JANET   270
        Control computers   270
        Crystallographic computing   271
    The canteen   275
    Institutions   280
        Laboratory talks   280
        Christmas party   280
        Christmas raffle   283
    Recreation   284

10 **Appendices**   **293**
    Growth of LMB   293
        Thirteen-bay extension   294
        Workshop extension   294
        Block 7   294
        The Clinical School   295
        CPE Building   295
        Max Perutz Lecture Theatre   295
        The Titanic   298
        The Hutch   299
        The Sanger Centre   299
    Administration   299
    Awards to Inventors   300
    Memories of LMB and earlier   300
        Sidney Altman   300
        Dick Dickerson   307
        Michael Levitt   312

Anand Sarabhai   315
Mitsuhiro Yanagida   320
Nikolai Kiselev   321
Jim Paulson   324
Andrås Fodor   326
Ron Morris   328
Bob Sweet   330
Leigh Anderson   330
Email from Tom Steitz to Richard Henderson on the death of Max   332
Keith Moffat's letter   335
Structure of globlglobin – Jerry Donohue   337
Farewell speech to Dan Brown by Greg Winter   343

Chronology   345
    Directors/Chairmen   345
    Timeline   346

List of Photographs   357

Index of Photographs   365
Index   369

Origin of the Book

When I started my ten years as Director at LMB, following on from Max Perutz, Sydney Brenner and Aaron Klug, I felt that the wonderful history of LMB, stretching back for 50 years or more, was beginning to fade from memory. The younger students and postdocs, who were naturally focused on the latest discoveries, knew little about the revolutionary achievements made by the founders of the Laboratory.

We started a small archive and history group and looked for someone to write a book about the origin and evolution of the Laboratory, and soon discovered that Soraya de Chadarevian, a member of the Department of History and Philosophy of Science at Cambridge, had already been working on a book, supported by a Wellcome Trust grant. Her topic was broader than we planned, covering the history of molecular biology in the UK. Her scholarly monograph, *Designs for Life: Molecular Biology after World War II*, was published in 2002 and has met with wide acclaim.

Soraya suggested that there might be another book to be written, providing more of an informal family history of the Laboratory including events and photographs of sentimental as well as historical interest.

As it happened, John Finch had just reached the normal retirement age, having joined the Laboratory when it opened on the Addenbrooke's site, so he was well acquainted with many of the people and events. After some thought, John agreed that this would be a great project, but I'm sure he did not imagine that it might take ten years to complete. It has been a massive undertaking. Annette Faux, our now full-time LMB archivist, has recently joined John in his project. Annette came to the Laboratory in 2001 and has worked on the assimilation and annotation of all the photographs.

This book captures and illuminates the excitement of the inception and development of molecular biology, to which LMB has made many key contributions. I am sure it will appeal to the many members of the Laboratory, present and past, who want to find out about or be reminded of earlier events and personalities. It will also appeal to people who seek an informal account of a remarkable period of scientific history.

Richard Henderson
25 April 2007

Author's Introduction

I retired officially in 1995 and, as well as finishing up the odd bits of science I was involved with, spent my first year of retirement organising a meeting in honour of Aaron Klug, marking his 70th birthday and the end of his ten years as Director of LMB. After a few months in Japan, in Masashi Suzuki's laboratory, I returned to LMB with an invitation to collaborate with Wes Sundquist, on the structure of tubes of the core protein of HIV that he was making in Utah. Richard Henderson, who was now the LMB Director, then asked if I would like to write a history of the laboratory. Since I had been in LMB since its beginning, and was now retired and had time for such things (and there was no one else), I seemed a good candidate for doing this, 'with the knowledge and perspective of an insider'. After some deliberation, I agreed, although it began very slowly for the first year or two, with most of my time being spent working on the HIV tubes and other things.

Richard's initial idea was that my book would follow what happened to the people and groups who made up the intake into the LMB when it was opened in 1962. The idea of following people rather than the strict science suggested more of a 'family history' of the laboratory than the academic history of molecular biology that was being written by Soraya in her *Designs for Life*. However, it seemed natural to put the family into context with its history, pre-LMB, and with other groups and people that have joined LMB later. But as about 3,000 scientists have worked at LMB since 1962, this has been rather selective and biased by my own knowledge (and lack of it).

The pre-LMB history is described in the first five chapters. The first two tell how Max Perutz came to work at the Cavendish in 1938, of the creation of the MRC Unit there in 1947 and of the first protein structures in 1958 and 1960. The third chapter tells of Watson and Crick and the DNA structure, and the fourth, of Crick's transition with Sydney Brenner towards molecular genetics. The fifth chapter describes the events leading up to the creation of the new LMB.

Chapters 6–8 record what happened to the groups after their installation in the three Divisions in the new laboratory. Chapter 6, dealing with the Structural Studies Division, is considerably larger than the others. This is partly because that Division has been numerically greater than the others, and partly because of the many different topics studied by Aaron Klug, but no doubt helped by my being a member of that Division myself. The various back-up sections, such as the workshops and library and some laboratory institutions, are described in Chapter 9, and other history and memories of LMB alumni are collected in Chapter 10.

The time span is rather variable – of the initial laboratory occupants, John Kendrew more-or-less ceased his research work on coming to LMB, although he continued on the organisational and administration sides until he left in 1975. Aaron Klug, at the other extreme still (in 2006) has a small research group. I have not included the Neurobiology Division which was set up in 1993, much later than the others, but its eldest LMB inhabitants, Nigel Unwin and Michel Goedert, are dealt with in their previous incarnations in Structural Studies and the Director's Section.

As with any family history and its photographic records, the most interested will be the family itself, and I hope the book will be a pleasant and useful reminder of life in LMB. Following the laboratory tradition, I have kept to first names as far as possible, although in some places surnames are used where they feel more suitable.

I have gathered much information from the laboratory archive collection of audio- and video-tapes of interviews with and talks by staff and ex-staff. Much of what I have written has been gathered from, and vetted and added to, by the people concerned. Various history books and articles have been consulted, as indicated in the text.

Most of the photographs are from the collection of our Visual Aids section, although quite a few of the earlier ones come from the Cold Spring Harbor Symposia and from people who were sufficiently farseeing to take them at the time and keep them.

Thanks to Sid Altman, Brad Amos, Uli Arndt, Joyce Baldwin, Bart Barrell, David Blow, Mark Bretscher, Dan Brown, George Brownlee, Jo Butler, Alan Coulson, Valerie Coulson, Bob Diamond, Wasi Faruqi, Mick Fordham, Michael Fuller, John Gurdon, Dave Hart, Brian Hartley, Ken Harvey, Richard Henderson, Jonathan Hodgkin, Terry Horsnell, Ross Jakes, Rob Kay, John Kendrick-Jones, John Kilmartin, Aaron Klug, Annette Lenton, Brian Matthews, Andrew McLachlan, Angela Mott, Hilary Muirhead, Michael Neuberger, David Neuhaus, Brian Pope, Terry Rabbitts, Michael Rossmann, David Secher, Jude Smith (now Jude Short), Wes Sundquist, Nichol Thomson, Andrew Travers, Alan Weeds, Tony Woollard and everyone else who provided material for inclusion and also those who allowed the reproduction of their mem-ories of LMB and letters in the Appendices in chapter 10. Thanks also to Soraya de Chadarevian, Richard Henderson, Tony Crowther, Mark Bretscher, Peter Lawrence, Cristina Rada and David Secher for reading through, correcting and commenting on large chunks of the text. Thanks too to Neil Grant who spent much time getting many of the photographs used in a form suitable for publication.

Thanks also to Robin Offord for providing me with the title; 'there's a Nobel Fellow on every floor' was a line in the song he wrote and sang at the celebrations for the four Nobel Prizes awarded to Max Perutz, John Kendrew, Francis Crick and Jim Watson in 1962.

I would like especially to thank Annette Faux, who had the mammoth tasks of locating and sorting out all the photographs included in this book and finding out the answers to queries that cropped up during the writing process.

John Finch
May 2007

CHAPTER ONE

How molecular biology came to the Cavendish

With its strong reputation for basic physics under Rutherford in the 1930s, the Cavendish Laboratory may seem an incongruous spawning ground for molecular biology. It came about because Cambridge was the birthplace of the use of X-ray diffraction for structure determination: W.L. (later Sir Lawrence) Bragg initiated its use for his work on salts and minerals, and J.D. Bernal began its application to protein crystals, and attracted Max Perutz and John Kendrew.

LAWRENCE BRAGG

W.L. Bragg was born in 1890 and educated in Adelaide, where his father, W.H. Bragg, was the Physics Professor (and his grandmother the Alice of Alice Springs). The family came to England in 1909 when his father was appointed to the Physics chair at Leeds, and Bragg began as an undergraduate at Cambridge.

He had just graduated in 1912 when the first X-ray diffraction photographs from a crystal (of zinc blende, ZnS) were reported from Friedrich and Knipping in Munich. The main aim of the experiment was to demonstrate the wave nature of X-rays, and their paper was accompanied by one from Max von Laue attempting to interpret the results in terms of the crystal structure. However, the structure was more complicated than von Laue assumed and there was also confusion on the mechanism of diffraction, so that even the proponents of wave X-rays did not find the explanation convincing.

Bragg's father had been interested in X-rays since their discovery in 1895 and because he believed they were particles, Bragg was initially also biased towards this view and suggested that the X-ray patterns were produced by particles being channelled down avenues between atoms. But on thinking of the treatment of light diffraction by a diffraction grating, he realised that the X-ray pattern could be explained by the selective reflection of specific wavelengths from a continuous spectrum of wave X-rays, from planes of atoms in the crystal according to the same equation $n\lambda = 2d\sin\theta$. This did not explain the ZnS pattern if a simple cubic lattice were assumed, but did so completely if the cubic lattice were face-centred. Thus Bragg confirmed that the phenomenon was diffraction, that X-rays were of a wave character, and also that they could be used to determine crystal structures. These results were presented at a meeting of the Cambridge Philosophical Society in November 1912, reported in *Nature* in December, and in more detail in a 1913 paper.

Bragg was keen to pursue the diffraction work and W.J. Pope, the Professor of Chemistry in Cambridge, who was interested in the theories of crystal lattices, suggested he work on NaCl, KCl, KBr and KI and obtained large crystals for him. The X-ray photographs obtained by Bragg were simpler than those from zinc blende and led to a complete solution of their structure. However, the conditions for experimental work at the Cavendish were not very satisfactory as Bragg later described:

1. *Lawrence Bragg, c. 1915.*
Courtesy of AIP Emilio Segrè Visual Archives,
Weber Collection.

> When I achieved the first X-ray reflections, I worked the Rumkorff coil too hard in my excitement and burnt out the platinum contact. Lincoln, the mechanic was very annoyed as a contact cost ten shillings (a week's wages at the time) and refused to provide me with another for a month. I could never have exploited my ideas about X-ray diffraction under such conditions.[1]

On the detection side too, the X-ray spectrometer at Leeds, built by his father, was far superior to the Laue-film set-up he had used earlier in Cambridge, and so he continued his work immediately in 1912 at Leeds. The crystals were 'supplied' by the Mineralogy Department at Cambridge – the Professor of Mineralogy had given strict orders that no minerals should ever leave the collections, but Arthur Hutchinson, who was then a lecturer in the Department, smuggled them out for Bragg. The structures of the selected halides, and of zinc blende (ZnS), fluorspar (CaF), iron pyrites (FeS) and calcite ($CaCO_3$) were published in 1913, but further work was interrupted by the start of the First World War in 1914.

Bragg spent most of the war working on a system of locating enemy guns by recording the arrival of their sounds at different places. Among the problems to solve were the identification of the sound of one particular gun, to distinguish between its report and the associated shock wave, and also to find a way of recording the time intervals precisely. The problems were solved sufficiently well that a fairly reliable system was in use from the beginning of 1917.

It was during this work, in 1915, that Bragg heard that he and his father had been jointly awarded the Nobel Prize for Physics, Bragg for his work on diffraction and crystal structure and his father for his study on the origin and properties of X-rays. Bragg's ideas on X-ray diffraction and his immediate application in using them to solve structures had made a great impression. It now became possible to establish structure at the atomic level. It was soon applied and resulted in dramatic advances in chemistry, mineralogy and metallurgy, and, more than a decade later, in biology.

After the war, Bragg (the son) succeeded Rutherford in the Physics Chair at Manchester – Rutherford having been appointed the Cavendish Professor at Cambridge. One of the people that Bragg had consulted on which crystals to investigate was the crystal-smuggler Hutchinson, who had remained greatly interested in the X-ray diffraction side of crystallography, and was now the Mineralogy Professor in Cambridge. In 1921, Hutchinson encouraged a graduate, W.A. (Bill) Astbury, to work with Bragg's father, W.H. Bragg, who was continuing with X-ray studies, now at University College in London, and in 1923 he similarly advised John Desmond Bernal.

J.D. BERNAL

Bernal was born in Ireland in 1901 into an Irish Catholic family and began his secondary education at the Jesuit public school, Stoneyhurst in Lancashire, but left after three months because no science was taught until the sixth form. He transferred to a Protestant English public school, Bedford School, which he also did not enjoy, but which did teach him chemistry and physics and provided him with a library of books to work through and a telescope to watch the stars. In his last year, he was shown Einstein's early papers on general relativity, and these impressed on him the changing nature of scientific knowledge. He came to Cambridge in 1919 with a mathematical scholarship to Emmanuel College and, because of his wide-ranging interests and knowledge, soon acquired the nickname 'Sage' – a name that remained with him for the rest of his life. Another lifetime acquisition was a belief in Marxism inspired by a talk by Henry Dickinson, the son of the curator of the Science Museum. The exuberance and enthusiasm of Bernal was later used by C.P. Snow as the basis of the character of Constantine in his novel *The Search*, published in 1934 – Constantine is on a committee trying to set up a National Institute of Biophysical Research.[2]

During his undergraduate studies in Mineralogy and Geology, Bernal had become fascinated with crystallography, and in particular with working out the various possible ways in which atoms or groups of them could be arranged regularly to form crystals – he re-derived algebraically, in his final year, the 230 ways of doing this, the 230 Space Groups. W.H. Bragg had now moved to the Royal Institution in London and Bernal joined his group there in the Davy-Faraday Laboratory in 1923. Bernal would later tell how he had diffidently asked WHB what he thought of his thesis on space groups. WHB replied, 'Good God man, you don't think I read it' – the first page evidently being sufficient to show that he was worth encouraging in research.[3]

2. *J.D. Bernal, 1932. Photo: Lettice Ramsey. Courtesy of Peter Lofts Photography.*

Both Astbury and Bernal were interested in pushing the X-ray technique towards biologically interesting molecules and in particular to proteins. Astbury concentrated on fibrous specimens and obtained X-ray fibre diagrams from wool and silk. Bernal investigated non-fibrous proteins and tried to get X-ray powder photographs from dried specimens of edestin, insulin and haemoglobin, but only obtained obscure bands.

In 1926, Hutchinson succeeded in creating the post of Lecturer in Structural Crystallography in the Mineralogy Department, for which both Astbury and Bernal applied. Bernal was successful and so returned to Cambridge. Thus in addition to supplying crystals for Bragg to develop the early X-ray diffraction work, Hutchinson played quite an important part in propagating the technique in Cambridge. Shortly after this, Astbury went to Leeds and began X-ray studies there.

Both Astbury and Bernal were still keen to try to get better X-ray results from proteins. Astbury was sent some crystals of pepsin from America for X-raying, but obtained very limited diffraction patterns from crystals carefully dried (and as a result, disordered!). On the fibre side he was more successful, and in 1934 published a long paper on the structure of hair, wool and related keratin fibres, demonstrating a contracted (α-) form and an extended (β-) form. It was suggested that both were built from extended polypeptide chains that became more pulled out in the β-form. The structure proposed for the α-form, although plausible, was incorrect, and the true α-helical structure was proposed by Pauling in 1951. However, in the 1934 paper, Astbury correctly proposed the β-structure of stretched out chains packed together to form β-sheets.

Bernal, in Cambridge, concentrated on crystals of the smaller globular proteins. In 1934 he was sent some crystals of pepsin from Uppsala. The grower, John Philpot from Oxford, had taken specimens there for centrifugation, and while he had been on holiday, crystals had grown up to 2mm in size. Again, dried crystals gave very disappointing results, but Bernal, following their drying in a microscope, could see that the crystals deteriorated considerably. There were some thin-walled glass capillaries being used in the laboratory for investigating ice crystals, so Bernal mounted a wet pepsin crystal into one of these, sealed it and obtained the first X-ray diffraction pattern from a well-ordered protein crystal – a film covered with spots from the diffracted beams. He was able to determine the unit cell as hexagonal with sides 67A × 67A × something much larger. Dorothy Hodgkin (then Dorothy Crowfoot) was a visitor to Bernal's group at that time from Oxford, and took further photographs. Notes of their results with the pepsin crystals and those of Astbury were published in *Nature*. The original Cambridge X-ray films have been lost; they probably went to Birkbeck College in London with Bernal in 1938 and were destroyed in the bombing of the College buildings during the war.

In 1934, Dorothy returned to Oxford, and her work in Cambridge was taken over by an American visitor, Isidor Fankuchen. Then, in 1936, Max Perutz joined the group. In the next four years, X-ray measurements were made on five different proteins: insulin and lactoglobulin (Crowfoot and Dennis Riley at Oxford), excelsin (Astbury, Dickinson and Bailey at Leeds) and chymotrypsin and haemoglobin (Bernal, Fankuchen and Perutz in Cambridge).

MAX PERUTZ

Max Perutz was born in Vienna in 1914. He was educated at the Theresianum (a grammar school originating from an earlier officers' academy). His parents suggested that he study law to prepare for entering the family business, but when a master sparked his interest in chemistry, he was allowed to change accordingly. In 1932, he entered Vienna University 'wasting five semesters in an exacting course of inorganic analysis'. His curiosity was aroused, however, by a course in organic chemistry in which the work of Frederick Gowland Hopkins in Cambridge on vitamins and enzymes was mentioned, and Max decided that Cambridge was the place where he wanted to work for his PhD.

The professor of physical chemistry in Vienna was Hermann Mark, a co-founder of polymer science who had shown that most polymers were flexible chains and had used X-ray diffraction in his studies. When Max heard that Mark was to visit Cambridge in 1935, he asked him to see if there was a place for him as a research student in the Biochemistry Department. Mark forgot about this when he was in Cambridge, but he had met Bernal and heard of his latest X-ray results and also that he would be willing to take on a student. Max knew nothing about crystallography but was attracted by hearing that it was being applied by Bernal to biological specimens. With financial help from his father, he joined Bernal's group in 1936 as a research student.

Bernal was away when he arrived in Cambridge and he was met by Fankuchen with the question 'What's your religion?' which took Max aback – his father had warned him never to ask an Englishman personal questions. His answer 'Roman

Catholic' provoked the response 'Don't you know the Pope is a bloody murderer'. Fankuchen, like Bernal, was a devout Communist, and his denunciation referred to the Pope's support for Franco in the Spanish Civil War. He regarded Max as a Capitalist because of his father's gift of £500 for his studies (this paid for living expenses and university fees for two years plus a term). However, between efforts to convert Max to communism, Fankuchen taught him some useful crystallography.[4]

At that point, Bernal had no useful biological specimens and Max was disappointed at being given some mineral specimens on which to cut his crystallographic teeth, but he remembered that 'Bernal's brilliance and boundless optimism about the powers of the X-ray method transformed the dingy rooms in the dilapidated grey-brick building into a fairy castle'[5] and, despite the minerals, he

3. Max Perutz at the conference on crystallographic computing held at Pennsylvania State University, 1950. Courtesy of Special Collections, Penn State University.

fell in love with Cambridge and remained there for the rest of his life.

Max's study of haemoglobin began after a summer holiday in 1937. He visited a cousin in Prague who was married to a professor of physical chemistry, Felix Haurowitz, who had studied the chemistry of haemoglobin and other proteins. Haurowitz suggested haemoglobin as a protein whose structure should be solved and Gilbert Adair, a physiologist in Cambridge, as someone who might well be able to supply some crystals for diffraction. On his return to Cambridge, Max approached Adair (after being properly introduced at a lunch party arranged by F.G. Hopkins' daughter, Barbara Holmes[6]) and, shortly after, Adair produced some suitable crystals of horse haemoglobin. Bernal and Fankuchen showed him how to mount them for X-raying, and also some chymotrypsin crystals that had been sent to Bernal by John Howard Northrop at the Rockefeller Institute. Max took X-ray pictures of both and determined their crystallographic parameters – the unit cell sizes and their space groups. This was really as far as one could go then. These parameters were sufficient to define the structures of the simplest crystals, with only one or two atoms per molecule. For the slightly more complex minerals with about a dozen atoms per molecule, the structure could be deduced from trial models – comparing the predicted and observed X-ray patterns. But no one knew what to expect for the structure of a protein molecule with hundreds or thousands of atoms. The detailed X-ray patterns did show, however, that the protein molecules in the crystals had a well-defined structure waiting to be determined.

Crystallography had been transferred from Mineralogy to the Cavendish Laboratory in 1931, probably not to the liking of Rutherford, the Cavendish Professor. Max recalled being disappointed that Rutherford never visited their group and assumed that he was only interested in atomic physics. But in fact,

> the conservative and puritanical Rutherford detested the undisciplined Bernal who was a Communist and a woman chaser and let his scientific imagination run wild. He had wanted to throw Bernal out of the Cavendish but was restrained from doing so by Bragg. If Bragg had not intervened, Bernal's pioneering work in molecular biology would not have started, John Kendrew and I would not have solved the structure of proteins, and Watson and Crick would not have met.[7]

Rutherford died in October 1937. Earlier in the year there had been a general professorial rearrangement. Bragg had moved from Manchester to the National Physical Laboratory (NPL) in London. He was succeeded in Manchester by Patrick Blackett from the Physics Department at Birkbeck College in London, and Bernal moved from the Cavendish to replace him at Birkbeck. Bragg had soon found the work at the NPL very disappointing, and when offered the Cavendish chair accepted it and moved to Cambridge in 1938.

Bernal had taken Fankuchen with him to Birkbeck, and so the only biological crystallographer left at the Cavendish was Max. He waited for a few weeks for Bragg to visit him after his arrival and then plucked up courage to call on him and show him the X-ray pictures from haemoglobin. Bragg was immediately enthused by the prospect of extending the X-ray diffraction method to biological molecules, and within three months had obtained a grant from the Rockefeller Foundation to continue the work and appointed Max his research assistant. This salary was vital for Max to continue his work – his parents, who had come to England to escape the effect of the Anschluss in Austria, could no longer provide for him, and in fact his salary enabled him to provide for them. However, his status was changed from a guest to a refugee, and because of the unemployment situation, he was not allowed to earn money in England – even as a college supervisor. However, he *could* receive the Rockefeller money, since it was from the USA and was designated specifically for him.

> The Rockefeller Foundation also bought me an X-ray tube for £99 and provided a modest supply grant. People often grumble now that it has become harder to get money for research, but they never knew those days when there just was not any. The Rockefeller Foundation supported all the pioneers in the subject for which Warren Weaver, its director of natural sciences, first coined the term 'molecular biology' in 1938. These included Theo Svedberg, Arne Tiselius, Kaj Linderstrom Lang, Bill Astbury and David Keilin. I remember the joy at the Molteno Institute when the Foundation bought Keilin the first Beckman spectrophotometer.[8]

Max was a keen mountaineer and skier and managed to spend the summer of 1938 in Switzerland with a travel grant to study glacier structure and flow, the results of which were published in the following year. When asked how, with such a love of the alpine, he could bear to live in flat, fenland Cambridge, he said he could enjoy wonderful holidays on the continent while living in Cambridge, but the reverse was not quite so tempting.

On the outbreak of war in 1939, most of the staff at the Cavendish became involved in war work, but Max, as an alien, was not immediately accepted for this. On the contrary, in 1940 he was arrested with about 100 others from Cambridge, and detained locally for a few weeks. They were then taken to join some 1,200 others before being transported by ship under dangerous and atrocious conditions to Canada. Max was interned in camps for some months with a group which included many other talented aliens, including Herman Bondi

4. *Max Perutz studying thin sections of glacier ice on the Jungfraujoch, 1938. Courtesy of Vivien and Robin Perutz.*

and Thomas Gold (who both later became professors with chairs in astronomy and maths) and organised a Camp University with these as teachers. He was allowed to return to Cambridge in 1941, and he wrote a striking account of this part of his life for the *New Yorker* magazine in 1985, reprinted in his book *Is Science Necessary?*[9]

Back in Cambridge, he met Gisela, herself a refugee, who was working for the Academic Assistance Council, which had been set up in 1933 to assist academic refugees. Max and Gisela were married in 1942. Later that year, as a consequence of his glaciology work, he became involved in Habakkuk – one of the schemes thought up by the eccentric man of ideas, Geoffrey Pyke. The aim of the project was to build assault weapons that could be used on ice and on the development of 'pykrete', a frozen mix of water and sawdust that Pyke thought could be used to build vast floating 'berg ships' and even a floating airbase. Research began in a large cold store in Smithfield Meat Market in London, and parallel work in Canada got as far as a model ice ship with insulation and refrigeration on Lake Patricia in Alberta. However, pykrete, like glaciers, suffered from creep and this, with other disadvantages and the fact that aircraft with larger ranges had been developed, doomed the project, and Max returned to Cambridge to continue his work on haemoglobin. He was joined in 1946 by John Kendrew.

JOHN KENDREW

John Kendrew was born in Oxford in 1917 and educated at the Dragon School and Clifton College, where an interest in chemistry persuaded him to focus on science and thus to aim for a place at Cambridge, which was then the 'real scientific university'.

Coming to Cambridge in 1935 for the scholarship exam, he found the facilities at Cambridge in the practical laboratories were very primitive compared to the modern science laboratories at Clifton. The Chemistry laboratory was lit by gas, and although the Cavendish had electricity, the equipment was very ancient. Towards the end of the exam, an old man came and sat by him and asked if he was interested in football – which he was not, since this was before the introduction of plastic lenses and John's eyesight was not good. Afterwards, the head assistant told him, 'Sir, that was Sir J.J. Thomson, Master of Trinity', and of course the most famous physicist of the Cavendish – he made a practice of talking to anyone who had put down Trinity and physics in their applications.[10]

John Kendrew was awarded a scholarship to Trinity College and graduated in chemistry in 1939. He began working for a PhD in physical chemistry, but this was soon interrupted by the war. He was diverted initially to work on radar, and then to more general operational research – as scientific adviser attached to one of the operational headquarters. He ended the war on the staff of Lord Mountbatten's South East Asian Command in Ceylon. This was a vital posting for Kendrew's future, since it brought him into contact with Bernal. Mountbatten and Bernal were good friends – Mountbatten was quite left-wing and sympathetic to Bernal's communist views, and Bernal was often called in for discussions and advice. It was during one of these visits that Bernal talked with Kendrew about how it should be possible to use X-rays to solve the structure of proteins and understand their biological functions. This so impressed Kendrew that he became keen to work in this field after the war. Bernal offered him a place in his laboratory at Birkbeck, but added that being a communist, it might be difficult for him to raise money for research and that Kendrew would do better to finish his Trinity scholarship in Cambridge and so directed him to Bragg and hence to Max.

Max was a little embarrassed by Kendrew's approach, since his work on the structure of haemoglobin did not seem to indicate that this was a quick route to a PhD. However, on meeting Joseph Barcroft, the distinguished

5. *John Kendrew at the Pasadena Conference on the Structure of Proteins, 1953. Courtesy of the Archives, California Institute of Technology.*

respiratory physiologist who was working at the nearby Molteno Institute for Parasitology and discussing the problem, Barcroft suggested a comparative study of adult and foetal sheep haemoglobin for which he could supply the blood. Kendrew was keen to become involved in the work, agreed to this project and became effectively Max's research student, although nominally under the direction of the Cavendish mineral crystallographer, W.H. Taylor.

The overall financial position at this stage was rather precarious. Kendrew's grant had two years to run and Max had been awarded an ICI fellowship, but this was again only for two years. Although Bragg had recommended Max for a University Lectureship, it took nine years to materialise. Max put this down to being a misfit – a chemist in a physics department working on a biological problem. However, it did give him the freedom to concentrate on his research. But for the future, while the Rockefeller grant provided vital money for equipment, etc., the Foundation thought that the University should provide Max's salary. So, between these, Max was out of a firm job.

1. W.L. Bragg, 1975. *The Development of X-Ray Analysis*. G. Bell and Sons Ltd, London, p. 54.
2. C.P. Snow, 1934. *The Search*. Victor Gollancz, London.
3. D. Hodgkin, 1980. John Desmond Bernal. *Biographical Memoirs of Fellows of the Royal Society*, 26, 17–84.
4. Max in his retirement lecture, 1979, reproduced in *New Scientist*, 85, 31 January 1980, 326–329.
5. *Ibid.*
6. *Ibid.*
7. *Ibid.*
8. *Ibid.*
9. M.F. Perutz, 1989. *Is Science Necessary? Essays on Science and Scientists*. Barrie and Jenkins, London.
10. In an interview with Ken Holmes at LMB in 1996.

Short biographies of Bragg, Bernal, Perutz and Kendrew are recorded in the *Biographical Memoirs of Fellows of the Royal Society*:

Bragg, by David Phillips in 25, 75–136, 1979.
Bernal, by Dorothy Hodgkin in 26, 17–84, 1980.
Perutz, by David Blow in 50, 227–256, 2004.
Kendrew, by Ken Holmes in 47, 311–332, 2001.
Max gave a biographical talk to the Peterhouse Kelvin Club in 1996 which was video-recorded.
A longer biography of Bernal was written by Andrew Brown in 2005: *J.D. Bernal: The Sage of Science* (Oxford University Press, Oxford), and one of Max by Georgina Ferry in 2007: *Max Perutz and the Secret of Life* (Chatto and Windus, London).

Chapter Two

The MRC Unit

The MRC began funding the unit in 1947, and it soon attracted students and visitors to work on haemoglobin and myoglobin. Hugh Huxley joined the unit in 1948, but soon became diverted into muscle research. Francis Crick joined in 1949. In 1953 there was a breakthrough in the X-ray diffraction work – Max showed how the structures of proteins could be solved by attaching heavy atoms to the molecules in the crystals. In 1957, myoglobin became the first protein to have its structure solved in this way by John Kendrew's group. The larger molecule, haemoglobin, was solved by Max's group in 1959; David Blow and Michael Rossmann were both involved in this.

MEDICAL RESEARCH COUNCIL UNIT FOR THE STUDY OF THE MOLECULAR STRUCTURE OF BIOLOGICAL SYSTEMS

The financial plights of Max Perutz and John Kendrew were overcome with the help of David Keilin, another distinguished Cambridge scientist. Keilin was a Russian-born biologist who had discovered the cytochromes and was the head of the Molteno Institute (a parasitology institute on the Downing site of the University off Free School Lane in Cambridge, set up in 1921, but incorporated into the Department of Pathology in 1987). Keilin had given Max and John bench space for their preparation of crystals. (Keilin was a very keen experimentalist and disapproved of theoreticians and, later, particularly of Crick. 'Keep him to the bench', he advised[1].) Max told him of their financial situation and that he thought he would have to find a job in industry. Keilin, who was friendly with Sir Edward Mellanby, the Secretary (the Executive Head) of the Medical Research Council, suggested that Bragg approach Mellanby for financial support. A meeting was arranged between them in the spring of 1947 at the Athenaeum Club, Mellanby submitted a paper to the Council for a 'preliminary run' and to his surprise the project was immediately adopted at their meeting in October 1947, establishing in the Cavendish Laboratory the 'Medical Research Council Unit for the Study of the Molecular Structure of Biological Systems'. The grant was for £2,550, rising to £2,650 per annum, to support Max and John and two research assistants for five years.

No one seemed very keen on the name. The address in papers continued mainly to be 'Cavendish Laboratory', though Max's paper in 1951 on the 1.5Å reflection from the α-helix gave the complete title. There was some discussion on the matter in 1953. Harold Himsworth, who had taken over from Mellanby as Secretary of the MRC in 1949, suggested 'Bio-molecular Research Unit'. Frank Young, the head of the Biochemistry Department, thought this rather vague and suggested 'Unit for Research on Bio-molecular Structure', but Max had a strong dislike for 'bio-molecular' and suggested 'Unit for Biological Structures'. The subject was then dropped. From 1953 to 1958, the complete earlier name tended to be used, but from 1958, the 'MRC Unit for Molecular Biology' became preferred. Warren Weaver's term 'Molecular Biology' was adopted as a compact title, and distinct from 'Biomolecular Structure', the name of Astbury's department in Leeds.[2]

The first research student attracted to the Unit was Hugh Huxley (1948), who began work on myoglobin but soon became more interested in muscle. His PhD supervisor was John Kendrew, who was then only one year into his own PhD. Francis Crick (1949), David Green (1953) and David Blow (1954) were all supervised by Max, with haemoglobin as their main subjects, although Francis was diverted into working on helical diffraction theory and coiled-coils and, when Jim Watson appeared in 1951, into DNA (chapter 3).

HUGH HUXLEY[3]

Hugh Huxley joined the Unit in 1948. As a schoolboy in Birkenhead in the 1930s, he became enthralled with the discoveries in atomic and nuclear physics and since Rutherford's laboratory was at the forefront of this work, Cambridge became his aim, which he achieved as an undergraduate in 1941. Although his ultimate aim was to do nuclear physics research, and in his second year he was able to go directly to Part II physics, he felt the need to be more closely involved in wartime events and in 1943 joined the RAF as a radar officer. The news of the dropping of the atomic bombs on Japan had a devastating effect on his desire to do nuclear physics research. Although on his return to Cambridge in 1947 he continued with Part II physics, and gained a first in the Tripos, making him eligible for a research studentship, he wanted to be far from the wartime applications. He was attracted more towards medical research, and so, in 1948, he joined the MRC Unit as a PhD student.

At first, he was incorporated into the team collecting X-ray data from myoglobin and haemoglobin, but reading about the problems of muscle structure and of the mechanism of its contraction, he became very interested in this. In particular, following the earlier experience of the protein crystallographers, there was the possibility of getting informative X-ray patterns from *wet* muscle specimens. John Kendrew had earlier suggested using a microcamera with a glass capillary collimator together with a microfocus X-ray tube, of the type being developed by Ehrenberg and Spear in Bernal's laboratory at Birkbeck, to look at diffraction from

6. *Cavendish staff in 1952 (section). In the second row from the front, Hugh Huxley, Jim Watson and Francis Crick are first, second and third from the left, and John Kendrew is first from the right. In the back row, Aaron Klug is on the extreme right. Courtesy of the Cavendish Laboratory, University of Cambridge.*

small biological specimens. Kendrew's friendship with Bernal yielded an early pro-totype of the X-ray tube. By that time, Hugh had decided to do low-angle diffraction on muscle using a miniaturised slit camera, and for this the microfocus tube was an excellent source, and he soon obtained X-ray patterns.

The first of these gave a number of equatorial reflections (i.e. perpendicular to the muscle fibrils) based on a hexagonal side of 400–450Å, which he interpreted as arising from a hexagonal array of contractile filaments, parallel to the length of the fibril. Later, with muscles in rigor (stiffened by lack of ATP), he found the same lattice but with considerably altered intensities, indicating a large lateral movement of material within the fibril. Hugh's interpretation, that the myosin filaments were located at the hexagonal lattice points with the actin filaments between – near the trigonal points – and becoming more fixed there in rigor by crosslinks, was broadly correct, except that the filaments are not continuous throughout the length of a muscle fibril, and it is largely the movement of the crosslinking material which changes the intensities of the hexagonal reflections.

Hugh found that the muscles of local Cambridgeshire Fen frogs gave stronger X-ray patterns than the laboratory-bred ones, especially in the meridional regions (along the length of the fibrils). Surprisingly, the spacings of these reflections did not alter as the relaxed muscle was stretched, and it was not clear how to assign them to the myosin and actin components.

After getting his PhD, Hugh went to MIT to learn electron microscopy at Frank Schmitt's laboratory and produced micrographs of cross-sections of fibrils showing the hexagonal array of filaments he had predicted from the X-ray work and suggestions of the crossbridges between them. A fellow visitor to the MIT laboratory in 1953 was Jean Hanson, who had been using the relatively new technique of phase contrast microscopy to photograph various types of muscle fibrils at King's College in London. Between them they established that the dense A-bands in longitudinal sections of muscle fibrils were not due to some material extra to myosin and actin filaments, but defined the location of the myosin filaments. Hugh pointed out that these results and his earlier X-ray data on constant axial periodicities were consistent with the sliding of the two types of filament past each other during stretching and possibly a similar process could occur during contraction. Later, they obtained evidence from band-pattern changes in isolated myofibrils that this was indeed what happened during contraction, and proposed the 'Sliding Filament Model',[4] simultaneously with a similar proposal from Andrew (A.F.) Huxley (no relation) and R. Niedergerke in the Physiology Department in Cambridge.

In 1954, both Hugh and Jean returned to England – Hugh at first back to Cambridge and then at the end of 1955 to the Biophysics Department at University College in London. He continued with the electron microscope work begun at MIT – looking at sections of embedded muscle specimens, sufficiently thin that with accurate alignment of the plane of sectioning, single thick and thin filaments could be seen and, clearly, the cross-bridges between them, in excellent agreement with the interdigitating, sliding filament model proposed earlier.

University College was close to Birkbeck College and, encouraged by Rosalind Franklin and Aaron Klug there, Hugh began looking at viruses in the electron microscope. In 1956, he found by chance that if tobacco mosaic virus were dried onto the carbon substrate from a solution containing phosphotungstic acid (or sometimes it happened with potassium chloride), the extra density produced by the dried salt showed a central hole along the rod-shaped particle. Cecil Hall at MIT had also noticed the effect with 'insufficiently washed' specimens of stained tomato bushy stunt virus. These were the first examples of negative staining in electron microscopy (surrounding and infusing a relatively low density biological specimen with a dense salt and so outlining the specimen in an electron beam). The method was developed in 1959 by Sydney Brenner in the MRC Unit with Bob Horne in the Cavendish, using sodium phosphotungstate as the stain, and in 1960 by Hugh using uranyl acetate. With the latter, he and Geoffrey Zubay produced images of ribosomes and of the small, spherical virus turnip yellow mosaic, showing the icosahedral pattern of the protein subunits on the surface of the virus particle. Hugh returned to Cambridge, to the new LMB, in February 1962.

THE PHASE PROBLEM

After taking the haemoglobin project of his PhD research as far as was then possible, John Kendrew took up the problem of myoglobin, a smaller protein that stored oxygen for use when muscles do work. Myoglobin is about a quarter of the size of haemoglobin and therefore seemed more hopeful to pursue by X-ray diffraction.

His first source, horse heart, provided little material and what there was grew poor crystals. They gave sufficient data to complete his thesis, but, with Bob Parrish, an early visitor, he began a survey of 24 different species, including diving mammals – he realised that these offered a good prospect since a tenth of their dry muscle weight is myoglobin needed for oxygen supplies during long undersea dives. Sperm whale looked promising; a chunk of sperm whale meat was located, and the myoglobin from this yielded large crystals which gave beautiful diffraction patterns.

As far as structure determination was concerned, both haemoglobin and myoglobin were more or less stuck at this point by the basic 'phase problem' of X-ray diffraction. The diffraction pattern records the intensities of the diffracted rays. The square roots of these intensities, the amplitudes, are proportional to the magnitudes of the sinusoidal electron density waves (the Fourier components) into which the crystal contents can be analysed – it is electron density that is measured, since it is electrons that scatter the X-rays. In order to build up a picture of the crystal structure in terms of the overall electron density variations in the crystal (a Fourier map), one has to combine the Fourier components in their correct spatial relationship, i.e. one needs to know the position, as indicated by the phase of each component wave, relative to some fixed point in the crystal. (The phase is expressed as an angle – the whole period of any one of the component sinusoidal electron density waves corresponds to 360° and so, in general, each wave can have any phase angle between 0° and 360°. Mathematically, the electron density is the Fourier transform of the *complex* amplitudes, i.e. including phases). Without the phases, only Patterson maps can be calculated. Patterson maps, which are the Fourier transforms of the distribution of the *intensities* of the X-ray reflections, show the distribution of vectors between atoms in the crystal and for large molecules they are not easily interpretable. The method commonly used for computing Fourier and Patterson maps at that time was with Beevers-Lipson strips on which the Fourier components were tabulated. The strips corresponding to a particular line in the map were aligned and the numbers in the columns summed with, at that time, a rather noisy adding machine, to give the values of the map along that line.

During the war (1942–3), Max had collected 7,000 reflections from haemoglobin crystals, out to a resolution of 2.8Å. These were recorded on films whose exposure times were one to two hours, and three sets of 45, 3° oscillation photographs about three different axes were taken. Sometimes he continued collecting all night when he was on duty fire-watching in the Cavendish (a wartime Civil Defence occupation), changing the film every two hours. The intensities were measured by eye – by comparing with a record on film of a reflection from an anthracene crystal exposed for different times. This task was shared with two assistants, Joy Boyes-Watson and Edna Davidson.

To calculate the Patterson map, Max began by using Beevers-Lipson strips, and with these it was only feasible to use the limited projection data and calculate the Patterson projections which were published in 1947. But the complete three-dimensional Patterson map was then calculated and published in 1949, the summation being made in London using a Hollerith punched card tabulator.

Overall, the interpretation of this map from such a large structure was not clear, but there was evidence for polypeptide chains in the proteins similar to those indicated in Astbury's X-ray pattern from α-keratin. Max concluded 'rashly'[5] that haemoglobin was constructed of a set of close-packed α-keratin-like chains parallel to the crystallographic a-axis. Shortly after this, Francis Crick joined the group and calculated that the density in the vector rod in the Patterson map interpreted on this basis was considerably lower than the interpretation required, and when the real structure emerged seven years later, it became clear that this vector rod arose from one of the α-helical stretches in the molecule (the G-helix) which makes up only 7 per cent of the molecule.

In 1950, Bragg, Kendrew and Perutz proposed a tentative common structure for proteins, but they did not consider non-integral helices and their argument was also flawed by allowing free rotation about the peptide bond. Later that year, Linus Pauling and Robert Corey pointed out this flaw and proposed two possible helical arrangements which fitted the available data. One of these was the α-helix with 3.6 amino acids per turn of the helix and pitch 5.4Å. Reading this in *PNAS* one Saturday morning at the Cavendish, Max was convinced of the existence of the α-helix, and was so angry at their making the earlier mistake that he immediately checked the prediction of the α-helical arrangement that there would be a 1.5Å reflection on the meridian of the X-ray fibre diagram by setting up a horse hair on the X-ray camera in the appropriate orientation. On being shown the reflection in the resulting picture and learning of Max's anger, Bragg commented, 'I wish I had made you angry earlier', a response used by Max for the title of his book of essays nearly 50 years later.[6]

THE PHASE PROBLEM SOLVED

In 1952, Bragg deduced the molecular shape of haemoglobin from variations in the intensities of the low resolution reflections with salt concentration, arriving at a spheroid with axial lengths 55×55×65Å. But the general way to solve the phase problem for proteins, by incorporating heavy atoms, was demonstrated by Max in 1953. Bernal, in a lecture at the Royal Institution in 1939, had indicated that this would in theory be the way to go, but without going into details of its practicality. Heavy atoms had already been used with smaller structures. Since they dominated the scattering density, the phases of the diffracted rays could all be taken, at least to a first approximation, to give a maximum at the heavy atom position, leading to a density map which could be interpreted and refined. This was not directly possible with a structure as big as a protein, and it was generally assumed that for such a big molecule the intensity differences in the diffraction pattern produced by a heavy atom would be too small to measure. However, Max measured the absolute amplitudes of the diffracted rays from a haemoglobin crystal relative to the incident beam and found that they were surprisingly low – the rays scattered by the many light atoms in the protein were more-or-less in random phase with respect to each other and so tended to cancel each other. As a result, a concentrated bunch of electrons at a heavy atom should in fact stand out and be detectable, and hence produce phase information. During the 1940s, Max had shared an office with Arthur Wilson, who was developing the statistics which were named after him, and which could have been used to calculate the absolute values of the intensities rather than determine them practically, 'but at that time I was busy collecting data for the three-dimensional Patterson, and it never occurred to me that Wilson's calculation would be relevant to the phase problem in haemoglobin, so that I had to determine the absolute intensities by laborious experiments'.[7]

In 1953, Max received a reprint from Austin Riggs, a biochemist at Harvard who was investigating possible differences between normal and sickle-cell haemoglobins. In the course of this he had shown that mercury atoms could be attached to sulphydryl groups on haemoglobin without affecting its oxygen uptake, and Max realised that this indicated that the structure had not been disturbed and if it crystallised was just what was required.

Vernon Ingram, a chemist in the group, made some of the mercury compound, and it was attached to haemoglobin before crystallisation. Max saw that the resulting X-ray picture had clear changes in the intensities of the reflections compared to those from native crystals, and when he showed it to Bragg, they both realised that this was indeed the way in which protein structures could be solved. With his student David Green, the locations of the mercury atoms in the unit cell were found and the signs of the 0kl reflections determined. (These reflections correspond to the projection of the crystal down its two-fold axis, and they can only have phases of 0° (plus) or 180° (minus) – the Fourier component cosine waves of density can only have peaks or troughs centred on a two-fold axis.) The paper recording this was published by the Royal Society in 1954,[8] and the same year Max was elected a Fellow of the Royal Society.

Although it was possible to calculate the phases and the density map corresponding to the projection down the two-fold axis of the haemoglobin crystal, the high density of atoms made it uninterpretable. Dorothy Hodgkin, visiting the laboratory to see the result, mentioned to Max that, in a recent paper, the Dutch crystallographer Bijvoet had pointed out that with two heavy atom derivatives one could determine all the phases. The search therefore began for more heavy atom derivatives. But, in pursuing the technique into three dimensions, the work on myoglobin had the advantage of a smaller sized molecule giving more robust crystals and simpler diffraction patterns.

THE STRUCTURE OF MYOGLOBIN

In 1951, John Kendrew had prospected in the USA for postdocs to amplify the work on myoglobin. One of the first visitors resulting from this was Jim Watson, but his lack of success in crystallising the protein left him time to think more about DNA. Another early visitor was Bob Parrish, who had helped John with the survey of different species of myoglobin – various whales, seal, penguin, carp and horse – for the most suitable crystals to pursue by X-ray diffraction.

After Max had demonstrated the feasibility of using the heavy atom procedure to phase the X-ray reflections from proteins, Gerhard Bodo and a heavy atom chemist, Howard Dintzis, were recruited by Kendrew to join the Unit in 1954. Dintzis specialised in complexes con-taining heavy atoms and the hope was that these might form a loose combination with the protein at pre-ferred specific sites – it was largely hit-and-miss, since myoglobin has no sulphydryl groups. Some of these were successful and led to the first map of the structure at 6Å resolution in 1957. Five different heavy atom sites were found and the phases cor-responding to the 400 reflections out to 6Å were calculated by hand. An electron density map was then calcu-lated using the Cambridge University computer, EDSAC1 (see chapter 9), taking 70 minutes. The calculation was checked by repeating it on the DEUCE computer at the National Physical Laboratory in London. The resulting first map of a protein struc-ture showed a number of rods of high electron density, which had the dimensions of α-helices – it was published in *Nature* in 1958.[9]

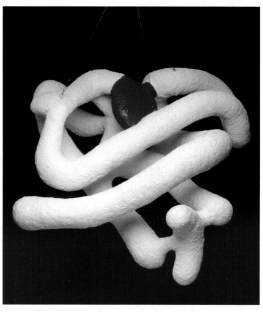

7. Model of the molecule of myoglobin built from a 6Å resolution map in 1957 – the first map of a protein structure. The haem group is shown in red and the white rods are lengths of α-helix.

The next stage was to extend the resolution to 2Å, involving about 10,000 reflections, or with five derivatives, about 60,000 measurements in all. The group was enlarged by the arrival of Dick Dickerson from Minnesota via Leeds (who recorded memories of his stay in an article in *Protein Science* in 1992, reproduced in chapter 10), Bror Strandberg from Stockholm and Roger Hart from Berkeley, and one of the data sets was collected at the Royal Institution by Vi Shore and David Phillips. The data were recorded on film using precession cameras. The intensities were now measured by densitometer rather than by eye and programs were written to calculate the phases using the new EDSAC2 computer.

David Davies from NIH arrived for a six-month stay during the final stages of this work. He remembers accompanying Dick and Bror (and everyone else who was involved with the myoglobin work) to the Maths Lab, where they tried to

8. *John Kendrew with the 'forest of rods' used as a basis of building the atomic structure of myoglobin, 1958.*

adapt Michael Rossmann's Fourier programs written for the new EDSAC2 computer to calculate the 2Å myoglobin map. This took some hours, but when they calculated a section through where John Kendrew thought the haem group was, from the 6Å map, and saw a peak corresponding to the iron, everyone cheered.[10] The complete map required about twelve hours to calculate, and the result was an enormous field of numbers that required contouring.

A preliminary calculation of a cylindrical section in the region corresponding to one of the rods in the 6Å map that had been interpreted as an α-helix clearly confirmed the interpretation. This was the first direct visualisation of an α-helix in a protein, and everyone was very excited and crowded into John and David's tiny office to see. Eventually the decision was made to build a complete model, and David and Bror bought wooden boards, which they drilled to take the steel rods on which coloured Meccano clips could be fixed to indicate the electron density – the original forest-of-rods model.[11] The new map was published in 1961[12] and in addition to verifying that all the earlier rods were indeed α-helices, it was possible to recognise the shapes of the polypeptide sidechains. Together with the sequence data obtained chemically by Allen Edmundson, who had joined the laboratory in 1960 from Moore and Stein's group at the Rockefeller Institute, a more or less complete amino acid sequence was traced in the map.

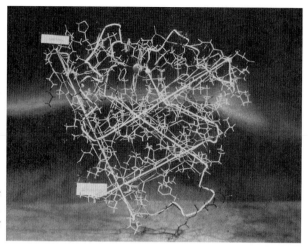

9. Atomic model of myoglobin, built from a 2Å map and published in 1961. Les Prix Nobel, 1962. Courtesy of the Nobel Foundation.

HAEMOGLOBIN

Initially none of the new heavy atom trials worked with haemoglobin, despite many attempts, especially by the visiting Larry Steinrauf from Caltech. However, after Dintzis' return to the USA, Max and his student Ann Cullis found that he had left a store of haemoglobin crystals which had been soaked in heavy atom solutions in a cupboard but which had not been photographed. Some of these gave intensity changes in the X-ray pictures. In all, six independent heavy atom derivatives were used to determine the haemoglobin phases with accuracy to 5.5Å resolution; 40,000 reflections were collected overall on 9° precession photographs. Several young assistants measured their intensities on a hand-operated, Joyce-Loebl, line-scanning microdensitometer designed at King's College, London. Tony North at the Royal Institution in London measured the absolute intensities of the 90 strongest reflections on Uli Arndt and David Phillips' Automatic Linear Diffractometer. Michael Rossmann determined and refined the heavy atom parameters and Hilary Muirhead, a PhD student, programmed Blow and Crick's method of phase determination (p. 22). The resulting 5.5Å map of haemoglobin was calculated in 1959 and published the following year.[13] It showed a cluster of four subunits, each very similar to the earlier struc-

10. Model of haemoglobin built from a 5.5Å map in 1959. The two white and two black molecules making up the structure are each very similar to myoglobin (Figure 7).

11. *Pasadena Conference on the Structure of Proteins, 1953. The participants included Max Perutz, John Kendrew, Hugh Huxley, Jim Watson and Francis Crick from the MRC Unit.*
Courtesy of the Archives, California Institute of Technology.

ture of myoglobin. In those early days, Max found this very reassuring – 'no conceivable combination of errors could have produced that striking similarity'.[14] The atomic structure of haemoglobin was not completed until 1967, in the new laboratory.

DAVID BLOW[15]

As a Cambridge undergraduate, David Blow had read Physics and had taken the Mineralogy and Crystallography course. He had also attended lectures by Bill Cochran, a Cavendish crystallographer, and by Bragg, so he was quite well-informed and interested in crystallography when he graduated in 1954. He wanted to get into research but did not get a sufficiently high degree to qualify automatically for a grant (except into Atmospheric Physics, which did not excite him). However, he heard from a friend that an Austrian at the Cavendish (Max Perutz) was good at getting money and so he made an appointment to see him. This was just after the mercury derivative of haemoglobin had enabled the h0l signs to be determined, and it all sounded quite exciting to him, and so, when he was offered a job in the Unit, he accepted, and began work in the Austin Wing. (An important influence on his decision to join Max was a talk with Sir George Thomson, son of J.J., who had won a Nobel Prize for his discovery of electron diffraction. Thomson

21

12. David Blow, c. 1967. Courtesy of the International Union of Crystallography.

urged him to accept the job, as he was convinced this was the way science would be going for the rest of the century.)

David spent the first year purifying haemoglobins from pig, dog and rabbit, crystallising them and working out the cell dimensions. This was a project to get into the feel of crystallography, but it was agreed that his main PhD project would be to generalise the sign determining method with heavy atom derivatives into a phasing method – aiming initially for 0kl reflections. There were two mercury derivatives of haemoglobin available, but they were very similar and so the intensity differences between them were correspondingly small. The intensities on the films were measured using the Joyce-Loebl microdensitometer, which David had, as one of his first jobs, set up and used to investigate the optical density response of the X-ray film commonly used (Ilford Industrial G).

Max's other research student, David Green (one year ahead), showed him how to use the local computer EDSAC1 before he went on a course himself.

Later in the year, Crick returned from the USA, where he had been for a year after the DNA work (chapter 3) and getting his PhD. He was keen to proceed with his own work, but he was asked by Max to watch over crystallographic matters – as a kind of theoretical adviser. Crick and David both had their desks in the same large room, shared by up to nine people, but Crick was in continual conversation with visitors and others. David remembers one key afternoon when he described his project and Crick put forward some fundamental concepts, especially that of the 'best Fourier', an electron density map that had the least error. This led to a method of phase estimation by calculating a probability function for the phase angle of each reflection and taking the centroid of this as the best amplitude and phase.

David Blow completed his thesis work in mid-1957. Although the new projection was again uninterpretable, since it was through a 50Å thickness, it did show many features above noise, indicating that application of the method in three dimensions should give interpretable information on the protein structure. He then went as a postdoc to the USA, initially for a year to NIH, working with Alex Rich and David Davis, and then on to MIT with Alex Rich for the second year.

In 1959, he returned to the MRC Unit and was staggered to find that his thesis had been consulted a great deal and that work into getting the phases of the rest of the reflections was well advanced. Michael Rossmann had joined the group (see next section) and had been writing programmes for this, and Hilary Muirhead had joined as a research student. So, feeling a bit superfluous to the main haemoglobin project, David suggested that he work on another protein. Max was happy with this, but suggested he tackle another haem protein. David chose cytochrome C and also, since that protein was a pretty unknown object crystallographically, chymotrypsin, which one could buy and was known to crystallise. Barbara Jeffery joined him at this time (early 1960) as a technician, and crystallisation experiments were well under way by the time of the move to the new laboratory in 1962.

David had remembered that as a second year research student he had considered writing a manuscript about haemoglobin being four myoglobins, a possibility first mooted by Francis in his 1953 thesis – but it was considered too speculative with no experimental basis. However, now that this had been confirmed by the 5.5Å map of haemoglobin, he suggested to Michael Rossmann that it should be evident in the X-ray diffraction patterns that haemoglobin had two similar units not related by the crystal symmetry in addition to those related by the exact two-fold axis of the crystal, and they both began to think of ways of investigating this and perhaps making use of it. Their first paper together – on determining the rotational relationship between two identical molecules not related crystallographically – was written just before the move to LMB. As part of the move, David was given the task of setting up the new library – choosing the furnishing and journals – and he became the first librarian.

MICHAEL ROSSMANN[16]

Michael Rossmann had joined Max's haemoglobin group in 1958. His first contact with crystallography had been at school at Saffron Walden, where one of the governors was Kathleen Lonsdale, who had worked with W H Bragg at the Royal Institution, and who now had her own crystallography group at University College in London. She took some of the top, interested pupils at the school to the Christmas Lectures at the RI and afterwards had shown them around the building and its many historical relics. After getting degrees in maths and physics at London University, Michael got a teaching job in the Department of Physics (then called Natural Philosophy) at the Royal Technical College in Glasgow (now the University of Strathclyde), hoping to be able to do some research. When no opportunity for this appeared, he was rather unhappy and wrote to Kathleen Lonsdale to see if there was any possibility of a job with her. She was keen to help, and applied for a DSIR grant for Michael who, when he learnt that she was working in crystallography, began reading up on the subject, in particular C.W. Bunn's *Chemical Crystallography*.[17] The DSIR application failed, but Michael in his reading had discovered that there was in fact, a crystallographic group nearby in the Chemistry Department of the University of Glasgow, under J. Monteath Robertson. Michael wrote to him saying he was interested in crystallography, was invited for an

13. Michael Rossmann and Tony North, Cold Spring Harbor, 1971.

interview, and was immediately offered a place in his group. Robertson was a member of the Governing Board of the Technical College and so it was arranged that Michael could continue with his teaching there in the afternoons, but in the mornings do his research in the University. His PhD was on 'A Study of Some Organic Crystal Structures' – these were aromatic hydrocarbons whose bond lengths and angles Robertson was particularly interested in. Michael solved three of them, one per year. Data were collected on home-made Weissenberg cameras, the intensities measured by eye, and calculations were done using Beevers-Lipson strips – one cycle of refinement taking about a week.

After getting his PhD, he wrote to Bill Lipscomb for a job – Lipscomb had visited Glasgow and given a lecture there – and in 1956, Michael moved to his laboratory in Minneapolis for two years. Michael remembers Lipscomb as 'proud of his Kentucky heritage and a member of the Kentucky Colonel philanthropic society. He generally favours a string tie, which, together with his upright and slender posture, was very reminiscent of the classical, post civil war image of a Kentucky colonel. As a consequence, most of his students and friends address him by his honorary title of 'Colonel'.[18] During his stay in Minneapolis, Michael worked on the structure of terpenoids – plant products with about 30 non-hydrogen atoms – and wrote computer programs (in machine code) for analysing structures on the early computer UNIVAC 1103 in the neighbouring St Paul. (Michael had not been very keen on the initial project proposed by Lipscomb and had made contact with Carl Djerassi, who had suggested and supplied the terpenoids.)

Hearing about the protein work in Cambridge, in a talk by Dorothy Hodgkin at an International Crystallography Meeting at Montreal, he thought the scale of the problem sounded very attractive and challenging and wrote to Max at the end of his two years to see if there was any possibility of joining his group. Max was very enthusiastic and offered him a job, which he took up in 1958. The group was at that time housed in the hut just outside the main Cavendish laboratory, and he remembers it 'as a cramped but happy place occupied by Max, John Kendrew, Francis Crick, Sydney Brenner, Ann Cullis, Mary Pinkerton and a few other post-docs and some young ladies who helped with the extensive hand calculations. Just across the yard from the hut was the mathematics laboratory building that housed the new EDSAC2 computer.'[19]

His first job was to determine the relative y-axis coordinates of the heavy atom sites for the different heavy-atom derivatives of haemoglobin, using data that had been collected by Max and Ann Cullis. The crystals were monoclinic (one two-fold axis) and so there were no symmetry-determined special points in the unit cell that could define an origin for these coordinates.

The functions proposed by Max, Francis and others to determine the relative y-axis coordinates of heavy atoms were complex expressions that did not appeal to my aesthetic sense. I had my own ideas. I predicted that a Patterson calculated with the symmetric $(|F_{PH1}| - |F_{PH2}|)^2$ Fourier coefficients would have negative peaks representing the vectors between the heavy atoms in the compound 1 and the heavy atoms in compound 2, where F_{PH1} and F_{PH2} are structure factors of the isomorphous derivatized compounds, respectively. Our turn at using the EDSAC2 computer was on Monday nights, which we shared with the radio astronomers. Thus, at the first Monday after I had completed checking my new Fourier program, I was ready to compute my type of three-dimensional 'correlation' function. The output was on punched five-hole paper tape used in telegraphic communications at that time. When I arrived in the laboratory the next day, the lady helpers had already printed out the results. It was obvious that there were no major peaks and that the symmetry of the maps was incorrect. Max was very supportive and encouraged me to search for my errors. Thus, two weeks later, I was ready for another night of computing. This time I saw immediately that the results were very easy to interpret. Here then was a method for determining the relative position of heavy atoms that left no doubt as to their positions. Max was delighted, and all visitors, including J.D. Bernal, Dorothy Hodgkin, and Sir Lawrence Bragg, were required to see these promising results.[20]

Subsequently, Michael developed a least-squares procedure based on the $(|F_{PH1}| - |F_{PH2}|)^2$ function to refine the heavy atom parameters. These provided the basis of the phase determination for the 5.5Å resolution map of haemoglobin which was calculated in 1959.[21]

1. Max's retirement lecture, September 1979, reproduced in *New Scientist*, 85, 31 January 1980, 326–329.
2. See also the discussion by de Chadarevian (2002. *Designs for Life*, Cambridge University Press, Cambridge, pp. 206–209).
3. Hugh Huxley has recorded his memories in the *Annual Review of Physiology*, 58, 1–19, 1996, and in the *European Journal of Biochemistry*, 271, 1403–1415, 2004.
4. H.E. Huxley and J. Hanson, 1954. Changes in the cross-striations of muscle during contraction and stretch and their structural interpretation. *Nature*, 173, 973–976.
5. M.F. Perutz, 1997. *Science is not a Quiet Life. Unravelling the Atomic Mechanism of Haemoglobin*. Imperial College Press, London, p. 40.
6. M.F. Perutz, 1998. *I Wish I'd Made You Angry Earlier: Essays on Science, Scientists, and Humanity*. Cold Spring Harbor Laboratory Press, New York.
7. Perutz 1997, *op. cit.*, p. 66.
8. D.W. Green, V.M. Ingram and M.F. Perutz, 1954. The structure of haemoglobin. IV. Sign determination by the isomorphous replacement method. *Proceedings of the Royal Society A*, 225, 287–307.
9. J.C. Kendrew, G. Bodo, H.M. Dintzis, R.G. Parrish, H. Wyckoff and D.C. Phillips, 1958. A three-dimensional model of the myoglobin molecule obtained by X-ray analysis. *Nature*, 181, 662–666.
10. D.R. Davies, 2005. A quiet life with proteins. *Annual Review of Biophysics and Biomolecular Structure*, 34, 1–20.
11. *Ibid.*
12. R.E. Dickerson, J.C. Kendrew and B.E. Strandberg, 1961. The crystal structure of myoglobin: phase determination to a resolution of 2Å by the method of isomorphous replacement. *Acta Crystallographica*, 14, 1188–1195.
13. M.F. Perutz, M.G. Rossmann, A.F. Cullis, H. Muirhead, G. Will and A.C.T. North, 1960. Structure of haemoglobin: a three-dimensional Fourier synthesis at 5.5Å resolution, obtained by X-ray analysis. *Nature*, 185, 416–422.
14. Perutz 1997, *op. cit.*, p. 157.
15. Much of the story involving David Blow is taken from an interview with him at Imperial College in July 2000.
16. Much of this section is from an interview with Michael Rossmann at LMB in December 2004.
17. C.W. Bunn, 1945. *Chemical Crystallography*. Clarendon Press, Oxford.
18. M. Rossmann, 2003. Origins. *Methods in Enzymology*, 368, 11–21.
19. *Ibid.*
20. *Ibid.*
21. M.F. Perutz *et al.*, *op. cit.*

CHAPTER THREE

Watson and Crick and DNA

The structure of DNA solved by Watson and Crick was one of the most important biological discoveries of the twentieth century. Apart from being very pleasing in itself, the complementary, double helical arrangement had the unexpected bonus of showing immediately how replication could occur, prompting Crick to announce in The Eagle that they had 'solved the secret of life'.[1] A talk by Jim Watson on 'The Structure of DNA' was added to the 1953 Cold Spring Harbor Symposium on Viruses (in the section on the Transition from Provirus to Vegetative Virus) and the model was well received by the phage group and geneticists. Biochemists tended to be cooler, still largely believing that proteins were the genetic material. Arthur Kornberg, then Chairman of the Department of Microbiology at Washington University, was struck by the biochemical naivety of the Nature *papers, and did not believe the replication mechanism until in 1961 when he was converted by his own experiments at Stanford that produced evidence that the two chains run in opposite directions.[2] Until 1960, the Wilkins group at King's College continued to improve DNA specimens for X-ray work and rigorously tested and refined the model, but crystallographic proof of the structure only appeared in 1979, with the work of Drew and Dickerson on single crystals of a defined dodecamer sequence.*

FRANCIS CRICK

Francis Crick joined the Unit in 1949. He was born in Northampton in 1916, and there were no strong scientific leanings in the family, although his grandfather belonged to the Northamptonshire Natural History Society, and had sent a small freshwater cockle attached to the leg of a water beetle that he had found in a pond to Charles Darwin, who was interested in such types of dispersal and cited it in his last publication – in *Nature* in 1882.[3] Crick's uncle had also written a pamphlet with Frederick Soddy (later a colleague of Rutherford at Montreal and Nobel Prizewinner for the discovery of isotopes), but their pamphlet was on the financial situation with the title *Abolish Private Money, or Drown in Debt*.[4]

Crick was educated at Northampton Grammar School and (a family tradition) at Mill Hill School in London. He read physics at University College in London

14. Crick and Watson in Cambridge, 1953. Courtesy of Cold Spring Harbor Laboratory Archives.

and began research for a PhD there under E.N. da C. Andrade, building apparatus to measure the viscosity of water at temperatures above 100°C. The work was interrupted by the outbreak of war in 1939.

At the beginning of the war he joined a group under Harrie Massey working on the sweeping of enemy mines, which was initially based at Teddington but later transferred to the Mine Design Department of the British Admiralty near Portsmouth, where Massey occasionally had to soothe the feelings of naval officers told by Crick that they were talking nonsense.

After the war he decided that applied physics was not for him – he had not enjoyed building apparatus and making measurements at UC (in fact, his apparatus and the whole laboratory at UC had been blown up by a landmine during the war) and he did not want to continue with weapons research in the Admiralty. On looking for a new field, however, he realised that he had no detailed knowledge of any particular scientific field at a modern level, but he felt this was an opportunity for a fresh start at any subject that appealed to him and looked for subjects that he felt had significance. He rejected fundamental particle physics – put off on the experimental side by the thought of large teams and large instruments, and he did not feel he had the ability to go into the theory side. Cosmology and astronomy seemed rather remote. Two areas on the biological side, however, attracted him, firstly the borderline between living and non-living (consequent to reading Schrödinger's book *What is Life?*[5]), and secondly consciousness and the nervous system, and after some agonising, decided on the first, since it was nearer to things he knew about already.

Crick left the Admiralty in 1947, and his first thought was to try to join Bernal's group in London, but Bernal was out of the country and his inquiry to Bernal's formidable secretary, Anita Rimel, brought the deflating reply 'Don't you realise that people all over the world want to come and work under the Professor? Why do you think he would take you on?'[6] Through Massey, he was introduced to A.V. Hill, the physiologist, at University College and to Edward Mellanby, the Secretary of the MRC. Mellanby was impressed by Crick's enthusiasm, but pointed out the difficulty of placing a man of his standing in the biological world with a commensurate salary. However, Crick was not discouraged and said he would be prepared to enter the research field by means of an MRC studentship – these were fixed at £350 untaxed, regardless of age and experience. Mellanby was opposed to his going straight into the structural side of biology without any previous biological experience, and Hill thought that Cambridge was the preferable educational centre in view of the considerable amount of work in progress there and, in particular, that the experimental cytology work in Honor Fell's group at the Strangeways Research Laboratory would give Crick the necessary basic experience in the biological field.

Crick visited the laboratories in Cambridge, and after talking with Honor Fell at Strangeways, it was arranged that he should start work there under her supervision in September 1947. His project was to work with Arthur Hughes, investigating the viscosity of protoplasm by studying the movement of magnetic particles ingested by chick fibroblasts in tissue culture. During the two years involved in this work, he read widely, educating himself in biology and chemistry. At the end of the two years, the MRC finally agreed that he had served his biological apprenticeship and that he would be allowed to move. He had to decide whether to join Murdoch Mitchison and Michael Swann working on mitosis in the Zoology Department, or the MRC Unit at the Cavendish. He had been attracted to the MRC Unit since he had first heard of their work, and inquired through a mutual friend, the mathematician George Kreisel, whether there was room for a physicist interested in biology. On meeting him, both Max Perutz and John Kendrew were keen for Crick to join them. Crick asked Mellanby for the MRC to transfer his studentship and this was done after a letter of agreement from Bragg, and an enthusiastic note from Max who wrote:

> I have known him ever since he decided to enter the field of biophysics and know that he has always been keenly interested in the problem of protein structure, and would have liked to join our Unit from the start, but was advised to gain some experience with living materials before making a final decision about his future line of research. After a thorough study of the subject he has now decided that X-ray analysis of protein structure really is the field that attracts him most.

I should be very glad to have Crick. I had many conversations with him and he has always struck me as an exceptionally intelligent person, with a lively interest, a remarkably clear analytical mind, and a capacity for quickly grasping the essence of any problem.[7]

Crick was offered a three-year appointment on the scientific staff of the Unit starting from June 1949. After some time as a scientific assistant, and some complications arising from his being paid by the MRC, he became a research student of Max. (This was partly to regularise his position in the Cavendish, but also because it was expected by Gonville and Caius College where he had been given dining rights.)

Initially, Crick began reading the work done by the group and learning about crystallography and proteins. On reading a recent paper written by Max in which he had proposed the 'hat-box' model for the structure of the haemoglobin molecule, consisting of straight, parallel polypeptide chains as in α-keratin, Crick calculated that the density in the resulting vector rods in the three-dimensional Patterson of the model would be ten times greater than that observed. After about a year he felt sufficiently confident to give a seminar criticising the methods the Unit had used to try to interpret the haemoglobin X-ray data, and their results – he tried to show that the methods were all hopeless, except, maybe, the isomorphous replacement method using a heavy atom derivative, if it were chemically possible. The title for the seminar 'What Mad Pursuit' was suggested by Kendrew and used again by Crick for his autobiographical book published in 1988. Bragg was initially indignant at Crick's criticisms and accused him of 'rocking the boat', but later agreed that their ideas of protein structure had been too simple and regular.

Crick collected some X-ray data from haemoglobin crystals, but at this time there was no direct way to progress from this and he tried to get some idea of the shape of the molecule from crystals in various shrinkage states. His work was given a jolt when Pauling's paper on the α-helix was published in April 1951. He began to investigate the haemoglobin X-ray data for evidence of the presence of α-helices and concluded that, if present in the molecule, they were not aligned. Pauling's paper also provoked Bragg to ask a Cavendish crystallographer, Bill Cochran, to work out the Fourier transform (the diffraction pattern) of an α-helical arrangement. But it was not until a paper on helical diffraction containing some errors was sent to the laboratory from Vladimir Vand in Glasgow that both Cochran and Crick were pushed (independently) into producing a correct version of the theory, and into writing up this[8] and its application to the α-helical poly-methyl glutamate, a synthetic polypeptide prepared and X-rayed by the Courtaulds research group. It was at this point that Jim Watson joined the laboratory.

JIM WATSON

Jim Watson was born in Chicago in 1928 and educated there in local grammar and high schools. He was extremely bright and at the age of 15 was accepted into the

University of Chicago, receiving a BSc in zoology in 1947. He had a great boyhood interest in birdwatching, but reading the Schrödinger book promoted a more serious desire to learn genetics rather than pursue ornithology, and he obtained a fellowship for graduate study at Indiana University, Bloomington, where the geneticist Hermann Müller had recently been awarded the Nobel Prize for his 1926 discovery that X-rays cause mutations. Although Müller was the initial attraction to Bloomington, and Watson attended his classes in gene mutations, he also took the course of Salvador Luria in bacteriology, and was drawn into Luria's research field of bacteriophage (viruses which infect bacteria). Luria, with Max Delbrück, then at Vanderbilt University in Nashville, had formed the Phage Group from those attending the Phage Courses at Cold Spring Harbor from 1945, the aim being to investigate genetic replication using phage as probably the simplest system. Watson began work in Luria's group in 1948, studying the effects of hard X-rays on the multiplication of phage, and gained his PhD in 1950.

At that time, there was an ambivalent feeling about what constituted genes. Although Avery, MacLeod and McCarty had in 1944 published their conclusion that it was DNA that caused a genetic transformation in the pneumococcal bacterium discovered in 1923 by Fred Griffith, changing it from one producing smooth, regular-shaped colonies (S) to one producing granular, irregular colonies (R), there was a reluctance to accept that the relevant changed gene had been provided as part of the added DNA – perhaps, for instance, there had been an undetected protein trace present. While working for his PhD, Watson had attended a course on proteins and nucleic acids by Felix Haurowitz (Max Perutz's earlier mentor). Haurowitz taught that proteins were so complex that only *they* could direct their assembly, and there was a general feeling that DNA was a rather dull molecule – an interminable repetition of units of only four types – compared with complex but precisely built protein molecules. But by 1950, more and more experiments were pointing towards DNA as the essential genetic material, though there was still the thought that it might not be exclusively so.

After attending the 1950 meeting of the Phage Group at Cold Spring Harbor, Watson was directed by Luria to Europe, to study nucleic acid chemistry under Herman Kalckar in Copenhagen, a move that Gunther Stent from Delbrück's laboratory (now at Caltech) had also made. Watson and Stent found Kalckar's English incomprehensible and anyway, they were not terribly interested in biochemistry. However, nearby was the laboratory of Ole Maaloe (a founder member of the Phage Group) and phage genetics – the temptation was too much, and they both effectively transferred to his laboratory for some months before Maaloe left for Caltech.

Kalckar decided to spend the spring of 1951 at the Zoological Station in Naples and invited Watson to accompany him. By chance there was a small local meeting there at which Maurice Wilkins from King's College, London showed his X-ray diffraction photographs from DNA. The photographs made a strong impression on Watson – his first indication that DNA, and therefore genes, might have a regular structure. It seemed a good idea to him to try to learn about X-ray diffraction as a way of finding out the DNA structure. He had heard of the work of the MRC Unit and wrote to Luria to try to get him an introduction. Shortly after this, Luria met John Kendrew at an Ann Arbor meeting. Kendrew was in fact looking for postdocs to help with the myoglobin work and Watson was invited to join him.

Although Luria had been keen on Watson learning X-ray crystallography, this had to be cleared with the Fellowship Board who were funding his stay in Europe. The head of this, Paul Weiss, was not impressed by his pulling out of biochemistry and thought that crystallography was too remote a subject for him to be tackling. However, Luria suggested that Watson pretend to be visiting Roy Markham, a biochemist working on plant viruses at the Molteno Institute in Cambridge, and this solved the problem. Watson arrived at Cambridge in October 1951, and as John Kendrew was still in the USA, he was introduced to the MRC Unit by Max. He met Bragg the following day, and was formally admitted to the Cavendish.

He was the first biologist to join the Unit – all the others being physicists or chemists. The primary aim of the Unit was, of course, to obtain the structure of a protein and although there was a vague assumption that this might indicate how the protein functioned, there was no deep biological feeling. Crick was interested in the basis of genetics – the relationship between genes and proteins, but for him too, the immediate concern was in protein structure.

Watson began trying to crystallise myoglobin but without much success, leaving a lot of time for discussion with Crick, whose office he was sharing. (When Crick arrived in 1949, the whole Unit was accommodated in one room, but soon after Max and John gained their own tiny private office, and in 1951 another room became available which they gave to Watson and Crick 'so that you can talk to each other without disturbing the rest of us'. As Crick wrote, 'a fortunate decision as it turned out'.[9]) At the end of October, Crick was working on the theory of helical diffraction. Pauling had deduced the α-helical arrangement of amino acids by model-building to fit the X-ray data from fibrous proteins and since DNA was also a polymer built from similar units, it seemed most likely that if DNA had a regular structure, as indicated by the X-ray pattern from King's, then that too was helical. However, to establish *which* helical structure required consistency with the X-ray patterns – very few of these had been published, and those that had were not very clear. Contact had therefore to be made with King's, and Maurice Wilkins.

MAURICE WILKINS

Wilkins had graduated in physics at Cambridge in 1938, and went to Birmingham for a PhD under John Randall studying luminescence of solids. From 1940 to 1944 he worked on the Manhattan Project in California. In 1944, he rejoined Randall at St Andrew's University, and went with him to the MRC Biophysics Unit in the Physics Department at King's College when it was set up in 1945, as Deputy Director.

The DNA work at King's effectively began there in 1950. Wilkins had a research group developing new optical instruments and in May 1950, he was given some long DNA by Rudolf Signer from Bern, for optical studies. Wilkins noticed that when touched with a glass rod, the DNA was drawn out into very thin uniform fibres. He took some of these to Raymond Gosling, a research student who was working on X-ray diffraction from ram sperm heads. Gosling cemented a bundle of these fibres together to get sufficient bulk for his X-ray set-up, and obtained a good crystalline diffraction pattern. Wilkins showed this pattern at a meeting organised by Max Perutz at the Cavendish in July, and mentioned the possibility of a helical arrangement. He had been struck by the marked gap in the low angle part of the meridian of the diffraction pattern, which a colleague at King's,

15. *Maurice Wilkins, c. 1960.*
Courtesy of Bettmann/CORBIS.

Alec Stokes, had pointed out as a characteristic feature of a helical arrangement. The pattern was probably the same one seen by Jim Watson at Naples.

Wilkins and Crick were good friends – both were physicists and both had worked under Sir Harrie Massey and had met after the war when both had consulted him about getting into biology. The Cricks therefore invited Wilkins for the weekend in early November 1951. Wilkins had no new X-ray pictures from DNA, but informed them of a DNA colloquium to be held at King's on 21 November, at which talks were to be given by Wilkins himself, Stokes, who had also worked out the theory of helical diffraction that summer, and Rosalind Franklin, who had joined the King's Unit earlier that year and who *did* have new X-ray pictures from DNA.

ROSALIND FRANKLIN

Rosalind Franklin was born in 1920, educated at St Paul's School in London and gained a place at Newnham College, Cambridge in 1938, reading chemistry. After graduating in 1941, she was directed, as was the practice during the war, into research – to the Coal Utilization Research Association, CURA, to work on the structure of carbons, for which she received a PhD in 1945. In 1947, she joined a government research group in Paris engaged in studying carbons by X-ray diffraction. Although very happy there, she realised that there would be no advancement

16. Rosalind Franklin on holiday in July 1950, photographed by Vittorio Luzzati.
Courtesy of the National Portrait Gallery, London.

for her in France and on looking for work in England became attracted towards the applications of X-ray diffraction to biological problems and accepted a research fellowship at King's College from the beginning of 1951. John Randall, the head of the MRC Unit, appointed Franklin to take up the X-ray diffraction study of DNA structure, and to take over Gosling as research student. They were given the long Signer DNA, a new Ehrenberg-Spear, microfocus X-ray set and a Philips micro-camera. With Franklin's X-ray experience, they were soon able to get improved patterns from smaller, more uniform bundles of the drawn-out fibres of DNA. Wilkins, however, after his initial involvement in this work was loath to withdraw from it. To Franklin's professional crystallographer's eye, he was an amateur – of no help and just intruding on her work. Relations between the two became rather strained and communication between them largely ceased.

Although Franklin believed that DNA had a basic helical structure – in her notes for her talk, she listed out points in its favour and wrote of helical bundles of two or three chains – she did not think that the data at that time gave sufficient evidence for this and so did not dwell on the molecular structure in her talk at the colloquium. She had controlled the water content of the DNA fibres as a means of getting at the number of DNA molecules in the crystallographic unit cell and the nature of the intermolecular bonding. In so doing, she discovered the distinct drier A- and wetter B-forms of DNA and was able to define the conditions for the transition between them. She was convinced that the behaviour of the fibres at high humidity indicated that the intermolecular contacts were via phosphate groups on the outside of the molecules.

DNA MODEL 1

Watson attended the King's colloquium hoping for structural information from Franklin's talk (Crick did not go). However, Watson was at this stage unfamiliar with crystallographic terminology and arguments, and in his usual way did not take notes. Thus Crick received some rather hazy answers when he later tried to question him. Particularly unfortunate was Watson's mis-remembering a far too low water content in the fibres. Nevertheless, within days, they had built a model. Influenced by the structure of the α-helix, they assumed that the regular part of the DNA polymer sequence – the phosphate–sugar backbone – would be the mainstay in a regular helical structure and thus lie at the centre, while the bases would lie on the outside where their irregular sequence could be accommodated without harming the regular, central part of the structure. On this basis, a three-strand model was built and the King's group was invited to see it. Franklin immediately pointed out that it disagreed with her evidence for the phosphates being on the outside of the structure, and that there was no lack of water in the structure and so no need for the Na^+ ions to be directly attached to the phosphates.

The two laboratory heads, Bragg and Randall, discussed the fiasco and agreed that the DNA structural work should be left to King's. Crick returned to writing his thesis and, in the course of thinking about helical diffraction work, deduced the coiled coil arrangement for the structure of α-keratin. The X-ray pattern of α-keratin has 5.15Å near-meridional intensity, whereas a straight α-helix would have 5.4Å layer line intensity on the meridian, but the 5.15Å intensity *would* be produced by the coiling of tilted α-helices around each other – two helices with the same sense of twist, especially if non-integral, would pack together at an angle rather than exactly parallel. Pauling and Corey came to the same conclusion at about the same time – the apparent discrepancy had delayed the publication of their α-helix paper by two years. Watson turned to X-ray work on the rod-shaped tobacco mosaic virus (TMV), hoping that the X-ray pattern would give clues, via the arrangement of the RNA it contained, to DNA structure. This hope was in vain. He did show that the structure was helical, though he underestimated the number of protein subunits per turn of the basic helix.

In May 1952, Franklin obtained the clear and much-reproduced X-ray pictures from the high humidity B-form of DNA (B51) and the lower humidity A-form. The B pattern was the simpler, with an X-shaped pattern near the equator and very strong meridional intensity at spacing 3.4Å. During the following months, Franklin became convinced that the B-form was helical, with a repeat of 34Å, and with a number of coaxial helical chains of nucleotides spaced 3.4Å apart, but the number of chains was not clear and the lack of crystallinity ruled out the possibility of determining this by standard crystallographic techniques. The A-form, however, *was* crystalline and did have sharp measurable X-ray reflections, and so she and Gosling began a crystallographic analysis of this, calculating the Patterson Function. But they found this difficult to interpret and only returned to the B-form in February 1953.

DNA MODEL 2

In June 1952, Watson reached his limit with TMV. He had obtained an X-ray picture which indicated that the TMV particle had a helical structure, but which gave no obvious clue to the RNA arrangement. He began to think again about DNA and of the chemical data and, prompted by a young Cambridge mathematician John Griffiths, so did Crick. Crick and Griffiths met in the tea queue at the Cavendish after a talk on 'The Perfect Cosmological Principle'. Discussing candidates for possible Perfect Biological Principles, Crick suggested base attraction might account for DNA replication and that Griffiths could perhaps try calculating whether there was any such effect. Griffiths tried calculating the forces between the flat faces of the bases and found attraction between A and T and between G and C. Crick concluded that this would lead to complementary replication, but the uncertainties in the calculation did not lead to a strong promotion of this idea until in July, when Erwin Chargaff visited Cambridge and was introduced to Watson and Crick by John Kendrew. Chargaff, from Columbia University, New York, had been working since 1945 on the analysis of DNA from various sources. In 1947, he had published a paper showing that the ratios of A/T and G/C were both unity for a wide variety of DNAs with differing ratios of A+T to G+C. When chaffed by Crick on the vast amount of chemical data on DNA which was not structurally helpful, Chargaff brought up these rules. Watson was familiar with them, but Crick was apparently not – he remembered that pairing had been suggested by Griffiths' calculations, but had to check what with what, and was surprised to find that the two agreed. Chargaff was impressed by their chemical naivety – not being able to remember the differences between the bases, for example – and because of their constant reference to helices called them 'two pitchmen in search of a helix'.[10] Crick became convinced that base pairing was the key to the structure, but by stacking rather than planar interaction. At this stage, hydrogen bonding was discounted, since it was widely accepted that bases existed in tautomeric forms (i.e. with different bonding arrangements), which would not all be consistent with a particular inter-base hydrogen bonding.

Meanwhile, Linus Pauling at Caltech had become interested in the DNA structure and following his reasoning for the α-helix, and like Watson and Crick in their earlier model, had put the regular part of the structure, the sugar–phosphate backbone, in the inside of the model, with hydrogen bonds between the phosphate groups holding the structure together. His model also needed three chains to pack reasonably into the space available. Pauling's son Peter had, by this time, joined the MRC Unit as a research student of John Kendrew and he received a letter from his father in December 1952 telling him that he and Corey had a structure for DNA in a paper submitted for publication and asking whether he would be interested in seeing it. A copy arrived in January with a note that it was to be published in the February issue of *Proceedings of the National Academy of Sciences of the USA*. Watson's gloom at being beaten, however, was dispelled by the arrival of the manuscript. Pauling had made a mistake – the phosphate groups in the model were not ionised as they should be under normal conditions, and it was critical for their model that they should not be!

Watson and Crick were fired up to try again before Pauling realised his mistake and restarted model building. Watson took the Pauling manuscript to King's to try to prompt a collaborative effort. His meeting with Franklin did not go well – she was not impressed by the similarities between Pauling's model and the earlier Watson–Crick model and insisted that there was no clear X-ray evidence for any helical arrangement.

Wilkins was, however, more receptive and showed Watson a copy of Franklin's best B-form X-ray pattern. This showed the very clear helical characteristics plus the intense 10th layer line at 3.4Å and a 20Å equatorial reflection indicating the molecular diameter. From the density of the specimens, the number of chains was either two or three – Watson was in favour of two. However, his argument that 'important biological objects come in pairs' did not persuade Crick to abandon three entirely when, afterwards in Cambridge, they were discussing what he had learned during his visit. Bragg did not frown on their taking up the DNA work again. He was persuaded by Watson's argument that Pauling would return – he did not like the idea of being pipped again by Pauling after the α-helical episode – and also he did not approve of the tensions at King's. So model-building began again in Cambridge.

Again, the attractions of a model with bases accessible on the outside and with no resultant need to pack them together was initially favoured, but did not get far. In the second week of February, however, Max passed on a copy of a report on the work of the King's group he had received as a member of an MRC inspecting committee, confirming what Watson had learned at King's, but also giving the space group (the crystallographic packing) of the A-form as C2. Crick knew this space group from his haemoglobin work, and that it had diad axes and these he deduced from the unit cell sides were perpendicular to the molecular axes and hence that there must be two chains in the molecule running in opposite directions. The report also gave Franklin's evidence for the bases being on the inside of the molecule. A single chain was built along these lines, but the problem remained – how to arrange the bases to accommodate their different sizes in the two chains and yet lead to a regular backbone on the outside.

Watson began to consider hydrogen bonding more seriously. He read of its existence between bases in even quite dilute solutions, so it could well be present to bind the molecule together in the polymers. He also read of the X-ray results of June Broomhead in her 1952 thesis from the Chemistry Department in Cambridge. This showed planar pairs of adenines and of guanines hydrogen bonded together at just the right distance to be accommodated in the double helix. The result of this would be a like-to-like, base-pairing structure. Watson's attempt to build this included wrong tautomeric forms – those with less stable locations of hydrogen atoms – for guanine, cytosine and uracil. He had copied these from Davidson's book *The Biochemistry of the Nucleic Acids*,[11] although the correct tautomeric forms for adenine and guanine had been presented in Broomhead's work. This was pointed out by Jerry Donohue, a crystallographer from Caltech (see chapter 10) who was sharing the office with Watson and Crick, and who had had much experience of hydrogen bonding in small molecules. Crick was also against the like-to-like pairing, since it gave no explanation for Chargaff's rules, and after some death throes, the like-to-like model was buried at the end of February. The exercise had however clarified the picture regarding the tautomeric forms – that there were particular, stable forms present for each base, making a hydrogen bonding arrangement feasible.

17. *Crick and Watson in their office in the Austin Wing of the Cavendish in 1953. Courtesy of A. Barrington Brown/Science Photo Library.*

The need to try to build something, at this stage, made Watson cut out the correct shapes of the bases from cardboard. After some shuffling of these, he noticed that A and T and G and C could both be hydrogen bonded together with two bonds to form pairs with identical shapes. Donohue could not find any fault in the pairing and Crick was convinced by its consistency with the C2 crystal symmetry and by its explanation of the Chargaff rules. Over the next two weeks metal components for model building were produced by the Cavendish workshop and an accurate model was built to check for possible stereochemical troubles. None were found and a paper was written for *Nature* with a copy sent to Wilkins. Wilkins suggested that accompanying papers should be sent from his group and from Franklin and Gosling showing the agreement with the X-ray data. As a result of the unsatisfactory relationships at King's, Franklin had just moved to Birkbeck College to work on TMV, but she and Gosling had written up their work on the B-form and this was easily adapted in support of the Watson–Crick model. The papers were received by the *Nature* editor at the end of March and were published in the issue of 25 April 1953.[12] At the end of their paper, Watson and Crick wrote 'It has not escaped our notice that the specific pairing we have postulated immediately suggests a possible copying mechanism for the genetic material'. Commenting on this sentence later, Crick wrote:

This has been described as 'coy', a word that few would normally associate with either of the authors, at least in their scientific work. In fact it was a compromise, reflecting a difference of opinion. I was keen that the paper should discuss the genetic implications. Jim was against it. He suffered from periodic fears that the structure might be wrong and that he had made an ass of himself. I yielded to his point of view but insisted that something be put in the paper, otherwise someone else would certainly write to make the suggestion, assuming we had been too blind to see it. In short, it was a claim to priority.[13]

The point was, however, elaborated five weeks later in a second *Nature* paper, 'Genetical Implications of the Structure of DNA'.[14] By then, they had seen the papers from King's showing how strongly the X-ray evidence supported the structure.

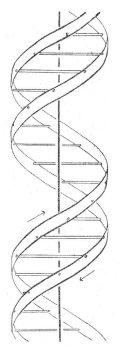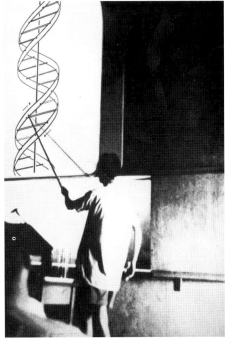

18. *(right) Diagram of the DNA structure from* Nature *171:737, 25 April 1953. Reprinted by permission from Macmillan Publishers Ltd.*

19. *(far right) Jim Watson giving the first public presentation of the DNA structure at Cold Spring Harbor, 1953. Courtesy of Cold Spring Harbor Laboratory Archives.*

Thus the year 1953 became what Max Perutz called the *annum mirabilis*. The Queen was crowned; Everest was climbed; the DNA structure was solved; Hugh Huxley and Jean Hanson discovered the sliding mechanism of muscular contraction; and Max himself had found a method for deciphering the X-ray diffraction patterns of crystalline proteins.

Crick was elected a Fellow of the Royal Society in 1959, and Watson a Foreign Fellow in 1981. In 1962, they received, with Maurice Wilkins, the Nobel Prize in Medicine and Physiology. Rosalind Franklin had died in 1958.

1. J.D. Watson, 1968. *Double Helix*. Weidenfeld and Nicolson, London/Atheneum, New York.
2. F.H.C. Crick, 1988. *What Mad Pursuit*. Basic Books, New York.
3. C. Darwin, 1882. On the dispersal of freshwater bivalves. *Nature*, 25, 529–530 (pointed out by Matt Ridley, 2004. Crick and Darwin's shared publication in *Nature*. *Nature*, 431, 244).
4. R. Olby, 1970. *The Twentieth Century Sciences – Studies in the Biography of Ideas*. WW Norton and Company, New York, pp. 227–280.
5. E. Schrödinger, 1944. *What is Life?* Cambridge University Press, Cambridge.
6. Crick, *op. cit.*
7. Olby, *op. cit.*
8. W. Cochran, F.H.C. Crick and V. Vand, 1952. The structure of synthetic polypeptides. I. The transform of atoms on a helix. *Acta Crystallographica*, 5, 581–586.
9. Crick, *op. cit.*
10. Erwin Chargaff resented the intrusion of the inexperienced and non-chemists Watson and Crick into his DNA field. He painted an unkind contemporary (1953) picture of Crick and Watson in *Heraclitean Fire* (1978. Rockefeller University Press, New York, p. 101ff.): 'One, thirty five years old; the looks of a fading racing tout; something out of Hogarth (The Rake's Progress) … an incessant falsetto, with occasional nuggets glittering in the turbid stream of prattle. The other, quite undeveloped at twenty-three, a grin more sly than sheepish; saying little, nothing of consequence … a gawky young figure…'. A later impression occurs in an oral interview of Chargaff for the American Philosophical Society in 1972: 'Crick and Watson are very different. Watson is now a very able, effective administrator. In that respect he represents the American entrepreneurial type very well. Crick is very different: brighter than Watson, but he talks a lot, and so he talks a lot of nonsense'.
11. J. Davidson, 1950. *The Biochemistry of the Nucleic Acids*. Methuen, London.
12. J.D. Watson and F.H.C. Crick, 1953. A structure for deoxyribose nucleic acid. *Nature*, 171, 737–738. M.H.F. Wilkins, A.R. Stokes and H.R. Wilson, 1953. Molecular structure of deoxypentose nucleic acids. *Nature*, 171, 738–740. R.E. Franklin and R.G. Gosling, 1953. Molecular configuration in sodium thymonucleate. *Nature*, 171, 740–741.
13. Crick, *op. cit.*
14. J.D. Watson and F.H.C. Crick, 1953. Genetical implications of the structure of deoxyribonucleic acid. *Nature*, 171, 964.

A biography of Watson was written by Victor K. McElheny: *Watson and DNA, Making a Scientific Revolution* (Wiley, New York, 2003). Biographies of Rosalind Franklin have been written by Ann Sayre: *Rosalind Franklin and DNA* (WW Norton and Company, New York, 1975) and by Brenda Maddox: *Rosalind Franklin, The Dark Lady of DNA* (HarperCollins, London, 2002).

Watson, Crick and Wilkins have each written their memories of this time, Watson (1968 *op. cit.*), Crick (1988 *op. cit.*), and Wilkins in his autobiography *The Third Man of the Double Helix* (Oxford University Press, Oxford, 2003).

Overall histories have been written by Robert Olby (*The Path to the Double Helix*, Macmillan Press, London, 1974) and Horace Freeland Judson (*The Eighth Day of Creation*, Jonathan Cape, London, 1979), and particularly on Rosalind Franklin's part in the DNA story, by Aaron Klug in the *Journal of Molecular Biology* (vol. 335, pp. 3–26, 2004).

In 1987, the BBC made a film for their Horizon Series on the unravelling of the DNA structure, largely based on Jim Watson's book the *Double Helix*. The film was called 'Life Story', and included Jeff Goldblum as Jim Watson, Tim Pigott-Smith as Francis Crick, Alan Howard as Maurice Wilkins and Juliet Stevenson as Rosalind Franklin.

20–51. DNA50 meetings in Lady Mitchell Hall, Cambridge, and at LMB, 2003.

THE STRUCTURE OF DNA
WAS DETERMINED HERE
IN 1953 BY
JAMES WATSON & FRANCIS CRICK
THIS PLAQUE WAS UNVEILED BY
H.R.H. THE DUKE OF EDINBURGH
CHANCELLOR OF THE UNIVERSITY
OF CAMBRIDGE ON 9 JUNE 1993

20. (right) Plaque outside Austin Wing. Courtesy of John Finch.

21. (below) The lecture room.

22. Aaron Klug.

23. John Sulston.

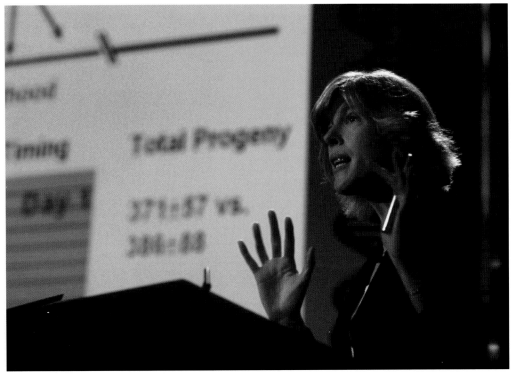

24. *Cynthia Kenyon.*

25. *Lord Sainsbury, Minister of Science (DTI), with Jim Watson unveiling a plaque outside The Eagle, the local pub for the Cavendish staff.*

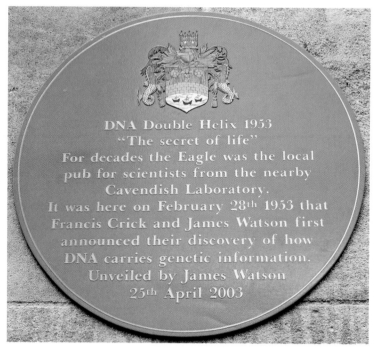

26. *The Eagle plaque. Courtesy of Richard Henderson.*

27. *Joan Steitz.*

28. Michael Rossmann and Venki Ramakrishnan.

29. Richard Durbin.

30. Sydney Brenner, Fred Sanger and Aaron Klug.

31. Allen Edmundson.

32. *Jon Widom, Tom Ceska and Soraya de Chadarevian.*

33. *Angelika Daser and Celia Milstein.*

34. David Secher.

35. Dan Brown and Henry Epstein.

36. Tim Richmond.

37. Sydney Brenner and Mary Osbourn.

38. Sydney Brenner.

39. Richard Perham and Hugh Huxley.

40. Suzanne Cory.

41. Elizabeth Blackburn.

42. *(above left) Mark Bretscher.*
43. *(above right) Gerry Rubin.*
44. *(left) Tom Steitz.*
45. *(below left) Sidney Altman.*
46. *(below right) Daniela Rhodes.*

47. *(top left) Brian Matthews.*
48. *(top right) Richard Henderson.*
49. *(right) Hugh Huxley.*
50. *(below left) Michael Rossmann.*
51. *(below right) Tim Richmond and Don Abrahams. Courtesy of Richard Henderson.*

CHAPTER FOUR

Post DNA

After a year in the USA, following the publication of the DNA structure, Crick was rejoined by Watson and with Don Caspar they began a brief examination of the structure of the small 'spherical viruses'. Crick's interest in demonstrating a direct genetic relationship between nucleic acid and protein led initially to some unrewarding investigations with Vernon Ingram, but prompted Ingram to analyse the difference between normal haemoglobin and the mutant sickle cell haemoglobin and show that the mutation produced a change in one amino acid. In 1957, Sydney Brenner joined the Unit, and prepared for an influx of phage workers and a build up of the molecular genetics side. Adaptor molecules (tRNAs), bridging between a nucleotide sequence and its appropriate amino acid, were proposed by Crick in 1956, but the three-base code was only established in 1961.

VIRUS STRUCTURE – DON CASPAR

Francis Crick completed his PhD thesis in July 1953 and left for Brooklyn Polytechnic to spend a year in David Harker's group working on the protein ribonuclease. Jim Watson, after a spell at Caltech, returned to Cambridge in July 1955, and he and Francis were joined by Don Caspar from Yale. All three were interested in virus structure. Watson had hoped that his earlier X-ray work on TMV would give some structural information on the RNA it contained and had also been working with isolated RNA in Caltech, but again without success. Caspar had also worked with TMV and had shown that the RNA was buried between turns of the helix of protein subunits at a radius of 40Å. But the lack of detailed information on the RNA structure from TMV led them to turn their attention to the small isometric ('spherical') plant viruses.

52. Don Caspar at Cold Spring Harbor, 1962. Courtesy of Cold Spring Harbor Laboratory Archives.

The first X-ray diffraction patterns from these viruses had been obtained by Bernal's group at Birkbeck College in London, using powders of tiny crystals of tomato bushy stunt (TBSV) and turnip yellow mosaic (TYMV) viruses in 1948 and 1950 respectively. The X-ray pictures indicated cube-shaped unit cells, but did not show whether the symmetry was also cubic. This was important for ideas on the substructure of the viruses because if it *was*, the virus particles themselves would have to have cubic symmetry and be made up of a number of identical subunits. To decide this, X-ray diffraction photographs from moving crystals to compare the intensities of reflections were required. Caspar found that Harry Carlisle, who had been involved in the earlier work at Birkbeck College, had large single crystals of TBSV and TYMV sitting in the fridge there, and it was agreed to divide them. TYMV remained with the virus group at Birkbeck (headed by Rosalind Franklin) and TBSV came to Cambridge.

Caspar managed to get X-ray precession photographs from the TBSV crystals and showed that they were indeed cubic, but in an X-ray picture from a disordered crystal he found rings of ten symmetrically arranged spots. This suggested that in addition to the basic cubic symmetry, the virus particles contained five-fold axes, and that they were built with a higher cubic symmetry, namely 532, or icosahedral symmetry. In pictures from more ordered crystals, spikes of strong reflections appeared along the directions of the 5-, 3- and two-fold axes of the 532 arrangement, as would be expected from this symmetry.

The cubic unit cells shown by the earlier work from the Birkbeck laboratory had suggested to Francis and Jim that the small isometric viruses could well be built with cubic symmetry and that the icosahedral member of the cubic family would cater for the largest number of structurally identical subunits, 60, in an isometric shell. They suggested that the adoption of a structure built with cubic symmetry could be a consequence of the desirability to build a protective shell around the nucleic acid out of a large number of relatively small protein subunits.[1] This would need a proportionately smaller amount of coding information than would be required for one, large shell-shaped molecule. These ideas and Caspar's results were presented at a Ciba Foundation meeting in London in 1956.[2] It was at this meeting that Heinz Fraenkel-Conrat and Robley Williams described experiments on taking apart the protein and RNA components of various strains of TMV and recombining them into hybrid particles which were infective and produced the same symptoms as the RNA they contained – nailing RNA in the genetic role.

The virus work marked the end of the direct collaborational work between Jim and Francis. In 1956, Jim returned to the USA – to the Harvard Biology Department, being promoted to Professor of Molecular Biology in 1961. He became Director of the Cold Spring Harbor Laboratory in 1968, and from 1994 has been its President.

In Cambridge, Francis had ideas on trying to make a direct correlation between a mutation in a gene and a corresponding change of sequence in the protein. For this, he enlisted Vernon Ingram, already part of the group, working on the bio-chemistry of haemoglobin.

VERNON INGRAM

Vernon Ingram graduated and received his PhD in organic chemistry at Birkbeck College in 1949. After a year at Yale and one at the Rockefeller Institute, he came to the MRC Unit in 1952. Following his attachment of mercury atoms to haemo-globin (Hb) and its resulting success as an isomorphous derivative for the X-ray work, his main task was trying to repeat this with other heavy atoms to get more and better phases. However, he was enticed away from this by talking with Francis about the lack of proof for the generally held assumption that a mutation in a gene altered an amino acid.

At first they concentrated on lysozyme, which was a well-studied molecule. The hope was that a mutant might be found by chance, but although lysozymes from various types of eggs (such as chicken, duck, goose) were looked at and differences found between them, all analyses of protein samples from any one species were identical. Similarly that from tears showed no variations. (One of the laboratory assistants, Rita Fishpool (see chapter 7), remembered Francis sniffing over a sliced-up onion while she collected tears from the corners of his eyes with a micro-pipette.[3])

At this point Ingram was given some sickle cell haemoglobin (HbS) by Max. Red cells from sufferers of sickle cell anaemia become deformed (sickle-shaped) when deoxygenated, aggregate and block the blood vessels, but recover in arterial blood. Pauling had proposed that this was a molecular disease caused by the muta-

53. Vernon Ingram at Cold Spring Harbor, 1969. Courtesy of Cold Spring Harbor Laboratory Archives.

tion of the haemoglobin gene which resulted in the HbS molecules aggregating into long fibres, and distorting the cell. His student, Harvey Itano, showed by elec-trophoresis that HbS was more positively charged than Hb, and these results had been presented at a meeting in 1949. James Neel of Michigan showed that the basic cause was a mutant gene following Mendelian statistics. However, the chem-ical difference between Hb and HbS was not immediately demonstrated – the Hb molecule was so large that individual amino acid changes were not detectable.

55

Ingram employed the technique that Fred Sanger had been using to chop insulin into reproducible short pieces that were manageable for analysis – trypsin digestion. Trypsin cuts polypeptide chains but only next to lysine or arginine, and in Hb this yielded about 30 peptides of various sizes but averaging about ten amino acids in length. Two-dimensional 'fingerprints' of the peptide families were produced by paper electrophoresis in one dimension and chromatography in the second. The fingerprints from Hb and HbS were extremely similar except for one spot '4' which had become more positively charged in HbS. This result was published in 1956 and the identification of the reason for this difference, the change of a glutamic acid residue in peptide 4 of normal Hb to valine in HbS, was determined and published in 1957[4] – the final proof that a mutation in a gene results in a change of amino acid. In 1958, Vernon Ingram left the Unit for MIT.

Other visitors at this time were Alex Rich and David Davies (see chapter 2), both from NIH. Alex was attracted by the power of the Broad X-ray tube – he had been given some synthesised polyadenylic acid made by Severa Ochoa and Marianne Grunberg-Manago, and had pulled small fibres of it, and hoped to get better X-ray pictures in Cambridge than were possible at Bethesda. Although a paper on the structure of polyA was published later (1961),[5] more of the immediate time was spent working on the structure of collagen, resulting in a *Nature* paper published in 1955 towards the end of Alex's six-month visit.[6]

SYDNEY BRENNER[7]

54. Sydney Brenner, c. mid-1970s.

Although the work of Francis and Jim on spherical viruses provided a basis for future ideas on the arrangement of protein in virus particles, in common with the earlier TMV work, there was little information on the RNA structure. But by now, Sydney Brenner had joined the group and raised interest in the nature of the genetic code and the mechanism of its operation.

Sydney Brenner was born in South Africa in 1927, won a scholarship in 1942 to Witwatersrand University in Johannesburg and received his first degree there in medicine. He was keen to get into basic medical research, and it was suggested that he apply to Sir Cyril Hinshelwood in Oxford. He was offered a one year research post there with encouragement to work on phage. He accepted and began work at Oxford in 1952. In April 1953, he came with a group (including Jack Dunitz and Leslie Orgel) from Oxford to see the DNA model in Cambridge and met Crick and Watson.

Sydney's thesis work included the repetition of experiments by Luria and Delbruck in the USA on phage-resistance produced in bacteria by mutations. Although disbelieved by Hinshelwood, this work caught the eye of the visiting Director of the Cold Spring Harbor Laboratory, Milislav Demerec, and Sydney was invited to the CSH laboratory for the summer of 1954. During this stay, he met Seymour Benzer who was working on mapping mutants in the *r*II gene of the T4 phage. Also, on a visit to Woods Hole, he became more acquainted with Watson and Crick. At the end of his stay, he called in at Cambridge on his way back to South Africa and Francis began moves to get him a post in the MRC Unit, which he joined at the beginning of 1957.

Max remembered that

> In 1956, I was asked by Crick to get Brenner a fellowship from the MRC. Things were so much simpler then. I went to see A. Landsborough Thomson, the deputy secretary of the MRC, and presented Crick's idea of a fellowship. Thomson replied: 'Why don't we take Brenner on our staff'. No panel, no referees, no interview, no lengthy report, just a few men with good judgement at the top.[8]

Sydney was initially involved in setting up a laboratory for phage work to be ready to receive visitors who had been invited from the USA. These included George Streisinger, Mahlon Hoagland and Seymour Benzer, all of whom came in 1957. Leslie Barnett was recruited from the crystallography computing side of the Unit, and Kate Wilkins was employed to run the kitchen – cleaning the glassware and making up supplies of standard solutions. (Kate moved with the Unit to LMB and continued running the Cell Biology kitchen until she retired in the late 1970s.)

During this time, Sydney became interested in the physiology of phage. For this he thought that the electron microscope would be useful, and so began collaborating with Bob Horne of the solid state physics group in the Cavendish. Because of their low density, biological specimens appear at very low contrast in the electron microscope and the standard method of increasing the contrast at that time was to evaporate a heavy metal such as platinum onto the specimen, but this was rather tedious. Sydney thought that adding a heavy metal stain might help improve the contrast and tried mixing the specimen with neutralised phosphotungstic acid (PTA). On looking at the resulting images, however, he recognised that in regions where there was a fair amount of the dense stain around, the specimens were embedded in it and were being made visible by their 'negative contrast' – or by negative staining as the effect was called in light microscopy. He and Bob Horne used the technique to look at various viruses as well as phage components in papers published in 1959.[9] The effect had been noted by Cecil Hall in 1955 (with the small spherical tomato bushy stunt virus in PTA) and by Hugh Huxley in 1956 (with tobacco mosaic virus in potassium chloride and in PTA). Hugh had in fact written 'The outlining technique would appear to be quite a useful one for this type of specimen, particularly as it is so simple and gives excellent contrast and resolution'.[10] But it was the striking images published by Brenner and Horne, particularly of the large and clearly icosahedral adenovirus, and their use of a defined concentration of PTA, which caused the method to take off, and helped bring the electron microscope from a specialist to an everyday tool.

Seymour Benzer had begun to follow up his study of the spontaneous rII phage mutants by studying those induced by incorporating 5-bromouracil acting as a base analogue, replacing thymine. In both cases, just the one base was affected. However, Sydney had been intrigued by published reports of many mutations being produced by proflavine. He persuaded Benzer with Leslie Barnett to look in the rII region for proflavine-induced mutants. These were found and mapped but their effects were quite distinct from the earlier ones; they were not, for example, capable of producing a slightly modified protein, but either no protein at all or a grossly altered one. The difference was a mystery until Francis and Sydney, discussing it in The Eagle, the public house conveniently close to the Cavendish in Bene't Street, realised that proflavine could intercalate between bases, and effectively add or delete a base – with a more devastating result than a change of one base. Resulting from this work, a paper on the 'Theory of Mutagenesis' was published in 1961[11] with Leslie Barnett and Alice Orgel.

THE GENETIC CODE

Since 1953, a major topic of interest had been the problem of the genetic code – how did the sequence of nucleotides in a gene carry the information for the amino acid sequence of the corresponding protein? It was generally considered that a code of three nucleotides per amino acid would be the most likely. A two-nucleotide code could only produce sixteen variations, whereas the number of amino acids was at least twenty – easily catered for by the 64 varieties of a three-nucleotide code. The triplet nature of the code was proved genetically in 1961 by Francis and Sydney with Leslie Barnett and Richard Watts-Tobin[12] – continuing their work on the rII region of T4, they showed that one or two additional bases in a gene resulted in nonsense, but three additions (or deletions) partly restored the wild-type function. (Since at that time it was not certain whether their mutations added or subtracted one base, or more than one base, they were careful to say that a higher-multiple-of-three code was possible, though unlikely.) At about the same time, Marshall Nirenberg and Heinrich Matthaei at NIH showed that a polymer of uridine coded for polyphenylalanine. So, between the two, the first codon (the term invented by Sydney) was established as UUU for Phe.

TRANSFER AND MESSENGER RNAs

There was still, however, the problem of how a three-base codon was able to cause the appropriate amino acid to be chosen in the synthesis. A direct structural association between amino acid and the coding sequence of nucleotides was initially suggested, but it seemed physically unfeasible to expect inter-nucleotide shapes to differentiate between the shapes of similar amino acids. Towards the end of his year in the USA, Francis had thought of the idea of two-part molecules which at one end could recognise a nucleotide sequence and, at the other end, attract the appropriate amino acid. The name 'adaptor molecules' was suggested by Sydney, but although much discussed, the adaptor hypothesis was not formally made public until February 1956 in a discussion at a Biochemical Society meeting. It was tentatively suggested that these were small pieces of nucleic acid and it turned out that such molecules had already been isolated by Mahlon Hoagland and Paul Zamecnik at Harvard Medical School – the transfer RNAs.

The idea of messenger RNA had been generally accepted by the later 1950s. The genetic data was encoded in the DNA within the cell nucleus, but the protein synthesis occurred in the cytoplasm where there was RNA but no DNA – thus the DNA sequence must be copied to RNA in the nucleus and this messenger transferred to the cytoplasm for protein synthesis. The largest amount of RNA was ribosomal and so it seemed that the ribosomes were the homes of the messengers. However, the composition of ribosomal RNA was worryingly constant and the so-called PaJaMo experiment (by Pardee, Jacob and Monod, at the Institut Pasteur) seemed inconsistent with this idea. In this, a known gene was introduced into a cell at a known time, and the corresponding synthesis was found to begin more or less immediately – not apparently waiting for the production of ribosomes. Francis and Sydney were reluctant to believe this. The French group came to see them in Cambridge on Good Friday, 1960, and there was a discussion at King's College. Francis and Sydney were forced to accept that ribosomal RNA was not the messenger. Both then remembered a paper presented at a meeting in 1956 by Volkin and Astrachan from the Oak Ridge National Laboratory reporting an RNA with an unusual composition which had been isolated from an *Escherichia coli* bacterium infected with the phage T4. Its base composition mirrored that of the T4 DNA and it was not present in uninfected bacteria. Francis and Sydney realised that this was the messenger for T4. Messengers had not been previously recognised, since their fast turnover stopped them reaching high and easily detectable concentrations.

The idea of a distinct mRNA was included by Jacob and Monod in their 1961 review of gene regulation in protein synthesis published in the *Journal of Molecular Biology*,[13] and experiments proving the existence of mRNA were published the same year by Sydney with Jacob and Meselson in *Nature*,[14] together with a companion paper by a group from the Pasteur Institute and Harvard. The collaboration with François Jacob in the field of gene replication continued and led in 1963 to the conclusion that there was a genetic unit of replication, a *replicon*, which could only replicate as a whole and whose capacity to replicate was controlled by specific determinants.

In 1957, Francis presented a classic paper at a symposium of the Society for Experimental Biology in London.[15] He summarised the state of current ideas on protein synthesis and gave the two general principles on which the current thinking was then based. The first of these was the Sequence Hypothesis – that the specificity of a piece of nucleic acid is expressed solely by the sequence of its bases, and that this sequence is a code for the amino acid sequence of a protein. The second was called the Central Dogma – that once information had gone into a protein, it could not get out again, i.e. that information went one way only, from nucleic acid to protein. Also included in this paper was a description of the adaptor hypothesis, which in its simplest form would require twenty adaptors, one for each amino acid.

1. F.H.C. Crick and J.D. Watson, 1956. Ciba Foundation Symposium: *The Nature of Viruses.* Churchill, London, pp. 5–13.
2. *Ibid.*
3. In an interview with Rita Fishpool and Eileen Southgate at LMB, 1999.
4. V.M. Ingram, 1956. A specific chemical difference between the globins of normal human and sickle cell anaemia haemoglobin. *Nature*, 178, 792–794.
5   A. Rich, D.R. Davies, F.H.C. Crick and J.D. Watson, 1961. Molecular structure of polyadenylic acid. *Journal of Molecular Biology*, 3, 71–86.
6. A. Rich and F.H.C. Crick, 1955. The structure of collagen. *Nature*, 176, 915–916.
7. A biographical interview of Sydney Brenner by Lewis Wolpert, *Sydney Brenner, a life in science*, was published by Science Archive Ltd, in 1997.
8. From Max's retirement lecture, September 1979.
9. S. Brenner and R.W. Horne, 1959. A negative staining method for high resolution electron microscopy of viruses. *Biochimica et Biophysica Acta*, 34, 103–110.
10. H.E. Huxley, 1956. Some observations on the structure of tobacco mosaic virus. *First European Conference on Electron Microscopy*, Stockholm, pp. 260–261.
11. S. Brenner, L. Barnett, F.H.C. Crick and A. Orgel, 1961. The theory of mutagenesis. *Journal of Molecular Biology*, 3, 121–124.
12. F.H.C. Crick, L. Barnett, S. Brenner and R.J. Watts-Tobin, 1961. General nature of the genetic code for proteins. *Nature*, 192, 1227–1232.
13. F. Jacob and J. Monod, 1961. Genetic regulatory mechanisms in the synthesis of proteins. *Journal of Molecular Biology*, 3, 318–356.
14. S. Brenner, F. Jacob and M. Meselson, 1961. An unstable intermediate carrying information from genes to ribosomes for protein synthesis. *Nature*, 190, 576–581. The companion paper is in *Nature*, 190, 581–585, 1961 by F. Gros, H. Hiatt, W. Gilbert, C.G. Kurland, R.W. Risebrough and J.D. Watson.
15. F.H.C. Crick, 1958. On protein synthesis. *Symposia of the Society for Experimental Biology*, 12, 138–163.

CHAPTER FIVE

Accommodation –
The new LMB

In 1957, the Unit was largely squeezed out of the main Cavendish building to the adjacent prefabricated hut, although the members wanted to expand their groups. They contacted Fred Sanger, who was also funded by the MRC and who was in a similar constricted position in the Biochemistry Department. A combined approach to the MRC was made suggesting a new building to house both groups, and after some years of negotiation with the University, the LMB was built on the site being developed for the new Addenbrooke's Hospital, and was occupied in 1962. In addition to the groups from the Cavendish and the Biochemistry Department, the new LMB also included Aaron Klug's group from Birkbeck College, and Hugh Huxley from University College in London. In May, the new laboratory was officially opened by the Queen, and in October, the Nobel Prize awards to Max Perutz and John Kendrew, and to Jim Watson and Francis Crick, with Maurice Wilkins were announced.

THE AUSTIN WING

Before 1957, the MRC Unit was inhabiting rooms and using laboratory space in the Austin Wing – a fairly new building occupied by the Cavendish. (The car manufacturer Herbert Austin had been persuaded to pay for this, the idea being possibly suggested by the site being close to an earlier Austin (Augustinian) Friary.) The Unit also had their X-ray tubes, the darkrooms for developing the X-ray films, and some preparation rooms and a small workshop in the basement and was able to draw supplies from the stores. (David Blow remembered that the senior technician in the Cavendish crystallography group was in charge of the X-ray film which was expensive to buy, and upon application one was allowed a few sheets – though always rather less than one hoped. His careful rationing led to the practice of using small fragments of film for exploratory and 'setting' photographs.)

In 1953, Bragg retired from the Cavendish, and was appointed Fullerian Professor at the Royal Institution in London. He had had a long connection with the RI, giving lectures there regularly since 1938, but it had lately been having financial and other problems, and Bragg was appointed with the aim of helping to sort these out. He took up the residential duties in January 1954. He wanted the MRC group to join him there, but both Max and John Kendrew considered the Cambridge environment essential for the continued vitality of the Unit.

Bragg's successor was Neville Mott – a solid state physicist. He wanted to bring his co-workers from Bristol, but he found that the department was already completely full and so he began looking for ways of making some space for them. The MRC Unit was the most vulnerable – it was the only group not directly connected to physics, it took up a good deal of space and wanted more, its staff did no teaching and its students did not help in the physics practical classes (Mott particularly remembered Francis Crick treating the suggestion that they might do more in this way with contempt[1]). Before coming to Cambridge, Mott asked the Unit to leave, but Max appealed to the General Board of the Faculties, pointing to the bright future ahead, and the Board backed him. Mott then wrote to the Board asking it to find a new site for the Unit, but they asked for it to remain at the Cavendish for at least another two years, until alternative accommodation could be found.

THE HUT[2]

In 1957 Mott's space problem became particularly acute, and he decided that he urgently needed the office and laboratory space in the Austin Wing for physicists. Next to the Austin Wing there was a prefabricated hut which Max thought could be a temporary solution. This had been occupied by a metal physics group whose leader Egon Orowan had moved to MIT. It was in a fairly seedy condition and lacked appreciable services and, at first, permission to occupy it was refused by the Secretary of the General Board, as it was due for demolition. However, with Mott's help, the demolition order was overruled and the hut was made habitable and useable for about £6,000, of which the University paid roughly half. (The hut still stands nearly 50 years later. It had a lean time after the MRC vacated it in 1962, when it became a bike shed, but it is now in a much-smartened state as the Rolls-Royce University Technology Centre. Michael Rossman, however, found it locked and empty when he tried to revisit it during the Memorial Meeting for Max in 2002 – a contrast to the open and busy atmosphere he remembered in the late 1950s. Max recalled that in the summer of 1959 a Biophysics Congress was held in Cambridge, which brought a delegation from the Soviet Union. One day they wanted to see the 'Institute of Molecular Biology' and when he took them to the hut they looked perplexed and went into a huddle. Finally they asked him 'And where do you work in the winter?'[3])

Half of the hut was converted to offices and half into a chemistry laboratory. Some space in an old Anatomy building (a conservatory) was given to Francis and

55. *The hut outside the Austin Wing of the Cavendish, c. 1960. Courtesy of Hans Boye.*

56. *The greenhouse, a conservatory outside the old Anatomy building used for phage work, c. 1960. Courtesy of Hans Boye.*

57. Max Perutz and some of the staff of the MRC unit outside the hut in 1958. From the left, Larry Steinrauf, Dick Dickerson, Hilary Muirhead, Michael Rossmann, Ann Cullis, Bror Strandberg and two unknown technicians. Sitting are Leslie Barnett and Mary Pinkerton. (Source unknown.)

Sydney for the genetic work. (Sydney remembers that through the windows one could see all the interesting people working at the University departments or visiting them – 'you see that man, that's Professor Dirac'.)[4] All that remained in the Austin Wing were the X-ray and workshop facilities.

The lack of space was, however, still very restricting for the members of the Unit who were wanting to expand their groups and studies. It was appreciated that the hut was only a temporary measure, but no long-term future locality had been identified. Mentions were made of a possibility in the new Chemistry laboratory being built at Lensfield Road 'if there is room'. Similarly there might have been a possibility in a new Physics Department – though even a site had not at that stage been decided. The members of the Unit also felt that they were short on biochemistry and so they approached Fred Sanger.

FRED SANGER

Fred was born in Rendcombe in Gloucestershire in 1918 and went initially to Downs School (a Quaker school) and then to Bryanston School, where he became interested in science, and especially in biology and chemistry. In a spare year before going to Cambridge, he spent much of his time in the chemistry laboratory at Bryanston, helping the master who was doing some research on dyestuffs, and Fred enjoyed the laboratory work, particularly growing beautifully coloured crystals. He came to Cambridge in 1936 (St John's College) and in choosing scientific subjects for his Part 1, came across 'biochemistry' for the first time and was greatly taken by the idea that biology could be explained by chemistry. After Part 1, he stayed on for a fourth year to take the Advanced Biochemistry course and obtained a first class degree. This news, conveyed to him by a cousin who had read it in *The Times*, surprised him since he had never done too well in exams, and he realised he was now sufficiently qualified for a research post.

58. *Fred Sanger, 1969.*

However, it was now 1940 and the war had begun. Being a Quaker and a registered conscientious objector, he was exempted from military service. He voluntarily worked in a military hospital for a time as a cleaner, but not finding this very inspiring, he wrote to the biochemistry professor in Cambridge – F. Gowland Hopkins – to see if there was any possibility of doing research there. Receiving no reply, he visited Cambridge and found several people there were willing to take him on. He chose to work with N.W. (Bill) Pirie – the protein expert in the laboratory – whose chief interest was trying to make edible protein from grass. Fred was given a large bucket of frozen grass, but almost immediately ('before it thawed') Pirie left Cambridge for Rothamsted and Fred was taken on by Albert Neuberger – his research project being on the 'Metabolism of Lysine'. He obtained his PhD in 1943 (the main criticism from the examiners being of the spelling – Fred had typed it himself).

Charles Chibnall took over the Cambridge Chair of Biochemistry in 1943. He was an expert in amino acid analysis and interested in protein structure, and brought a protein group with him from London. Neuberger had left the laboratory and Chibnall suggested that Fred try to obtain a quantitative estimation and identification of the amino acids in insulin with free amino groups. In London, Chibnall's group had found this number to be appreciably larger than could be accounted for on the basis of lysines alone, and suggested that the balance was due to free amino groups at the ends of the chains, and hence that the polypeptide chains were short.

At that time, almost nothing was known about sequencing. In fact, the position of only one amino acid in any protein was known: this was a phenylalanine residue at the N-terminus of insulin which had been detected by H Jensen and E A Evans in 1935. – It was fairly generally agreed that amino acids were linked by peptide bonds, according to the theory of Fischer and Hofmeister – although there were some doubts.

Another point of some contention was whether proteins could be regarded as pure chemical entities with all the molecules of one protein being identical, or whether they were heterogeneous mixtures of closely related molecules. It was not known how proteins were synthesized. The most popular theory was that it was some sort of reversal of the action of the proteolytic enzymes, and it was difficult to see how this could be completely specific.[5]

Fred developed a new chromatographic method for determining end-groups and his results on the free amino groups of insulin were published in 1945. Exploiting the techniques further, he determined the N-terminal sequences of the two insulin chains in 1949. The complete sequence of the phenylalanine (B) chain was obtained with an Austrian postdoc, Hans Tuppy, and published in 1951, and that of the glycyl (A) chain obtained with an Australian postdoc, Ted Thompson, was published in 1953. The rounding-off paper, locating the disulphide bonds between the chains, was published in 1955, with A.P. Ryle, Leslie Smith and Ruth Kitai.[6] The work established biochemically the uniformity of a protein species and resulted in the award to Fred of the Nobel Prize for Chemistry in 1958 'for his work on the structure of proteins, especially that of insulin'.

From 1944 to 1951, Fred was funded by a Beit Memorial Fellowship for Medical Research, and from 1951 he was a member of the external scientific staff of the Medical Research Council.

MOVES FOR A NEW BUILDING

As with Max, Fred Sanger was frustrated by the limitation of his space in the Biochemistry Department. He and other members of his group needed to expand, but there was no promise of any extra space becoming available. (The new bio-chemistry block – the Sanger Building – did not in fact appear until 1997, 48 years later.) Fred therefore agreed that both groups should join forces and approach the MRC for a more satisfactory solution.

Encouraged by Fred's enthusiasm, Max wrote to the MRC in 1957. The MRC was funding both the Sanger and Perutz groups, and as both groups were keen to combine, Max suggested the possibility of a new building to house them together. In response, Sir Harold Himsworth, who had replaced Mellanby as Secretary of the MRC, came to visit the Unit with Quintin Hogg (later Lord Hailsham), who as Lord President was answerable to parliament for the Research Councils. In early 1958, Himsworth asked Max to present the group's case to the MRC, which he did in the form of two memoranda, one drafted by Francis and Max and approved by all the senior staff in both the Cavendish group and in Fred's group, as a formal presentation to the MRC of their needs, and another by Max alone on 'Recent Advances in Molecular Biology'. Max was greeted in London by several members of Council who had found the memorandum most exciting, and the following morning Himsworth phoned to say that the plan had Council's approval. The next problem was a building site and the approval of the University – a much greater problem than winning over the MRC. It took more than two years of further negotiations before agreement was reached.

Himsworth first tested the opinion of the interested Department heads in Cambridge. He found Mott, the head of the Cavendish, uncomfortable about things – he was enthusiastic about the MRC research, but felt he could spare no space: he didn't disfavour a new Institute, but he thought there should still be some connection with the Physics Department. Alexander Todd at the Chemistry Department had no objection in principle, but thought the groups would benefit from strong contacts with Chemistry. However, Chibnall had resigned his chair in Biochemistry in 1949 and been replaced by Frank Young, who was very much against the idea of an independent Institute. He thought that such establishments formed to house a few top specialist research people tended to decline as those people became older. He also thought that research workers should take their full share of the University chores of teaching etc., and not be able to opt out, and that it would also increase the competition for the small number of technical assistants available in the relatively small Cambridge area. He thought that if the MRC wanted to set up a large combined laboratory, they should do it in places like the large MRC Institute, NIMR at Mill Hill in London, located on a separate site with a correspondingly large critical mass of workers. Within the groups, John Kendrew was the least in favour of a possible Institute of Molecular Biology – he did not like the idea of being cut off from the University and losing the possibility of attracting PhD students.

By June (1958), Joseph Mitchell, the Regius Professor of Physic at Cambridge (the head of University Medicine) and head of a new Department of Radiotherapeutics, had become involved. He was 100 per cent in favour of forming a new laboratory combined with his own Department, and at a University meeting suggested possible sites. Young was still anti-, and in September he again argued that as the leaders lost their vigour, such purpose-built Institutes tended to become backwaters. He was still in favour of either keeping Sanger's group in Biochemistry (with little chance of its enlargement) and the Perutz group in the Cavendish, or setting up a University Department of Molecular Biology (or sending the lot to the NIMR at Mill Hill). However, the next month (the month in which Fred was awarded his first Nobel Prize) he told Himsworth that if he was in a minority of one, he would aquiesce. Himsworth thought it was now time to communicate officially with the University, but thought that it might be a good idea to avoid the word 'Institute'. Max agreed and decided on the name 'Laboratory of

Molecular Biology', and a report was sent to the University Board on numbers of workers, areas of working space and a plan of the building. A four-level building was proposed to house 35 research workers in three main groups – protein chemistry, protein crystallography and molecular genetics. (Max also told Himsworth that he had been approached by Hans Krebs and Dorothy Hodgkin, who thought that a site for the proposed laboratory could probably be found at Oxford.)

Appreciating how slowly the wheels of the University turn, Mott got himself elected to the General Board and persuaded them to set up a subcommittee including himself, Todd and Young, and it was agreed in March 1959 that a site should be found for the laboratory. In April, some space close to the old Addenbrooke's Hospital in Trumpington Street was suggested, but this proved too small upon inspection by Max and Himsworth (and it turned out not to belong to the University anyway, but to the Department of Health). It was agreed that the alternative proposal of building on the newly developing hospital site off Hills Road, two miles south of the city centre, was the best option.[7]

In July 1959 a working party including Mitchell, Max, representatives of the University and Hospital and architects met, and it was proposed to build a joint building for the MRC laboratory and for the Department of Radiotherapy. This would be financed mainly by the MRC, with the Wellcome Trust providing a grant for equipment, and the University Grants Committee contributing to the site works. The buildings and site would be the subject of a direct lease (99 years suggested) between the Minister of Health, the University and the MRC. The building was slightly larger than originally planned, to accommodate Hugh Huxley from University College and Aaron Klug's 'virus' group from Bernal's laboratory at Birkbeck College in London, both of whom being funded by the MRC.

(Part of the MRC's contribution was paid out of the largest single private benefaction ever received by the Council, amounting to £160,000 – from the estate of Lady (Julia) Wadia, who died in 1957 leaving the money to form a fund named after her late husband, Sir Cusrow Wadia, a Parsee who had been a prominent millowner and philanthropist in Bombay.)

THE BIRKBECK GROUP

Birkbeck College was launched in 1823 by George Birkbeck as London's first Mechanics Institution, dedicated to the education of working men. In 1858, the ratification of the charter of the University of London enabled any student to sit degree examinations and Birkbeck soon emerged as the main promoter of university education for people unable to afford full-time study. Since 1925, it has been an exclusively evening-class college, mainly for undergraduates but with some part-time PhD students.

It was to the Physics Department of Birkbeck that Bernal came as Professor in 1937. During the war (1941) the college premises were bombed, and a new building was opened in 1952 alongside the University Senate House in Malet Street, in the Bloomsbury area of London. There was, however, insufficient room for the crystallography laboratory that Bernal was building up, and this was housed in 21–22 Torrington Square, the remains of a bomb-damaged and semi-redeveloped Georgian Square close to the new building. Bernal had a flat over No. 22, a favourite calling place for visiting communists and Bloomsburians. In 1950, on his way to a Peace Conference, Picasso drew a mural on the wall which was preserved when the houses were demolished, and later transferred to a new building in the Square. Aaron Klug remembers a visit by the Soviet crystallographer, Belov, at the time of the fall of Beria, the head of the Soviet secret police under Stalin. Bernal kept a copy of the *Soviet Encyclopaedia* – a continuously updated publication – on his shelves, and Belov seeing it, reached out for the Be- section and turned through the pages and pointed out that Beria had been removed and replaced by an article on the Bering Straits. But next to it he noticed the entry for Bernal: 'Ah ha, Bernal is alright, he is still there!'

The Birkbeck virus group had been started by Rosalind Franklin in Bernal's laboratory after she left King's in 1953. The crystallography laboratory was a research department, which was then composed of seven or eight small groups. Bernal, at that time, was more involved in external affairs and travelling than personal research. Apart from the dilapidated condition of the buildings, the polluted London atmosphere added its grime – a first attempt at cooling a crystal by blowing air from outside onto the capillary tube enclosing it, resulted in a layer of soot after an hour or so. Once in the X-ray room, one of the part-time PhD students came in to see Aaron and myself in a rather distressed state – on trying to track down a strange smell from his X-ray set, he had sniffed the anode before earthing it and received a high voltage shock on his nose. He was fearful that his face was badly damaged, but too scared to look. Aaron calmed him down and said such shocks had been common in the Cape Town department where he had worked – the X-ray sets were served by a common high-voltage supply, and workers from time to time accidentally touched these and were thrown about the laboratory, until one day one was thrown out of the window. This prompted a feeling that something should be done – and so bars were put over the windows!

Rosalind was housed in a not-quite-rainproof attic room at the top of No. 21. She had begun work on improving the X-ray pictures from the rod-shaped tobacco mosaic virus (TMV) and in 1955 had taken on two PhD students, John Finch and Ken Holmes. (Since Rosalind had no University of London status, the nominal supervisor was Bernal. He could never remember our names, but did keep an interest in the work of the group. On reading my thesis, however, his only comment was to insist that I put in a reference to Euclid when the icosahedron was mentioned.) Ken Holmes was to continue work with TMV and I was to work on the small spherical viruses. Rosalind was also collaborating with Aaron Klug, whose office was in the neighbouring attic room. Aaron had become interested in the virus work and several joint papers on TMV and on the spherical virus, turnip yellow mosaic (TYMV), were published.

59. Arthur Page, John Finch and Ken Holmes at Birkbeck, during the building of the TMV model for the Brussels Exposition in 1957. The model is now on the first floor of LMB. Courtesy of John Finch.

The plant viruses were isolated from plants grown in the University of London Botanical Supply Unit at Egham in Surrey, for which we bought a greenhouse. They were rather scornful that it was framed with aluminium rather than their normal wood, and no doubt felt justified when the plants refused to grow in it – but grew well after being thrown out on a nearby compost heap. However, the Unit allowed us to use one of their wooden greenhouses temporarily until the inside of ours had been decontaminated.

The X-ray diffraction photographs from TMV were much improved by Ken Holmes, who set up an X-ray focusing arrangement with a bent quartz crystal monochromator on a fine focus Beaudouin X-ray set. Reuben Leberman, the group's biochemist, produced a mercury derivative of the virus and with this, the helical parameters of the virus particle were established – there are close to 49 sub-units in three turns of the basic helix.

However, it was the spherical virus work in particular that generated a close contact with Crick, Watson and Don Caspar in the Cambridge Unit – the X-ray patterns from TYMV showing evidence for icosahedral symmetry in the virus particle, predicted as a possibility by Crick and Watson.

On her last visit to the USA in 1957, Rosalind discussed the possibility of a crystallographic study of poliovirus with Fred Schaeffer and Carlton Schwerdt, who had grown tiny crystals at Berkeley. These were sent to her, but having been grown in very low salt conditions they dissolved when introduced into the thin-walled glass capillary tubes for X-raying. Rosalind wrote to suppliers to try to get neutral glass capillaries, but later Aaron introduced the idea of using quartz capillaries in which the crystals were stable. When larger crystals were grown, they were brought to Aaron in 1959 by Carlton and Patsy Schwerdt. This apparently worried the air-port officials at Heathrow – it was before mass polio immunisation – but they became much happier in allowing the virus into the country after being told by Patsy that it was in the form of crystals. However, the staff at Birkbeck were not very happy with the polio work being done in their laboratory. They did not feel it was properly equipped to have the virus around and the crystals were banished to the nearby London School of Hygiene and Tropical Medicine, and the X-ray work to the Royal Institution where the director, Bragg, was happy for the more powerful rotating anode X-ray sets there to be used. (He was, however, mildly crit-ical of the 'waste' of X-ray film – some of the patterns were very small, only a few millimetres in diameter, but one still needed a five-inch strip to locate in the film cassette.)

Again, the X-ray patterns showed indications of icosahedral symmetry, but unhappily Rosalind did not live to see these – she died of cancer in April 1958, aged 37. Unhappily too, she was unable to join in the plans for her group to be accommodated in the new Cambridge laboratory. Aaron Klug took over the lead-ership of the group, and the interaction with the MRC Unit was extended by his collaboration with Crick and Harold Wyckoff. They developed the helical diffrac-tion theory in practically useful forms, in particular by introducing the ideas of radial and helical projections. In addition to Klug, Finch and Holmes, the group moving to Cambridge at the beginning of 1962 also included Bill Longley, a crys-tallography student, and Reuben Leberman, the group's biochemist.

THE NEW LMB

Max was appointed Chairman of the new laboratory, with John Kendrew as deputy. Max was insistent on not being a Director, as he later wrote:

> Since there was no difference in age or distinction between us, I persuaded the Medical Research Council to appoint me Chairman of a Governing Board rather than a Director, a Board to be made up of Crick, Kendrew, Sanger and me. This arrangement reserved major decisions of scientific policy to the Board and left their execution and financial responsibility vis-à-vis the Medical Research Council to me. The Board met only rarely, when such decisions needed to be taken. This worked smoothly and left me free to pursue my own research. Seeing the Chairman stand-ing at the laboratory bench or the X-ray tube, rather than sitting at his desk, set a good example and raised morale. The Board never directed the laboratory's research but tried to attract, or keep, talented young people and gave them a free hand. My job was to make sure that they had the means to carry it out.[8]

Being a Chairman paid off when Max retired. It was an MRC policy that Directors should not continue to work in their laboratories after retiring and Max was able to say that he had never been the Director.

60. The brand-new LMB in 1962.

61. The Governing Board, which consisted initially of all the LMB Fellows of the Royal Society. From the left, Hugh Huxley, John Kendrew, Max Perutz, Francis Crick, Fred Sanger and Sydney Brenner (1967).

Max and John Kendrew were joint heads of the Structural Studies Division (briefly referred to in earlier plans as the 'Protein Crystallography Division', but since Hugh Huxley's work was involving electron microscopy, he suggested the name Structural Studies, and this it has remained). Francis Crick and (after a year) Sydney Brenner were the joint heads of the Molecular Genetics (later Cell Biology) Division and Fred Sanger headed the Protein (later Protein and Nucleic Acid) Chemistry Division. There were three main floors as well as the ground floor and basement. The ground floor housed the general stores and workshop and the large Structural Studies equipment rooms – the X-ray sets and Hugh Huxley's electron microscope and laboratory. The first floor was mainly offices, plus rooms for model building and for the computing girls – for densitometering the X-ray films and plotting density maps. (An early visitor, Vittorio Luzatti, was intrigued by the label 'computers' on their room and queried 'you have new machines?' but on opening the door and seeing the computer girls said 'oh no, … very old designs.') The second floor was mainly for Molecular Genetics plus a lecture room, and the third for Fred's Division plus a library. Above the west end of the third floor was built the canteen (which now houses the Visual Aids department). Much of the logistics of moving in were organised by Michael Fuller – he acted as a middle man between the architects and the scientists and looked after the local details of services and equipment. The Cavendish wanted nothing left behind and so, for example, the benches in the laboratory end of the hut were stripped out and reassembled in one of the new laboratories.

MICHAEL FULLER

62. *Michael Fuller, c. 1970.*

Michael Fuller was born in Cambridge and educated at the Central Grammar School (now Parkside) which then had a technical bias. Reading about the nuclear physics work that had been done at the Cavendish made him enthusiastic about trying to get a job there and, when he was fifteen, he wrote asking if there were any vacancies. The letter reached Max, who wrote back inviting him to an interview for the post of apprentice technician. Just before Christmas 1951 he was interviewed by Max with John Kendrew and Tony Broad, who had designed the Unit's rotating anode X-ray tube (based on one built by A. Taylor at the Mond Nickel Company in Birmingham[9]) and was in process of getting it going. Michael was offered the job and began work on 2 January 1952.

73

His main job was helping Tony Broad with the final stages of the X-ray tube construction and installation, and, after the first of these began running in 1952, with its maintenance. (However, he was available for other general odd jobs for anyone in the Unit – he remembers on his first day fetching horse blood for Max from Pink's slaughterhouse in Coldham's Lane.) Most of the construction work was carried out by the Cavendish staff in their mechanical workshop – only relatively small jobs could be done in the students' workshop. This resulted in delays; for example, the parts for the DNA models in 1953 had to wait for some months for their turn in the main workshop. (Michael remembers that there was little interest in the DNA structure among the physicists at the Cavendish – someone on a visit to the USA had brought back a 'Slinky' metal spring that 'walked' down the stairs, and there was more interest and discussion on that.) In 1956, the Unit was able to appoint their own qualified instrument maker, Len Hayward. By this time, the X-ray sets were running fairly smoothly and Michael became involved in the construction of other instruments, often with local companies who later developed and marketed them – fraction collecters, dry block heaters and water baths.

In 1957, Michael was called up for National (military) Service and because of his medical connections (working for the MRC) he was allotted to the army medical corps. Eventually he became an acting sergeant in charge at night of a 400-bed hospital on the south coast. Although tempted by an offer to stay on in the army with the prospect of officer training, when he visited the Unit in Cambridge on a week's leave and learnt of the plans for the new building, he asked if he could have his old job back when his two years of service were up. He was employed again as a technician, but was immediately involved in setting up the new laboratory.

THE MOVE

The move into the new LMB began at the end of 1961. The stores and workshop were the first parts to be set up. Michael Fuller equipped the stores (he was allotted £500 for chemicals), and Len Hayward, the Unit's instrument maker, organised the fitting-out of the mechanical workshop. The various research groups then followed – no research being interrupted for more than a week.

The first Head of Maintenance, from 1962, was Jack Peacock – who had been the Site Engineer during the construction of the building – with a staff of three. (Dave Claxton took over from 1968 and Robert Robertson from 1993 until 2006, with an overall staff of twelve.)

Although Michael Fuller remained in charge of the stores and of general purchasing, the actual workers in the stores were recruited from shopkeepers and publicans – used to dealing with people – and they provided a general information centre for the laboratory. Michael's purchasing side was virtually half of the local administration in these early days – the other half was Audrey Martin, the laboratory secretary, recruited from the Dunn Nutritional Laboratory (with her dog Slippers, who was accommodated beside her desk). The staff numbers were fairly small – about 25 scientists and the same number of visitors – and much of the financial side was conducted at the MRC head office in London. As the laboratory has grown, and more MRC-funded Units established nearby, more responsibility has been taken over locally, and the number of administrators correspondingly increased (see chapter 10).

The LMB was officially opened by the Queen in May 1962, and the work of the laboratory was described to her by the Divisional Heads, except for Crick and Brenner who had absented themselves. Jim Watson, on the other hand, made a special journey from the USA to be involved.

The LMB opening in 1962

63. *The Queen and Max. (Source unknown.)*

64. *John Kendrew showing the atomic model of myoglobin to the Queen, with onlookers (from the left) Mavis Blow, Gisela Perutz, Charlotte and Sir Harold Himsworth (Secretary of the MRC) and Lord Shawcross.*

FOUR NOBEL PRIZES

As soon as the new laboratory was occupied, in October 1962, the first major celebration occurred – on the award of the Nobel Prizes in Chemistry to Max Perutz and John Kendrew 'for their studies of the structures of globular proteins' and in Physiology or Medicine to Francis Crick and Jim Watson (with Maurice Wilkins) 'for their discoveries concerning the molecular structure of nucleic acid and its significance for information transfer in living material'. At what has become the traditional celebratory canteen party, Robin Offord, a student of Ieuan Harris, lauded the laboratory and the prizewinners with a guitar and song containing the line '... and there's a Nobel Fellow on every floor'. Although Fellows have dispersed, and some have died, new creations kept the number fairly constant for the next 35 years.

65. Nobel Prizewinners, 1962. From the left, Maurice Wilkins, John Steinbeck, John Kendrew, Max Perutz, Francis Crick and Jim Watson. Courtesy of TopFoto, UK.

66–69. Nobel celebration at LMB, 1962

66. (top) Sydney Brenner and Francis Crick. Courtesy of
Hans Boye.
67. (below) Max with David Green (immediate left), Leslie
Barnett (extreme right) and others. Courtesy of Hans Boye.
68. (top right) Max Perutz. Courtesy of Hans Boye.
69. (bottom right) John Kendrew. Courtesy of Hans Boye.

1.   E.A. Davis, ed., 1998. *Neville Mott – Reminiscences and Appreciations.* Taylor and Francis, London, p. 110.
2.   Memories of life in the hut were recorded by R.E. Dickerson, 1992. A little ancient history. *Protein Science*, 1, 182–186. Part of this is reproduced in Chapter 10.
3.   M.F. Perutz, 1996. The Medical Research Council Laboratory of Molecular Biology. *Molecular Medicine*, 2, 659–662.
4.   From a biographical interview. L. Wolpert, 1997. *Sydney Brenner, A Life in Science.* Science Archive Ltd, London.
5.   F. Sanger, 1996. *Selected Papers of Frederick Sanger.* World Scientific Series in 20th Century Biology – Vol. 1, p. 3. World Scientific, Singapore.
6.   The three papers are: F. Sanger and H. Tuppy, *Bioch. J.*, 49, 481–490, 1951; F. Sanger and E.O.P. Thompson, *Bioch. J.*, 53, 353–366, 1953; A.P. Ryle, F. Sanger, L.F. Smith and Ruth Kitai, *Bioch. J.*, 60, 541–556, 1955.
7.   The site being developed for the new Addenbrooke's Hospital consisted of nearly 44 acres, mainly part of the Pemberton Estate with a frontage owned by Trinity College. It was bought by the hospital in 1952, with £2,259 15s. 5d. being paid to the Pemberton Trustees and £2,394 19s. 6d. to Trinity. It was agreed that part of the land should be leased to the University for their use. 'In 1960 the [hospital] Board of Governors and the University agreed a peppercorn rent for leasing the area at Hills Road to be used for University teaching and research purposes.' (A. Rook, M. Carlton and W.G. Cannon, 1991. *The History of Addenbrooke's Hospital Cambridge.* Cambridge University Press, Cambridge, p. 422.
8.   Perutz, *op. cit.*
9.   A. Taylor, 1949. A 5kW crystallographic X-ray tube with a rotating anode. *Journal of Scientific Instruments*, 26, 225–229.

CHAPTER SIX

Structural Studies

The first heads of the Structural Studies Division were Max Perutz and John Kendrew. Initially, in 1962, the Division consisted of the groups of Max continuing the work on haemoglobin, John Kendrew continuing with myoglobin and Michael Rossmann who was becoming interested in using non-crystallographic symmetry to solve protein structures, collaborating with David Blow who was also continuing with chymotrypsin – all from the hut. In addition, Aaron Klug and his group came from Birkbeck, working mainly on viruses, and Hugh Huxley from University College continuing with his muscle work. Uli Arndt was also invited, and joined the laboratory from the Royal Institution in 1963, with a general remit to design new techniques and new instrumentation for protein crystallography.

The longevity and interests of these groups have varied enormously. The haemoglobin work continued well after Max's retirement in 1979, and Max himself was actively involved in research until his death in 2002. John Kendrew soon became interested in external scientific affairs, did no scientific research after 1962, and left to become the Director General of EMBL in 1975. His group had disintegrated with the departure of Herman Watson for Bristol in 1968. Michael Rossmann left for Purdue in 1964, but David Blow's group continued until David moved to Imperial College in 1977. Hugh Huxley carried on with the structural work on muscle, but left LMB in 1987, to continue his research at Brandeis University, in Massachusetts. Aaron Klug's group soon grew and branched out from virus structure into a variety of topics and Aaron still (2005) has a small group working on zinc finger proteins. Uli Arndt was involved in the design and development of many of the instruments used in the X-ray structural side.

As staff have left the laboratory, new people and groups have joined, producing a continuing and steady growth in overall size. As well as keeping up with the advances in X-ray diffraction and electron microscopy, newer techniques have been introduced, notably NMR, and many structures of proteins and other molecules have been analysed and published.

MAX PERUTZ AND THE HAEMOGLOBIN GROUP

Transferring with Max from the hut to the new laboratory were his student Hilary Muirhead and Ed McGandy, a postdoc visitor from Boston. In mid-1962, Gwynne Goaman from University College, Cardiff joined the group.

The molecular structure of oxygenated horse haemoglobin determined in the hut in 1959 had shown the subunit arrangement, and the 5.5Å resolution was sufficient to see the α-helical sections within the subunits. In the following year, chemical data enabled the four subunits to be identified as the two α- and the two β-chains. But clearly, to establish how the molecule worked, two directions had to be pursued – the resolution had to be pushed to atomic dimensions (2 or 3Å) and a comparison made between the oxy- and deoxy- forms.

The deoxy- form of horse haemoglobin did not initially crystallise in a favourable form, but human deoxy- was more amenable and had been given to Hilary Muirhead as her project when she had joined the group as a student in the hut in 1958. Her 5.5Å map, completed late in 1962, showed a rearrangement of the subunits – the β-chains had moved appreciably further apart (later, in 1967, the overall movement was shown by Joyce Cox (now Baldwin) to be a rotation and translation of the $\alpha_1\beta_1$ dimer relative to the $\alpha_2\beta_2$ dimer). There was some initial controversy over the interpretation – since the oxy- and deoxy- forms were from different species, it was argued that the rearrangement might be due to this, but a simpler crystal form of the horse deoxyhaemoglobin was found later (1963) and this showed identical heavy atom attachments. Its density map was subsequently (1968) shown to superpose on that of the human deoxy- form.

One of the properties of haemoglobin of great interest in understanding how it worked was the cooperative effect in its oxygen uptake – initial oxygenation promotes further uptake, and initial deoxygenation promotes further release – ensuring that most of the molecules in solution are either fully oxygenated or fully deoxygenated. The phenomenon is similar to that found for certain enzymes which also show cooperative binding to their substrates, and which Monod had called allostery – he called haemoglobin an 'honorary allosteric enzyme'. The relative subunit shifts observed in the transition suggested that these might be involved in the effect. However, the detailed structural mechanism could not be explained without a high resolution map, and this now became the main aim of the group.

Although the earlier horse deoxy- data to 5.5Å had been collected on film with precession cameras, it was not easy to collect the extended data in this way, as had been done with myoglobin, because of the larger size of the haemoglobin molecule and unit cell. Preliminary data from crystals of the horse oxyhaemoglobin, collected with a linear diffractometer by Gwynne Goaman and Scott Mathews, a postdoc from MIT, were not sufficiently accurate and so Max decided to collect the new data himself – 100,000 reflections overall for the native crystals and three heavy atom derivatives – on a Hilger and Watts four-circle diffractometer (see p. 97). But this needed a controlling computer.

At that time, it was not felt that the laboratory could accommodate a large computer (with an attendant large number of maintainance staff) that could take over the crystallographic computing and also be used to control the diffractometer. Small computers were, however, just beginning to appear, and it was decided to buy one of these for use with the diffractometer. The choice was between the Ferranti Argus, developed in the UK for military use in controlling the

70. Max setting a crystal on the diffractometer, 1980. Courtesy of Cambridge Newspapers Ltd.

Bloodhound Rocket, and a machine called PDP4, made by the then relatively unknown US firm, the Digital Equipment Corporation. Helped by pressure to 'buy British', a Ferranti Argus 400 machine was chosen and installed in 1963. David Blow wrote the programs to calculate the diffractometer settings and Tim Gossling was recruited from Ferranti to write cosine and other basic routines. The Ferranti control circuits supplied for the diffractometer were very unreliable and were rebuilt by Frank Mallett who had joined the laboratory from Harwell. Paper tapes – initially five-hole and later eight-hole – containing the setting instructions were produced by the Argus to be fed into the diffractometer reader, and the output was again on paper tape.

The punched tapes were, however, very prone to errors, with the occasional disk of paper failing to be cleanly removed, and the reliability of the system was greatly improved when a direct link was made between Argus and the diffractometer. The data collection took 15 months continuously, the diffractometer being kept going by Uli Arndt and Frank Mallett. Nowadays (~2005) one hour at a synchrotron would be ample.

The data were processed by Hilary Muirhead (who returned to the LMB in 1966 after two years at Harvard in the laboratory of Bill Lipscomb) and Joyce Cox, using the Titan computer at the Maths Laboratory and an IBM7090 at Imperial College (see chapter 9). Hilary with Max took

71. Ferranti Argus 400, control box, teleprinter and tape reader, 1966. (Source unknown.)

three months to build a wire model. The 2.8Å map of horse oxyhaemoglobin was published in 1968,[1] and a 2.8Å map of horse deoxyhaemoglobin in 1970 by Bill Bolton and Max.[2] A map of human deoxyhaemoglobin was published by Hilary Muirhead and Jonathan Greer at 3.5Å in 1970[3] and the resolution increased to 2.5Å by Lynn TenEyck and Arthur Arnone in 1972 (published in 1976).[4] The atomic model based on the latter was refined by Judd Fermi as one of his first jobs at LMB,[5] firstly by using Bob Diamond's recently introduced real-space method of fitting coordinates to the map, calculating a new map from phases now predicted, and symmetry averaging about the non-crystallographic molecular dyad axis.

From the 1968 map, Max concluded that the functional unit of haemoglobin was the tetramer – there are significant contacts between members of opposite dimers, for example between $\alpha1\beta2$. In 1970, Max proposed a mechanism explaining the cooperative effect in oxygen uptake, detailing the structural changes in the subunits produced by oxygenation which destabilise the deoxy- structure.[6] Previous work, particularly by a haemoglobin group in Rome, had seemed to show that individual *dimers* exhibited the complete cooperative effect. However, in 1971, ultracentrifugation analysis by George Kellett at Bristol, of haemoglobin in the high salt 'dissociating' conditions used by the Rome group, failed to find any dissociation into dimers, and, in 1972 John Kilmartin and John Hewitt in LMB showed that a partially cleaved haemoglobin could be dissociated in magnesium chloride, but lost cooperativity – which was regained when the salt was removed. These and other results provided convincing evidence that the overall tetramer *was* the cooperative unit, but more objections arose to the proposed cooperativity mechanism, which lingered on over some years. Thus, for example, R.J.P. Williams in Oxford argued that oxy-crystals used in the X-ray work would have become oxidised to met-haemoglobin and that CO-haemoglobin should have been used, but in 1972, Betsy Goldsmith-Heidner and Bob Ladner showed that CO- and met- were structurally the same.

Across the road from LMB, in Addenbrooke's Hospital, was the Department of Clinical Biochemistry, whose head was Hermann Lehmann – a world authority on abnormal haemoglobins. Most of these are point mutations, and he and Max were able to correlate the substitution with abnormal properties and clinical symptoms – the first time that the causes of human disease could be seen at the atomic level.

After retirement

In 1979, Max retired as Chairman of LMB, but taking advantage of the fact that he had not been Director, he sidestepped the MRC policy of not encouraging Directors to continue in their laboratories after retirement, and carried on working in LMB. At a meeting in Washington in 1980, the possibility of vetting drugs to counter the insolubility of deoxy-sickle-haemoglobin was discussed. Several compounds that increased the solubility were sent to Max to determine the binding sites and possibly give information on improving them. The X-ray work was done with Judd Fermi, but no compound was found that produced a useful anti-sickling effect at tolerable doses. However, work on ligand binding to haemoglobin led to the development by Don Abrahams and others of a clinically useful drug for increasing oxygen delivery to hypoxic tumours for radiation therapy and to oxygen-deprived tissues in general. A collection of Max's haemoglobin papers with a commentary by him, *Science is not a Quiet Life*,[7] was published in 1997 and also contained his papers on glacier flow and one on the proposed iceberg/aircraft carrier.

Around 1990, Max became interested in the abnormally expanded repeats of glutamines near the N-termini of the affected proteins in neurodegenerative diseases such as Huntington's disease. In all cases, the disease becomes more severe and begins earlier when there are longer glutamine repeats. In 1992, while pondering over the aggregation of the Hb molecules of the nematode worm *Ascaris*, he noticed that a run of glutamines would generate alternate partial positive and negative charges on two sides of a β-strand, forming what he called a polar zipper. In 1994, with Tony Johnson, Masashi Suzuki and John Finch, he showed that polyglutamine polymers could form β-sheets with glutamines in neighbouring strands being linked by hydrogen bonds. He suggested that proteins with long runs of glutamines could in this way form aggregates harmful to the cell.[8]

In the case of Huntington's disease, although aggregates of the protein called huntingtin have been observed in intranuclear inclusions in the brains of patients, it had not yet been established that they were themselves the cause of neuronal death. In an article in *Nature* in 2001,[9] Max and Alan Windle presented a model for the formation of the aggregates in which their nucleation is the critical event leading to neuronal death. The model explained the finding that the age of onset of the disease is lower for longer lengths of glutamine repeats in the pathological protein, since it is energetically more favourable for aggregates to grow from the larger nuclei these would produce.

In addition to his scientific work, Max was a contributor to both the *New York* and *London Review of Books* and a collection from these and other articles on notable scientists was published in 1998 under the title *I Wish I'd Made You Angry Earlier*.[10] In another collection, *Is Science Necessary?*, published in 1989, the main article describes how science has played a great part in health, energy and food production.[11] It also includes the article, reprinted from the *New Yorker*, describing his experience as an alien in 1940.

From 1949, Max suffered increasingly acute digestive troubles, which for periods restricted his work in the laboratory. There was no useful medical advice from doctors, but he himself discovered that the cause was an allergic reaction to certain foods, and developed a diet that enabled him to get back to normal work. Later, he suffered trouble from his back which became painful on sitting. Because of this he used a high drawing board to enable him to stand for reading and writing in his office, and he stood in the canteen for meals. For lectures he also stood or lay flat on the floor in the front of the lecture room, which could be disconcerting for an

72. Max, at his retirement in 1979, presenting the key of the laboratory to Sydney. The key was suitably inscribed with the initiator codon AUG.

unsuspecting speaker – and, as Uli Arndt commented, gave a new meaning to 'questions from the floor', since it did not inhibit Max from querying the lecturer.

On his retirement in 1979, the Max Perutz Fund was set up from donations. Max asked that it be used consistent with his enthusiasm for encouraging young scientists, and prizes are therefore awarded annually for outstanding work by scientists not older than 36, and by students. Travel grants are also made available from the Fund to younger scientists. The presentations are made at the beginning of the annual Laboratory Lectures.

'The new Marxism' – defending the MRC

Max was always pleased to acknowledge the financial support and encouragement he had received from the MRC, from the initial setting up of the Unit at the Cavendish when its aim of getting a high resolution structure of a protein seemed rather remote, through to the setting up of LMB and funding its subsequent growth. He was therefore rather shocked in 1989 when he read a review of a committee set up by the Advisory Board for the Research Councils 'Research Councils' Responsibilities for Biological Sciences'. The committee, composed of business men and scientists chaired by an engineer, J.R.S. Morris, proposed an overall National Research Council, with separate divisions for different sciences. It would be headed by a Chief Scientific Adviser who, within guidance from the council, would be responsible for developing, promulgating and implementing a coordinated policy for science and engineering. He would be responsible for allocating resource allocations to the six divisions. Those appointed to senior positions should be scientists or engineers who have had training and experience in management so as to equip them with the necessary knowledge to carry out their accounting, marketing and policy roles. The new council would present a Five Year Plan to the Secretary of State and monitor annual progress against that plan. The MRC would be abolished in favour of a Medical and Biological Sciences Division in the new organisation.

No mention was made of experience in research, and overall the Review reminded Max of a document by the Soviet Politburo and provoked him to write an article for the *New Scientist* called 'The new Marxism'.[12] He pointed out that the MRC commanded a degree of international respect and admiration that was the envy of the scientific world. Its unique reputation had been built up by a succession of outstanding heads with distinguished records of research and a council that is an autonomous body which had included the leading figures in the biomedical sciences of the day. He compared the more successful MRC policy of finding talented individuals doing promising work in a field in which the Council was interested, and supporting them by giving them a free hand, with that of the SERC (Science and Engineering Research Council) which selected subjects for development and offered funds to people willing to work on them.

He listed some of the MRC's fundamental contributions to both epidemiology and clinical medicine as well as its support for molecular biology, and ended with a plea that

> the ABRC will defend the institutions and values that have made British science great – the pluralism, the freedom, the support of talent wherever you find it, the pragmatic scepticism of planning and of uniform precepts; that it will reject policies designed to regiment science and that it will not suppress the MRC which is one of the world's most successful and internationally acknowledged research organisations.[13]

The subsequent reorganisation of research funding left the MRC virtually untouched, but closed the SERC and the Agricultural Research Council.

Max was elected a Fellow of the Royal Society in 1954. He and John Kendrew were awarded the Nobel Prize for Chemistry in 1962. Both were much involved in the creation of EMBO in 1963, and Max was its first Chairman. Max was appointed a CBE in 1963, became a Companion of Honour in 1975, and was appointed to the Order of Merit in 1988. He died in 2002 aged 87, still much involved in research.

73. *Max with Dorothy Hodgkin and the members of an EMBO workshop on Stereochemical Mechanisms of Allostery held in honour of Max, Cambridge, 1980. (Source unknown.)*

74. *Max with Margaret and Denis Thatcher in the LMB model room, c. 1980.*

JOHN KENDREW AND THE MYOGLOBIN GROUP

Although his group carried on with work on myoglobin and other proteins, John Kendrew did no direct scientific research himself after 1962, but became more interested in external scientific affairs. In 1958 he had become the founding editor of the *Journal of Molecular Biology* and remained editor-in-chief for twenty years. In 1962 he became part-time deputy to Solly Zuckermann, the Chief Scientific Adviser to the Ministry of Defence, and in 1971 he became the chairman of the Defence Scientific Advisory Council. (Hermann Bondi remembers Kendrew chairing a meeting in which the subject of tanks cropped up and he asked what their purpose was. When after a considerable delay the answer came that they were needed to fight enemy tanks, Kendrew suggested that we scrap our tanks and the Soviet tank armies would then be devoid of significance.[14]) Later, he became primarily concerned with international scientific collaboration. In particular, he was concerned that European research institutes and universities were slow in taking up molecular biology, and Europe was falling behind the USA in training young people in the subject.

In 1963, he and Max were both founders of the European Molecular Biology Organization, which started the continuing, successful programme of summer schools and travelling fellowships. In 1974, after eleven more years of skilful diplomacy, John persuaded governments to build the European Molecular Biology Laboratory in Heidelberg and became its first Director General in 1975, when he left LMB. EMBL-Heidelberg was soon followed by the outstations at Hamburg and Grenoble to exploit their respective synchrotron X-ray and neutron sources. He retired from Heidelberg in 1982 and for five years became President of St John's College in Oxford. In 1987, he returned to his house at Linton near Cambridge, where he died in 1997 aged 80.

The myoglobin group

After the publication of the high resolution structure of myoglobin, John Kendrew's group, at the time of its transfer to the LMB in 1962, had whittled down to Herman Watson, Charles Coulter, Lubert Stryer and Allen Edmundson. Visiting scientists were, however, still keen to join and from 1962, various crystallographic binding studies on myoglobin were made with visitors, Len Banaszak, Chris Nobbs and Benno Schoenborn. Allen Edmundson published the amino acid sequence in 1965, and in 1966, Watson and Nobbs published a comparison of oxy- and deoxy- forms. To try to improve the myoglobin model, data were collected to 1.4Å on a diffractometer at the Royal Institution by Colin Blake and David Phillips. The LMB group assigned phases to the new reflections on the basis of the atomic positions determined from the earlier 2Å model, and although the resulting map showed new atoms, the original (2Å) ones remained in the same positions. Herman Watson published coordinates based on this map in 1969. Later, Bob Diamond partially refined the structure starting from these coordinates and this was the starting point for work published in 1976 by Tsuni Takano. By this time, advances and experience in diffractometer techniques made it possible to collect data more accurately and Bob Diamond and others had further developed structural refinement methods. Takano re-collected the data to 2Å and refined the structure. The C-terminal residues, not very clear in the earlier map, were located and details in the side-chains were more clearly visible as well as 82 solvent molecules.

In 1968, however, a break in the work on myoglobin led Herman Watson towards crystals of other proteins that were being studied in the Protein Chemistry Division on the third floor. One of these, GPDH (D glyceraldehyde-3-phosphate dehydrogenase) from Ieuan Harris's laboratory, was studied with Len Banaszak and Paul Wassarman, but was not immediately solvable. By contrast, elastase, an enzyme being studied in Brian Hartley's laboratory, was a great success.

Brian and his student David Shotton purified the enzyme in 1968, and crystallised it – growing large crystals, up to a millimetre, in two days. With the help of the protein crystallographers, Shotton took X-ray diffraction photographs which extended further than 2Å and showed an ideally small unit cell. Shotton then collaborated with Herman Watson, and drawing on the experience of David Blow's group with α-chymotrypsin, a mercury derivative was prepared (PCMBS-elastase) and another derivative by soaking in uranyl nitrate, and data were collected to 3.5Å on the four circle diffractometer, all within the space of a few weeks. The data were processed and a Fourier map calculated by Hilary Muirhead and Joyce Cox, but soon after, Watson and Shotton moved to Bristol (in 1968) and the map was interpreted there, drawing on the sequence data which had been produced in parallel by Shotton and Brian Hartley. Later, in 1979, this model was refined by Bob Diamond and Bob Ladner using data to 2.5Å that were collected in Bristol.

HUGH HUXLEY AND THE MUSCLE GROUP

Electron microscopy

Hugh Huxley's success with the negative stain technique in the electron microscopy of viruses and ribosomes in London prompted him to apply it to muscle structures. When he first looked at a preparation of homogenised muscle, he was gratified to see many thick filaments of the length expected from sectioned material. There were also thin filaments (actin) often paired about the vestiges of the Z-band – their meeting point in micrographs of sections. These thin filaments after isolation could be recombined (decorated) with the myosin head moiety HMM, with an obvious polarity which reversed at the Z-band – exactly as one would expect from a sliding filament system for muscle contraction.

The microscopy work continued when Hugh arrived at LMB. The microscope installed for him was a Siemens Elmiscop I. Among the first visitors to the group were Arthur Rowe in 1962, looking at individual muscle proteins, and in 1964,

75. Hugh Huxley, 1987. New Scientist *114: 45, 1987. Courtesy of Pete Addis/Photofusion Picture Library.*

76. Peter Moore. Courtesy of Peter Moore/ Yale University.

Mike Reedy, working on insect flight muscle. Hugh's earlier work on ribosomes was continued by Martin Lubin, who came in 1967, using electron microscopy to study the shape of the 50S subunit and also the structure of RNA polymerase and its interaction with DNA.

In 1967, Peter Moore joined the group, coming from Alfred Tissières' laboratory in Geneva, and became involved in three-dimensional reconstruction work. This was being developed at that time by David DeRosier with Aaron Klug, and in 1968, the first application was to the helical tail of the phage T4, using programs based on those written for the X-ray work on TMV by Ken Holmes. The various helical particles in the electron micrographs of muscle proteins taken by Hugh were obvious candidates for reconstruction and Peter Moore and David DeRosier collaborated on this. Their first reconstruction was of an F-actin filament using mainly the earlier programs, but for subsequent reconstructions of thin filaments, both naked and decorated with the myosin subfragment 1, a new system of programs was written using the Fast Fourier algorithms and introducing techniques for dealing with electron microscope images such as boxing (masking the required part of the image), floating (to make the average density around the box zero and so minimise the effect of the box shape on the Fourier transform) and correcting for possible tilt of the original particle out of the horizontal plane. The structures

77. *Jim Spudich at Cold Spring Harbor,*
1972. Courtesy of Cold Spring Harbor
Laboratory Archives.

78. *John Haselgrove, c. 1970.*

obtained, although at lower resolution, compare well with those obtained using more recent technology.

Another visitor to Hugh's group around this time was Jim Spudich. He came originally as a postdoc in 1971 and studied the interaction of the tropomyposin-troponin complex with actin, biochemically with Susan Watt, and structurally with Hugh and John Finch by electron microscopy leading to 3D reconstruction. He left for San Francisco in 1972, but returned for a sabbatical in 1979, working with Linda Amos on the structure of actin filament bundles from microvilli of sea urchin eggs.

Although the electron microscope techniques available at this time produced a lot of indirect information, it was clear that they did not offer much hope of finding out directly what happened during a muscle contraction. As a consequence, there began to be more emphasis on low-angle X-ray diffraction work, for which, in 1965, Wyn Brown joined the group, and John Haselgrove began as a research student.

X-ray work – more powerful sources

The problem with X-rays was the intensity – muscle does not diffract strongly, and to investigate parts of its contraction cycle very short exposure times were needed, since structural changes occur on a millisecond time scale. Some help could be obtained by superposing over several exposures, but this only scratched at the surface of the problem of producing a time-resolved system.

The first advances were in the laboratory X-ray source. The main X-ray sources in the laboratory were the rotating anode tubes designed for the MRC Unit in the Cavendish by Tony Broad. But a more finely focused X-ray source was produced on the fixed anode Beaudouin X-ray tube which had been brought with the virus group from Birkbeck. So, in 1964, Ken Holmes and Bill Longley grafted a Beaudouin cathode assembly onto a Broad tube to take advantage of the rotating anode, with a resulting factor of ten increase in intensity. It was effectively this design that was taken over and produced by Elliot Bros. and later by Nonius. A further considerable increase in intensity was found by Hugh Huxley and Ken Holmes if the X-ray beam were focused on to the film, firstly by a bent glass mirror and then with a focusing quartz crystal monochromator. Low-angle X-ray patterns down to several hundred Ångströms could be recorded.

The next modification was to increase the diameter of the rotating anode so that a greater power could be conducted away from the focus point before it came into the electron beam again. The anode diameter was increased from 4 inches to 24 inches, spinning at about 1,500 rpm – this was operated in an old high-speed centrifuge containment vessel in case of anode explosion. It was a terrifying device

79. *The Big Wheel rotating anode built at LMB, c. 1965, to produce a higher power X-ray source.*

91

to operate, although it did lead to the big-wheel rotating anode X-ray set later produced commercially by Elliot Bros.

It did not seem possible to improve the laboratory source further, but the possibility of a more sensitive detector was explored. At hand was Wasi Faruqi with experience in this field from his high energy nuclear physics work. From about 1971, Hugh with Wasi, John Haselgrove and Chris Bond developed position-sensitive electronic detectors with time resolution down to about 10 msec. With the laboratory X-ray source it was necessary to collect over many cycles of contraction, but the set-up did begin to produce interesting results and the experience was invaluable when similar detectors were used with more powerful X-ray sources.

It had occurred to Ken Holmes around 1965–66 that useful X-ray intensity might be obtained from a synchrotron – known to produce radiation over a broad range of wavelengths, but at that time calculation suggested that it would be of power only comparable to a laboratory source. In 1968, Ken moved to Heidelberg as the Director of the Department of Biophysics at the Max Planck Institute for Medical Research and was joined the following year by Gerd Rosenbaum, who had previously worked as a graduate student at DESY – the synchrotron radiation facility in Hamburg. In discussions, it emerged that the updated characteristics of DESY should in theory provide a much more intense X-ray source than a laboratory tube, and they realised that the mirror–monochromator combination would efficiently monochromatise and focus the synchrotron radiation. An experimental single-focusing monochromator camera was built with Jean Witz (an earlier visitor to LMB, from Vittorio Luzzati's laboratory in Strasbourg, and an expert in monochromator design) at DESY and a specimen of insect flight muscle was exposed in September 1970. The result was at least ten times more intense than with any existing laboratory source and at least two more orders of magnitude could be expected from a doubly-focusing set-up and other improvements.[15]

Prompted by this, the LMB group, with Uli Arndt, designed a low-angle camera to take advantage of the similar electron synchrotron, NINA, at Daresbury in Cheshire (home of the Cat: Lewis Carroll had been born in Daresbury) and experiments with a beamline were begun there in late 1973 with John Haselgrove and Wasi Faruqi, but the results were weaker than with the big-wheel in LMB.

John Haselgrove had joined Hugh's group as a PhD student in 1965. His thesis was involved with X-ray work on muscle, investigating the behaviour of the equatorial reflections on contraction, using the laboratory X-ray sources. After a spell as a postdoc in Jack Lowy's muscle group in Aarhus, he returned to Hugh's group and became involved in the development of new X-ray detectors and later in using them at the new synchrotron source at Daresbury. However, the intensity of the beam was never as high as was hoped for a variety of reasons. The installation was intended for particle physicists looking at what was emitted after pulses of electrons were accelerated and made to collide with a target. The X-ray workers were tolerated with second-class priority, and the X-ray camera was sited some way from the electron beam. X-rays were only emitted from the electrons in the final part of their acceleration – only a few per cent of the total time. Even so, the beam was weaker than expected. John became frustrated with the paucity of results, and in 1977 he left for a very successful subsequent career in Philadelphia, where he died in 2003.

In 1976, experiments at the Stanford storage ring, SPEAR, showed that the continuous beam from a storage ring was a great advantage over the pulsed intensity available from a synchrotron. Plans were made to use the radiation from DORIS, the storage ring at DESY in Hamburg for which an EMBL outstation had been set up in 1977. By then, when DORIS became operational, the LMB group had whittled down to Hugh Huxley and Wasi Faruqi, later joined by Marcus Kress. Initially the beam was very faint due to an obstruction upstream, but the major problem over the next two years was the unreliability of the circulating electron and positron beams (the beamline was on the positron side) – the storage ring, and all priority in controlling its behaviour, was dedicated to collision experiments for high-energy physicists and these required constant adjustments to DORIS. Much experience was gained from these experiments, but the beamline being used, X12, was rather distant from the storage ring, and so operations were switched to the more favourable beamlines X11 and X13. On X11, there was a camera designed by Rosenbaum and Harmsen, consisting of a glass mirror and a curved germanium crystal monochromator, and using this, good quality low-angle patterns could be obtained from muscle on film in a few minutes compared with about 24 hours with the best laboratory set-up.

Electronic detectors of various sorts were, however, now being used and notably an X-ray image intensifier TV detector brought by Jim Milch from Princeton gave a two-dimensional display of the myosin layer line pattern from muscle with an integration time of about one second in which changes could be seen more or less in real time as the muscle was stimulated and relaxed. Ideally, though, for time-resolved work, where only a part of the muscle cycle was being studied, a two-dimensional detector with a high counting rate and rapid readout system was required. Hugh outlined the required specification at a detector meeting in 1978, and was given forecasts ranging from a few months to two years, but in fact it was ten years before a useful detector was realised.

Time-resolved measurements (at low time-resolution) were begun on laboratory X-ray sources in LMB in the mid-1970s using firstly a point and then a linear detector, adapted from a design by André Gabriel at EMBL. This was based on an RC-delay line in which the anode wire was made of a carbon-coated quartz fibre. (The difference between the times of emergence of an injected pulse from each end of the wire was proportional to the positional coordinate of the pulse along the wire.) An unfortunate consequence of beam damage was the gradual removal of the carbon coating, necessitating quite frequent renewal.

By 1978, higher time resolution measurements were made possible at DORIS, much of it with a similar linear detector from EMBL, but with muscle physiology controlled by LMB electronics. The delay line was later converted to LC operation that used a more robust, gold-plated tungsten wire anode. A faster, multiwire detector along these lines was built at LMB by Wasi Faruqi and Chris Bond in 1981, and was capable of considerably higher counting rates. The group also used a similar multiwire linear detector which was built by Jules Hendrix at EMBL, Hamburg.

Two experiments at this time have remained outstanding in Hugh's memory. Firstly, Bob Simmons, from University College, London, had designed a device to change muscle length extremely rapidly, with quick releases within 1 msec. With him, they found that the large and abrupt drop in the intensity of the 143Å meridional reflection takes place almost simultaneously with the rapid release of tension – strong evidence for axial changes in the crossbridge structure associated with the working stroke. The other memory was of seeing the changes in the actin second layer line with the evidence it provides that tropomyosin movement is responsible for switching on the actin filaments as Hugh and John Haselgrove had suggested earlier. 'To see that reflection flashing up immediately after electrical stimulation of the muscle, at a time significantly before any tension had developed, was a thrilling experience for Marcus Kress, Wasi Faruqi and myself.'[16]

Marcus Kress began as a research student of Hugh in 1982, working on actin. He was a very good experimentalist and theoretician and became involved in the synchrotron work. About halfway through writing up his thesis, however, he was missed from the laboratory and on investigation appeared to have vanished, leaving no indication why, either at his rooms or at LMB. It was not until about a month later that his body was found near a path that he could have been using on the way to LMB. His death remains a tragic mystery. The autopsy found nothing to account for it. He was a diabetic, but he had it well under control. He had become an important part of the muscle group – Hugh had found him a useful person to discuss experimental projects and theoretical aspects with, and help decide whether a particular direction was worth pursuing, and found his death a great loss.

Around 1986, as the storage ring beams became more reliable and the installations more user-friendly, protein crystallographers realised the advantage of them for collecting data – the high intensity made smaller crystals useable and allowed more data to be collected before radiation damage became apparent – and that was further reduced by freezing crystals. So more beamlines and time were dedicated to this rather than to the more specialised cameras for muscle work. However, this problem has now been alleviated by the greater number of synchrotrons, and their higher, useful power – the latest beamlines (2003) have useful intensities for crystallographic work about 10^5 greater than those of laboratory rotating anode X-ray tubes.

Hugh Huxley was awarded the MBE in 1948 (for technical work on radar in the RAF during the war). He was elected a Fellow of the Royal Society in 1960. He became Joint Director of the Division of Structural Studies with Aaron Klug in 1978 and was Deputy Director of LMB from 1977. He left the laboratory in 1987 and has since continued his research at Brandeis University, Massachusetts. In the early 1980s, there was an LMB policy not to allow senior members to continue working in the laboratory after retirement. However, Hugh wanted to continue working and queried the policy with the MRC, who replied that they backed up the local Director in such matters. Hugh was quite angry since he had continued to work at LMB in spite of getting very tempting offers over the years to work in the USA. He contacted Brandeis and committed himself to accept their offer of a research position, although by 1987 the LMB policy had changed. After Hugh retired, the muscle section has continued to expand and diversify via Alan Weeds, Jake Kendrick-Jones and Murray Stewart.

Electron microscopes

Although electron microscopy was introduced into LMB in Hugh Huxley's muscle group, it soon became more popular and began spreading outside the muscle interests. The first electron microscope was a Siemens Elmiskop I, in Hugh's laboratory in 1962, and a second Siemens machine was bought around 1965. Some of the original tilting work was done on these microscopes – following the changes in the images of particular particles as the specimen grid was tilted, and so getting strong evidence for (or against) proposed models – but the tilt mechanism was indirectly operated, and not easily controlled.

In 1968, we bought a Philips 300. This was more user-friendly than the Siemens, and had a tilt stage directly connected to an external angle-dial. This stage was very vibration-sensitive, and occasionally unusable when drilling or other maintenance work was going on nearby – which seemed quite often. However, I remember trying to use it one day when drilling began outside in the car park in preparation for the workshop extension, and being sent a message that my microscopy was interfering with the drilling – the water output pipe outside had been cut and my turning on the microscope resulted in a flood where the drillers were working. The improved version, the Philips 301, arrived in 1973 – not so vibration-sensitive, very user-friendly and used fairly continuously until 1996, by which time it had taken close to 100,000 films. It was replaced by a Philips 208.

The 301 had been used for the first low-dose work by Nigel Unwin and Richard Henderson in 1974, with modifications built by Chris Raeburn, but for this it was superseded by the Philips 400 which arrived in 1981, with a cold stage which could be used for the liquid nitrogen temperature cryo-work, following its development at EMBL by Dubochet in 1983. The 400 was followed by a 420 in 1984, and a CM12 in 1987. The CM12 is still being used (in 2007), for the development of electron detectors by Wasi Faruqi and Richard Henderson. The Cell Biologists traded in their AE5, used by Nichol Thomson for looking at his 20,000 thin sections through the nematode worm (see chapter 7), for a CM10 in 1984. Other, current, high resolution data collection machines are FEI Tecnai 12, F20 and F30, the latter two being 200 and 300kV field emission gun microscopes. In 2007, the F20 was scrapped for a 300keV Polara.

ULI ARNDT

Uli Arndt was born in Berlin in 1924. His parents found the developing Nazi Germany intolerable and in 1936 his father succeeded in appointing himself head of a British subsidiary of the company he worked for, and the family came to England. After a few weeks coaching he passed the exam for Dulwich College, but in 1939 the family moved to Birmingham and he went to the King Edward VI School there. In 1942 he gained a place at Cambridge and graduated in Physics in 1944. He was keen to stay in Cambridge in research and Henry Lipson, who was then running the Department of Crystallography, suggested a project correlating structure and properties of iron–copper–nickel alloys for which the Electrical Research Association would pay a salary of £200 a year. He found the suggested technique of taking X-ray powder photographs and densitometering them inadequate, and the manual densitometry particularly boring, and so began to construct his own apparatus mainly from the large supply of war surplus equipment then available to research laboratories. From this he built his first prototype X-ray powder diffractometer with a Geiger tube detector and recorded one single powder diffraction line before his time in Cambridge was up in 1948.

He was invited to join a group in the Department of Metallurgy in Birmingham University using X-ray diffraction to investigate transformations in steels. They had seen his prototype diffractometer and engaged him to build a precision instrument in collaboration with W.H. Hall, and with this he soon had enough material to complete his thesis. However, he missed the camaraderie he had enjoyed among the large number of research students in Cambridge and was attracted to the idea of life in London when invited by Dennis Riley, whom he had known in Cambridge, to join him and Bill Coates (his technical assistant) at the Royal Institution (RI). Riley was taking low- and medium-angle X-ray patterns from proteins in amorphous (freeze-dried) conditions or in solution, hoping to analyse the conformation and shape and so by-pass laborious crystallography. The main tool was to be a 50kW rotating anode X-ray tube built at the RI by A. Müller in the 1930s. But Uli found that the local X-ray intensity over its large emitting area was smaller than that of a standard sealed X-ray tube and so he designed a 5kW rotating anode tube with a more compact focus, based (like the Broad tube) on a prototype built by A. Taylor at the Mond Nickel Company in Birmingham.[17] A series of automatic diffractometers was also built for recording the X-ray patterns – initially with Geiger counters, built to Uli's design by 20th Century Electronics to detect the relatively soft X-rays, and later with proportional counters, built by themselves in the RI, which, unlike the Geiger tubes, were capable of discriminating the characteristic copper radiation, which was being used for the data collection, from the other wavelengths also being produced by the X-ray tube.

With Bragg's arrival as director in 1953, Uli's interest shifted towards crystallography of single crystals of proteins and he applied his diffractometer experience to this problem. He constructed a manually operated three-circle diffractometer –

the three circles were the three crystal-orienting shafts and in addition there was the shaft for setting the proportional counter. However, the calculation of the setting angles for these shafts for each reflection was extremely tedious and when David Phillips arrived in 1955, they devised a way of finding them graphically. This involved a drawing of the reciprocal lattice (the pattern of reflections), rotating protractors over this and reading off the setting angles. Uli remembers that

> David looked at this one day and said it was a pity that one could not automate it. I said 'I expect one can', but he replied 'oh no, you could never do it properly'. I used to spend a lot of time with an old friend of mine who lived just outside London and who had a small boy. That weekend I commandeered his meccano set and built an arrangement of parallelograms out of it and proudly presented it to David on Monday morning, showing how the problem could be solved.[18]

The mechanism was then expanded into three dimensions and resulted in the Linear Diffractometer (so called since the reflections were measured along lines in the diffraction pattern). A set of data for the first, 5.5Å, map of myoglobin was collected with it at the Royal Institution for John Kendrew by David Phillips in 1957, and later the data for the first enzyme structure, lysozyme, which was solved at the RI in 1965. The machine was commercially produced by Hilger and Watts and about 40 to 50 were sold.

Initially, a great strength of the Linear Diffractometer was that it did not need a digital computer to work out the settings, since it incorporated a mechanical

80. Uli Arndt and the three-circle diffractometer built at the Royal Institution in 1956. Courtesy of Elizabeth Arndt and family.

97

analogue computer, and access to a digital computer was not always easy or convenient. However, a digitally controlled, three- or four-circle diffractometer was capable of a more accurate setting, and it was possible to collect more of the diffraction data. (The more sophisticated four-circle diffractometer, with an extra degree of freedom to rotate the crystal, allowed one to optimise the setting of the crystal to collect a particular reflection and reduced the 'blind' region of reflections physically blocked by parts of the instrument.) Soon, digital computers became more common and began to be used to control machine tools, and it was realised that the shafts of three- or four-circle diffractometers could be set by the control instruments developed by Ferranti Ltd for automatic milling machines. A three-circle diffractometer controlled on this basis was built at the RI – the setting information being fed in via five-hole paper tape, and the output of intensity measurements via a paper-tape punch.

This largely home-built, three-circle diffractometer was not mechanically very precise, and a chance meeting with an earlier Cambridge friend, Terry Willis, who was now working at the Atomic Energy Research Establishment at Harwell, prompted Uli to suggest that a neutron diffractometer should be built on this basis – the Harwell laboratory had plenty of money and a very good engineering division. A collaboration developed and, as a result, a four-circle diffractometer was built at Harwell in 1963. This was also developed for X-ray use and again marketed by Hilger and Watts, and became for many years the workhorse for protein crystallography. The LMB soon acquired two, initially with paper tape input and output, but later controlled directly by a computer (a Ferranti Argus).

In 1962 Uli had been invited by Max to join LMB and he made the move from the RI in 1963. He began to look again at the photographic method of X-ray data collection. For large unit cells it was clear that the collection by diffractometer of the intensities of thousands of reflections one at a time was relatively slow and inefficient. Photographs recorded many more reflections at a time but required densitometry. The current method at that time was to use the mechanical Joyce-Loebl densitometer, which plotted the intensity along straight rows of spots on the film and had to be reset row by row. Each spot had to be indexed and its peak height measured by hand. Precession photographs were being used, since they recorded the reflections along straight lines of spots – however, these did not collect the data in a very efficient way, and were not feasible for large unit cells and high resolution.

The densitometry was speeded up with the construction of the automatic densitometer known as the 'Flying Spot', built in 1966 with Tony Crowther and Frank Mallett (p. 104). A computer-controlled mechanical densitometer, based on a Nikon projection microscope, was also built in 1969 with John Barrington Leigh, Frank Mallett and Keith Twinn. It was used first for measuring the continuous (non-spotty) X-ray patterns from the aligned specimens of TMV. (A hybrid of these two densitometers, combining the accurate, long range, positioning of the mechanical stage with the local high speed of scanning by the cathode ray spot, was built in 1972. Frank Mallett designed the electronics, Tim Gossling the mechanical side, Wasi Faruqi the optics, and John Champness commissioned it by collecting data from crystals of TMV protein.)

It was soon appreciated, however, that a computer-controlled instrument was not confined to measuring along the straight lines of a precession photograph and Uli's student, Paul Phizackerley, was given the task of exploring the method of rotating (or oscillating) the crystal through a small angle during its X-ray exposure – sufficiently small that no overlap of spots from different reflections occurred. So, unlike the precession method, no layer-selecting screen was required and all the diffracted beams heading towards the film were recorded, and their locations on the film could be calculated on the computer, and their intensities measured. Uli's initial idea was to use a rotation camera as a test-bed for an electronic area detector based on a TV camera. However, largely due to the enthusiasm of Alan Wonacott, and with John Champness, the photographic film version, with a carousel of film holders, was built in 1973 and this Arndt-Wonacott camera became popular in itself. It was marketed by Enraf-Nonius.

Uli had spent the year 1972–73 at the ILL neutron establishment in Grenoble mainly designing the electronics of the TV detector. Although this was never taken up for neutron work, the X-ray version was developed at LMB, with Uli's postdoc, David Gilmore, and Stan Boutle in the workshop, and was also taken up commercially by Enraf-Nonius, who in the end produced an automatic X-ray television diffractometer which they called FAST, the software being written by another of Uli's students, David Thomas. Around this time Uli was also involved with the muscle group in developing the camera for low angle studies at NINA, the synchrotron X-ray source at Daresbury.

Uli Arndt was elected a Fellow of the Royal Society in 1982. He retired officially in 1989, but after his retirement, he became occupied with, among other things, producing a small, intense X-ray source by combining a small toroidal-mirror focusing arrangement with a microfocus X-ray tube. In this he collaborated with Peter Duncumb and Jim Long in the University Department of Earth Sciences, who produced much of the design of the miniature X-ray tube. The combination produced an X-ray intensity comparable to that with a conventional collimator on a rotating anode tube running at 150 times the power. From 1998, the overall system was marketed by Bede Scientific Instruments. Uli died in 2006, aged 81.

81. Uli with the Microsource X-ray generator he designed in 1997.

DAVID BLOW

Rossmann and Blow

When David Blow and Michael Rossmann moved to the new LMB in 1962, they planned to follow up their work on non-crystallographic symmetry, with Michael concentrating on the theory side and David on the application to α-chymotrypsin. The original idea for this had arisen from the appearance of four myoglobin-like molecules in the 5.5Å haemoglobin map. The two α and two β subunits of haemoglobin were not identical and not related to each other by crystallographic symmetry operations, but they were very similar and this should have some effect on the X-ray diffraction pattern, and conversely from the diffraction pattern one should be able to calculate the relationship between them in terms of a translation (a straight shift between their centres of gravities) and a rotation, and by this means, useful phase information obtained. α-Chymotrypsin and presumably other proteins had more than one identical molecule in the crystallographic unit and so there should be similar phase constraints in these crystals.

The first paper stating this had been written in the hut and a following paper analysed the haemoglobin data to determine the angle of rotation between the two molecules, α and β, in the asymmetric unit. The result from the rotation function search agreed with the arrangement in the Fourier map – the complete angular search, on EDSAC2, took all night and because of the sequence of searching, the peak showing the relationship did not appear until about 6 o'clock in the morning. On Max's suggestion, the analysis was next applied to insulin, being studied by Dorothy Hodgkin's group at Oxford. With Marjorie Harding and Eleanor Coller (now Dodson) of the Oxford group, evidence for a non-crystallographic two-fold axis was found in rhombohedral zinc insulin. Michael's hope was that the method could be used to solve the α-chymotrypsin structure, but later, David Blow with Brian Matthews showed that two molecules in the asymmetric unit were not enough to 'solve' a structure, although they provided a powerful way to improve it.

Michael Rossmann had joined the Unit at the hut in 1958, and when David Blow returned from the USA the following year they got on extremely well, possibly a result of their complementary personalities – Michael was very enthusiastic and would go roaring off at the least idea, whereas David would want to mull over things a bit first. Michael fell naturally into computing and started with EDSAC2, but, when they moved to LMB, he and David and Ken Holmes applied for a special (sprat) grant from IBM to have some hours of free computing time on their 7090 machine in London. They were convinced that they would do better using FORTRAN on the IBM machine, with its relative ease of programming complex calculations, than with the EDSAC2 machine code. Another crucial factor was the amount of memory available for programs in the IBM machine.

When the free time was used up, they persuaded Max to pay for more time at the IBM full price. But by now the rotation function calculations were taking longer and longer, and Max found that a correspondingly larger and larger proportion of his budget was disappearing into this and so he put an upper limit to the computing time that they could pay for. David and Michael both began to have the feeling that they were being urged to leave LMB for new pastures. At about this time, one Henry Koffler came from Purdue recruiting. He had plenty of money and wanted to spend it setting up a new crystallography department. Both Michael and David were interested, and were offered exploratory visits to Indiana, but David then learnt, from a conversation that his wife, Mavis, had with Max's wife, Gisela, that Max would be sorry to see him go. This surprised David – there had been no intimation from Max himself – and he decided to stay. Michael, however, went to Purdue in 1964 and set up his own very successful laboratory.

α-Chymotrypsin

Much of David's time was initially taken up with writing software for the Argus computer – programs to calculate the setting angles for the new four-circle diffractometer. However, when these programs were complete and the overall system working, it became clear that the diffractometer was needed full time for the haemoglobin work and so the α-chymotrypsin data were collected photographically.

α-Chymotrypsin had been chosen originally because it was known to crystallise easily and the prospects for making derivatives were good – substitutions could be made straightforwardly at a serine residue at the active site. Both of these proved to be wrong. Although it did crystallise readily, virtually all the crystals were twinned – a mixture of two orientations which gave two superposed X-ray patterns on the film. (This had in fact been noted by Bernal, Fankuchen and Perutz in their 1938 paper.) The two orientations adopted the same crystal shape, so that only by taking an X-ray picture could it be seen whether the crystal under test was sufficiently dominant in one orientation to be worth proceeding with. This was a great bane until by chance Barbara Jeffery and David included dioxane, used as a solvent for some of the heavy atom compounds tested, in the crystallisation mix. This produced untwinned crystals which, for the first time, made it possible to collect data at atomic resolution. But, some of the derivatives aimed at the serine residue substitution proved to be unstable under the crystallisation conditions and did not survive the length of time of the X-ray exposures.

Brian Matthews and Paul Sigler

At about this time, Brian Matthews (1963–66) and Paul Sigler (1964–67) joined David's group. Brian, an Australian, came as a postdoc, and Paul as a PhD student from NIH. By 1965, data from the native crystals and from a $PtCl_4$ derivative had been collected. The process was extremely slow – four films were required to span the intensity range, and each film from the pack contained about 2,500 reflections. These were measured by a computer girl using the Joyce-Loebl densitometer,

82. The chymotrypsin group, c. 1965. From the left, Jill Collard (now Dawes), Diana Singleton (now Watson), Paul Sigler, Brian Matthews, David Blow, Sue Simpson and Sue Wickham. Courtesy of Brian Matthews.

which produced a recorder trace, row by row – and each peak along a row had to be indexed and measured, taking in all about a day for each film. With four films per pack and the associated bookkeeping, a full week was needed to get the data to the point of recording the intensity onto IBM punched cards. A complete 2Å data set consisted of 40 film packs – effectively a person-year (the computer girls included Jill Collard, Valerie Coulson, Angela Mott, Sue Simpson, Diana Singleton and Sue Wickham). In the following year a data set from an iodine derivative, from reaction with the active site serine, was added, but the map calculated from these was disappointingly uninterpretable. Paul Sigler suggested that ammonium ions in the crystallisation mix might be competing for many of the heavy atoms in the earlier trials and, sure enough, a change to potassium produced another derivative. Another nine months were needed before a three-derivative map could be calculated, in March 1967. This map was now interpretable. It was particularly striking to David how little difference there was between the contours on the sheets of this map and those of the previous map, but suddenly it was interpretable.

However, there was now a problem of finding space to build a model. Although there was a model room, it was full with the large models of myoglobin and haemoglobin, and David wrote to John Kendrew threatening to build the model in his garage at home before myoglobin was cleared out to make room. A model was then built and the results published in 1967.[19]

Brian Matthews left the group at the end of 1966 and went to NIH. Besides being involved with the chymotrypsin work, particularly on the data collection and computing sides, he had worked on methods for locating atoms that scattered anomalously (having an abnormally high absorption at the incident X-ray wavelength, which shows up in the diffraction pattern and gives more phase information). He had also begun X-ray work on chymotrypsinogen B (a close relative of α-chymotrypsin), and wrote up a paper on this for the *Journal of Molecular Biology*, listing the various crystal forms he had obtained. The solvent content of one of these suggested that there were two molecules in its asymmetric unit – but the evidence for this was challenged by a referee. This prompted Brian to analyse the solvent content of the 116 crystal forms of globular proteins that had been published, the results of which clearly showed that the crystal in question required two molecules in the asymmetric unit to be within the ranges indicated by the analysis. He published the analysis in a paper preceding the chymotrypsinogen one and it became a very useful reference paper for crystallographers and has been by far the most cited of all his papers.

Paul Sigler left in 1968 to form a group in Chicago. Before coming to the LMB he had spent a year at NIH with David Davies working on γ-chymotrypsin (then thought to be differently cleaved from α-chymotrypsin). He had reacted crystals of this with pipsylfluoride and so introduced iodine as a heavy atom derivative. When he came to LMB, he used the same procedure to produce a derivative for α-chymotrypsin. He also had strong ideas contributing to the hypothesis of the activation mechanism of the enzyme. But he also made a big impression on the laboratory in general, and not just because of his large dimensions. He was interested in other people's problems. One of the virus crystals I was trying to work with then was very radiation-sensitive – not lasting sufficiently long in the X-ray beam to get a useful diffraction photograph. Paul suggested adding ferrous sulphate to the crystal solution to react with any hydroxyl radicals formed, and it worked. (Inexplicably, in later work the ferrous sulphate was omitted with no obvious consequences.) I also remember him staring mystified at a pile of about 30 56-pound weights being used to test the lift – 'why should anyone want to make one 56-pound weight let alone 30?' But the outstanding memory for most at LMB at the time will be the squash of his great frame into a tutu for a ballet scene in one of the Christmas parties (see chapter 9). He stayed at Chicago until 1989, when he moved to Yale where he died suddenly in 2000 aged 65.

In 1968, a more accurate model of α-chymotrypsin was built from the 1967 map by Jens Birktoft, from Denmark, using a Richards Box. Until now, the skeletal models had been built from measurements of the contour plots. The Richards Box (designed by Fred Richards when he visited Oxford, on sabbatical in 1967 from Yale – it was commonly known as Fred's Folly) incorporated a large 45° semi-silvered mirror so that the contour plot drawn on large perspex sheets (about a metre square) could be slotted in and viewed in the same plane as the atoms in the model being built. The laboratory had two of these large contraptions until model building using graphics display took over in the early 1980s. (Andrew Leslie remembers that in Purdue at this time, they had three enormous 'Follies' constructed to build southern bean mosaic virus, but, being overtaken by the computer graphics, they were only used to build one stretch of α-helix.)

There was no structural refinement at this stage, but in 1969, the map was improved by refining the heavy atom parameters – a bug (a mistake in a sign) in the FORTRAN refinement program had shifted some of these by an Ångström or two – and in 1970, an improved model was built, again by Jens Birktoft. During this rebuilding, which took about two months, the height coordinate was read off a plumb line marked in centimetres. However, when the model was complete the plumb line was checked and found to have stretched – so, assuming that Jens' progress and the stretching had both been uniform with time, a linear correction was applied to the z-coordinate according to the amino acid number. (Jens had also brought a Danish ruler with him, which caused some confusion at one point since Danish inches are somewhat different to British ones.) The model building on α-chymotrypsin proceeded with constant reference to the amino acid sequence that had been determined by Brian Hartley. But Birktoft was worried about the region of the active site where an asparagine in the sequence was aspartic acid in all the related proteins. It was checked by Hartley and was in fact confirmed as aspartic acid. This led to a much better understanding of the stereochemistry in this region, and a proposal for the mechanism, the 'charge relay system', to increase the nucleophilicity of the serine hydroxyl.

Flying Spot densitometer

Although the α-chymotrypsin data had to be collected photographically since the four-circle diffractometer was needed for the haemoglobin work, the time for processing films was considerably reduced by the advent of the 'Flying Spot' densitometer, which came into action in 1966. The idea was suggested by the provision of a plotting system with the Argus computer, based on a precision cathode ray tube whose spot position was controlled by Argus. This had been installed as a device for plotting electron density maps, but it was soon realised that it could also be used as a flexible light source for film scanning, providing a good example of the enabling power of new technology. The X-ray film

83. Flying Spot densitometer, 1967.
Courtesy of Tony Crowther.

was illuminated by the spot on the CRT, whose location could be set to a particular reflection on the film. Only the computed position of each reflection with its immediate neighbourhood was scanned by the spot, and the optical density digitised.

The mechanical side of the densitometer was designed by Uli Arndt with his student Paul Phizackerley, and built by Ernie Norman in the workshop, and the electronics were designed by Frank Mallett. Tony Crowther arrived at this time as a research student – he had been attracted by the prospect of writing programs for Argus and was given, as part of his thesis project, the job of making the densitometer work. This involved mainly producing control programs with the help of Tim Gossling who had written the 'Initial Orders' for Argus after having been poached from Ferranti. The main task of the computer was to measure the integrated intensity in each reflection spot (required since the spot shape varied over the film) and the local background, and also to make allowances for irregularities, such as those in the phosphor over the screen area, spatial distortion over the screen and variations in the light paths of beams from different parts of the screen. The densitometer was not confined to X-ray film measurement and was also, for example, programmed to digitise electron microscope images for the first three-dimensional reconstructions by Aaron Klug and David DeRosier in 1968.

Richard Henderson and Tom Steitz

Richard Henderson joined David Blow's group in 1966, and Tom Steitz in 1967. Both began investigating the binding of inhibitors at the active site of α-chymotrypsin using precession and diffractometer data respectively. However neither was able to find any clear evidence of binding in the X-ray maps. On a brief return visit, Brian Matthews suggested that as the native data had been collected in the presence of dioxane, this might be binding to the active site and stop the inhibitor showing up. So Richard and Tom collected a native data set using crystals from which dioxane had been removed and, sure enough, the substrates were now visible in difference maps. The mode of binding was consistent with the mechanism proposed soon after by David with Jens Birktoft and Brian Hartley, and the residue responsible for the difference in specificity between trypsin and chymotrypsin was seen clearly at the bottom of the binding pocket.

This work led on to the study of the reaction between the related enzyme trypsin and trypsin inhibitors. Robert Huber in Germany had been trying to dock his model of trypsin inhibitor into a model of trypsin from Bob Stroud in the USA, but errors in the trypsin structure were frustrating these attempts. David had now (1970) been joined by Christine and Tonie Wright, postdocs from Princeton. Christine found, by model building, that there was a natural docking between the trypsin inhibitor and chymotrypsin structures, and this was followed up in 1974 by an X-ray structure of the complex of soybean trypsin inhibitor and porcine trypsin to 2.6Å by David with Tonie Wright, Bob Sweet, Joel Janin and Cyrus Chothia.

84–86. Chymotrypsin group punting, 1969.

84. *(top left)*
Richard Henderson.
Courtesy of Jens
Birktoft.
85. *(top right)*
Penny Henderson,
Tom and Joan
Steitz. Courtesy of
Jens Birktoft.
86. *(right) David*
Blow, Betty Wulff
Birktoft, Jude Smith,
Jane (surname
unknown), and
Prakash Cashmore.
Courtesy of Jens
Birktoft.

tRNA synthetase

When Tom Steitz arrived in 1968, he had suggested working on an amino-acyl tRNA synthetase, but David had thought the logistics of the problem at that time were not feasible. Brian Hartley had been working on the biochemistry of the methionyl- enzyme from 1966 with Robert Heinrikson and later Chris Bruton – starting from large scale productions of *E. coli* from the Microbiological Research Establishment at Porton. Brian Hartley was very keen on this family of enzymes, which he considered to be the 'secret of life' since they were responsible for the recognition of an amino acid and its cognate tRNA and corresponding anti-codon. Around 1972, he persuaded David that it would be worth putting in a lot of effort into crystallising them. By then, other laboratories had produced crystals from the *E. coli* enzymes, but these tended to be very labile regarding both temperature and X-rays. To try to get over this problem, tyrosyl-tRNA synthetase was purified from a Porton preparation of the thermophilic *Bacillus stearothermophilus*. In 1973, Brian Reid and Gordon Koch grew large crystals which indeed proved to be stable, and a 2.7Å structure was determined with a student, Mike Irwin, in 1976.

Alan Wonacott

87. Alan Wonacott, 1975.

Alan Wonacott joined David's group in 1969, working initially on lysyl-tRNA synthetase from yeast. He had gained his PhD working in the group of Watson Fuller at King's College, London, with an X-ray diffraction study of fibres of poly-L-alanine, and in 1968 he had gone to Michael Rossmann in Purdue. In Cambridge, he soon became greatly involved with the design and development of the Rotation Camera with Uli Arndt. He then took up the problem of GPDH that had been partly solved by Herman Watson's group and investigated first the structural changes that occur on binding the coenzyme NAD$^+$ (nicotinamide adenine dinucleotide, a major electron acceptor) and then the differences in the structures of the enzymes from moderate and extreme thermophiles compared to that from the normal temperature rabbit muscle. GPDH from the extreme *B. thermusaquaticus* is stable at 90°C (and even has a half life of 30 min at 95°C) and has many more interactions between the subunits making up the tetrameric enzyme than the enzyme from muscle, whereas that from the moderate thermophile *B. stearothermophilus* has a stability and structure somewhere in between. Alan went to Imperial College with David in 1977.

Tony Jack

Tony Jack had initially come to LMB in 1969 as a PhD student of Aaron Klug, working on the crystals of TMV (tobacco mosaic virus) protein, but he had become

88. Tony Jack, 1975.

more interested in the idea of using the 17-fold symmetry of the disk aggregates in the crystal to solve the structure than in the standard crystallographic methods. He thought these ideas more appropriate to David's group and switched supervisors. However, he continued with the TMV protein crystals and by imposing the 17-fold symmetry on the disks, he obtained a 7Å projection map comparable to the projection calculated from a single heavy atom derivative. He also applied non-crystallographic symmetry to barnase – a small ribonuclease with only 110 residues, brought to the LMB by Bob Hartley from Bethesda. Hartley had grown crystals of this and collected data to 4Å from the native and a heavy atom derivative. The resulting map was sharpened by applying non-crystallographic symmetry elements between the three molecules in the crystallographic unit, but the method was limited, probably mainly by the difficulty in defining the molecular boundary, and the structure remained unsolved until some years later.

From 1972 to 1974, Tony Jack visited Steve Harrison at Harvard as a postdoc, and the structure of the small, spherical virus, tomato bushy stunt, was solved to 16Å using heavy atom derivatives and the non-crystallographic icosahedral symmetry of the virus particles. With Tony Crowther, a comparison map was calculated to 28Å, using phases from an electron microscope reconstruction calculated from negative stain images – the differences between the two could be interpreted as artifacts arising from the stain in the electron microscope samples.

When he returned to the LMB in 1974, he rejoined Aaron Klug's group and became involved in the computing side of the yeast phenylalanine tRNA work. He modified Bob Diamond's programs for real space refinement of protein structures for use with RNA. (The first stage in the structure determination from an electron density map is to interpret it in terms of the known monomers – amino acids for proteins and bases for nucleic acids – and the aim of real space refinement is to fit ideal monomers preserving as near as possible bond lengths and angles.) He later included terms for energy minimisation (from work with Michael Levitt) and least squares refinement (minimising functions involving the differences between observed and calculated intensities, and ideal and calculated distances). Unhappily, after such an extremely promising start, Tony Jack died suddenly in 1978 from a heart condition he had had for many years.

Move to Imperial

In 1974, Brian Hartley left LMB to take up a chair in Biochemistry at Imperial College, London, and in 1976, they wanted to set up a Department of Biophysics for which David was invited to be the head. There were three main reasons that persuaded him to accept. First, it seemed that LMB was becoming more oriented towards nucleic acid work, gene expression and general cell biology, and the structural side was being limited, so that although he could continue running a group, it did not seem likely that he would be able to enlarge it appreciably. Second, he found it frustrating that the tripos structure at Cambridge did not attract crystallographic students (whom he supervised for Trinity College) towards biological subjects. Third, the Phillips Report was published about this time. With Max due to retire in 1979, the MRC set up a committee under David Phillips to formulate future policy for the support of molecular biology. Perhaps envy of LMB's secure support by the MRC compared with that for groups in relatively insecure university departments made the Report critical of the way LMB was run and in particular it recommended that a quarter of the permanent posts at LMB should be removed and that the budget be reduced by 25 per cent. Thus there seemed little possibility of expansion at LMB, but the chance of a modest expansion at Imperial, and so he left in 1977, with Alan Wonacott. He built up a flourishing group there including Bhat (employed by Daresbury to organise the CCP4 set of crystallographic programs), Peter Brick and Andrew Leslie.

David Blow was elected a Fellow of the Royal Society in 1972. He was much involved with the setting up of the British Crystallographic Association (BCA) in 1982. Up until this time crystallographic meetings in this country were arranged by sub groups of the Institute of Physics and of the Royal Society of Chemistry, which occasionally led to clashes of meetings on similar subjects. A committee was set up to try to sort this out and it proposed a single crystallographic body, the BCA, but the problem was the lack of money for it to function – neither of the parent bodies would want to lose subscription money to fund it. David thought of the idea of offering life membership for a £100 subscription. This in fact became a ten-year membership subscription, but with 52 Founder members on this basis, and 31 Founder Sponsors (industrial companies) contributing an average of £400 each, the BCA became solvent and operative.

David retired in 1994 with a serious heart problem, but continued to work part-time at Imperial College, rounding off projects he had begun, and drawing on his long experience to write an excellent book, *Outline of Crystallography for Biologists*.[20] In 1997, a 30th Anniversary Meeting was held in Cambridge to commemorate the publication of the chymotrypsin structure. In 2003, while coping with lung cancer, he wrote a biographical memoir of Max Perutz for the Royal Society,[21] and a short novel. He died in 2004, aged 72.

Alan Fersht

Alan Fersht had joined David Blow's group in 1969. He had read physical chemistry in Cambridge, but had also studied biochemistry and advanced physics. He worked on models for enzyme catalysis for his PhD, and was then 'headhunted' by LMB as a chemist who could study the mechanism of enzymes whose structures were being solved. He came to LMB after a year at Brandeis with Bill Jencks. For the first four years he was mainly studying chymotrypsin and then concentrated more on aminoacyl tRNA synthetases in which he was joined by Colin Dingwall. In 1978, Alan also moved to Imperial – taking up a Royal Society Research Professorship after being proposed by David and Brian Hartley. With Greg Winter at LMB, there was a collaboration using site-directed mutagenesis as a probe of enzyme structure and catalysis with tyrosyl-tRNA synthetase as the specimen. Alan remembers this as his proudest moment as a protein chemist – one of the referees of the paper describing the work as a landmark in the history of proteins. Alan returned to Cambridge in 1989 and became Director of the MRC Centre for Protein Engineering in a building alongside LMB. He was knighted in 2003.

89. Alan Fersht, 1971.

Gerard Bricogne

Gerard had joined David's group in 1972 as a student, and was interested in developing the application of non-crystallographic symmetry in X-ray diffraction. Later, he became interested in trying to determine protein structures from the X-ray data directly, without heavy atoms, and built up a small group working on this. He left LMB in 1998 and formed a small crystallographic computation firm, Global Phasing Ltd, in Cambridge.

90. Gerard Bricogne, 1975.

110

Jude Smith

Jude Smith came to LMB in 1969, initially working in David Blow's group as a general assistant, building balsa wood models and producing pictures on the Argus plotter as well as writing software. When David left for Imperial in 1977, she transferred to Aaron Klug's group and became involved in the reconstruction of the histone octamer from electron micrographs of tubular aggregates. From 1982, she joined Anne Bloomer and concentrated more on writing software – the database programmes Cellbase for César to keep track of his cell lines, and Oligonet for ordering oligonucleotides. Geltrack, for measuring bands along one-dimensional gels was written originally for Daniela Rhodes. Ximdisp, one of the basic programmes for image analysis, began life at about this time, and has been continuously updated since. In 1987, she joined Terry Horsnell in System Management, but since 1997 she has been involved more in her own projects of analysis of electron microscope images of single particles and helical aggregates.

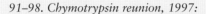

91–98. Chymotrypsin reunion, 1997:

91. Participant group photograph. Courtesy of Eaden Lilley Photography (Ref GK230).
From the left, front row: Richard Henderson, Brian Matthews, David Blow, Jo Sigler, Paul Sigler, Mavis Blow, Pat Hutchings (née Masters), Tom Steitz, Brian Hartley, Jens Birktoft, Michael Rossmann, George Hess, Uli Arndt, Sue Hess, Barbara Harris (née Jeffrey), Diana Watson (née Singleton), Tony Kossiakoff. Second row: Bill Butler, Carla Butler, Helen Matthews, John Wickham, Sue Simpson, Sue Wickham, Gwynne Johnson (née Goaman), Tim Gossling, Bob Diamond, Ross Jakes, Jim Brown, Katie Brown, Val King (née Coulson), Tim Bullock, Jenny Brightwell, Janet Jubb, Jade Li, Cyrus Chothia, Sue Kossiakoff, unnamed. Third row: Airlie McCoy, Phil Evans, Hilary Muirhead, Bob Stroud, Frank Mallet, Tony Crowther, Michael Green, Jens Nyborg, Jacques Fastrez, Joyce Baldwin, Angela Mott, Jude Smith, Tony Broad, Ann Diamond, Kristine Matthews. Fourth row: Peter Moody, unnamed, Hua Chang-Ming, Joel Janin, Andrew McLachlan, David Trentham, Ken Holmes, Phil Rodgers, Ken Harvey, Alan Barrett, Tonie Wright, Wasi Faruqi, Gill Mallett, Hilary Wallace, Ian Watson.

92. *Paul Sigler, Brian Matthews and Richard Henderson with David Blow holding the* Nature *paper with the chymotrypsin structure. Courtesy of Jens Birktoft.*
93. *David Blow, Tom Steitz and Richard Henderson. Courtesy of Jens Birktoft.*
94. *Uli Arndt, Brian Matthews and Ken Holmes. Courtesy of Jens Birktoft.*
95. *Cyrus Chothia. Courtesy of Jens Birktoft.*
96. *Ken Harvey and Angela Mott. Courtesy of Bob Diamond.*
97. *Gwynne Goaman and Hilary Muirhead. Courtesy of Bob Diamond.*
98. *Michael Rossmann. Courtesy of Richard Henderson.*

AARON KLUG

Aaron Klug was born in 1926 in Lithuania, but in 1928 his family emigrated to Durban, South Africa, and he was educated at Durban High School. The book *Microbe Hunters* by Paul de Kruif[22] influenced him to begin medicine at university as a way into microbiology. At the University of Witwatersrand in Johannesburg he took the pre-medical course, and in the second year, among other subjects, physiology and biochemistry. However, feeling the lack of a deeper foundation, he moved to chemistry and thence to physics and mathematics, and so to a science degree.

99. *Aaron Klug, 1982. Courtesy of Cambridge Newspapers Ltd.*

Deciding to do physics research he went to the University of Cape Town to obtain an MSc degree under Professor R.W. James, a crystallographer from Bragg's school in Manchester, and acquired a good knowledge of X-ray diffraction from his own work and by checking the proofs of James' classic book *The Optical Principles of the Diffraction of X-rays.*[23] His project for the MSc was on the structure of para-bromochlorobenzene, which he solved and published in *Nature*, in 1947. He decided to stay on at Cape Town for a PhD, which was on the structure of triphenylene – he calculated (by hand) the Fourier Transform of the four molecules in the unit cell and found the best fit to the diffraction pattern. The work sufficiently impressed James that an appropriate appendix on the Fourier Transform was added to a later edition of his book. The triphenylene work was published in *Acta Crystallographica*, in 1950,[24] but he did not bother to write it up for his PhD – he had won a studentship to Cambridge and had decided he would go straight there.

In 1949, Aaron came to the Cavendish Laboratory wanting to do some 'unorthodox' X-ray crystallography: for example, on proteins with Perutz and Kendrew (James kept in touch with Bragg), but he was told that the MRC Unit was full (a recent, difficult visitor had made Bragg rather wary about who he accepted into that group). Instead, his PhD was obtained in solid state physics under D.R. Hartree – on the cooling of steel through the austenite–pearlite transition. The idea of nucleation and growth in a phase change became relevant later in the work on the assembly of tobacco mosaic virus. After taking his PhD, Aaron spent a year in the Colloid Science department, working with F.J.W. Roughton studying the problem of simultaneous diffusion and chemical reaction occurring when oxygen enters a red blood cell. This work made him more and more interested in biological matters and he decided he really wanted to work on the X-ray analysis of biological molecules.

In 1954, he obtained a Nuffield Fellowship to work in Bernal's department in Birkbeck College, initially to join Harry Carlisle in his crystallographic work on ribonuclease. However, he soon met Rosalind Franklin there and interest in her work drew him into the study of macromolecular assemblies, initially the rod-shaped tobacco mosaic virus (TMV), on which there were several collaborative papers and, later, spherical viruses. After Rosalind's untimely death in 1958, he became leader of the Virus group and moved to the new LMB in 1962.

With him from Birkbeck came the group's X-ray workers. John Finch and Ken Holmes and their biochemist, Reuben Leberman, and a little later Bill Longley, after he had finished his PhD in London. Initially, the group's work was confined to viruses – John Finch and Bill Longley on small spherical viruses and Ken Holmes on TMV.

100. *Group at the International Union of Crystallography Meeting, Madrid, 1956. From the left, Ann Cullis, Francis Crick, Don Caspar, Aaron Klug, Rosalind Franklin, Odile Crick and John Kendrew. (Photo: Don Caspar)*

Ken Holmes

101. Ken Holmes, 1967.
Courtesy of Valerie King.

Besides continuing the X-ray work on TMV, Ken Holmes had become interested in the muscle field. During a year (1960–61) at Don Caspar's laboratory, then in Boston, he had worked with Carolyn Cohen and found X-ray evidence for α-helical coiled coils in native muscle. At LMB he collaborated in low-angle X-ray work with Wyn Brown and Hugh Huxley and on insect flight muscle with Mike Reedy and Richard Tregear. As described in chapter 6, he worked with Bill Longley and Hugh Huxley on increasing the useable X-ray intensity from the rotating anode tubes.

On the TMV front, he and Reuben Leberman attached a uranyl fluoride group to the virus to produce a new heavy atom derivative. With Judith Gregory, he studied the conditions for preparing optimally oriented sols for X-ray work. In 1972, a 10Å map of TMV was published with John Barrington Leigh and Peter von Sengbusch. Ken had already left LMB by then – to become the Director of the Department of Biophysics at the Max-Plank-Institut für Medizinische Forschung in Heidelberg in 1968.

Reuben Leberman

At LMB, Reuben Leberman was responsible for the virus preparations used by the group, but he was also much involved in the structural studies. He suggested the use of uranyl formate as a negative stain as an alternative to the uranyl acetate which Hugh usually employed – with this it was possible to see the 23Å pitch periodicity along the particles of TMV in the electron microscope. Reuben was also involved with the crystallisation of the several viruses the group was interested in and of TMV protein.

In the case of TMV protein, Aaron's intention had been to crystallise the relatively small trimer of subunits, named A-protein. Instead, the unit in the crystals turned out to be a two-turn disk aggregate of the protein of about the same diameter as the virus particle. The crystals were studied by myself, Aaron and Zhang Youshang, a visitor from Shanghai. X-ray diffraction showed that the disks had 17-fold symmetry (close to the $16\frac{1}{3}$ subunits per turn of the basic helix in the virus

115

102. Reuben Leberman in the foreground, at a rounders game in 1965. In the background from the left are Ken Holmes, Bill Longley (hidden) and Allen Edmundson. Courtesy of Diana Watson.

rod). The arrangement of disks in the crystal was determined with Peter Gilbert and Jean Witz. In 1969, Reuben Leberman joined Ken Holmes in Heidelberg and was succeeded by Jo Butler, from Ieuan Harris's group.

One of the early visitors to Aaron's group was Steve Harrison from Harvard. He contacted Aaron after graduating in 1963 and came to LMB in 1964–65. Aaron suggested that he work with Reuben Leberman investigating the path of assembly of the small spherical plant virus turnip crinkle. This did not attract Steve, who wanted to do crystallography – he had heard Max give a talk at Harvard on the structures of myoglobin and haemoglobin and had been impressed by these results. The remainder of his time at LMB was spent studying the turnip crinkle virus by X-ray diffraction. In 1964 he returned to the USA, to Don Caspar's laboratory in Boston, to work on tomato bushy stunt virus, the structure of which was solved at gradually increasing resolution, ultimately at 2.8Å in 1977. By this time Steve had moved back to Harvard, where the data were collected, but much of the computing and plotting of the sections of the resulting map was done in the summer of 1977 at LMB.

Caspar and Klug – quasi-equivalence

From 1961, Aaron had been collaborating with Don Caspar in extending the Crick and Watson ideas on virus structure – that the small viruses were built from symmetrical arrangements of identical protein subunits. However, it had become apparent that several of the small spherical viruses, although exhibiting the predicted icosahedral symmetry, were built from more than the 60 subunits that the symmetry required. Caspar and Klug introduced the idea of quasi-equivalence[25] – subunits being related by local hexagonal planar symmetry (p. 6) but with curvature introduced regularly by the periodic inclusion of a pentagonal group instead of a hexagonal one, resulting in a spherical shell accommodating 60T subunits, where T (the triangulation number) could take values 1, 3, 4, 7, 9, etc. ($h^2 + k^2 + hk$). The asymmetric unit of the icosahedral symmetry would contain T subunits in nearly or quasi-equivalent environments. The theory explained the 32 surface unit structure seen in the electron microscopy of TYMV (turnip yellow mosaic virus) by Hugh Huxley and Geoffrey Zubay in London and Nixon and Gibbs at Rothamsted, as a clustering of 180 biochemically identical subunits in the virus particle (T=3) into 12 pentamers and 20 hexamers. But the explanation was not universally accepted until the number of subunits was established (as 180 ± 5) in 1966, when the overall particle weight of the virus was determined by David DeRosier and Bob Haselkorn in Chicago.

A greenhouse was erected close to the LMB building to grow plants for the viruses used by the group, *Nicotiana* for TMV and Chinese cabbage, *Brassica rapa*, for TYMV. The easiest way to monitor the preparations was by electron microscopy of negatively stained specimens, and taking advantage of this, the group began looking at the micrographs for structural detail.

Optical diffraction and filtering

It was not obvious at first what one was seeing in the images of negatively stained particles. It was initially thought by Brenner and Horne and by Huxley that the virus particles left a footprint-like impression in the film of stain, and that the image was a picture of this – an impression of the bottom of the particle. The first objective demonstration that the particles could be completely submerged in the stain and the resulting image a superposition of detail from both the near and far side of the particle was obtained with Jack Berger in 1964[26] – by using an optical diffractometer designed by Henry Lipson and Charles Taylor at Manchester University. The diffraction patterns from electron microscope images of negatively stained actin filaments and TMV both showed spots arising from periodicities on both the top and the bottom of the particles. The method was soon applied to analyse the images of T4 polyheads – long cylindrical shells of the major head protein formed by mutants of the T4 phage, made by Tony Stretton – and the patterns showed the polyhead lattice to have local hexagonal symmetry.

117

Optical diffraction techniques were developed further with the arrival in the laboratory in 1964 of David DeRosier, a postdoc from Bob Haselkorn's laboratory in Chicago. A commercial version of the Manchester diffractometer (by Pullen Ltd) was bought and installed in the ground and basement sections of a narrow lift shaft meant to serve the canteen when that was originally planned to be on the third floor. In subsequent planning, the canteen was moved to the fourth floor – beyond the height that the lift was allowed by the planners (see chapter 9), and so this lift shaft was initially vacant. In order to get a reasonably sized diffraction pattern, the instrument needed to be rather long, and so folding it up in a vertical shaft was quite economical in terms of space. The light source was a mercury arc and the exposures required were about an hour – even using enlargements of the electron micrographs. By 1971, Aaron and David DeRosier had introduced a laser as light source and as a result the micrographs themselves could be used as the diffracting subjects. The optical diffraction patterns could now be recorded on film in about a second.

103. *Hugh Huxley and David DeRosier at Cold Spring Harbor, 1971. Courtesy of Cold Spring Harbor Laboratory Archives.*

The next stage was to produce a filtered image – either filtering out noise from a single image or separating the confusing detail from two overlapping images, for example the near and far sides of a helical particle seen on its side. The parts of the diffraction pattern arising from one image were selected and punched out of the film, which could then be used as a mask and reintroduced into the diffractometer.

This allowed only the selected parts of the diffraction pattern to be combined with a subsequent lens to produce a filtered version of the chosen image. The practice was adopted of submerging the electron microscope film in oil at this stage so that artifactual diffraction from emulsion thickness variations did not introduce artifactual detail. In this (inclined to be rather messy) way, filtered images of the near and far sides of the tail of T4 phage were obtained.

A more compact scanning diffractometer was also designed by Aaron and David in 1971 and built in the LMB workshop by Dave Hart and Len Hayward. This also had a laser light source and all the controls at hand so that micrographs could (and can) be scanned rapidly to pick out areas suitable for further work. This was all that was needed optically, since the further work was soon being done computationally rather than by optics, and despite needing occasional re-alignments and dusting, and the need to work in the dark to see the fainter diffracted beams, the instrument has remained in continuous use, although recently a more robust and versatile benchtop diffractometer has been designed and introduced by Brad Amos for this work.

Optical diffraction and filtering soon became a useful tool for analysing micrographs of negatively stained helical particles and 2D arrays. Several courses on this work were run in the laboratory with both lecture and practical sessions. (One of the last of these was held in Cambridge, with lectures in Peterhouse and the practical demonstrations in a temporarily empty room which had been previously used by the Cavendish, but was now being made ready for housing computational equipment for the Maths Lab. Amongst the junk we found a tube of powder labelled 'Frederick Soddy' – which, being curious, we tested with a Geiger counter, and obtained quite a strong signal.)

In 1967, micrographs of bacterial cell walls taken by Milan Nermut at NIMR in Mill Hill were optically filtered to show square arrays of surface units. Moreover, optical diffraction from images of overlapping layers showed that though multiple scattering (diffraction by the second layer of the diffracted rays from the first) could be detected, it was only at the level of a few per cent, and hence an electron micrograph of a typical specimen could really be treated as a simple projection. The work on polyheads was extended with Mitsuhiro Yanagida in 1972 and with Uli Laemmli in 1976. In 1972 too, helical arrays of glutamic dehydrogenase were studied by Bob Josephs and Gary Borisy and of gastropod haemocyanin by Jan Mellema and Aaron.

In 1971, Tony Crowther and Linda Amos introduced a technique for analysing electron microscope images for rotational symmetry.[27] One of the first applications was to enhance the detail in the hexagonal baseplate of the T4 phage using micrographs provided by the visiting Jonathan King. It was also used to confirm the X-ray work indicating that the disc of TMV protein had 17-fold symmetry. (In the early 1960s, Roy Markham, at the ARC Virus Research Unit, had used photographic superposition to enhance the details on images with rotational or translational symmetry, but since there was no initial analysis to determine the repeating symmetry parameters, a wrong choice was liable to produce an artifactual result.) Rotational filtering was subsequently used by Tony in a collaboration with Jonathan King (by then at MIT) to locate various gene products in the T4 baseplate and to study the hexagon to star transition associated with tail contraction.

Towards 3D reconstruction

Optical diffraction, however, was of no use for the spherical viruses being studied by the group. Initially we looked at small plant viruses built on symmetric surface lattices, and views in symmetry directions could show clear interpretable patterns, but away from these the details in the images were confused and difficult to interpret. We also looked at poliovirus – one of the conditions being that immunisation was offered to everyone in the laboratory. (The laboratory van driver at that time, Dick Tompkins, was very grateful – after being vaccinated he no longer suffered from rheumatism and was convinced it was due to the vaccine.)

The apparent confusion in the images was, in the light of the parallel work on helical structures, recognised as the superposition of detail from the near and far sides – and this was particularly apparent in the papilloma virus images, where the particle structure is based on a skew lattice (T=7) resulting in little superposition of the positions of the units on the near and far sides. Initially we looked for particles in thin stain so that we had dominantly one-side images to analyse. This worked for the human wart virus, but with the rabbit virus we misinterpreted the image detail and concluded that the lattice was based on the opposite hand to the human virus. (The correct hand was later obtained by Tim Baker's group in Purdue, using electron cryomicroscopy.)

(Bragg, visiting the laboratory at that time, was interested in the wart virus work. His daughter had suffered from a wart infection on her arm when young, and the doctor had recommended stroking the arm with a feather every night. The warts had vanished and Bragg wondered if we had an explanation – it was probably a delaying tactic since a high proportion of warts clear up in a few weeks without treatment.)

The striking superposition patterns from particles in thick stain prompted the next stage – guessing a likely model based on the quasi-equivalence theory, building a skeletal version of it and photographing shadows from it as it was rotated in a light beam. This was superseded by using the plotting facility of the Argus computer to display the superposition pattern calculated for a particular model put together in the computer – model refining was much easier with this. It was also possible to follow the changes in the patterns in micrographs taken as the specimen was tilted in the microscope, and so establish the hand of a skew lattice. (The T=7 models were based on the clustering of subunits on the T=7 lattice into pentamers and hexamers as predicted by the quasi-equivalence theory, but in fact, later X-ray work by Don Caspar's group in Brandeis, Massachusetts and cryo-electron microscopy by Tim Baker and his group have shown that the virus shells are not built in this way, but that all the clusters are pentamers.)

The more objective method of 3D-reconstruction from the projections of the particles seen in the electron microscope images, using Fourier methods, was introduced from 1968 onwards. It was first applied to helical particles by David DeRosier and Aaron[28] – helical particles are particularly suitable for this since, effectively, many projections are contained in each image (the subunits are seen in many different views). The computational methods used for helical reconstructions were further developed by Peter Moore and Linda Amos – and included, where relevant, the programs written by Ken Holmes for his X-ray work on TMV. The overall procedure is similar to that used to produce Fourier maps of proteins from X-ray diffraction data, with the advantage that phase information as well as the amplitudes of the Fourier components can be calculated from the images.

The methods were applied to spherical viruses in 1970.[29] Tony Crowther had returned to LMB to work with Aaron on image processing, as David DeRosier was returning to the USA. Tony was largely responsible for the mathematical analysis and Linda Amos for programming. The spherical viruses, having icosahedral symmetry, again contained many different views of the subunits in one image, but reasonable reconstruction required the data from more than one image. Thus programs were needed both for identifying an image (the orientation parameters) from symmetry relationships, using the so-called common lines, and for combining data from different images, for which Tony devised a least squares method.

The first spherical viruses to be reconstructed (in 1970) were tomato bushy stunt virus – showing a dimer clustering pattern on the T=3 icosahedral surface lattice – and human wart virus. Jan Mellema and Linda Amos reconstructed TYMV in 1972, confirming the hexamer–pentamer clustering on the T=3 lattice. In 1974, members of the group reconstructed polyoma, cowpea mosaic and *Nudauralia capensis* β (a virus of the Pine Tree Emperor Moth) viruses – the latter being the first found to be based on a T=4 lattice.

Tobacco mosaic virus

The assembly of TMV

In 1971, Aaron initiated, with Jo Butler and Tony Durham, a study of the aggregation of TMV protein – he had in mind the underlying project of investigating the nucleation and growth of the virus. TMV has a very simple structure, consisting of 2,132 identical protein subunits arranged in a helical framework, 16⅓ per turn, packaging the single RNA molecule (6,395 nucleotides) in a rod-shaped particle. Such a simple structure suggests a simple method of assembly – that the subunits add on to the growing helix one or a few at a time, enclosing the RNA in the process – and in 1955, Heinz Fraenkel-Conrat and Robley Williams at Berkeley had demonstrated that TMV could be reassembled from its isolated protein and nucleic acid components. Thus all the information necessary to assemble the particle must be contained in its components – the virus 'self-assembles'.

But there were one or two problems. Firstly, in 1956, Roger Hart and John Smith, at Berkeley, showed that foreign RNAs, for example from yeast, and also synthetic polyribonucleotides, could be incorporated into virus-like rods. This cast doubt in the belief that the specificity required for the formation of identical virus particles *in vivo* was achievable during the assembly itself. Also, the slow rate of assembly in the reconstitution experiments – about six hours or more were required for maximum yields – suggested that there were missing elements in the story. Another difficulty was the starting point – getting at least seventeen subunits to bind to the flexible RNA molecule before the assembling structure could close round on itself and start off the helical growth.

It occurred to Aaron that the two-turn disk aggregate of protein (see previous section) could provide a jig on which the first turns of the viral helix could assemble. From the group's systematic survey of the aggregation states of TMV protein, it was found that while at low pH the protein alone forms helices of indefinite length that are structurally similar to the virus except for the lack of RNA, at physiological pH and ionic strength, the disk aggregate was the stable form. Furthermore, using disks and RNA, complete virus particles were formed in minutes rather than hours, and there was a preference by several orders of magnitude for RNA from TMV over RNAs from other sources. It was also found that disks enhanced the rate of elongation and so were actively involved in growth.

The preference for TMV-RNA suggested the presence of a unique site on the viral RNA optimised for interaction with the protein disk and so initiating growth. In 1977, David Zimmern and Jo Butler isolated this sequence – surprisingly, it was not at the end of the RNA strand but about one-sixth of the way along. Thus, having bound to a disk, more than 5,000 nucleotides had to be coated in one direction and about 1,000 in the opposite direction. So the conclusion was reached that nucleation occurred by the insertion of a hairpin of RNA – the nucleation region – into the central hole of a protein disk and between the two layers of subunits. The loop binds around the first turn and causes the disk to dislocate into a short helix (or lockwasher), which then encloses the RNA between its turns. This complex gives a start to the virus helix, which can rapidly elongate by adding disks and repeating the process.[30]

X-ray work
The significance of the disk aggregate of TMV protein in the nucleation and growth of the virus spurred on the interest in the crystals of the disks. The crystallisation results were rather variable until it was realised that better crystals grew after cold nights and when this was incorporated into the routine – cooling the crystallisation mix to 15°C for the first night – the results became more reliable.

Aaron's student, Peter Gilbert, collected data to 6Å on precession films. An initial attempt at phasing was made by Tony Jack by direct methods, using the 17-fold non-crystallographic symmetry on the hk0 projection – normal to the planes of the disks. However, a heavy atom derivative was made with methyl mercury nitrate, which had been used on the X-ray work on the virus, and the phases given by this (in the main projections) extended, again using the 17-fold symmetry, into three dimensions. The results of this study were published in 1974[31] – the arrangement of the disks in the crystal being established from the X-ray work and from my electron micrographs of negatively stained, crushed crystals, and a 6Å electron density map obtained.

In 1976, the limitations of the precession method of collecting data from the large unit cell (200×200×180Å) were overcome by the introduction of the Arndt-Wonacott camera enabling a complete set of three-dimensional data to 5Å to be collected. Anne Bloomer and John Champness had by then joined the group, and Gerard Bricogne, who used the 17-fold symmetry to phase completely – in the resulting map, most of the polypeptide chain could be traced. In 1978, the resolution was pushed to 2.8Å[32] – at the time this was the largest protein structure (600kD) to be solved by X-ray crystallography – and a comparison was made with a 4Å map of the virus from Ken Holmes' group in Heidelberg.

tRNA

Around 1967, several laboratories were trying to crystallise tRNAs, although it was not universally accepted that the molecules had a fixed physical structure. At LMB, however, Francis Crick was convinced that they had, and, having a paternal interest in the molecules, persuaded Aaron (since he was familiar with RNA in TMV) to become involved. Attempts at crystallisation were therefore begun by Ken Holmes with an assistant, Shirley Morris, using material from Brian Clark and his group in the Molecular Genetics Division. Brian Clark had joined LMB in 1964 to work on protein synthesis, and had become interested in investigating the role of the mysterious n-formyl-methionyl- tRNA discovered by Kjeld Marcker and Fred Sanger (p. 210). Large-scale preparations of tRNAs were obtained from the Microbiological Research Establishment at Porton, and individual species were separated and purified by countercurrent distribution (making use of the slightly different solubilities of tRNAs in solvents – a technique developed for tRNAs by Robert Holley's group in Ithaca and set up in the LMB by Brian with Bhupendra Doctor, known, of course, as 'Doc').

Reports were heard that a young German research worker, Hasko Paradies, had grown crystals of yeast tRNA^Ser by dialysing solutions against dioxane in the presence of cadmium or copper. So he was invited to LMB to participate – although by the time he arrived, his crystals had disappeared 'lost in an accident on the ferry'. Subsequent work of Paradies did appear to be fraudulent (for example, an X-ray pattern published by him in 1970 and attributed to valyl tRNA was in fact from a protein crystal), but it is not impossible that there was some truth in the earlier work. Although the LMB group were not able to reproduce his protocol, they were influenced into pursuing dioxane as precipitant, and with this Brian Clark managed to grow tiny spherulites of even tinier crystals of tRNA^fMet in 1968, from which it

104. Daniela Rhodes, 1973.

was possible to get X-ray powder patterns, and determine the unit cell parameters. However, no bigger crystals appeared for a while. Ken Holmes went off to Heidelberg, and Daniela Rhodes joined the group. With a visitor from the USSR, Andrei Mirzabekov, crystals of several tRNAs were grown in 1971 by precipitating with Cetavlon, but they were not of very good order. Jacques Fresco, from Princeton, was visiting Cell Biology at this time, involved in tRNA sequencing. Before coming to LMB, however, he had had some indications that crystals could be grown from a mixture of tRNAs, implying a common structure. He tried unsuccessfully to reproduce this result here, but it later turned out that there was one dominant species present in the earlier crystals.

In the absence of a firm crystal structure for tRNA, a number of model structures were proposed to explain the large amount of data appearing on the molecular properties. The most satisfying of these was built by Michael Levitt and published in 1969, only a year after joining the laboratory as a research student, and it proved to be a useful prelude to the model building when the X-ray map appeared later.

In 1972, Ray Brown had joined the group and he succeeded in crystallising several species of tRNA using dioxane or spermine as precipitant, but of these, only tRNA^{Phe} from *E. coli* diffracted to high resolution – to about 3Å. In 1970, crystals of yeast tRNA^{Phe} had also been reported to diffract to 3Å (by the laboratories of Rich and Sundaralingam in the USA). This tRNA was available commercially, and since its anti-codon was partially complementary to that of one of the tRNAs that were being produced in the laboratory, Jane Ladner, on her arrival, was given the project of trying to cocrystallise the two, in the hope that interaction between them could stabilise the structures. Well-ordered crystals were obtained, but were of tRNA^{Phe} only. The crystallisation of this as a function of spermine and magnesium was investigated, and a monoclinic form was chosen as the most promising to pursue.

Data from native crystals and four heavy atom derivatives were collected by Jon Robertus, a postdoc from Joe Kraut's laboratory in San Diego – the crystals were very thin plates and had to be bolstered with Sephadex beads to stop them bending against the walls of the capillary tube. The crystals were grown in the cold

105. Jon Robertus, 1973.

room and cooled by a cold air stream on the diffractometer and so the long-winded mounting procedure also had to be carried out in the cold room. A 3Å map and structure were obtained in 1974 – the structure disagreeing considerably with one published earlier that year by the Rich group at MIT. A paper was submitted to *Nature* in June,[33] and, the same month, Jon Robertus and Brian Clark described the results at a meeting at Madison. Rich and Sung-Hou Kim were at this meeting and immediately afterwards wrote a paper revising their structure and submitted it to *Science*, who published it two weeks before the LMB-*Nature* paper.

The work continued at LMB and, in 1975, the resolution was increased to 2.5Å. In the following year, the structure

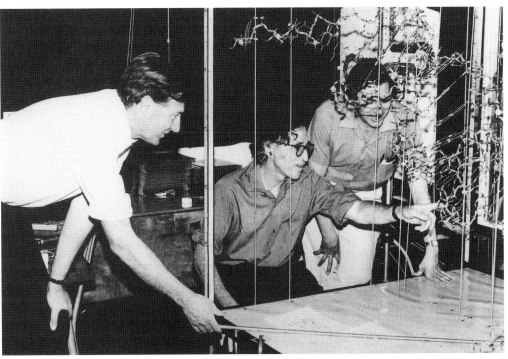

106. John Finch, Aaron Klug and Brian Clark looking at the tRNA model, 1975.

was refined by Michael Levitt and Tony Jack. In 1977, the binding to tRNA of various metals was studied, following up the work of Jacques Fresco in Princeton, who had shown that they stabilised the tertiary structure. This study was returned to in 1982 with Brian Hingerty and John Dewan, when the cleavage of the sugar–phosphate backbone catalysed by lead was proposed to imply a self-splicing possibility. A similar site was found in 1995, for a magnesium ion in the hammerhead ribozyme structure determined by Bill Scott,[34] and was a critical part of the explanation of the mechanism of the ribozyme catalytic cleavage.

Memories of the tRNA work were recorded by Brian Clark in TIBS in 2001.[35]

Other nucleic acid work

In the 1970s, there was some debate on whether native DNA in the 'wet' B-form had a constant local structure along its length, or whether it had local structural features arising from special sequences which, for example, could be recognised by a regulatory protein such as a repressor. Research into this was mainly on defined oligonucleotide structures, or on DNA under different conditions. Aaron recognised that there were indications in physico-chemical data (NMR, X-ray diffraction and nuclease digestion patterns) that in an alternating sequence of A and T residues there was a structural distinction between the neighbouring A–T and T–A dimers. Just before his death in 1978, Tony Jack did some energy calculations on the structure of the alternating copolymer which were completed by Michael Levitt. These suggested that the sugar–phosphate backbone alternated between common B-type and an abnormal form – the first positive indication of local structural variations – and this was confirmed later by the pattern of DNAseI digestion determined by George Lomonossoff and Jo Butler.

In 1987, postdoc Hillary Nelson solved the structure of an oligo(dA).oligo(dT) tract. The sequence is peculiar in that its helical repeat in solution is 10.0, compared with 10.5 for random DNA, and the axial rise is 3.2Å compared with 3.4Å for other B-type fibres. The sequence cannot undergo the B- to A-type transition and cannot be associated into nucleosomes. Runs of four or five base pairs of the sequence placed every ten to eleven base pairs (the helical repeat) cause an overall bending of the DNA configuration. From the crystal structure it was found that the bending occurs at the ends of the runs rather than within them. The other features are a consequence of good base-stacking with additional hydrogen bonds producing a more rigid structure than normal, B-type DNA.

(During that year we moved house to Swaffham Prior on the edge of the fens, and held a housewarming party. Bill Turnell, who was living on a boat in Cambridge at that time, offered to bring Hillary by water. The section on the Cam was straightforward, but the lodes (side channels) leading towards us were rather overgrown with weed which clogged the propeller – Hillary had to earn her passage by trying to keep the weed clear until they seized up completely on the wrong side of the lode and had a long walk around to reach the house. Bill Turnell was initially a visitor from Mark Pepys' laboratory at Hammersmith Hospital, but stayed on for a few years after that connection ceased, working on amyloid proteins, and helping Anne Bloomer with the crystallisation of C-reactive protein. He was an excellent violinist and had earlier to decide between a career in science and one in the Royal Philharmonic Orchestra.)

In 1989, Wes Sundquist, a postdoc from MIT, investigated the telomeric ends of chromosomes – a special maintained G-rich sequence at the ends of linear chromosomes that ensures continual replication from the ends. It had been suggested that the telomeric sequences at the ends of sister chromatids might associate as a parallel guanine quadraplex to facilitate their alignment. He confirmed that telomeric sequences dimerise to form stable complexes in solution – guanine tetrads between hairpin loops.

Wes and his wife were theatre fans and booked seats at the Arts Theatre soon after arriving in Cambridge, not really knowing what they were booking for. Their first visit was to the pantomime. Wes, being rather thin on top, and sitting in the front row, was an irresistible target for the Dame. Another experience was the triennial Greek Play staged by the university students – only at the theatre did they appreciate that it was to be performed in the original classical Greek language.

Chromatin and the nucleosome

Work on chromatin had begun from the opening of LMB – John Hindley, in Ieuan Harris's group in the Protein Chemistry Division, had tried reconstituting chromatin from DNA and extracted histone protein (then fractionated into slightly lysine-rich, very lysine-rich and arginine-rich) and Aaron Klug had tried pulling fibres from the results but without any success. There was then a gap until 1972, when Roger Kornberg came to Aaron's group. He asked for a messy subject to work on and Aaron suggested chromatin. About ten years before this, X-ray diffraction studies on chromosomes and extracted chromatin, by the Wilkins group at King's College, London, and Vittorio Luzzati's group in Paris, had found evidence for a repeating structure of about 110Å. Beyond this, the X-ray pictures were not very informative, leading to a variety of model structures being proposed, including a speculative one from Crick in 1971. The trouble with chromatin was that at near physiological conditions, samples at reasonable concentration for X-raying formed a gel in which individual fibres were firmly stuck together in random orientations and resisted reasonable methods of producing some preferred orientation which would enable the X-ray pattern to be disentangled and interpreted in some detail. To try to get more precise structural detail, Roger began by trying to get better X-ray pictures, but a year at this did not improve matters and he then abandoned it in favour of biochemical studies.

In 1973, Roger began isolating histones using the mild conditions that had been published in 1971 by van der Westhuyzen and von Holt working in Cape Town. It was now known that the chromatin of most organisms had roughly equal amounts of the histones H2A, H2B, H3 and H4 – one molecule of each for every 100 base pairs of DNA, plus about half as much of the histone H1. Cross-linking studies with Jean Thomas, who had been a postdoc with Ieuan Harris, and was now at the Biochemistry Department, showed that H3 and H4 associated in solution as a tetramer, $(H3)_2(H4)_2$ and H2A and H2B as a dimer. This was a very illuminating discovery – it showed that the histones were not simply forming a protective coat around the outside of the DNA. Hewish and Burgoyne in Australia had just published the results of nuclease digestion studies on chromatin which showed a preferential cutting of the DNA at a periodicity of about 200 base pairs, suggesting a repetitive shielding by the protein between these sites. Roger realised that

107. *Roger Kornberg at Cold Spring Harbor, 1977. Courtesy of Cold Spring Harbor Laboratory Archives.*

Hewish and Burgoyne's results would be explained if the DNA were wrapped around a histone aggregate, and in 1974 proposed what was later to be called the nucleosome[36] – a subunit structure in chromatin, consisting of a histone octamer made up of the (H3, H4) tetramer and two of the (H2A, H2B) dimers, plus about 200 base pairs of DNA (the exact amount depending on the species of cell). Roger suggested that as the amount of H1 was close to half of the others, it too could be associated, one per subunit in chromatin. This was confirmed with Markus Noll by prolonged nuclease digestion studies, which showed pauses at DNA lengths 160 and 140 base pairs, between which the H1 was released.

An open beads-on-a-string appearance had been seen in the electron microscope for chromatin which had been sheared as it was ejected from nuclei, or which had been depleted of H1. But the definitive experiment correlating these with the units proposed by Roger was the '1–2–3–4' experiment of Finch, Noll and Kornberg.[37] In this, chromatin was cut with micrococcal nuclease and the smallest fractions – containing 200, 400, 600 and 800 base pairs of DNA were isolated and shown by electron microscopy to contain 1, 2, 3 and 4 bead units respectively.

Intact chromatin under physiological conditions appeared in the electron microscope as a thick (about 300Å diameter) filament. In 1976, Finch and Klug studied the relationship between this and the more open structures seen in chromatin at non-physiological, low salt concentration, by electron microscopy and proposed that the compact form was a helical twisting of the open form with about six nucleosomes per turn, which they called the solenoid.[38] The solenoidal model has remained the most commonly accepted, although many other models have been proposed.

The existence of the nucleosome as the structural unit of chromatin promoted attempts to crystallise them. Len Lutter developed a technique for large-scale preparations of the 140-base pair particles for biochemical studies and, in 1977, these were found sufficiently uniform for crystallisation. Initially the crystals were poorly ordered – only to about 20Å, but a combination of X-ray diffraction and electron microscopy revealed the nucleosomes as rather flat pillbox-shaped, about 50Å high and about 110Å in diameter. A model was proposed with $1\frac{3}{4}$ turns of DNA wrapped in a superhelix around the histone octamer core.[39]

108. *Len Lutter, 1975.*

The $1\frac{3}{4}$ superhelical turns of DNA in the nucleosome introduced what became known as the linkage number problem. Several studies had shown that when the DNA superhelix was unwound from the nucleosome, the change in the twist of the DNA was between –1 and $-1\frac{1}{4}$ turns per nucleosome. (The minus sign signifying that the supercoiling had been left-handed.) Why didn't this agree with the $1\frac{3}{4}$ turns of superhelix on the nucleosome? Crick pointed out that these unwinding experiments measured the change in linkage number – the number of times that one strand of the DNA double helix is wound round the other strand, and that the technique could not separate the contributions of changes in the superhelical coiling and any associated change in the local twist of the DNA. So, it was proposed that the twist of DNA – the helical screw – did in fact change when bound into nucleosomes from solution.

The cutting of the DNA on the nucleosome by the nuclease DNAse-1 produced a pattern of cuts at ten base pair intervals, suggesting that the number of base pairs per turn was close to 10.0. The linkage number change would require that DNA in solution had about 10.7 base pairs per turn. In 1980, Daniela Rhodes and Aaron found that the DNAseI cutting pattern of naked DNA in solution (actually bound from solution onto three different inorganic surfaces) *was*, in fact, close to this – 10.6 base pairs per turn. This satisfactory state of affairs was shattered when more accurate work by Len Lutter in Cambridge and Roger Kornberg and Ariel Prunell in Stanford produced average cutting patterns of DNA on the nucleosome close to 10.4 bases apart. However, all these figures were shown to be too large when steric hindrance effects were taken into account – the histones and the neighbouring DNA strands should push the nuclease cutting points away from a line parallel to the (local) DNA axis. Taking this into account, Aaron, Len and Daniela showed that a DNA structure on the nucleosome with 10.0 base pairs per turn, measured along the axis of the duplex (the local frame of reference) fitted the observed cutting pattern best and 10.5 was impossible.

The almost 50:50 make-up of the nucleosome from DNA and protein made it an ideal candidate for investigation by neutron diffraction using the method of contrast variation. This makes use of the variation in the degree of scattering of neutrons with the proportion of D_2O present. So, by changing the ratio of D_2O to H_2O in the background solution of a crystal, this background can be made to match either the protein or DNA scattering at low resolution, and so effectively show up only the other component. In this way, the v-shaped side view of the DNA superhelix appeared at the protein-matching contrast, and at the DNA-matching contrast, the protein appeared as if it were a helical ramp on which the DNA could coil. The experiment was done in 1980 at the neutron source at ILL, Grenoble, with Anita Lewit and Graham Bentley. Although with the widespread use of synchrotron radiation for crystallography this has become commonplace, it was very striking at the time how insignificant our tiny 0.5 mm crystal seemed, buried somewhere among the massive shielding, collimating and filtering equipment required at neutron sources.

At about the same time, attempts were being made to crystallise the histone octamer by itself, and although useable crystals were not grown, electron micrographs of precipitates which formed showed helical aggregates. With Jude Smith, the 3D reconstruction technique was applied to these. A map at about 25Å resolution showed a shape similar to that deduced for the protein component of the nucleosome from the neutron scattering work.

X-ray work from chromatin was returned to in 1976 by Linda Sperling. She, with Annette Tardieu in Luzzati's laboratory in Paris, measured the low angle scattering from solutions at low ionic strength and their data indicated a rod-shaped structure with a diameter of about 100Å. Linda and Aaron deduced that the 110Å diffraction found with samples under more *in vivo* conditions arose from the spacing between turns of the solenoid rather than the distance between nucleosomes along the nucleofilament. This was confirmed in 1985 when Jon Widom managed to produce specimens with some orientation by sucking into a capillary tube samples from a dilute isotropic gel produced by spinning down from dilute solutions – the 110Å diffraction did turn out to be meridional as one would expect from a solenoidal type of arrangement.

In 1980, Tim Richmond had joined the group and, with Daniela Rhodes and Ray Brown, better ordered crystals of the nucleosome core were grown, diffracting to about 5Å in the best direction, and with a smaller unit cell than the earlier one. Data were collected to 7Å and a map to this resolution was published in 1984.[40] The overall

109. Tim Richmond, 1980.

structure concluded from the earlier, more subjective methods was confirmed. Much of the DNA duplex was visible, showing the superhelix bent (quite sharply) around the histone octamer. In 1985, Tim Richmond left LMB for the ETH in Zurich with his student Song Tan, and continued work on the nucleosome, publishing a 2.8Å structure in 1997, and a 1.9Å structure in 2002.

Zinc finger

In the 1980s, Aaron became more interested in 'active chromatin' and turned to the TFIIIA-5S RNA system pioneered by Don Brown at the Carnegie Institute in Washington and Bob Roeder at St Louis. TFIIIA is a protein required for the correct initiation of the transcription of the 5S RNA gene in *Xenopus* oocytes. Although the protein is relatively small, the binding site to the gene DNA covers about 45 base pairs. It was also available in fairly large amounts and so was proposed as a suitable project for Jonathan Miller, who came as a PhD student in 1984. Initially Jonathan found his protein yield was very small, but this was traced to a need for zinc, which had been eliminated in his preparations. He found that for stability, the 7S complex required from seven to eleven atoms of zinc per complex. He also found that prolonged proteolysis produced fragments of molecular weight about 3kD and that limited proteolysis produced periodic intermediates with this spacing. These results suggested that TFIIIA was built almost entirely from a string of tandem 3kD segments each folded about a zinc ion into a small, compact RNA-binding domain. (Jonathan Miller was new to gels and did not recognise the significance of the periodic ladder. He did notice it, however, and consulted a more experienced person in the laboratory who told him not to worry about it – 'such ghost artifacts often occurred'. Fortunately, Aaron asked to see the gel and recognised its significance.)

At about this time, the sequence of the protein was published. It showed an abnormally large number of Cys and His residues and with Andrew McLachlan, the sequence was analysed and found to show a pattern of 30 residue repeats, the best alignment showing nine similar units. Aaron concluded that each of these units bound zinc atoms in a tetrahedral coordination by (2Cys + 2His) residues, forming extended RNA-binding fingers linked by a flexible joint enabling the protein to bind to the relatively long (45bp) stretch of RNA.[41] Since they gripped the RNA, or the cognate DNA, these minidomains were later called zinc fingers. Louise Fairall confirmed that the fingers of TFIIIA made

110. Louise Fairall, 2000.

131

repeated contacts with the DNA by footprint studies – finding where the DNA could not be cut by nuclease because it was shielded by the protein bound to it – and showed that the fingers made multiple contacts with the DNA, about five base pairs apart. (The nine fingers are spread fairly uniformly along the 45 base pair binding site on the DNA, where short runs of Gs occur.) The resolution of this type of study was increased by Mair Churchill using the considerably smaller (and low sequence specificity) hydroxyl radical footprinting.

Hundreds of zinc finger motifs have since been discovered – it has been estimated that as much as 3 per cent of the genes in the human genome contain regions which specify zinc fingers, and in chromosome 19 it is as high as 8 per cent. In some cases, like TFIIIA, they make up the bulk of a DNA-binding protein, and in others, a relatively few fingers are present on a more globular DNA-binding molecule. The number of fingers per protein range from as few as two to as many as 37.

In the case of SWI5, a yeast transcription factor with three fingers on a larger globular protein, the region containing the fingers was isolated with Kiyoshi Nagai and an NMR study with David Neuhaus and Yukinobu Nakaseko showed that this region was sufficient to locate the binding site to DNA without any of the rest of the protein, and that at least two fingers were required to attach to the correct length.

Grant Jacobs compared the amino acid sequences of more than 1,000 zinc finger motifs and found that the amino acids in three positions are particularly variable and these are precisely those used to make contact in the DNA-binding domain of the transcription factor Zif268 for which an X-ray structure had been published. These sites dictate the specificity to the appropriate DNA binding site. In 1994, Aaron with Yen Choo demonstrated, by phage display, the selection of specific zinc fingers by given DNA triplets, and also the converse – the selection of specific DNA binding sites by given zinc fingers.

By 1987, investigators had sequenced several members of a large family of transcription factors known as nuclear hormone receptors. These must be bound by a particular steroid or thyroid hormone or vitamin before they can activate a gene. Each sequence contained a similar domain of about 80 amino acids, each of which included two subsections reminiscent of the zinc finger. However, the zinc binding region consisted of cysteines only – not cysteine and histidine. In 1990, NMR was applied to determine the structures of the DNA-binding domains of the rat cortisone receptor by a group in Utrecht, and of the human oestrogen receptor in LMB by John Schwabe, David Neuhaus and Daniela Rhodes. In both cases, the two zinc-finger-like motifs merge into a single structural unit and though there is some structural similarity to TFIIIA-like zinc fingers, and they participate in DNA-binding, they are also involved in forming the protein dimers which recognise the specific binding sites on DNA. The crystal structure of the DNA-binding domain of the oestrogen receptor was determined in 1993 by John Schwabe, and Daniela Rhodes, with John Finch and Linda Chapman.

Alzheimer's disease

In 1984, the Professor of Psychiatry, Sir Martin Roth, discussed with Aaron and Tony Crowther the possibilities of structural work on the proteins involved in Alzheimer's disease. The two characteristics of Alzheimer-affected brains are senile plaques – amyloid deposits of beta protein (or A4) – and neurofibrillary tangles, seen in electron micrographs to be composed of paired helical filaments (PHFs). As a result of the discussion, Claude Wischik came from the Psychiatry Department as a student with Tony, and they analysed in detail the morphology of PHFs. Subsequently, in collaboration with Michel Goedert and John Walker, the PHF protein was shown in 1988 to be the microtubule-associated protein tau. Tony Crowther has continued his electron microscopy of neurofibrillar deposits, and biochemical and genetic work on these and other abnormal neuronal fibrils has continued in the group of Michel Goedert.

111. Michel Goedert, 1997.

Michel had joined the Director's Section of the laboratory in 1985 and initially collaborated with Stephen Hunt in the MRC Molecular Neurobiology Unit, studying the regulation of biosynthesis of neuropeptides at the cellular level. Abnormal production of nerve growth factor mRNA had been suggested to be involved in producing Alzheimer-type abnormality, but they found no evidence for this. Michel also found no difference between control and Alzheimer brains in the cellular localisation of the mRNA for the precursor of beta protein. From 1989, he was joined by Maria Spillantini and Ross Jakes. Ross had worked in the groups of Brian Hartley (from 1970), Alan Fersht, Alan Weeds and Jake Kendrick-Jones, but remained with Michel's group from 1989 until he retired in 2005. The group was incorporated into the new Neurobiology Division when it was formed in 1993, and since 2003 Michel has been a joint Head of the Division with Nigel Unwin.

Uli Laemmli and Jake Maizel – 'SDS gels'

Both Uli and Jake were visitors to Aaron's group in 1971. Uli had been working on the T4 phage in Geneva and at LMB he was trying to study the protein components of which there were about eleven in the phage head. He had already found that the four major head proteins were cleaved during the process of assembly, and in following this up, there was a problem in separating them on gels. Jake suggested the use of disc-electrophoresis to increase the resolution. In this, the first part of

112. *Alfred Tissières and Uli Laemmli at Cold Spring Harbor, 1977.*
Courtesy of Cold Spring Harbor Laboratory Archives.

113. *Jake Maizel.*

the gel is made more dilute and the proteins in the added specimen quickly migrate under the electric field to form a thin layer at the start of the normal gel. However, although the resolution capability of the system is improved, in practice the variable shape factor of the proteins tended to blur out the bands. To get over this, Uli heated the sample in SDS before loading, to eliminate aggregation and open out the molecules in a uniform way into polypeptide chains. The resulting gel patterns were a great success, enabling Uli to allot more reliable molecular weights to the proteins than had previously been reported. The technique of 'SDS gels' was quickly taken up universally.

Aaron Klug became joint head of the Structural Studies Division of LMB with Hugh Huxley, in 1978, and became the Director of the laboratory from 1986 to 1996. One of the major achievements of his direc-torship arose from his encouragement of John Sulston and Alan Coulson to begin sequencing the genome of the nematode *Caenorhabditis elegans*. This led, via a col-laboration between the MRC and the Wellcome Trust, to the setting up of the Sanger Centre and its participation in the sequencing of the (almost) complete nematode and human genomes (see chapter 7). While Aaron was director, there was a considerable growth of interest in organising the transfer of technology developed in LMB to industry, with the realisation of the possible financial rewards for the inventor, and for LMB and MRC. He was much involved in the development and implementation of the MRC's Awards to Inventors scheme in 1987 (see chapter 10). Aaron was also a major influence in breaking the monopoly that Celltech had on developing antibody inventions. It was felt that Greg Winter's method of creating humanised antibodies in 1988 could be exploited in many more ways than Celltech could by itself and a procedure for licensing to other companies was established. The MRC itself, much against its wish, was persuaded by Aaron to take a share in the equity of a new company, Cambridge Antibody Technology, formed in 1989, to produce completely human antibodies selected by Greg's development of using phage display (see chapter 8).

Aaron was elected a Fellow of the Royal Society in 1969, and became its President in 1995–2000. He was knighted in 1988 and appointed to the Order of Merit in 1995. In 1982, he was awarded the Nobel Prize for Chemistry 'for his development of crystallographic electron microscopy and his structural elucidation of biologically important nucleic acid-protein complexes'.

In 1996, a meeting was held in Cambridge to mark Aaron's 70th birthday and his retirement as Director – about 80 past members of his group were able to attend. Several have continued in their own research in LMB, as described below.

114–134. Aaron Klug's 70th Birthday Meeting, 1996:

114. Speakers. Clockwise around Aaron from top left: Ken Holmes, Tim Richmond, Uli Laemmli, David DeRosier, Steve Harrison, Hillary Nelson, Alfonso Mondragon, Michael Levitt, Roger Kornberg and Tim Baker.

115. *Don Caspar, Roger Kornberg and David DeRosier.*

116. *Kiyoshi Nagai and Mitsuhiro Yanagida.*

117. *Don Caspar and Tim Baker.*

118. *Moira Cockell and Hans Christian Thøgersen.*

119. *Rafael Giraldo-Suarez, Hillary Nelson and Gabriel Varani.*

120. *Lu Duo, Steven Brenner, Murray Stewart and Nigel Unwin.*

121. *Bill Scott.*

122. *Jonathan King and Cyrus Chothia.*

123. *Bill Turnell and Anne Bloomer.*

124. *Jake Kendrick-Jones and Jo Butler.*

125. *Michel Goedert and Maria Spillantini.*

126. *Uli Arndt and Nikolai Kiselev.*

127. *Rodger Staden and Len Lutter.*

128. *Bob Diamond and Reuben Leberman.*

129. *John Kilmartin and Brian Clark.*

130. *Mair Churchill and Andrew Leslie.*

131. Tony Durham and Jo Butler.

132. Jo Butler and Joyce Baldwin.

133. Steve Lippard, Wes Sundquist and Aaron.

134. Joyce Baldwin, David DeRosier and Tony Crowther.

Linda Amos

Linda was recruited via the courses that were run at the laboratory in the early days of optical diffraction and filtering. Brad Amos attended one of these and asked if there were any vacancies suitable for Linda on the computing side, assuring the powers-that-be of her FORTRAN knowledge. Linda was at the time programming in a rather boring job at the Central Electricity Generating Board, although not in FORTRAN, but a quick-guide book provided sufficient information for her to begin programming when she arrived at the laboratory in 1968. It was at this time that programs were being written for three-dimensional reconstruction from electron micrographs, and Linda collaborated with David DeRosier and Peter Moore on programs for helical particles and with Tony

135. Linda Amos, 1975.

Crowther for spherical viruses. On applying the latter, she collaborated with Jan Mellema on the reconstruction of the spherical turnip yellow mosaic virus and with Tony and John Finch on the phages R17 and f2. In 1974, she began working on the structure of flagella microtubules with Aaron and Richard Linck, and her group continues to work mainly on microtubules and tubulin and the associated protein, kinesin. She has, however, collaborated with Ken Taylor and Hugh Huxley on the binding of myosin crossbridges to muscle thin filaments.

Anne Bloomer

Anne joined Aaron's group in 1971 and became involved in the X-ray diffraction work on crystals of the disk aggregate of tobacco mosaic virus. This continued as the major part of her work, with John Champness, Gerard Bricogne, Jo Butler and Jim Graham, until the 2.8Å map was published in 1978. With this, it was possible to study (with Sven Hovmoller) the binding of nucleotides to the disk for the light it might give to the assembly and structure of the virus. With Daniele Altschuh and Dino Moras at Strasbourg, and Alfonso Mondragon, a study of the crystallographic data from TMV and other proteins showed that sites of antigenicity tended to be those associated with high mobility.

136. Anne Bloomer and David Phillips at Cold Spring Harbor, 1971. Courtesy of Cold Spring Harbor Laboratory Archives.

A crystallographic study of C-reactive protein was taken up with Graham Cheetham, Bill Turnell and others outside the laboratory. This pentameric protein normally occurs in trace amounts in the plasma, but is expressed rapidly as part of the acute phase response to infection or injury, although its function was unknown. Anne also determined the crystal structures of an Fab fragment of a therapeutic monoclonal antibody Campath-1H (see chapter 8) in both the rat and humanised versions. This is one of a series of antibodies used for the treatment of immuno-logically mediated diseases.

From 1999, she worked with Uli Arndt on the development of his new micro-focus X-ray sources and improved mirror focusing devices. Anne retired in 2003.

Jo Butler

Jo Butler has carried on with biochemical and physical chemical studies on interactions between proteins and between nucleic acids and proteins, particularly in viruses – recent subjects being hep-atitis B virus and HIV.

Jo came to LMB in 1964 as a research student of Ieuan Harris. He had been in contact with sev-eral LMB people while in the Biochemistry Department as an undergraduate. Ieuan organ-ised some of the practical classes in which Robin Offord and Richard Perham were demonstrators, and Jo's biochemistry supervisor at Queen's College was Brian Hartley. Sydney Brenner had informal discussion evenings for interested stu-dents and Jo remembers Mark Bretscher and Tony Stretton contributing to these. Not surpris-ingly, therefore, when the time came to organise a postgraduate research position, Jo wrote to Fred Sanger and was put in touch with Ieuan

137. Jo Butler, 1987.

Harris, who applied to the MRC for a studentship grant. A little after this, Jo was invited to talk with Professor Frank Young, who had been very much against the setting up of LMB, about applying for a studentship in the Biochemistry Department. Not knowing of Young's antagonism, Jo asked if he could wait for the outcome of the MRC application first. Young became very frosty at this and 'sup-posed that [Jo] could try applying later', and the interview was over![42] The antag-onism, however, was quite personal; in general there was a very good relationship between the staff of the two laboratories.

Jo's thesis project under Ieuan Harris was on the structure of yeast alcohol dehydrogenase, and during this the idea of using maleic anhydride as a reagent for the reversible blocking of peptide amino groups was conceived with Ieuan, Brian

Hartley and Reuben Leberman. Jo obtained his PhD in 1968, and the following year Reuben left for Heidelberg, and Jo replaced him as the biochemist in Aaron's virus group.

His initial work in the group was on the plant viruses being studied, a selection of small spherical viruses and the rod-shaped tobacco mosaic whose assembly became the dominant field of study in the early 1970s. Through the virus work, Jo made great use of the analytical ultracentrifuge and has become the laboratory expert in its use. Since 1978, he has been the Biological Safety Officer.

Tony Crowther

Tony Crowther first came to the LMB in 1964. When the first laboratory computer, the Ferranti Argus was bought, someone was required to write software for it. Although it was hoped that Tim Gossling, who had written the Initial Orders for the machine at Ferranti, could be persuaded to come, it was not immediately clear whether he would, and so the post was advertised. Tony, who had just graduated in Maths at Cambridge and was doing the Diploma in Computing, was one of the applicants. At a late stage, Tim agreed to accept, and since he had so much experience with the machine, he was the clear choice. David Blow, however, was very impressed by Tony, who was clearly interested in the work they were doing, and invited him to come as a research student, and Tony accepted. He started by writing a faster and more general three-dimensional Fourier program than

138. *Tony Crowther, 1987.*

was then available (MOFOUR), and this was used to calculate a number of the subsequent crystallographic electron density maps.

As the first part of his thesis project, Tony was given the job of making the Flying Spot densitometer work (p. 104). The second part was an analysis of non-crystallographic symmetry and some preliminary development of its application to phase determination. During this time he invented the translation function for positioning a molecule of known structure and orientation in an unknown crystal structure. He returned to this area in 1971, writing a program to calculate the Rossmann and Blow rotation function relating non-crystallographic subunits which, by introducing spherical harmonics, speeded up its calculation by some hundred times – the *fast rotation function*. As more and more protein structures were solved, the translation and fast rotation function formed key parts of what became known as the Molecular Replacement solution of protein structures.

Tony spent 1968 as a postdoc in Edinburgh, but then returned to Aaron Klug's group, and became involved with Aaron, David DeRosier and Linda Amos in developing the methods of three-dimensional reconstruction of objects from their projections seen in electron micrographs (p. 121). These were applied to the reconstruction of a variety of virus particles in the 1970s. He also worked with visitors Bill Earnshaw and Eddie Goldberg on the tail fibres and the triggering of the tail of phage T4, including isolating and mapping baseplate mutants. With Barbara Pearse and John Finch, he began a study of the structure and assembly of the clathrin coats of vesicles. This was returned to in 1986 with Guy Vigers, a research student; the three-dimensional reconstruction method was applied to electron micrographs of unstained clathrin cages in ice. These maps were among the first to be made from cryo-micrographs of single particles.

From 1984, Tony became involved with Alzheimer's disease (p. 133). With Claude Wischik, the image reconstruction methods were applied to the paired helical filaments associated with the disease, and the work in this field has continued in collaboration with Michel Goedert and his group. Another interest has been the core of hepatitis B virus – in 1997 with Bettina Böttcher the three-dimensional structure of this was determined from electron cryo-micrographs to produce a numbered fold,[43] which was later confirmed by X-ray diffraction with Sam Wynne and Andrew Leslie. This was the first example of such a detailed structure determination from single particles.

Tony Crowther was elected a Fellow of the Royal Society in 1993, and was joint Head of the Structural Studies Division from 1994 to 2005.

Daniela Rhodes

Daniela joined Aaron's group in 1969, and became involved in the tRNA work, particularly on the preparation side with Brian Clark, and in the crystallisation – purifying different species and trying different precipitants and conditions to grow well-ordered crystals. After the crystal structure of yeast tRNA^{Phe} was determined in 1974, the main interest of the group turned towards chromatin and the nucleosome. Len Lutter found conditions for producing fairly uniform preparations of the nucleosome core, and again, Daniela's role was to produce well-ordered crystals. After many attempts, crystals were grown which were ordered to about 7Å, and an electron density map was obtained by the group in 1984. The crystal work was taken by Tim Richmond to Zurich in 1985, but Daniela has remained interested in the chromatin field and has continued the study of the '300Å' chromatin filaments – attempts have been made to construct uniform examples for structural studies with her students Van Huynh and Phil Robinson.

Following the establishment of the zinc finger DNA-binding domain by Aaron with Jonathan Miller and Andrew McLachlan in 1985, Daniela began a study of

139. Kiyoshi Nagai and Daniela Rhodes, 1989.

proteins containing them, starting with the *Xenopus* transcription factor TFIIIA, with Louise Fairall. Another, the oestrogen receptor, was studied with John Schwabe, David Neuhaus and Lynda Chapman, both by NMR and X-ray diffraction. Another major interest of her group has been the telomere.

From 2000 to 2006, Daniela chaired the EMBO fellowship committee. She was elected a Fellow of the Royal Society in 2007.

LATER GROUPS AND PEOPLE

Brad Amos

Brad came to work at LMB, unofficially, in 1981. Officially, he had been involved in research and teaching in the Department of Zoology in Cambridge using the advanced microscopy apparatus of Professor Torkel Weis-Fogh until his sudden death in 1975. Brad then obtained short-term grant support, and came to LMB while the recipient of an MRC Project Grant in the Department of Zoology. The subject of the grant was an investigation of antigens in the mitotic spindle of HeLa cells using monoclonal antibodies. The work was done in collaboration with John

140. Brad Amos using a confocal microscope in 1992. Courtesy of John Cole, Perseverance Works.

Kilmartin in Cell Biology. Difficulties in imaging the HeLa spindle led to discussions with John White, who was having similar imaging problems in his research on *C. elegans*. After the expiry of the MRC project grant in 1983, Brad (without salary) joined in the development of the confocal microscope with John White and Mick Fordham (see chapter 9). He continued with promoting and improving the microscope with Bio-Rad until they sold out in 2004 to Zeiss, who discontinued it. Brad had become a staff member in Structural Studies in 1987 and continues as an inventor of optical instruments. In 1997, he designed a diffractometer using a combination of coherent and incoherent illumination and dual CCD cameras for rapidly scanning electron micrographs for evidence of periodicities and/or other properties.

Brad was elected a Fellow of the Royal Society in 2007.

Joyce Baldwin

Joyce (then Cox) joined the haemoglobin group in 1964. She had read physics in Cambridge and began computing work in industry. However, after two years she decided that she would like to transfer to work connected with medicine and wrote to the Director of NIMR – the MRC laboratory at Mill Hill. He replied that he had no relevant posts, but suggested that she contact Max in Cambridge. Max invited her to come for a chat one Saturday morning to see what was going on at LMB and in the haemoglobin group, and offered her a job.

Her first project was to use the noncrystallographic symmetry of the haemoglobin molecule to sharpen the 5.5Å map of the deoxy- form, and then became involved in calculating the high resolution, 2.8Å map of the oxy-form, and in 1980, the 2.7Å map of the carbonmonoxy- form with data collected by Leigh Anderson.

From 1980, Joyce worked with Richard Henderson on the structure of bacteriorhodopsin using high resolution electron cryo-microscopy. With Tom Ceska, Ken Downing and others, she helped to develop the computer programs required to produce an atomic model for the structure obtained in 1990, and with Niko Grigorieff this was refined against electron diffraction data in 1996. From 1990,

141. Joyce Baldwin and Steve Harrison at Cold Spring Harbor, 1971. Courtesy of Cold Spring Harbor Laboratory Archives.

Joyce began an overall study of the structure of G protein-coupled receptors, the large family of integral membrane proteins which, like bacteriorhodopsin, have a seven transmembrane α-helix arrangement. With Vinzenz Unger and Gebhard Schertler, the disposition of these helices in rhodopsin – the photo receptor in rod cells – was obtained in 1997, from a low resolution three-dimensional map using cryo-electron micrographs. A model was proposed for the arrangement of the α-carbon positions in this receptor family, based on the map and the analysis of the sequences of 500 receptors.

Joyce retired in 2004.

Chris Calladine

Although he was based in the Department of Engineering in Cambridge, and not a member of LMB, Chris Calladine has been involved in several collaborations with members of LMB, and so can be thought of as an honorary member. As a fellow of Peterhouse, he frequently met Aaron Klug at the college and conversation often turned to structural problems. One of the first, around 1970, involved bacterial flagella. These are rigid corkscrew-shaped, slender filaments, which are rotated by the bacterium to propel it through water. They are made out of a single type of protein subunit, flagellin, the subunits being close-packed in a filament. However, if they were identically bound together, they would form a *straight* filament. Chris suggested that the problem of the corkscrew shape could be solved if the subunits existed in two states – most simply in the form of alternative connection points to neighbouring subunits. He designed a model built of subunits with such a bistable connection property, which reproduced all the main aspects of the flagellum structure, and also explained the family of different helical shapes adopted by various mutants, and by wild-type filaments at different pH, and under torsional stress.

The second major system to which Chris applied his mechanics approach was that of DNA structure. In the early 1980s, it was becoming recognised that, although the overall or average structure of DNA in solution was the B-form, the local structure depended on the precise sequence of bases there. In a paper in 1982, Chris explained the local variations in helix twist in terms of one simple cause – the

142. Chris Calladine. Courtesy of Chris Calladine.

steric hindrance or clash in the minor-groove between the large purine bases on opposite strands of the double helix at adjacent base pairs. He introduced the local motions of *roll* and *slide* (using a local system of coordinates rather than 'laboratory' coordinates based on the overall helix axis) to add to helical *twist* as the most important parameters describing the relative arrangement of adjacent base pairs. With Horace Drew, the mechanics of the transition from the (wet) B-form to the (dry) A-form were described in 1984 in terms of these parameters.

Chris showed that it is the degree and sense of the roll parameter that mainly decides the curvature of DNA. It had been shown in 1977 that the nucleosome core consists of about 140 base pairs of DNA wound into about 1¾ turns of a superhelix of diameter 110Å, around a core of histone protein. In 1985, Chris explained that curvature was proportional to the Fourier component of *roll* at a period equal to the helical repeat of DNA; and this encouraged Horace with Andrew Travers and Sandra Satchwell to sequence nucleosomal DNA, and look for periodicities which could explain its curvature into the superhelix. They found highly periodic distributions of particular dinucleotide steps having the expected double-helical repeat of 10.2 base pairs, and with a preferred high or low roll, located where it would promote the bending of the DNA around the histone core. Chris and Horace also explained the slow-running in gel electrophoresis of DNA having a sequence-repeat of about 10, in terms of intrinsic superhelical coils of large diameter.

Chris has also collaborated with Ben Luisi and others at the Biochemistry Department, investigating the geometrical principles of the architecture of the *E. coli* outer membrane protein, TolC. Part of this protein consists of twelve α-helices packed in an anti-parallel fashion to form a hollow cylinder of nearly uniform radius. The α-helices pack together in a 'knobs-into-holes' manner reminiscent of that in the normal two-strand coiled coil; but their particular sequence of amino acids causes them to untwist and adopt an almost parallel packing.

143. *Cyrus Chothia.*

Cyrus Chothia

Cyrus Chothia first visited LMB to collect precession camera data from crystals of lysergic acid (LSD) as part of his PhD work as a student of Peter Pauling at University College, London, and then joined LMB for three years from 1970 as a postdoc. In 1973 he became a Royal Society Research Fellow, dividing his time between Birkbeck College and LMB until his permanent appointment to the Research Staff at LMB in 1990, where he has built up a group studying structural patterns in proteins and the relationship between amino acid sequence and three-dimensional structure.

Bob Diamond

Bob Diamond came to LMB in 1963, working on computational aspects of crystallography. He was initially involved with Max's haemoglobin group and then went on to more general topics, writing programs for refining protein structures in real space. In the late 1970s he developed the computer graphics program Bilder, which was initially used by Phil Evans in 1978 on phosphofructokinase, and by Anne Bloomer's group on the TMV protein work published in 1980. Several computer graphics programs were being developed at around this time, including Alwyn Jones' FRODO (which became the favourite until his O took over around 1991). The trigger for these was the availability of graphics display systems which occurred about this time. The leader was the Evans and Sutherland Vector Graphics display, which cost the laboratory about £50,000. The crystallography departments at York, Sheffield and Leeds could only afford one between them, and

144. Bob Diamond, 1987.

it trundled around between the three places in a bus. The system had been developed for US military use and at the same time we bought our *one*, McDonnell Douglas ordered some hundreds! Graphics systems are considerably cheaper these days – spin-offs from computer games and TV monitors rather than from the military.

For many years, Bob was involved with the International Union of Crystallography (IUCr), the body that is responsible for organising international crystallographic affairs. It runs triennial scientific meetings (Congresses) and General Assemblies which attend to the management of the Union and to interaction with the outside world. Its members are the national academies of science – for the UK this is the Royal Society, though the Council of the British Crystallographic Association has taken over the practicalities since it was founded in 1982. The Assemblies appoint Commissions such as the Journal Commission which runs *Acta Crystallographica*, the *Journal of Applied Crystallography* and the *Journal of Synchrotron Radiation*, and the Computing Commission which aims to promote the spread of good or advanced computing practices. Bob was appointed to the Computing Commission in 1975 and became its chairman in 1978. In 1984 he became a member of the Executive of the IUCr and the Convenor of the Finance Committee, signing some 731 cheques or other payment authorisations and some 4,662 items of other Union correspondence between 1985 and 1994. He stood down at the Beijing Congress in 1993. In 1992, Bob was invited by the Executive Committee to accept nomination as Vice President, but since he would be losing his operational base at LMB on his retirement in 1995, felt he had to decline.

Phil Evans

Phil Evans had previously worked in Colin Blake's group at Oxford, and came to LMB in 1978, to boost the crystallography side after the departure of David Blow to Imperial College. At LMB, he began work on the structure of phosphofructokinase with Peter Hudson and has continued with other protein and nucleoprotein complexes, including collaboration with Kiyoshi Nagai on components of the mRNA splicing mechanism. Recently he has been studying the proteins involved in exo- and endocytosis, with Harvey McMahon and David Owen. Phil was elected a Fellow of the Royal Society in 2005.

145. Phil Evans and Paul McLaughlin, 1993.

Wasi Faruqi

146. Wasi Faruqi, 1999.

Wasi Faruqi joined the LMB in 1969. He had gained his first degree in physics at Lahore in 1959, and his PhD in High Energy Physics nominally at Imperial College, London in 1965, although the actual work was using the high energy machine NIMROD, a 7GeV proton synchrotron at the Rutherford Laboratory at Chilton. After a year in Pakistan, working on low energy nuclear physics with the Pakistan Atomic Energy Commision, he returned to IC for three years as a postdoc, again mainly based at the Rutherford laboratory. The end of this, 1969, was one of the relatively down periods in high-energy physics and having watched and been very interested in John Kendrew's television series 'The Thread of Life', he enthusiastically replied to an advertisement for a position at LMB.

This position had been created by the prolonged absence of Frank Mallett in Chicago. Frank had devised the electronics for the Flying Spot densitometer which had come into use for measuring X-ray films while Paul Sigler was working in the

149

laboratory, and Paul had been sufficiently impressed to borrow Frank for a year to set up something similar for him when he left to set up his own laboratory in Chicago. But the year had overrun and the Flying Spot at LMB periodically needed repairing. No specific project had been mentioned at his interview, although Wasi remembers that at lunch, Max, in particular, was keen on his coming. However, when he began at LMB, his first call was in fact to the Flying Spot.

In 1970, Frank returned from the USA, and it was decided to update the Flying Spot. The result was the 'Hybrid', combining the positional accuracy of the mechanical densitometer based on the Nikon projection microscope with the fast scanning speed of the CRT, scanning only close to the CRT centre so that there was less problem from stray light. Wasi designed the optics for this.

From the 1970s, Wasi was involved with the development of faster detectors for Hugh Huxley and the muscle group, until 1989, after Hugh had left LMB. He then became involved in various aspects of electron microscopy, firstly evaluating tunnelling and force, scanning microscopes and later developing CCDs as faster detectors in our more standard electron microscopes. He is now investigating the possibility of direct pixel detection for faster and zero noise recording.

Judd Fermi

Judd (Giulio) Fermi, the son of the Italian nuclear physicist Enrico Fermi, joined Max's group in 1971, and remained at the LMB until his death in 1997.

He had attended Oberlin College and Princeton University (MS, Mathematics, 1957), and received his PhD in 1961, working with Gunther Stent at Berkeley, studying the role of the initial proteins synthesised after infection by the phage T4. His postdoctural work was done at the Max Plank Institute für Biologie in Tübingen (1961 –63), working in Werner Reichardt's group studying the optical nervous system of the common housefly.

In 1963, he returned to the USA and was employed as a systems analyst at the Institute for Defence Analysis and later at the Center for Naval Analysis in Washington, DC. But by 1970, Judd had become disillusioned with this type of work and began to look for a low-stress scientific job in Europe. When Max offered him a post as a technician at

147. Judd Fermi, 1994.

LMB, he promptly accepted, and the whole family (wife and two children) moved to Cambridge in the spring of 1971. Within a year he was promoted to the senior staff.

He began work on the refinement of the 2.5Å model of human deoxyhaemoglobin, which had been produced by Lynn Ten Eyck and Arthur Arnone, the refined structure being published in 1975, Judd continued to work in the data collection and computing work on many different aspects of the structure of haemoglobins. After his death in 1997, Max said, 'He was my mathematical arm'.

Richard Henderson

After being involved with the structure work on chymotrypsin, Richard Henderson became interested in membrane proteins, and in particular the purple membrane from *Halobacterium halobium*, a light-driven proton pump involved in photosynthesis. The membrane sheets tended to crack on being dried down for electron microscopy and, to prevent this, a method was devised with Nigel Unwin in 1975, using glucose to replace water. With this and keeping electron exposure to a minimum, images of the membrane were obtained ordered to 7Å.[44] Later that year a three-dimensional map was calculated, showing for the first time by electron microscopy the transmembrane helices. Various visitors contributed to the work, including Don Engelman, Michael Rossmann, David Agard, Bob Glaeser, Tom

148. Richard Henderson at Cold Spring Harbor, 1971.
Courtesy of Cold Spring Harbor Laboratory Archives.

Ceska and Ken Downing. Janet Jubb had also joined the group and Joyce Baldwin from the haemoglobin section. An atomic model of the structure from 3.5Å data was published in 1990.[45]

Jim Deatherage and Rod Capaldi worked with Richard on cytochrome-C oxidase vesicle crystals. In 1989, Gebhard Schertler began work on the visual pigment rhodopsin, an example of the many G protein-coupled receptors for neurotransmitters and hormones. Richard is also interested in pushing the determination of structure by electron microscopy of individual particles rather than arrays.

Richard became joint head of the Structural Studies Division with Hugh Huxley in 1986, and with Nigel Unwin from 1987. He became Director of LMB in 1996. He was elected a Fellow of the Royal Society in 1983.

Terry Horsnell

149. Terry Horsnell and Jude Smith, 1995.

Terry joined LMB in 1972. He had graduated in Sheffield University in 1965, and worked for a PhD in the Department of Electrical Engineering on the design of an electromagnetic Shot Blaster for cleaning castings. In 1968 he joined British Steel, but at the end of a project developing the computer control of a rolling mill at Scunthorpe, during which he had been involved with Ferranti Argus computers, British Steel began one of its periodic upheavals and Terry thought it a good time to move on. In 1972, Tim Gossling, who had done much of the early programming for the laboratory Argus, left LMB, and the post of Systems Manager to replace him was advertised. Terry applied, and after being interviewed by David Blow, Tony Crowther and Alan Wonacott, was given the job.

At this time all the interfaces from Argus were home-built, devised by Tim Gossling and Frank Mallett. Terry's first problem was to improve the connection between Argus and the X-ray diffractometer. He remembers Leigh Anderson on his knees setting control numbers by handswitches and feeding them individually into the machine and begging that this chore be removed.

Other control computers began to appear quite quickly, the first being a PDP11 to control the Optronics X-ray film densitometer. And another to run the Evans and Sutherland Vector Graphics display system for building molecular models.

However, most of the instrumentation needed to pursue the science of molecular biology at this time involved new techniques and had to be built in-house, using our comprehensive electronics and mechanical workshops. Frank Mallett was much involved in the design and construction of numerous pieces of data-collection hardware, for which he then designed the electronics to enable them to be connected to computers. Terry would then write the software to drive the devices to enable the automatic collection and processing of data.

The PDP11s were superseded by the LSI11 (a miniaturised version, with the processor on a single large-scale integrated-circuit) and it was this computer which became the standard instrumentation machine in the laboratory. But disk space was still very expensive, and so Frank (hardware) and Terry (software) set up our own 10Mbytes/sec network and central disk store. When ethernet arrived at the laboratory, some five years later, Frank's network was still running at ten times the ethernet speed.

When our first in-house large computer, the Vax11/780, was bought in 1982, micro-Vaxs began to appear for local control.

John (Jake) Kendrick-Jones

Jake joined the muscle section in 1970. He had obtained his PhD with Sam Perry at Birmingham, studying the contractile proteins in developing skeletal muscle. As a postdoc, he worked with Carolyn Cohen and Andrew Szent-Gyorgyi in Boston investigating how paramyosin self assembles to form the cores of thick filaments in molluscan muscles.

At LMB, Jake set up his own group and established that the calcium regulatory components on the molluscan myosins were small subunits called light chains associated with the neck region (now referred to as the lever arm) of the myosin head and named them the regulatory light chains (RLCs). Focusing on non-muscle myosins, his group identified another novel mechanism for regulating contractility/force generation in vertebrate cells. They showed that phosphorylation of the RLCs of myosins purified from non-muscle cells not only regulated myosin interaction with actin but also the assembly of these myosins into force-generating filaments. These important results illustrating the dynamic nature of these myosins have crucial

150. Jake Kendrick-Jones, 1975.

implications for a wide variety of processes in vertebrate cells where dynamic cytoskeletal structures are required to be assembled and then disassembled at specific times during the cell cycle, e.g. cytokinesis.

Jake's group was the first to employ the newly developed bacterial protein expression systems to prepare myosin RLCs and generate mutants which could be exchanged into myosin to probe the regulatory mechanism and in collaboration with David Trentham (NIMR), Malcom Irving (London) and Yale Goldman (Philadelphia) could be exchanged into muscle fibres to monitor myosin cross-bridge motions in these fibres on the physiological time-scale.

In the early nineties he and other groups discovered new classes of myosins confirming that myosin exists as a superfamily of motor proteins and identified eighteen major classes. To probe the cellular functions of these myosins he focused on the myosins in class VI, since they are unique in moving towards the minus ends of actin filaments (all other myosins move towards the plus end) and appear to be associated with hearing, cardiomyopathy and ovarian cancer. In collaboration with Folma Buss (CIMR), Claudia Veigel (NIMR) and John Trinick (Leeds), using molecular biological, cell biological, single molecule imaging and mechanical approaches, they have shown that myosin VI is involved in receptor mediated endocytosis, in maintaining Golgi organisation and exocytosis/secretion, in membrane ruffling and cell motility and in mitotic spindle organisation and cytokinesis. These intriguing results demonstrate that myosin VI is a multifunctional motor involved in a diverse range of cellular processes.

Jake has also studied the structure and function of dystrophin localised at the muscle plasma membrane, and emerin present in the inner nuclear membrane, proteins whose absence or mutation leads to the major forms of X-linked muscular dystrophy.

Andrew Leslie

151. Andrew Leslie, 1999.

Andrew came to LMB in 1988 from David Blow's crystallography group at Imperial where he had worked with Alan Wonacott and others from 1980. Before that, he had been at Purdue working in Struther Arnott's group on the relationship between the various forms of the DNA double helix, and in Michael Rossmann's group working on the structure of southern bean mosaic virus. At LMB, he began with the structure of ovalbumin with Penny Stein, published in 1991. In 1993, with Jan Pieter Abrahams he solved the structure of the catalytic domain, F1, of the ATP synthase complex, from crystals grown by John Walker's group, and since then the structure has been solved in a variety of states to give insight into the remarkable rotary, catalytic mechanism. In 1999, the structure of the hepatitis B virus capsid was solved to 3.3Å resolution, with Sam Wynne and Tony Crowther. Andrew was elected a Fellow of the Royal Society in 2001.

152. Mike Levitt, 1975.

Michael Levitt

Michael came to LMB in 1968 as a research student of Bob Diamond. His thesis project was the conformation analysis of proteins, but much of his first year was spent in building a tRNA model, which was published in 1969. He spent 1971–74 as a postdoc at the Weizmann Institute working on protein folding with Shneior Lifson, and then returned to the LMB until 1979. He worked with Cyrus Chothia on the classification and analysis of protein structure and with Tony Jack developing ways of refining the structures of large molecules. He is now in the department of Structural Biology at Stanford University. In 2001, Michael recorded his memories of LMB and of the birth of computational structural biology in a paper which is reproduced in chapter 10. He was elected a Fellow of the Royal Society in 2001.

153. Jade Li.

Jade Li

Jade Li came to LMB in 1985 from Columbia University, New York, although she had previously worked with Don Caspar at Brandeis. Here, she began with electron microscopy of arrays of lactose permease from *E. coli* prepared with Phil Tooth. However, she soon became involved with X-ray diffraction work on the crystalline toxin inclusions in *B. thuringiensis* with Joe Carroll and David Ellar at the Biochemistry Department. This is a membrane toxin which forms pores in the midgut membrane of particular insects, killing them through starvation and septicemia, and work continues, investigating the structural basis of its action. Jade has also collaborated in X-ray diffraction studies with Gebhard

155

Schertler on bovine rhodopsin, and with Phil Evans and Kiyoshi Nagai's group on small nuclear ribonuclear particles (snurps).

Andrew McLachlan

154. Andrew McLachlan, 1987.

Andrew McLachlan read Maths and Physics with Theoretical Physics at Cambridge and graduated in 1956. He began research under Christopher Longuet-Higgins in the Department of Theoretical Chemistry, working on the Molecular Orbital Theory of aromatic hydrocarbon radicals, their electron spin distributions and their Electron Spin Resonance (ESR) spectra, obtaining his PhD in 1959. He then spent a year in the USA working with Harden McConnell at the California Institute of Technology on ESR, and another at Harvard with E. Bright Wilson who was interested in infra-red spectra. Andrew returned to CalTech in 1964–65 and wrote a book – *Introduction to Magnetic Resonance* – with Alan Carrington, an ex-colleague from Cambridge.

Although continuing to work in Theoretical Chemistry, Andrew became increasingly interested in molecular biology. He had had discussions at Trinity College with Richard Watts-Tobin, who was working with Sydney Brenner and Leslie Barnett on the genetic code, and wrote to Max from California inquiring about the possibility of working at LMB. Max suggested he spoke with Francis Crick who was visiting CalTech in 1965, and as a result was invited to work with Max on the mechanisms of haem–haem interaction in haemoglobin, and joined LMB in 1967.

Andrew has been to a large extent involved in the analysis of sequences, initially from proteins, and later, when they became available indirectly, from DNA. This has involved collaborative work with many other groups and people in the laboratory, including, for example, Murray Stewart with work on tropomyosin and John Walker on serum albumin. In 1980, with Don Engelman, Richard Henderson and Bonnie Wallace, the different ways of connecting the seven trans-membrane α-helices, found by Richard with Nigel Unwin from the electron microscopy of bacteriorhodopsin, were examined and, from the electron density and the charge nature along the amino acid sequence, the correctly connected arrangement from the 5,040 possibles was predicted. In 1982, with Jon Karn the periodic charge distribution in the amino acid sequence along the myosin rod was shown to match the cross-bridge spacings in muscle, and with Rodger Staden, he devised a computer program to help find protein coding regions in a long DNA sequence.

Andrew also studied the sequences of proteins for signs of their origin – via evolution and gene duplication – their similarity to other proteins, and for their structural implications. With Ross Boswell, he developed methods for comparing sequences and establishing homology.

In 1986, in collaboration with David Eisenberg in Los Angeles, Andrew investigated hydrophobicity in protein structure as a criterion for testing proposed folding, and solvation energy as a means of calculating the stability of a protein structure in water.

He became interested in direct methods of solving structures (methods that do not involve the experimental determination of phases of the X-ray reflections) using the 'Pair-Functional Principle' of classical statistical mechanics, which states that the ensemble of atoms which fits the unphased observed X-ray intensity data of a crystal structure is that with the maximum entropy, and wrote three papers developing this before retiring in 2000.

Hilary Muirhead

Hilary Muirhead joined Max as a PhD student in 1958. She had read physics at Cambridge and after graduating heard of research positions in the Low Temperature section and at the MRC, and opted for the latter. Her project was to work on the deoxy- form of haemoglobin, but began learning the techniques with Ann Cullis, growing crystals and collecting data by precession photography on the oxy-form.

The rotating anode X-ray tubes were in the basement of the Austin Wing, the darkroom was on the first floor and the laboratory for growing and mounting crystals was next door in the hut. She shared an office in the hut with Anne Stockell and Stanley Glauser who were working on foetal haemoglobin. Max made her calculate one of the Patterson projections using Beevers Lipson strips, which she found quite educational, if a bit slow. The final summations were made with a mechanical computer which was very noisy and made everyone else get out of the room. However, most of the processing was with EDSACII, to which she was introduced by Michael Rossman.

She was one of the last of the group to leave the Cavendish, so that she could complete the data collection, densitometer the films and begin processing the data. On moving to the new LMB, the first jobs were contouring the map, making the balsa wood model and writing up. The result, published in 1963, was a 5.5Å map showing an appreciable movement between the subunits compared to the oxy-form.

In 1964, she moved for a postdoctoral period of two years, to Harvard, working in Bill Lipscomb's group on carboxypeptidase and introduced the Fourier programs that had been used in Cambridge. She returned to LMB in 1966 at Max's invitation. One of her first jobs was to examine the processing of the high resolution, 2.8Å, oxyhaemoglobin data which was not going well. She found that after a program update, one of the corrections to the data (the temperature factor) was being applied the wrong way around, and with this corrected, processing was much improved. Her main project later, however, was with Jonathan Greer, collecting the data for a 3.5Å map of human deoxyhaemoglobin. She also became involved with Joyce Baldwin in processing the elastase data of David Shotton and Herman Watson.

In 1969, Hilary left LMB and went to Bristol, when a lectureship became available – she was keen to teach rather than do full-time research. This also became evident in her interest in organising summer schools in protein crystallography through the Biological Section of the British Crystallographic Association, of which she was a founder member.

Kiyoshi Nagai

Kiyoshi Nagai came initially to join Max's group in 1976 for eighteen months working on the biochemistry of haemoglobin. He returned to this in 1981 using genetic engineering to make artificial mutants of haemoglobin in E. coli which were extensively analysed in terms of both their structure and function. From 1990, he began work on crystallising the small nuclear ribonuclear particles (snurps) which are involved in removing the non-coding intervening sequences, the introns, from the precursors of messenger RNA – the spliceosome. Crystal structures of several of these have been determined with Phil Evans, Stephen Price and Chris Oubridge. Kiyoshi was elected a Fellow of the Royal Society in 2000, and became joint head of Structural Studies with Tony Crowther in 2001.

David Neuhaus – NMR

It became clear by the late 1980s that NMR spectroscopy had developed to the extent that it was capable of generating reliable structural information from biological macromolecules, and collaborations were beginning with people who had access to NMR machines. The advantage over X-ray diffraction was the lack of need for crystals – they need not be grown and there were no resulting intermolecular contacts to be taken into account. The structures of isolated molecules and possible interactions could be determined, not necessarily in conditions where crystals grew. Our first NMR machine, a 500MHz spectrometer, was bought in 1988 and housed in the University Department of Medicinal Chemistry (on the nearby Forvie Site), headed by Professor Laurie Hall. Later, an NMR suite was fitted out in the old Pharmacology building to accommodate a 300MHz and a 600MHz spectrometer, and in 2001, a dedicated MRS (magnetic resonance spectroscopy) building was put up, housing a new 800MHz spectrometer (shared with Alan

155. Aaron Klug, David Neuhaus and John Ionides, 1995.

Fersht) and the re-located 500MHz spectrometer, now moved out from Laurie Hall's laboratory.

David Neuhaus brought his expertise to LMB in 1988, having completed NMR postdocs with Kurt Wüthrich in Zürich and Ray Freeman in Oxford. Among the first results was the solution structure of the DNA-binding domain of the oestrogen receptor, determined in 1990 with John Schwabe and Daniela Rhodes (the mode of binding to DNA was determined by crystallography in 1993). The solution structure of two zinc finger domains from SWI5 was determined in 1992, with Yukinobu Nakaseko, Daniela Rhodes, Kiyoshi Nagai and Aaron Klug. David and his group have concentrated their studies mainly on proteins, and interactions of proteins with other proteins and DNA. Gabriele Varani, who was a group header at LMB from 1993 to 2000, concentrated the work of his group on RNA and protein-RNA complexes, some of the latter in collaboration with David.

Venki Ramakrishnan

Venki came initially to LMB in 1992 for a sabbatical in Aaron Klug's group, during which he solved the structure of histone H5 using MAD 9 (multiwavelength anomolous diffraction) crystallographic data collected at Brookhaven on a selenium derivative. On his return to the USA, at Brookhaven and later in Utah where

he became a Professor in the same department as Wes Sundquist, he began working on ribosome proteins. He returned to LMB in 1997, and with his group successfully crystallised the 30S ribosomal subunit and solved its structure, and has gone on to pursue a study of the mechanism of translation culminating in a high resolution structure of the complete 70S ribosome: tRNA complex in 2006. Venki was elected a Fellow of the Royal Society in 2003.

156. Venki Ramakrishnan.

Clarence Schutt

Schutt was at LMB from 1977 to 1985. He came from Steve Harrison's group at Harvard, working on the structure of tomato bushy stunt virus, collaborating with Gerard Bricogne. While at LMB, he improved the low-angle camera equipment which was used for work on chicken erythrocyte chromatin with John Langmore, and on reovirus with Bill Earnshaw. He also became interested in crystallographic work on the profilin:actin complex and acted as thesis adviser to Hugh Huxley's PhD student Nick Strauss. Crystals had been grown by Uno Lindberg at Stockholm and collaboration on this work continued when Schutt left LMB for Princeton. The profilin:actin structure was finally solved in 1990.

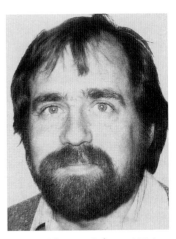

157. Clarence Schutt, 1984.

158. Murray Stewart, 2005.

Murray Stewart

Murray Stewart came from Australia in 1973, and began structural work on tropomyosin, paramyosin, myosin and other muscle-related projects as well as non-muscle filaments. Since 1990, he has also exploited nematode sperm to probe the mechanisms of producing force in amoeboid cell motility.

Nigel Unwin

Nigel Unwin gained his PhD in 1968 in the Metallurgy Department in Cambridge, with work on grain boundaries in alloys, using the electron microscope. Hugh Huxley heard he was interested in using the electron microscope for biological specimens and invited him to come to LMB. His first innovative idea was to improve phase contrast by using a quarter wave plate, made from a single strand from a spider's web stretched across an aperture in the microscope. He then investigated improving negative stains by using mixed salts, and studied how the stain distribution changed under electron exposure. In 1975, he and Richard Henderson devised the stainless, glucose method of preserving specimens in the microscope. In 1977, he took up work on two-dimensional arrays of ribosomes with Werner Kuhlbrandt. These were from lizards, and escapees are still living free around the outside of the laboratory. He had also hoped to get some from bats, but was refused permission to capture them in Ely Cathedral.

In 1978, he began a collaboration with Guido Zampighi from Duke University, working on gap junction channels. These channels span the gaps between adjacent cells forming a leakproof connection between them for the passage of ions and small molecules. Nigel continued with this study at Stanford University, where he worked from 1980 to 1987, with Ron Milligan, and Peter Ennis. They showed by electron crystallography of frozen specimens that the channel pore contracts in the

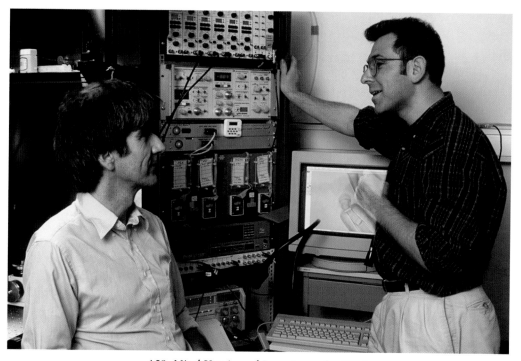

159. Nigel Unwin and Leon Lagnado, 1995.

presence of calcium. Nigel also began work on the acetylcholine receptor from the postsynaptic membrane of *Torpedo marmorata* with Allain Brisson and, later, Chikashi Toyoshima.

Nigel returned to LMB in 1987. He carried on with both projects initially, the gap junction study was pursued with Kathrin Stauffer, but later he concentrated on the acetylcholine receptor. This membrane-spanning pore acts as a gate to control electrical signalling between nerve and muscle cells. Work with Rameen Beroukhim and Michael Stowell in Cambridge and Atsuo Miyazawa and Yoshinori Fujiyoshi in Japan culminated in 2003 in an atomic model of the closed pore,[46] which was refined to 4Å resolution in 2005.[47] It has a girdle-like gate at the middle of the lipid bilayer, which becomes broken apart when acetylcholine enters. The structure was determined by electron crystallography of frozen specimens of tubular crystals of the receptor, photographed at low electron dose on a liquid helium microscope stage in Japan.

Nigel became joint Head of the Structural Studies Division with Richard Henderson in 1987 and Head of the new Division of Neurobiology when it was formed in 1993. He was elected a Fellow of the Royal Society in 1983.

Alan Weeds

160. Alan Weeds, 1987.

Alan Weeds came as a research student to work on myosin with Brian Hartley in the Protein Chemistry Division in 1962. Following a post-doctoral fellowship at Harvard Medical School with Susan Lowey, he transferred to Hugh Huxley's group in Structural Studies in 1969 and was joined almost immediately by Brian Pope working on myosin sub-fragments and isoenzymes. His focus changed to studying non-muscle motility in the late 1970s with an emphasis on actin binding proteins. He was joined by John Gooch in 1980. He discovered gelsolin in blood plasma and, with Jim Bamburg, another depoly-merising protein (ADF/cofilin) in brain. His principal focus for the rest of his career was on the structure, localisation and functions of these proteins. Apart from a brief spell away from LMB and another working with John Kendrick-Jones, Brian Pope remained with Alan until both retired in 2005. John Gooch moved to John Schwabe's group in 1997, and retired in 2007, when John Schwabe moved to Leicester.

1. M.F. Perutz, H. Muirhead, J.M. Cox, L.C.G. Goaman, F.S. Matthews, E.L. McGandy and L.E. Webb, 1968. Three-dimensional Fourier synthesis of horse oxyhaemoglobin at 2.8Å resolution. *Nature*, 219, 29–32 and 131–139.
2. W. Bolton and M.F. Perutz, 1970. Three-dimensional Fourier synthesis of horse deoxyhaemoglobin at 2.8Å resolution. *Nature*, 228, 551–552.
3. H. Muirhead and J. Greer, 1970. Three-dimensional Fourier synthesis of human deoxyhaemoglobin at 3.5Å resolution. *Nature*, 228, 516–519.
4. L. TenEyck and A. Arnone, 1976. Three-dimensional Fourier synthesis of human deoxyhemoglobin at 2.5Å resolution. I. X-ray analysis. *Journal of Molecular Biology*, 100, 3–11.
5. G. Fermi, 1975. Three-dimensional Fourier synthesis of human deoxyhaemoglobin at 2.5Å resolution: refinement of the atomic model. *Journal of Molecular Biology*, 97, 237–256.
6. M.F. Perutz, 1970. Stereochemistry of cooperative effects in haemoglobin. *Nature*, 228, 726–739.
7. M.F. Perutz, 1997. *Science is not a Quiet Life. Unravelling the Atomic Mechanism of Haemoglobin*. Imperial College Press, London
8. M.F. Perutz, T. Johnson, M. Suzuki and J.T. Finch, 1994. Glutamine repeats as polar zippers: their possible role in inherited neurodegenerative diseases. *Proceedings of the National Academy of Sciences of the USA*, 91, 5355–5358.
9. M.F. Perutz and A.H. Windle, 2001. Cause of neural death in neurodegenerative diseases attributable to expansion of glutamine repeats. *Nature*, 412, 143–144.
10. M.F. Perutz, 1998. *I Wish I'd Made You Angry Earlier: Essays on Science, Scientists, and Humanity*. Cold Spring Harbor Laboratory Press, New York.
11. M.F. Perutz, 1989. *Is Science Necessary? Essays on Science and Scientists*. Barrie and Jenkins, London.
12. M.F. Perutz, 1989. The new Marxism. *New Scientist*, 15 July, 72–73.
13. *Ibid*.
14. K.C. Holmes, 2001. Sir John Kendrew. *Biographical Memoirs of Fellows of the Royal Society*, 47, 311–332.
15. G. Rosenbaum, K.C. Holmes and J. Witz, 1971. Synchrotron radiation as a source for X-ray diffraction. *Nature*, 230, 434–437. The history and development of synchrotron use are described in papers by H.E. Huxley and K.C. Holmes, 1997. Development of synchrotron radiation as a high-intensity source for X-ray diffraction. *Journal of Synchrotron Radiation*, 4, 366–379, and K.C. Holmes and G. Rosenbaum, 1998. How

X-ray diffraction with synchrotron radiation got started. *Journal of Synchrotron Radiation*, 5, 147–153.

16. H.E. Huxley, 1966. A personal view of muscle and motility mechanisms. *Annual Review of Physiology*, 58, 1–19.

17. A. Taylor, 1949. A 5kW crystallographic X-ray tube with a rotating anode. *Journal of Scientific Instruments*, 26, 225–229.

18. From an interview with Uli Arndt in LMB, 1998.

19. B.W. Matthews, P.B. Sigler, R. Henderson and D.M. Blow, 1967. Three-dimensional structure of tosyl-alpha-chymotrypsin. *Nature*, 214, 652–656.

20. D. Blow, 2002. *Outline of Crystallography for Biologists*. Oxford University Press, Oxford.

21. D. Blow, 2004. Max Perutz. *Biographical Memoirs of Fellows of the Royal Society*, 50, 227–256.

22. P. de Kruif, 1926. *Microbe Hunters*. Harcourt, Brace, Jovanovich, New York.

23. R.W. James, 1948. *The Optical Principles of the Diffraction of X-Rays*. G. Bell and Sons, London.

24. A. Klug, 1950. The application of the Fourier-transform method to the analysis of the structure of triphenylene, $C_{18}H_{12}$. *Acta Crystallographica*, 3, 176–181.

25. D.L.D. Caspar and A. Klug, 1962. Physical principles in the construction of regular viruses. *Cold Spring Harbor Symposia on Quantitative Biology*, 27, 1–24.

26. A. Klug and J.E. Berger, 1964. An optical method for the analysis of periodicities in electron micrographs, and some observations on the mechanism of negative staining. *Journal of Molecular Biology*, 10, 565–569.

27. R.A. Crowther and L.A. Amos, 1971. Harmonic analysis of electron microscope images with rotational symmetry. *Journal of Molecular Biology*, 60, 123–130.

28. D.J. Derosier and A. Klug, 1968. Reconstruction of three dimensional structures from electron micrographs. *Nature*, 217, 130–134.

29. R.A. Crowther, L.A. Amos, J.T. Finch, D.J. DeRosier and A. Klug, 1970. Reconstruction of three dimensional structures from electron micrographs. *Nature*, 226, 421–425.

30. Reviewed by A. Klug, 1999. The tobacco mosaic virus particle: structure and assembly. *Philosophical Transactions of the Royal Society of London Series B*, 354, 531–535.

31. P.F.C. Gilbert and A. Klug, 1974. X-ray analysis of the disk of tobacco mosaic virus protein. III. A low resolution electron density map. *Journal of Molecular Biology*, 86, 193–207.

32. A.C. Bloomer, J.N. Champness, G. Bricogne, R. Staden and A. Klug, 1978. Protein disk of tobacco mosaic virus at 2.8 Ångstrom resolution showing the interactions within and between subunits. *Nature*, 276, 362–368.

33. J.D. Robertus, J.E. Ladner, J.T. Finch, D. Rhodes, R.S. Brown, B.F.C. Clark and A. Klug, 1974. Structure of yeast phenylalanine tRNA at 3Å resolution. *Nature*, 250, 546–551.

34. W.G. Scott, J.T. Finch and A. Klug, 1995. The crystal structure of an all-RNA hammerhead ribozyme: a proposed mechanism for RNA catalytic cleavage. *Cell*, 81, 991–1002.
35. B.F.C. Clark, 2001. The crystallization and structural determination of tRNA. *Trends in Biochemical Sciences*, 26, 511–514.
36. R. Kornberg, 1994. Chromatin structure: a repeating unit of histones and DNA. *Science*, 184, 868–871.
37. J.T. Finch, M. Noll and R.D. Kornberg, 1975. Electron microscopy of defined lengths of chromatin. *Proceedings of the National Academy of Sciences of the USA*, 72, 3320–3322.
38. J.T. Finch and A. Klug, 1976. Solenoidal model for superstructure in chromatin. *Proceedings of the National Academy of Sciences of the USA*, 73, 1897–1901.
39. J.T. Finch, L.C. Lutter, D. Rhodes, R.S. Brown, B. Rushton, M. Levitt and A. Klug, 1977. Structure of nucleosome core particles of chromatin. *Nature*, 269, 29–36.
40. T.J. Richmond, J.T. Finch, B. Rushton, D. Rhodes and A. Klug, 1984. Structure of the nucleosome core particle at 7Å resolution. *Nature*, 311, 532–537.
41. J. Miller, A.D. McLachlan and A. Klug, 1985. Repetitive zinc-binding domains in the protein transcription factor IIIA from *Xenopus* oocytes. *Embo Journal*, 4, 1609–1614.
42. From an interview with Jo Butler and Andrew Travers in LMB, 2003.
43. B. Bottcher, S.A. Wynne and R.A. Crowther, 1997. Determination of the fold of the core protein of hepatitis B virus by electron cryomicroscopy. *Nature*, 386, 88–91.
44. R. Henderson and P.N.T. Unwin, 1975. Three-dimensional model of purple membrane obtained by electron microscopy. *Nature*, 257, 28–32.
45. R. Henderson, J.M. Baldwin, T.A. Ceska, F. Zemlin, E. Beckmann and K.H. Downing, 1990. Model for the structure of bacteriorhodopsin based on high-resolution electron cryo-microscopy. *Journal of Molecular Biology*, 213, 899–929.
46. A. Miyazawa, Y. Fujiyoshi and P.N.T. Unwin, 2003. Structure and gating mechanism of the acetylcholine receptor pore. *Nature*, 423, 949–955.
47. P.N.T. Unwin, 2005. Refined structure of the nicotinic acetylcholine receptor at 4Å resolution. *Journal of Molecular Biology*, 346, 967–989.

CHAPTER SEVEN

Molecular Genetics (became Cell Biology in 1970)

161. Francis and Sydney, Joint Divisional Heads, 1975.

The head of the Division in 1962 was Francis Crick, despite his having an aversion for administration, and to share the burden he was joined, after a year, by Sydney Brenner as joint-head. Also in the Division were John Smith, Richard Watts-Tobin, Tony Stretton and Robin Monro, Sydney's students Mark Bretscher and Anand Sarabhai, and Francis's students Ed O'Brien and Hans Boye, technical helpers Leslie Barnett, Rita Fishpool, Eileen Southgate and Muriel Wigby. Among the visitors were Hildegard Lamfrom, Alex Shedlovsky, Rob Traut and Alfred Tissières.

Francis continued working with Sydney on the genetic code and on mutagenesis, and his interest in DNA structure led on into chromatin. He also became interested in the more cell-biological subject of pattern formation. After a sabbatical in the US, he left LMB in 1977 for the Salk Institute. Sydney took up the nematode C. elegans, initiating studies on its genetics and tracing the nervous system, leaving these projects behind when he left LMB in 1986. Richard Watts-Tobin was involved in the mutagenesis work and in a theoretical study of haemoglobin oxidation and haem–haem interaction, and Robin Monro worked on protein synthesis, but both left LMB in 1967. Mark Bretscher began work in protein synthesis, but from 1970 switched interest to cell membranes, investigating their structure and role in cell motilty. John Smith was recruited by Francis and Sydney from Caltech in 1962 for his expertise in nucleic acid chemistry, and became involved mainly in work on tRNAs, retiring in 1986. Tony Stretton returned to Cambridge in 1962, and was initially involved in genetics work with Sydney, and from 1968 he joined in the nematode work, but left for Madison in 1971. Later arrivals on the molecular side were Brian Clark in 1964, working on tRNAs, and Andrew Travers in 1965, who later specialised in transcription and chromatin structure.

With the change in emphasis towards cell biology, the newer groups of Peter Lawrence and Michael Wilcox studying pattern formation began in 1969, and that of John Gurdon and Ron Laskey working on nuclear transplantation in 1972, and other groups have since been set up, continuing the enlargement of the Division.

FRANCIS CRICK

Following the double helical DNA work and the subsequent Nobel Prize, Francis was inundated with requests of various sorts. For written requests he had a universal refusal card printed (fig. 162), but there were many phone calls for interviews and queries of various sorts. Francis and Sydney were initially in a combined office on the first floor opposite that of Max and John Kendrew. Sydney maintained that on answering phone calls for Francis, he would say 'there's no such person – he's a committee'. In one interview, Francis was questioned about his entry in *Who's Who*, where he described his favourite recreation as 'conversation – especially with pretty women'. He commented that there wasn't much opportunity to do this in the laboratory – provoking an outcry from some of the female staff and resulting in an apology from Francis. (Sydney gives his recreation in *Who's Who* as 'rumination'.) It was said that by the large TMV model (close to their office) was a dangerous place for the computer girls to be cornered, although one or two of them now regret rejecting his propositions. He had a habit of saying to any female spotted yawning 'Early to bed again last night eh? Heh heh heh.' At the DNA-50 meeting, the very striking Suzanne Cory described writing to Francis directly for a place in the Division, and being accepted immediately – she added that she did not send her photograph! In the mid- or early 1960s, Francis drove to the laboratory in a white Lotus Elite – the envy of the younger students. It was one car that was not entrusted to Mick Fordham (in the workshop) for repair or servicing.

On the research side, Francis continued with his interest in DNA. Initially he was largely concerned with the genetic code until this was completed in 1967. In 1966 he proposed the Wobble Hypothesis to explain the general nature of the degeneracy of the genetic code.[1] Of the 64 possible triplets of nucleotides forming the codons in the mRNA molecule, three are stop-codons, specifying the termination

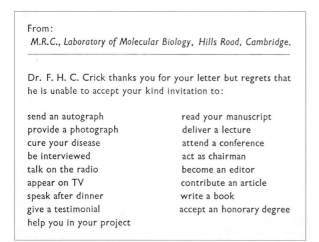

From:

M.R.C., *Laboratory of Molecular Biology, Hills Road, Cambridge.*

Dr. F. H. C. Crick thanks you for your letter but regrets that he is unable to accept your kind invitation to:

send an autograph	read your manuscript
provide a photograph	deliver a lecture
cure your disease	attend a conference
be interviewed	act as chairman
talk on the radio	become an editor
appear on TV	contribute an article
speak after dinner	write a book
give a testimonial	accept an honorary degree
help you in your project	

162. Francis' all-purpose reply card, 1963.

of the polypeptide chain, leaving 61 codons to specify only 20 different amino acids. It was found that most amino acids are represented by more than one codon – a fixed first two nucleotides and some variation in the third. This degeneracy of the code implies that either there is more than one tRNA for these amino acids, or a single tRNA molecule can base pair with more than one codon. It was to explain the latter that wobble was proposed – the nucleotides in the first two positions of the anti-codons of these tRNAs require accurate base-pairing with those in the codon, but a mismatch (wobble) can be tolerated at the third position.

Francis was also interested in the organisation of DNA in the chromosome, and in 1971 published a speculative model for chromatin structure. When Roger Kornberg joined Aaron Klug's group in 1972 and began work in this field, Francis joined in the periodic group meetings of those involved. When the nucleosome particle as a subunit of chromatin was proposed by Kornberg in 1974, there was speculation on how the DNA could be wound up in such a compact (~100Å) particle. The feasibility of bending DNA into a radius of about 40Å was not known and Francis, with Aaron Klug, investigated the possibility of kinking the DNA structure. They found a family of reasonable kinks that could be produced involving the unstacking of one base pair per kink. Shortly after this, however, Michael Levitt made some energy calculations which showed that DNA could in fact be smoothly bent to a radius of 45Å with a local geometry very similar to straight B-DNA and energy only slightly higher.

In 1976, Francis wrote a paper on writhing, linking and twist – topological terms applied to the ribbon picture of the DNA duplex. This was prompted by the published results of work on the circular mini-chromosome of the virus SV40 from which it was estimated that there were -1 to $-1\frac{1}{4}$ supercoils of DNA per nucleosome (negative denotes left-handed supercoiling), rather smaller than the $1\frac{3}{4}$ in our proposed nucleosome structure (chapter 6). The SV40 work followed, in gels, the change in the DNA supercoiling as nucleosomes were removed from the mini-chromosome. Francis pointed out that what was being measured was the change in Linking Number, L – the number of times one strand of the DNA duplex goes around the other – and not necessarily supercoiling (see chromatin section, chapter 6).

Francis was also interested in the general mode of condensation of DNA in the mitotic chromosome – by a factor of about 10,000 overall. The coiling in the nucleosome and of the string of nucleosomes into the 300Å diameter fibre, accounted for a factor of about 40. In a paper with the Arne Bak and Jesper Zeuthen in Denmark, it was proposed that the remaining factor of 250 was attained by the 300Å fibres being further coiled up into a super-solenoid.

During this time, Francis also became involved in ideas on pattern formation in developing insects with Peter Lawrence, who had been recruited in 1969. With Mary Munro, they investigated the feasibility and limitations of a gradient system (a gradient in the concentration of a chemical – a morphogen) as the basis for the formation of patterns during development, and in 1972 they concluded that, for the pattern of folds or ripples on the adult cuticle in the insect *Rhodnius*, a blood-sucking South American bug, the gradient could be a concentration gradient that diffused.

In 1977, Francis left LMB for the Salk Institute, with a chair in Psychology at the University of California, San Diego, and his main interests since then have been in neurobiology. Francis died in 2004 aged 88.

SYDNEY BRENNER

For the first years at LMB, Sydney Brenner continued with work on the genetic code, mutagenesis and the regulation of DNA replication. One of the first results, with Anand Sarabhai and Tony Stretton and with A. Bolle in Geneva, was to show a co-linearity between the codons along the gene and the amino acids along the polypeptide chain for which it was coding. They used a set of closely spaced *amber* mutants in the gene for the head protein of the phage T4. The *amber* mutants result from the premature occurrence of a stop codon, and segments of the polypeptide chain were found to be produced in the same order as the positions of the mutants on the genetic map of the gene. (Luckily there were no splicing complications in bacteriophage.)

The *amber* mutants occur in susceptible bacteria (*su+*), but are suppressed in other strains (*su−*) where a normal amino acid is inserted in place of the stop. Another class of suppressible mutants, called *ochre*, was isolated by Jon Beckwith and these required distinctly different suppressors. In 1965, Sydney, with Tony Stretton and Sam Kaplan, deduced that the stop-codon involved in *amber* mutants is UAG and in *ochre*, UAA. The final member of the codon table, UGA, was added in 1967, when Sydney, with Leslie Barnett, Gene Katz and Francis showed it to be a third stop-codon.[2] Again, suppressor strains of *E. coli* were found.

It had been shown in 1965–67 that for three *amber* suppressors, $su^+_{I, II, III}$, the suppression is caused by the presence of an altered tRNA which inserted the amino acids serine, glutamine and tyrosine respectively instead of terminating. In 1968, Howard Goodman, John Abelson, Art Landy with Sydney and John Smith showed that for su_{III}, the mutation causing suppression (*su−* to *su+*) results in a base change in the anti-codon of the tRNA, changing it from recognising the stop-codon UAG to recognising the tyrosine codon UAC. Similar results were found for tRNAs in other suppressors with visitors, Malcolm Gefter, Joe Sambrook, David Fan and Dick Russell. In 1968 too, Harvey Lodish, who had worked at the Rockefeller Institute with Norton Zinder on the bacteriophage f2, came for a year to LMB and continued the study of the translation of the RNA of the phage, before returning to the USA, to MIT.

The mechanism of suppression of UGA was studied by David Hirsh, with unexpected results. Genetic data had indicated that the amino acid substituted in the suppressors for the stop was tryptophan, and in one of these it had been shown that, as before, the suppression resided in the tRNA fraction. However, Hirsh found that the difference in the tryptophan tRNA in the suppressor was not in the anti-codon but in the stem of the dihydrouracil loop – the anti-codon–codon recognition is altered by this change elsewhere in the tRNA molecule. This was confirmed by an *in vitro* suppression study with Larry Gold. (Both papers were published in 1971.)

In 1967, continuing their work on the *r*II region of T4 phage DNA (see chapter 4), a detailed study with Leslie Barnett, Francis, Bob Shulman and Richard Watts-Tobin located 243 mutants. The mutants were either from local miscoding produced by including base analogues in the DNA, or phase shift mutants produced by intercalation of flat dye molecules, such as the acridine-derivative proflavin, between bases, which upset the reading sequence mechanism. (Some bias in the selection procedure in this work was blamed on 'the inexperience of one of us (F.H.C.C.)'.)

In a base analogue mutant, a wrong base is inserted, and this can be corrected by the inclusion of another base analogue. A phase shift mutant can be corrected by an opposite phase shift. One would not expect that a given mutant would be revertible by both methods, but a number of such mutants were found by Sydney with Alice Orgel in 1961, and these were rather worrying. They were all base substitution mutants, and in 1972, Sydney with Roger Freedman showed that the acridine-induced suppression was produced by a phase shift in a phage gene with a limited *r*II function, away from the *r*II region.

A PhD student at this time (1964–68) was Steve (G. Steven) Martin, now at Berkeley. His thesis project involved a study of RNA synthesis in *E. coli*, with genetic and biochemical investigations of appropriate mutants.

Sidney Altman

One of the visitors involved in the tRNA work was Sid Altman. Initially a physicist, he had become interested in molecular biology and had worked with Leonard Lerman at Colorado on the intercalation effects on DNA of acridines. In 1966, he met Sydney Brenner when he visited the Colorado laboratory and had asked for a job at LMB. There were no vacancies at that time, but in 1968, after he had moved to Meselson's laboratory at Harvard, he was recruited by Sydney to do some structural studies on tRNA – presumably by NMR. However, by the time he arrived at

163. Sidney Altman. Courtesy of Sidney Altman/Michael Marshland, Yale University.

LMB in 1969, Aaron Klug's group had crystals of tRNA, and so Francis and Sydney suggested he decide on another project.

Sid chose to join John Smith's group working on acridine-induced mutants of tRNA^{Tyr}. John was working on the suppressor tRNA^{Tyr} and had shown that the mutation in going from su^+ to su^- involved a base change in the anti-codon. Together, they were studying the biosynthesis of tRNA^{Tyr} when Sid discovered precursor molecules – longer than normal by about 40 nucleotides. John and Sid determined the overall sequence, and with Hugh Robertson, an RNA processing hydrolytic activity was isolated, which trimmed the extra nucleotides from the 5' end of the molecule – RNAse P.[3] The investigation of this was continued when Sid returned to the USA, and the discovery that the enzyme was part protein and part RNA (M1 RNA) and that the catalytic activity lies in the RNA led to the award of the Nobel Prize for Chemistry (with Tom Cech) in 1989.

Sidney Altman gave a reminiscing talk in LMB during the DNA50 celebrations in April 2003 of which a modified version was written up for *Genetics* and is reproduced in chapter 10.

Joan Steitz

Joan Steitz came to LMB as a postdoc with Mark Bretscher in 1967. She had been working on the bacteriophage R17 at Harvard, and using the techniques being developed in Fred Sanger's group, her initial work at LMB was the sequencing of the three ribosomal binding sites in the RNA of the virus. During her stay, she helped determine the gene order in the R17-RNA, and became interested in the *in vitro* reconstitution of R17, MS2, f2 and other RNA phages.

MARK BRETSCHER

Mark Bretscher's research has spanned the Molecular Genetics–Cell Biology fields. He began as a PhD student of Sydney Brenner in 1961, just before the move to the new laboratory. (Coming from the Chemistry Department, he applied to work for

164. Mark Bretscher, 1973. Courtesy of Mark Bretscher.

a PhD with Francis and at the interview it was suggested he choose his own project. After some deliberation, he came back suggesting he did some chemistry on DNA (cross-linking base pairs or ...) to check the double helical structure, and was told 'No, we all believe it here'.)

The first work for his PhD, completed in 1964, was investigating and checking the genetic code using polynucleotides prepared by Marianne Grunberg-Manago in Paris, and identifying their products produced in a cell-free protein synthesising system. He then showed that incomplete polypeptide chains are attached to a molecule of tRNA during the synthesis of a polypeptide, and chemically characterised the complex. He went on to show that the bond between the polypeptide chain and tRNA is cleaved for chain termination, and using a selection of synthetic polynucleotides (poly-U, poly-UA, etc.) that the terminating code was composed of a combination of 'A's and 'U's[4] – cited as support for the *ochre* stop-codon, UAA, by Stretton, Kaplan and Brenner in 1966.[5]

In 1968, Mark proposed a model for how the translocation of tRNA between the two binding sites on the ribosome, P- (where the nascent polypeptide chain plus its last-used tRNA are bound) and A- (where the current tRNA is bound), is effected during protein synthesis – in his scheme, the movement is eased by an intermediate hybrid binding of the tRNA between the sites.[6] Experimental support for this idea was published in 1989 by Moazed and Noller at Santa Cruz.

Mark then moved on to work on chain initiation. Brian Clark and Kjeld Marcker had shown that a special tRNA, formyl-methionyl-tRNA, was required to initiate the polypeptide chain synthesis in *E. coli*. Mark and Kjeld Marcker showed that it bound to the ribosomal P-site, and not to the A-site. With Jim Dahlberg, who was at LMB as a two-year postdoc, the process of initiation was further studied, with ribosomes directed by the RNA of the f2 phage.

Around 1970, Mark began to feel that the obvious and interesting work on protein biosynthesis had been done and looked around for another field of research. There was a feeling that all the results from the Division at that time were spin-offs from Francis and Sydney and so he looked for a subject outside their fields. Perhaps prompted by the change in the Divisional title, he thought cell membranes would be an interesting area. No one else in the laboratory was working on this and so it required a fair amount of preliminary study.

In one of his first investigations, Mark established that a large protein (called component *a*, now known to be the anion channel) was spanning the human erythrocyte membrane. For this he used a label which could not get through the intact cell membrane and compared the labelling from intact cells with that from ghost (leaky) cells. He also showed that the same was true for an erythrocyte glycoprotein. In 1972, using the results of his own work and others, he was the first to put forward the idea that the lipid bilayer structure for biological membranes was asymmetric – that different phospholipids are chiefly located on the inner and outer halves of the bilayer. Thus Mark was the first to establish that cell membranes consist of an asymmetric lipid bilayer, spanned by specific membrane proteins.

Mark then became interested in cell movement or motility. It had been proposed in 1970, by Michael Abercrombie and his group at University College, London, that this was achieved by a membrane being added from the cytoplasmic interior of the cell to the leading edge, giving rise to a continuous surface flow of membrane from the leading edge to the trailing edge (relative to the centre of the cell). Membrane translocation was accomplished by the budding off of small areas forming vesicles, used for transporting receptor/ligand complexes inside the cell, and their eventual rejoining the surface at its leading front – endocytosis and exocytosis. Mark calculated that if this were so, ferritin receptors continuously liberated in this way near the leading edge as vesicles budded into the membrane would not have time to diffuse away into uniformity. This was confirmed with Nichol Thomson – electron micrographs of the leading edge region were taken and, as predicted, higher concentrations of the receptors were found, showing that exocytosis occurs at the front of a moving cell.

Coated vesicles had been studied by Barbara Pearse, who in 1975 found that their coats contained one major protein species – clathrin. These vesicles originated as coated indentations or pits on the membrane and in 1980, she, with Mark and Nichol Thomson, showed that these coated pits acted as molecular filters, selecting specific receptors but excluding other plasma membrane proteins[7] and subsequently budded off with their contents for transport.

Mark has continued to work on endocytosis and its relation to cell locomotion. He was Joint Head of the Cell Biology Division from 1984 to 1994, initially with Peter Lawrence and later with Hugh Pelham. He was elected a Fellow of the Royal Society in 1985.

JOHN SMITH

John Smith was brought into the LMB at its start in 1962 as an expert in nucleic acid chemistry. He had graduated in Cambridge in 1945, having read physics, chemistry and botany, and his first class honours prompted an offer of a research position in the ARC (Agricultural Research Council)-funded Virus Research Unit housed in the Molteno Institute in Cambridge. The head of the Unit was the plant virus expert Kenneth M. Smith, but John's research was redirected by the Molteno Director, David Keilin, towards leg-haemoglobin (a haemoglobin-like molecule in the root nodules of leguminous plants) and bacteriophage. Keilin probably felt he was fair game, since Kenneth Smith had asked for temporary space while his laboratory on the Huntingdon Road was being redecorated, and was still there some ten years later.

165. John Smith, c. 1980.

After getting his PhD in 1948, John officially became part of the Virus Unit and began collaborating with Roy Markham. Markham and Kenneth Smith had isolated the spherical virus turnip yellow mosaic, and found two sorts of particles – the bottom component containing RNA and infectious and the top component without RNA and not infectious. (Top and bottom referring to their locations in tubes after centrifugation.) Although they were very cautious about interpreting this result, it did at least indicate that the RNA played a leading part in virus multiplication and led Markham and John to begin a joint study of RNAs from yeast and from the plant viruses they were studying. They began by hydrolysing the RNAs and were the first to develop paper chromatography techniques and solvent conditions to separate individual nucleotides. This was sufficient to see that the RNA from each virus had a specific, but individual base composition, continuing the demolition of the tetranucleotide structural hypothesis. This hypothesis had been put forward by P.A. Levene at the Rockefeller Institute in 1931 – since both RNA and DNA contained only four nucleotides, it was proposed that they were built of strings of identical tetramers. However, the work of Chargaff and his group from 1948, apart from discovering the A:T and G:C ratios, also found species differences in DNA composition, inconsistent with the tetranucleotide hypothesis. Roy Markham and John went on to study the DNA in the phages T4 and λ. John discovered that Dan Brown, who he met at lunch in The Eagle, and Todd in the Chemistry Department, were studying the mechanism of alkaline hydrolysis of RNA and following this there was much interaction between the two groups.

Through being at the Molteno, John came into contact with several of the scientists who would be in the future LMB. Max Perutz and John Kendrew had bench space there for growing their crystals, and Markham introduced him to Fred Sanger in the Biochemistry Department. He met Francis socially, and later Sydney who visited Alfred Tissières, then working in the Molteno. Jim Watson also nominally came there to fulfil the terms of his fellowship. Later, John advised Rosalind Franklin and Aaron Klug at Birkbeck on growing turnip yellow mosaic virus for crystallisation purposes.

In 1958, the ARC group moved to their new laboratories in Huntingdon Road, and with his research student, David Dunn, John discovered that occasional bases in bacterial DNA were methylated, which was later found to be a defence marker against their own restriction enzymes – nucleases intended to digest invading foreign DNA.

After short spells at the Pasteur Institute and at Berkeley, John decided to emigrate and in 1959 went to Caltech, working with Renato Dulbecco and Giuseppe Attardi. However, in 1961, he received letters from Max, Francis and Sydney inviting him to come to the new LMB and these (along with a personal invitation and description of the new laboratory from John Kendrew who came to give a lecture) persuaded him to leave Caltech and join LMB. He arrived in October 1962, and joined the Molecular Genetics Division.

Initially he was interested in the genetic code and the mechanism of protein synthesis, and started by finding out what oligolysine peptides were encoded by defined lengths of poly A messenger. From 1967 he became interested in the involvement of mutant bacterial tRNAs in suppressing the effects of mis-sense and chain terminating codons in mutants of phage and this converted into a more general interest in tRNAs and their precursors, as described above.

John Smith was elected a Fellow of the Royal Society in 1976. He retired from LMB in 1986 and died in 2003.

TONY STRETTON

Tony had read Chemistry in Cambridge and began work with the MRC in 1957, joining Vernon Ingram as a PhD student in the hut at the Cavendish. His PhD project was the study of the A_2 component of human haemoglobin. When, in 1958, Vernon moved to MIT, Tony accompanied him. He returned to LMB in 1962, to Sydney's group, and after the work showing the co-linearity of codon and polypeptide chain was involved in the study of *amber* and *ochre* mutations and their suppression. Around 1969, he began work on the muscle and neuronal structure of the nematode *Ascaris*, and he carried on with this after transferring to the University of Madison, Wisconsin in 1971, initially, continuing the connection with LMB via Rita Fishpool and Eileen Southgate.

166. Tony Stretton, c. 1960.

RITA FISHPOOL, EILEEN SOUTHGATE, LESLIE BARNETT, MURIEL WIGBY

Rita Fishpool

Rita began work with the MRC Unit in 1954 as a general laboratory assistant. From 1957, she worked exclusively for Vernon Ingram until he left in 1958, and transferred to Sydney's group, working with Jim Ofengand until 1961. After this she worked with Tony Stretton until his departure in 1971. For two years she worked on the muscle proteins of *C. elegans* with Henry Epstein, and then on other aspects of the *C. elegans* work with Sydney, Sandy Macleod, Jon Karn and Donna Albertson, moving with Donna to Sydney's new Molecular Genetics Unit in Addenbrooke's from 1986 to 1991. She then returned with Donna to John Sulston's group to assist in the mapping of *C. elegans*. Rita retired in 1995.

Eileen Southgate

Eileen began work as a laboratory assistant in 1956, employed on Max's three-year Rockefeller grant. Initially her job was helping in the preparation of the haemoglobin and myoglobin for the crystallography work, but she also helped Vernon Ingram in his sickle cell investigation. When the new laboratory opened in 1962,

167. *Eileen Southgate and Rita Fishpool, c. 1960. Courtesy of Eileen Southgate.*

168. *Eileen Southgate, c. 1987. Courtesy of Eileen Southgate.*

she worked for a time with Reuben Leberman, growing the plants in the nearby greenhouse for infection with plant viruses and harvesting them and purifying the viruses for crystallography and other studies. She then joined Tony Stretton, first working on β-galactosidase and later in his *Ascaris* work. *Ascaris* is a large nematode worm living in the intestines of pigs – supplies had to be fetched from Sainsbury's slaughterhouse at West Wratting, near Haverhill. After Tony's departure, she joined John White on reconstructing the nervous system of *C. elegans* from micrographs of thousands of sections through the worm. She retired in 1993.

Leslie Barnett

169. Leslie Barnett, c. 1973. Courtesy of Mark Bretscher.

Leslie joined the MRC Unit at the Cavendish in 1957 as a technician, originally to help on the computing side for the crystallographers, but she was soon recruited by Sydney on his arrival when he began setting up for phage work to be ready to receive invited visitors from the USA. She became immersed in the practical side of producing and analysing mutants, and sufficiently involved that she was a co-author with Francis and Sydney on the 'Theory of Mutagenesis' and the 'General Nature of the Genetic Code for Proteins' papers and on that showing that UGA was the third stop-codon.

Leslie became one of the laboratory's repositories of phage folk lore which she taught to numerous visitors and she had an invaluable knowledge of the bacterial strain collection, which was erratically catalogued on a semi-historical basis with new strain series beginning almost at random. In the days before computer databases, only Leslie could be relied on to remember that the precursor for a 'U' series strain was to be found in the 'CA' collection. In Leslie's lexicon the paper strips used to streak out phages on agar plates were always 'Benzer' strips in honour of their creator. It was also always important when adding phage to a bacterial culture to hold it up to your ear and say in the Brenner/Benzer tradition, 'hear them screaming'. Somehow the experiments never quite worked if this ritual was not followed.

Around 1969–70, she participated with John Smith and several visitors in the work of characterising tyrosine tRNAs, which were able to suppress UAG stop-activity. In the early 1980s, she collaborated with Sydney and Jon Karn on developing a method of using bacteriophage λ as a vector for recombinant DNA. Starting with a mixture of DNA fragments prepared from a restriction enzyme digest, the genome of an entire organism could be represented as a collection of overlapping fragments. One of the first of these so-called libraries that was ever prepared was a representation of the entire nematode genome made by Jon Karn. By using a specific probe, it was possible to select particular clones representing genes. Leslie worked again with Jon on characterising the heavy-chain gene of the myosin of the *unc-54* mutant of *C. elegans*, and on finding a tRNA that suppresses a nonsense mutation in the worm. The original phage collection was used for many years to clone nematode genes, but Sydney would complain, 'it's just a heap of books until you create a card catalogue'. Spurred on by the challenge, Jon Karn, Alan Coulson and John Sulston developed a method that allowed ordering of genomic clones into a physical map. This project eventually led to a complete map of the genome of *C. elegans*, and eventually to its complete sequence, the first higher eukaryote to be sequenced in its entirety.

When Clare Hall, the graduate college, was established in Cambridge in 1966, Leslie was made Senior Tutor, a job she fitted into very well and thoroughly enjoyed, and she became very popular with the students. When Sydney retired from LMB in 1986, she moved with him to the new MRC Molecular Genetics Unit across the road in the main Addenbrooke's hospital building, and retired when that Unit closed in 1992.

Muriel Wigby

Muriel worked as a technician in Sydney's bacteriophage work while the group were in the Cavendish, and continued in this at LMB from 1962. However, in the late 1960s, Sydney was becoming more interested in nematodes, and Muriel became involved in growing these and, when *C. elegans* was chosen, identifying mutants after chemical treatment, so that by 1973 about 300 had been characterised. She retired from LMB in 1980 to start her own business in grooming dogs.

ANDREW TRAVERS

Andrew Travers joined LMB initially in 1965 as a research student of John Smith, studying the 5' terminal nucleotide sequences of RNA sythesised *in vitro*. In addition to investigating the function of this sequence, part of the aim was to feel the way towards the complete sequencing of a messenger RNA. After gaining his PhD, he spent two years in the Biological Laboratories at Harvard, working with Dick Burgess on RNA polymerase. Andrew showed that one of the components of the enzyme, σ, was the initiation factor of the system, and it was shown to be reused

170. Andrew Travers, c. 1960s.

cyclically. He returned to LMB in 1970 and continued work on transcription.

In the mid-1980s Andrew became interested in the effects and biological significance of variations on the local structure of DNA. He collaborated with Horace Drew, a postdoc visitor with Aaron Klug from Dick Dickerson's laboratory in Los Angeles, on a study of the interactions of three different nucleases with a fixed sequence of DNA (the bacterial promotor, *tyrT* from *E. coli*) and they concluded that all three seemed sensitive to DNA backbone geometry rather than base sequence *per se*. Angus Lamond showed that the transcriptional activity of the same promotor was strongly enhanced when it was underwound (by including it in a negatively supercoiled plasmid) and Horace and Andrew with John Weeks showed that the variation in activity went in parallel with sensitivity to S1 nuclease digestion, which is normally centred on a TpA doublet, and so both correlated with sequence-dependent structural properties of the DNA.

Andrew and Horace then investigated local DNA structure and in particular the ability it conveyed to allow bending, in connection with nucleosome positioning. They found that in a closed circle of DNA, short runs of AT tended to have minor grooves facing inward and those with runs of GC, outward. (Outer minor grooves were located by their being blocked to DNAse1 cutting by first reacting with antibiotic drugs of known sequence specificity, whereas inner minor grooves were inaccessible to the drugs.) This angular orientation was conserved when the same DNA was wound around a histone core to reconstitute a nucleosome. They also found the same tendency in DNA from native chicken nucleosome cores. With Sandra Satchwell, they cloned and sequenced 177 DNA molecules cut from chicken erythrocyte cores and found that ApApA/TpTpT and ApApT/ApTpT runs were predominantly located where, in the core particles, they would have minor grooves facing in towards the protein and those of GpGpC/GpCpC and ApGpC/GpCpT where minor grooves faced outwards.[8] Long runs of the homopolymer AT preferred to occupy the ends of the core DNA. All of these results gave a good indication that it is the DNA sequence *itself* which is responsible for deciding where the nucleosomes are located.

These investigations have continued with further work on nucleosomal DNA as well as interactions with other proteins and complexes, notably on the role of

HMG1, an essential abundant non-histone component of chromatin, in the regulation of chromatin structure, but in general on the relationship between chromatin structure and transcription.

BRIAN CLARK

171. Brian Clark, c. 1969.

Brian Clark gained his PhD in 1961, working with Dan Brown in the Department of Chemistry in Cambridge, on the chemistry of phosphoinositides. After postdoctoral work at MIT and with Nirenberg at the NIH National Heart Institute in Bethesda, he joined LMB in the Molecular Genetics Division in 1964. He became interested in a 'strange' tRNA, shown to be formylmethionyl-tRNA (fMet-tRNA) that had recently been discovered by Kjeld Marcker and Fred Sanger. In 1966, Clark and Marcker showed that it was a prokaryotic initiator. (Prokaryotes are the simpler bacterial cells without nuclei, and the initiator tRNA provides the amino acid that starts the polypeptide chain.)

As described in chapter 6, Brian Clark was largely responsible for the large-scale preparation and purification schemes that provided sufficient quantities of tRNAs for crystallisation studies that eventually led to the structure determination (see chapter 6). He was also involved in sequence and biochemical work on tRNAs with his students Suzanne Cory, Peter Piper and David Ish-Horowicz. Brian left LMB to take up a position at Aarhus University in 1975.

DIVISION OF CELL BIOLOGY

In 1970, the name of the Division was changed. Following the events of the 1950s and early 1960s – the unravelling of the DNA structure and the determination of the Genetic Code – there was a feeling of anticlimax among molecular geneticists. In 1963, the Principal Medical Officer of the MRC came to the LMB to discuss plans for future expansion (which was to lead to the thirteen-bay extension of the original building towards Hills Road). This prompted Sydney and Francis to discuss the future lines of research for their Division. Both 'felt strongly that most of the classical problems of molecular biology had been solved, and that the future lay in tackling more complex biological problems. ... and decided against working on animal viruses, on the structure of ribosomes, on membranes, and other similar trivial problems in molecular biology'.[9] They concluded that the most interesting fields to branch out into would be development and the nervous system. This conclusion was presented by Sydney in a letter to the director, Max Perutz, in June 1963.[10] His idea was to try to use the techniques of genetic analysis, then in current use in bacterial genetics, to isolate the individual steps in the development of a higher organism.

By October 1963, when the general laboratory proposal for future expansion was presented to the MRC, Sydney's ideas had become firmer. He wrote:

> It is probably true to say that no major discovery comparable in importance to that of, say, messenger RNA, now lies ahead in this field, but the elucidation of the mechanisms already discovered is nevertheless vital. The new major problem in molecular biology is the genetics and biochemistry of control mechanisms in cellular development. We propose to start work in this field and gradually make it the Division's main research.
>
> In the first place, control mechanisms can be studied most easily in microorganisms, and this work has already begun. In addition we should like to start exploratory work on one or two model systems. We have in mind small metazoa, chosen because they would be suitable for rapid genetic and biochemical analysis. Proposals for such work, which we plan to begin in the next few months, are set out in Appendix I.

Appendix I
Differentiation in a Nematode Worm
Part of the success of molecular genetics was due to the use of extremely small organisms which could be handled in large numbers: bacteria and bacterial viruses. The processes of genetic replication and transcription, of genetic recombination and mutagenesis, and the synthesis of enzymes could be studied in their most elementary form, and having once been discovered, their applicability to the higher forms of life could be tested afterwards. We should like to attack the problem of cellular development in a similar fashion, choosing the simplest possible differentiated organism and subjecting it to the analytical methods of microbial genetics.

Thus we want a multicellular organism which has a short life cycle, can be easily cultivated, and is small enough to be handled in large numbers, like a microorganism. It should have relatively few cells, so that exhaustive studies of lineage and patterns can be made, and should be amenable to genetic analysis.

We think we have a good candidate in the form of a small nematode worm, *Caenorhabditis briggsiae*, which has the following properties. It is a self-fertilising hermaphrodite, and sexual propagation is therefore independent of population size. Males are also found (0.1%) which can fertilise the hermaphrodites, allowing stocks to be constructed by genetic crosses. Each worm lays up to 200 eggs which hatch in buffer in twelve hours, producing larvae 80μ in length. These larvae grow to a length of 1mm in three and a half days, and reach sexual maturity. However, there is no increase in cell number, only in cell mass. The number of nuclei becomes constant at a late stage of development, and divisions occur only in the germ line. Although the total number of cells is only about a thousand, the organism is differentiated and has an epidermis, intestine, excretory system, nerve and muscle cells. Reports in the literature describe the approximate number of cells as follows: 200 cells in the gut, 200 epidermal cells, 60 muscle cells, 200 nerve cells. The organism normally feeds on bacteria, but can also be grown in large quantities in liver extract broth. It has not yet been grown in a defined synthetic medium.

To start with we propose to identify every cell in the worm and trace lineages. We shall also investigate the constancy of development and study its genetic control by looking for mutants.[11]

The last paragraph summarised the work done in the field for the next twenty years or so. In fact Sydney had not at that stage decided whether the *briggsiae* strain was the one to concentrate on, but a search began for a worm with the best properties for a laboratory investigation. The group then consisted of Sydney and his technician, Muriel Wigby, but they were shortly joined by Nichol Thomson.

Nichol Thomson

Nichol had been a technician at the Scottish Marine Biological Association, located on an island in the Firth of Clyde, helping visiting scientists including Lord Rothschild, from the Department of Zoology in Cambridge, who came to study the fertilisation of sea urchins. In 1954, Rothschild brought Nichol (with his wife of three weeks) to Cambridge as his technician. Rothschild was interested in looking at sea urchin sperm, and was keen to get some electron micrographs, but had no electron microscope at that stage, so Nichol learnt how to cut sections and looked at them in the microscope of the Cavendish laboratory. When Rothschild retired from the zoology department in 1964, he recommended Nichol to Sydney, who was keen to make use of his experience in microscopy and found him an LMB appointment. It was not until after this was arranged that Rothschild phoned Nichol to tell him of his new employment.

Nichol's first job in LMB was to join in the search for the optimum nematode. Worms were collected from dozens of soil samples and compost heaps, and tested to see

172. Nichol Thomson, c. 1975.

how easily they would adapt to growth conditions in the laboratory and whether they were amenable to optical and electron microscope investigation.

The nematode *C. elegans* was in fact chosen, largely because it grew better in laboratory culture than the *briggsae* strain and was therefore easier to manipulate, and it proved outstandingly good for fixation and sectioning for electron microscopy. Actually, Nichol Thomson's initial conclusion was that *C. elegans* was terrible for electron microscopy purposes. But Sydney was so pleased with its vigorous growth that he insisted that Nichol try again, and this time the results were excellent. The reason the first attempt failed was due to their inexperience with feeding them – the worms had exhausted the nutrient and entered the 'dauer' or starvation state, which has a highly impermeable cuticle and fixes very badly.[12]

The ultimate intention was for Nichol to section the worm along its length so that the structure and location of individual cells could be followed along it – about 20,000 sections in all. However, before this was accomplished, a long time was spent in developing suitable techniques of staining and sectioning. The initial results of cutting sections using glass knives, for example, were frustratingly inadequate until diamond knives were obtained. The first reconstruction from serial sections (1,600 in number) was put together with Sam Ward who, with John White and Sydney, reconstructed the anatomy of the anterior sensory nervous system of *C. elegans* in 1975.

In addition to the serial section work, Nichol provided the electron microscopy in other studies of *C. elegans*, with Donna Albertson, Martin Chalfie and Jim Priess, and his expertise in sectioning brought him in as a collaborator with work on many other specimens (for example, with Mark Bretscher and Barbara Pearse) and as a general laboratory adviser on the technique.

Nichol retired in 1989.

John White

John White came to LMB in 1971 from NIMR at Mill Hill, where he had been an instrumentation engineer. He and Sydney had initially intended to develop a computer system to record and follow the nerve cells through the sections of the worm, and this formed the first part of John's thesis. However, although much time was spent on its development, in the end it proved more satisfactory to follow the sections by eye and Eileen Southgate was brought in for this.

When procedures had settled into a routine, Nichol spent his time cutting serial sections, and Eileen did much of the microscopy, printing the micrographs and determining the register between between them, with John interpreting the result. The structure of the ventral nerve cord was determined in 1976 and in 1986 a mammoth paper (340 pages) was published recording the 302 nerve cells and 8,000 connections.[13]

From 1985, John White was much involved in the development of the confocal microscope (see chapter 9). He moved to Wisconsin in 1994 and was elected a Fellow of the Royal Society in 2005.

173. Mick Fordham, Richard Durbin and John White with prototype confocal microscope, 1987.
Courtesy of Eileen Southgate.

Mutants

Having settled on *C. elegans*, Sydney began a search for mutants. The first was produced in October 1967 – a short 'dumpy' animal among the long, thin wild-type worms, obtained by soaking a culture in ethyl methane sulphonate. By 1973, with help from Muriel Wigby, he had characterised about 300 mutants, in descriptively named classes including dumpy, uncoordinated, roller, long, blistered and abnormal (morphologically aberrant). He continued with more detailed mutant studies with Jonathan Hodgkin, who joined the group in 1976, Sandy MacLeod from 1976, Jon Karn from 1979 and with visiting workers including Donna Albertson, Philip Anderson, Padmanabhan Babu, Henry Epstein, K. Gergyo, H. Hagawa, Graham Hudson, Bob Horvitz, Bob Herman, J. Kaxen, Andrew Roberts, Maria Salvato, Robert Sheldon, Gerrit Voordouw and Bob Waterston, as well as with Leslie Barnett and Rita Fishpool, who continued from earlier Molecular Genetics days. Martin Chalfie, from 1978, investigated the developmental genetics of the worm, in particular studying the neuronal microtubules, with Nichol Thomson, John Sulston, Bob Horvitz and other members in the group. Cynthia Kenyon, from 1983, was also involved with the genetics and the control of development in the worm. Her group at UCSF in San Francisco now studies the genes and cells that regulate the lifespan of *C. elegans*.

Bob Waterston first came to LMB as a postdoc in 1972 for two years, and became involved in the identification of mutants of myosin and paramyosin, with Sydney and Henry Epstein. This work was carried on during another visit in 1975, and continued then by collaboration with his laboratory in the Washington University School of Medicine in St Louis. From 1986, the collaboration focused on mapping and then sequencing the *C. elegans* genome.

JOHN SULSTON

John Sulston had graduated in 1963 at Cambridge, and gained his PhD in the Chemistry Department for research in nucleotide chemistry. He continued in this field, as a postdoc with Leslie Orgel at the Salk Institute, for three years, studying the early prebiotic chemistry of life. He was hired by Sydney in 1969 to analyse the neurochemistry of the worm, and began by producing a plot of the patterns of some of the neurons by microscopy of specimens with fluorescent, derivatised neurotransmittters. He then determined that the total worm genome was twenty times larger than that of *E. coli* (i.e. 100,000kb).

John also collaborated with Gerry Rubin, a PhD student at this time, investigating the RNA of ribosomes from the yeast *Saccharomyces cerevisiae*. (Gerry returned to the USA in 1974 and, with the advent of restriction enzymes and cloning, became one of the leading workers on the molecular genetics of *Drosophila*, running the *Drosophila* genome sequencing project which was completed in 2000. He was until recently the scientific director of the Howard Hughes Medical Institute and has

174. *Bob Waterston, c. 1972.*

175. *John Sulston, c. 1985.*

now become the director of their new offshoot, the HHMI Janelia Farm Research Campus.)

John became interested in working out the complete cell lineage of the worm. According to the textbook this was established in the embryo stage, but, fortunately, not knowing this, John examined nematodes at different developmental stages, and found there to be fifteen neurons in the ventral cord in young larvae, and 57 in older animals. Using a light microscope (with Nomarski optics) he 'tethered' live young worms by providing a limited lawn of bacteria on a slide and watched their growth – over one weekend he was able to account for the origins of the 42 post embryonic neural cells, and the entire development of the ventral cord. (Unlike some other species of nematode, *C. elegans* proved to be particularly transparent, and an excellent subject for light microscopy.) With Bob Horvitz, the larval cell lineage was completed and published in 1977[14] (with the exception of the gonad lineage, which was worked out by Judith Kimble and David Hirsh at Boulder, Colorado, and published in 1979). The embryonic cell lineage was published in 1983.

176. Judy Kimble, 1982.

177. Bob Horvitz, 1976.

Bob Horvitz had joined the group in 1974 as a postdoc, coming from the molecular biology laboratory of Wally Gilbert, Jim Watson and Klaus Weber at Harvard, where he had studied T4 phage induced modifications of the RNA polymerase of *E. coli*. After working with radioactivity, gels and molecules, he was initially not greatly attracted to the idea of watching cells divide, but was soon won over by 'the thrill of directly watching development and the elegance and intriguing nature of the cell lineage diagrams that resulted'.[15]

In addition to determining the precise pattern of growth via cell division and differentiation, programmed cell death, where the cells visibly rounded up and became optically dense before dying, turned out to be an important feature of the growth sequence. For this work, Sydney Brenner, John Sulston and Bob Horvitz were awarded a Nobel Prize in 2002. John Sulston had been elected a Fellow of the Royal Society in 1986.

GENETIC ENGINEERING

In 1974, Sydney became involved in the controversy over genetic engineering. At the Gordon Conference on nucleic acids in 1973, the recent advances in producing biologically active recombinant DNA molecules *in vitro* had been reported. Several groups planned to use the technology in research projects, and this raised concerns that there might be some unforeseen biological hazards connected with such work. For example, the cloning of recombinant molecules in bacteria like *E. coli* could lead to their wide dispersion, since strains of *E. coli* commonly reside in the human intestinal tract. A call was made for the Academy of Sciences to consider this situation, resulting in a Committee on Recombinant DNA Molecules being created, who published a letter in *Science* in 1974[16] calling for a voluntary deferment of certain of the possibly more hazardous experiments until the potential hazards were evaluated, and guidelines devised. A meeting was called in the USA for February 1975 by the NIH, the NAS and the NSF at Asilomar in California for scientists around the world to help evaluate the scientific opportunities and potential risks in the technology, and consider the ethical and legal issues.

On publication of the letter in *Science*, the MRC declared all the experiments described in the letter virtually illegal in the UK until the risks could be evaluated. However, the MRC (and ABRC – the Advisory Board for the Research Councils) acted quickly and invited Eric (Lord) Ashby to chair a working party to which Sydney gave evidence. Before the end of 1974, the working party reported – they recommended that genetic modification techniques should be allowed to continue but with rigorous safeguards. These were spelt out by another working party set up for this under (Sir) Robert Williams, the director of the Public Health Laboratory Service, including Sydney as a member. The resulting Williams Report, published in January 1975, defined four degrees of possible hazard with corresponding degrees of recommended containment. It was proposed to start on a voluntary basis to see how it worked, and statutory force was in fact only introduced in 1989.

To ensure consistency between the USA and the UK, Sydney was invited to join the Asilomar organising committee and contribute to the general discussions. The chairman, Paul Berg, thinks that this was perhaps the committee's wisest decision – 'Sydney's unique brand of humour kept us going; his creative way of attacking scientific issues inspired us all. And his deeply felt ethical responsibilities motivated many to forgo their more selfish instincts'.[17] The resulting recommendations were very similar to those in the Williams Report, and were approved by the Assembly of Life Sciences of the National Academy of Sciences in May 1975.

SYDNEY – DIRECTOR

In 1979, Max retired as Head of LMB and Sydney took over as Director, which looking back he regards as a big mistake. Two years earlier, when he had been chosen as the Director-elect, LMB had run into financial difficulties. Before this, funding by the MRC had been sufficiently generous that the fairly relaxed way of dealing with the finances, largely by Michael Fuller on the buying side, Frances Taylor (Audrey Martin had retired in 1973) and her assistants on the invoice side and MRC Headquarters doing the actual paying, had worked pretty well. However, with a tighter money situation in the late 1970s, the delays in the system masked a considerable overspending, and suddenly it was realised that the laboratory owed about a half a million pounds. Sydney was asked to oversee getting the financial situation into a satisfactory state, together with the then Administrative Director, Bronwen Loder. Much of the overspend was paid by the MRC by allowing an early borrow from the following year's budget, but this meant a tight rein on spending over both years. Sydney urged the staff to thoroughly think through proposed experiments to be sure that they were really worth doing (he also suggested that to save experimental costs, it might be a good idea if everyone stayed at home for a few weeks). For three months no orders were placed at all – a system of searching the laboratory for chemicals was set up (a paper version of the present e-mails). For the next few months all orders of value greater than £2 had to be approved by Divisional Heads and then by Sydney or Bronwen. The conditions were gradually eased after about six months.

Two days before he was due to take over as Director in 1979, Sydney was knocked off his motor cycle on his way home and broke a leg. He was in the hospital for many months before being able to get about on crutches and still uses a walking stick. But while in hospital he remembers being impressed that the new technology era had arrived – he was visited by Fred Sanger, who asked for a new disk drive for the sequencing work. (More in keeping with Fred's attitude to technology was the reminiscence of Elizabeth Blackburn at the DNA50 meeting, of seeing Fred in the corridor examining a new centrifuge and commenting 'too many knobs'.)

Sydney resigned as Director in 1986, a few years earlier than was planned – he had become bored with the administrative side, frustrated by being thwarted in innovative ideas to finance the laboratory and wanted to get back to science. With John Sulston, a project of mapping the C. elegans genome had been started, but Sydney withdrew from this and left the laboratory to set up a new MRC Molecular Genetics Unit, in the main hospital building. He left the MRC altogether in 1992, for the Scripps Research Institute, in La Jolla, closing the Unit before its first quinquennial review. He founded the Molecular Sciences Institute at Berkeley in 1996,

178. *Francis and Sydney, 1986.*

and has had a host of interests in Singapore, Japan, California and Cambridge since then. As was said of Queen Victoria, the sun never sets on Sydney's empire.

Sydney was elected a Fellow of the Royal Society in 1965. In 2002, he was awarded the Nobel Prize in Physiology or Medicine jointly with Bob Horvitz and John Sulston 'for their discoveries concerning the genetic regulation of organ development and programmed cell death in *C. elegans*'. He became a Companion of Honour in 1987.

Sydney became Assistant Editor to John Kendrew of the *Journal of Molecular Biology* from Volume 3 in 1961 until 1985, when he became co-Editor and in 1987 he took over as Editor in Chief until 1990 (Volume 210). From 1993 to 2000, he wrote a monthly column, 'Loose Ends', for *Current Biology* to give vent to his inexhaustible supply of humour and new ideas. However, he could be very slow in writing up scientific papers – Jon Karn remembered trying to get him to look up some details for a paper on work done two years earlier – these were eventually produced, but the paper was turned down by the editor for *Journal of Molecular Biology* and appeared later in *Gene*.

GENOMES – THE SANGER CENTRE

The determination of the cell lineage of *C. elegans* accelerated investigation of the molecular interactions involved in the development of the worm, and of the genetic programming controlling it. To start with, isolated genes were identified whose mutants caused detectable changes, and beginnings were made towards a physical genome map of the locations of these and those reported from other laboratories. In 1983, Fred Sanger retired and his assistant in developing nucleic acid sequencing methods, Alan Coulson, joined the worm team. Both John Sulston and Alan Coulson were keen on completing the genome map to help co-workers locate genes.

The map was initially based on methods developed with Jon Karn and Sydney. Overlapping genomic fragments were cloned in cosmid vectors (vectors that accept large DNA inserts for replication in a bacterium). Overlaps between clones were determined by the separation of radiolabelled restriction fragments in polyacrylamide gels, providing a characteristic band pattern for each clone. Programs were written for seeking matches between the patterns by Rodger Staden and later by

John Sulston and Richard Durbin, who was then a PhD student of John White and had written software for the confocal microscope (see chapter 9). Collaboration with Bob Waterston introduced fragments cloned in yeast artificial chromosomes (YACs), which proved to be essential to fill gaps in the cosmid map. Yuji Kohara also collaborated at this stage. The entire map became available in 1989.

John Sulston, Alan Coulson and Bob Waterston were keen to follow up the mapping with sequencing. In 1986, Sydney Brenner had retired from LMB and the new Director, Aaron Klug, encouraged John and Alan to determine the complete genome sequence, rather than the easier path of just sequencing expressed genes (mRNAs or the complementary cDNAs). Athough these would have been the most immediately useful to the nematode community, the complete genome would enable all genes to be recognised rather than just those detected by their expression, and also the control sequences occurring in non-coding regions. Aaron's initial thought was that *Drosophila* would be a more useful subject for a complete genome sequence than *C. elegans*, but John was adamant on tackling the worm, since that was his subject and it was a much less competitive area, and Aaron agreed to give his support – 'John was the standard bearer [for genome studies] and that's why it had to be the worm'.[18]

At 10^8 base pairs, the complete genome was quite a jump from the viral sequences around 10^5 base pairs then being tackled in Bart Barrell's PNAC group, and a substantial amount of money would be required to finance the staff and facilities that would be required. Aaron organised more room for the group, in space created by the closing of the Neurochemical Pharmacology Unit, and formed a new LMB section called Genome Studies. In addition to a million pound grant from MRC, Jim Watson, who was then the Director of the National Center for Human Genome Research at NIH, was persuaded to organise a £2 million grant over three years, to both John and Bob Waterston in St Louis for their groups to begin this work as a pilot project for sequencing the human genome. If the price per base could be reduced to 50 cents or less, Jim could get the go-ahead for human genome sequencing to begin in the USA.

Serious sequencing of the worm genome began in 1991, in collaboration with Bob Waterston's laboratory. Automated machines were beginning to appear on the market using fluorescent rather than radioactive tags on the DNA fragments, and the group began with two of these machines.

By 1992, the cost of the nematode sequencing had come down and although sequences totalling 3 million bases had been determined, these made up only about 3 per cent of the genome, and the NIH grant was due to run out. (There were also moves in the USA to poach John Sulston and Bob Waterston and form a company for genome sequencing that would profit from its immediate access to the data obtained.) It was clear that much more money, staff and facilities were required in Cambridge to continue at a reasonable rate. Aaron looked to the Wellcome Trust for help, and was allowed by Dai Rees, the MRC Chief Executive, to approach Bridget Ogilvie, the Director of the Trust. In 1992, the Trust had become the wealthiest medical charity in the world, by selling its shares from what had originally been the pharmaceutical company, the Wellcome Foundation, and more than doubling its budget to £200 million. Aaron and John proposed that they begin sequencing the human genome, based on the experience with the nematode. The Trust indicated that they were interested in building up a large sequencing effort on human DNA, but would also provide space for the worm genome project. The MRC agreed a grant of £10 million over five years for the worm sequencing to continue. A company was set up in 1992 called Genome Research Limited with representatives from MRC and Wellcome, to manage the financial and legal sides of the partnership. It was set up as a charity 'limited by Guarantee', requiring each guarantor to contribute £1.

The problem at this stage was the lack of a site for a laboratory to expand into. John Sulston and Michael Fuller looked around Cambridge for possibilities, but none of those inspected were very suitable, until, on an afternoon drive through Hinxton, about nine miles south of Cambridge, Michael noticed that Hinxton Hall, with its surrounding 55 acre parkland estate, was for sale. The estate had earlier housed a research centre for the metallurgy and engineering firm Tube Investments, but had been empty for some years. A plan to develop it as a business site had foundered with the property slump and the developer had put the whole site back on the market. The Wellcome Trust agreed that Genome Research Limited could take on a year lease on the estate and convert the existing research laboratories for genome research as a temporary measure. As the refurbishment began, in 1992, another complication arose. The DNA Data Library of EMBL was outgrowing its space in Heidelberg. Although the general assumption was that the proposed, new European Bioinformatics Institute should be built in Germany, the relevant EMBL committee were persuaded, largely by Michael Ashburner, the fly geneticist, backed up by John Sulston and Aaron, that it should be located in the UK. The Wellcome Trust and MRC were both enthusiastic, and the Trust solved the problem of a site by immediately buying the complete Hinxton estate.

The LMB genome sequencing group, including John Sulston, Alan Coulson, Richard Durbin and Bart Barrell, moved into the refurbished laboratories in 1993. John phoned Fred Sanger to ask if he would permit the new research centre to be named after him, and Fred agreed on one condition, 'It had better be good'.[19] The Sanger Centre was opened by Fred in October 1993, with John Sulston as Director. A new laboratory to house the Centre was built and occupied in 1995. Since the Wellcome Trust was by now the principal financial supporter of the sequencing efforts, it took over the whole management: the Sanger Centre is now called the Wellcome Trust Sanger Institute and is part of the overall Hinxton site known as the Wellcome Trust Genome Campus.

As well as continuing the worm sequencing, work on human DNA began almost immediately, new recruits being trained by the worm group. One of the earliest new workers to join the group was David Bentley from the genetics department at Guy's Hospital, who had been studying mutations in a human gene causing a form of haemophilia. From the initial seventeen staff, the numbers grew to 500 by 1999. The (virtually complete) sequence of the worm genome was published in December 1998 by the Cambridge and St Louis laboratories[20] – the first multicellular organism to have its genome sequenced. The first draft of the human sequence, of which the Cambridge group contributed about one-third, was announced in 2001.[21]

Much of this section is culled from a detailed and personal account of the genome story (both worm and human) by John Sulston with Georgina Ferry in their book *The Common Thread*[22] and from a review of the human genome project written by Aaron Klug.[23] Alan Coulson returned to LMB in 2002.

NEW GROUPS AND PEOPLE

In addition to the worm projects, other new workers and groups appeared in the Division as a result of the change in emphasis towards cell biology and to development in particular. In 1969 Peter Lawrence and Michael Wilcox joined the division.

Peter Lawrence

Peter Lawrence had graduated in Cambridge and gained his PhD in 1965 in the Department of Zoology under the supervision of the Professor Sir Vincent Wigglesworth. His project was on the development of hairs and bristles on *Oncopeltus*, a milkweed bug. He spent two years in the Department of Biology at Western Reserve University in Cleveland, Ohio, and at Charlottesville, Virginia, and during this became convinced that genetics was the best way forward for the study of development. Thus appropriately, when he returned to Cambridge in 1967, it was to the Department of Genetics. He had been transplanting pieces of *Oncopeltus* cuticle to study aspects of pattern – such as how hormones influence bristle development, and decided, with some success, to try X-rays to make mutations mark his grafts.

In 1969, he was invited to LMB by Francis and Sydney. Initially, Peter continued with his work on *Oncopeltus*, but soon became involved with Francis in developing ideas on molecular gradients and pattern formation, and in 1975 they reviewed the relatively new findings of separately-developing compartments in insects and their origins in polyclones.[24]

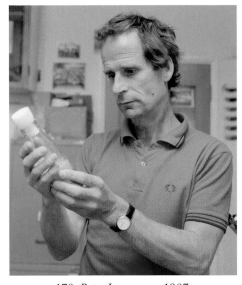

179. Peter Lawrence, 1987.

With Sheila Green, the inter-segmental boundary in *Oncopeltus* was studied as an example of a compartment border.

However, the study turned more towards *Drosophila* and continued after the arrival of Gines Morata in 1974, and Gary Struhl in 1976, with the investigation of *Drosophila* development via compartmentalisation, focusing on genetics and cell lineage. The interest in the function of morphogen (chemical) gradients in pattern formation has also continued – directed to a large extent at the gene *engrailed* (Tom Kornberg was involved in the study of its characteristics in 1983) and the protein Hedgehog. Hedgehog is produced in the rear compartments of the banding pattern of the epidermis of *Drosophila*, is taken up by cells in the front compartments, and becomes a line source of a diffusing morphogen forming a gradient with a peak near the compartment boundary. This gradient delivers information, directly or indirectly, about position, polarity (with respect to the main axes of the body) and dimension, in both types of compartment so that the underlying plan for pattern development can be created, in which genes are activated in appropriate places and elements such as bristles are arranged with precision.

Peter Lawrence was joint head of Cell Biology with Mark Bretscher from 1984 until he resigned in 1987. He was elected a Fellow of the Royal Society in 1983.

Michael Wilcox

180. Michael Wilcox, c. 1970.

Michael Wilcox obtained his first degree and PhD in Chemistry at the University of Manchester. He then went as a postdoc to the Chemisches Institut of the University of Zurich under Professor A.S. Dreiding, and determined the structure of betanin, a red pigment from beetroot. From 1965 to 1969, he was a visiting fellow to Marshall Nirenberg's group at NIH, where he studied glutaminyl-tRNA in bacteria such as *B. subtilis*. He found that no corresponding synthetase exists, but glutamic acid itself is placed on tRNA^{gln} and then amidated.

In a complete change when he came to LMB, Michael began working on pattern formation. He was soon joined by Richard Smith and the initial subject of study was the filamentous blue-green alga *Anabaena*, in collaboration with Graeme Mitchison. *Anabaena* consists of a linear array of dividing cells, with occasional non-dividing heterocysts in between, which fix nitrogen

195

for use by their neighbours. They showed that heterocysts arise when a sufficiently large gap occurs between them – there is in fact a tendency for all cells to become heterocysts, but most are prevented by a long-range inhibitor produced by the hererocysts themselves (later found to be an 11 amino acid peptide).

From the late 1970s, the group concentrated more on *Drosophila*, and in particular studied the imaginal disks – small groups of cells which are the precursors of external organs. In 1980, they were joined by Danny Brower, and began using monoclonal antibodies to locate position-specific cell surface antigens on the disks, which were later found to be integrins – involved in cell adhesion. Mutations of a particular one, PS2, showed it to be required for muscle attachment and for correct wing morphogenesis. Another visitor was Rob White, who with Michael studied the distribution of ultrabithorax proteins in *Drosophila* and its regulation.

Michael died in 1992.

John Gurdon and Ron Laskey

A larger group, headed by John Gurdon and including Ron Laskey was imported from the Zoology Department at Oxford in 1972. In 1968, John Gurdon had been the first to clone an animal. Working on *Xenopus laevis* (the South African clawed frog which had become firmly established in laboratories as a result of its widespread use in pregnancy testing), he had destroyed the nucleus of an unfertilised egg with UV, and replaced it with the nucleus of an intestinal cell of another frog and the egg developed, generating a fertile adult frog – a genetic twin of the frog that donated the nucleus. In this way, numerous male and female adult, fertile frogs were obtained.

Max thought that the group, already funded by the MRC in Oxford, would make a

181. John Gurdon, 1982.

very appropriate addition to LMB, extending the developmental work in the Cell Biology Division and making a suitable filling for some of the laboratory space in the first (thirteen-bay) building extension which had remained empty since 1968. John had strong domestic ties to Oxford and wavered a lot before accepting Max's offer. But Max was exemplary in his tolerance of John's indecision. When he finally accepted, John's Professor at Oxford wrote to Max to tell him what a difficult fellow he was.

At LMB, the group continued with work involving nuclear transplantation and the study of transcription and chromatin assembly using *Xenopus* eggs and oocytes. Others in the group included Colin Dingwall, Eddy DeRobertis, Larry Korn (founder of the biopharmaceutical company Protein Design Labs), Andrew Wyllie (of apop-tosis fame, and now a Professor in the Pathology Department in Cambridge) and Doug Melton (who came as a PhD student and is now a senior Professor at Harvard).

When Princess Margaret came formally to open the new Clinical School next door to LMB, there was a spare hour in her timetable during which the planners decided she could visit LMB. John Gurdon was the only senior staff member pres-ent and so hosted her during her visit. Joy Fordham remembers that no one in LMB seemed very interested in her visit and feeling sorry for her, the canteen staff gath-ered by the stairwell as she arrived and scuttled along the corridor to greet her at the other end – hoping she did not recognise them as a rent-a-crowd. Apparently she was not very taken with the appearance of *Xenopus*, and her only comment during the whole visit was to ask why there was an empty bottle on top of a fridge! John could not think of an immediate answer.

During the colder winters of that time, John used to take Max ice-skating in the fens. One time, the senior staff challenged a group of very young people (mostly under twenty) to an ice hockey match at Sutton Gault. With the benefit of Max and César Milstein in the team, the seniors actually won, even though they were mostly more than twice the age of the juniors.

John Gurdon became head of the Cell Biology Division in 1979, but the group moved in 1983 to a Cancer Research Campaign Unit in the Zoology Department in Cambridge: John became Professor of Cell Biology and Ron Laskey, Professor of Animal Embryology. In 1991, the Wellcome/CRC Institute was opened in Tennis Court Road, with John as Chairman and Ron as Director. John was elected a Fellow of the Royal Society in 1971, he was knighted in 1985, and became Master of Magdalene College until 2002.

182. Mariann Bienz, 2003.

Ron Laskey was elected a Fellow of the Royal Society in 1984. In 2002 he became joint Director (with Bruce Ponder) of the Hutchison/MRC Research Centre close to LMB.

Mariann Bienz

Mariann came initially in 1981, as an EMBO Fellow to work with John Gurdon on the heat-shock response in *Xenopus* oocytes, and continued work on this, partly with Hugh Pelham, until she went back to Zurich in 1986. She returned to LMB in 1991 working on developmental path-ways in *Drosophila* – investigating molecular mechanisms of cell differentiation, and more recently signalling pathways and transcriptional control. Mariann was elected a Fellow of the Royal Society in 2003.

Matthew Freeman

Matthew graduated in Biochemistry at Oxford in 1983, and obtained his PhD with David Glover at Imperial College, London, working on *Drosophila* cell cycle genes. In a spell as a postdoc in Gerry Rubin's laboratory at Berkeley, he cloned a gene called *argos* and showed that it regulated cell recruitment in the developing eye. After joining LMB in 1992, he discovered that *argos* was an inhibitor of the EGF (Epidermal Growth Factor) receptor, and subsequently his group has focused on the genetics, cell biology and biochemistry of intercellular signalling, eye development, EGF receptor function and rhomboid – discovered as an activator of EGF receptor signalling in *Drosophila*. Rhomboids are a family of serine proteases that cleave substrates within trans-membrane domains and exist throughout evolution, from bacteria to humans.

Matthew was elected a Fellow of the Royal Society in 2006.

183. Matthew Freeman, 1992.

Jonathan Hodgkin

Jonathan came to LMB in 1971 as a PhD student of Sydney, working on the *C. elegans* project, studying the anatomy and mutagenesis. After gaining his PhD in 1974, he continued with the developmental and molecular genetics of the worm. In particular, he discovered a novel and complex pathway relating the chromosomal nature of the individual worm to its physical structure as a male or hermaphrodite. He was elected a Fellow of the Royal Society in 1990 and left LMB in 2000 to become Professor of Genetics at Oxford.

184. Jonathan Hodgkin, 1983.

Jon Karn

Jon first came to the MRC as a Helen Hay Whitney Fellow in 1976, but joined the laboratory staff in 1979. He collaborated closely with Sydney Brenner on developing novel methods for cloning genes, a significant challenge in the early days of recombinant DNA. One of his notable achievements came in 1982. With Sandy MacLeod, the gene for the *unc-54* mutant of *C. elegans* was discovered to code for the heavy chain of the muscle myosin of the nematode. Together with Leslie Barnett, Jon was able to clone and sequence the gene, leading to a prediction of the first complete amino acid sequence of myosin. Andrew McLachlan analysed the sequence in terms of periodicities of charged amino acids and showed how these led to a prediction of the packing of myosin rods into thick filaments. The model of the myosin rods built by Andrew

185. Jon Karn, 2000.

and Jon became a particular favourite of Max, since it was a modern variant of Francis Crick's coiled-coil prediction.

From 1984 Jon was drawn more into problems concerning retroviruses and gene regulation in mammalian cells, and in 1987, at the urging of Aaron Klug, he began leading the laboratory's effort into AIDS and formed a group investigating the control of gene expression in HIV-1. Working closely with Mike Gait, Jon's group discovered that the regulatory proteins *tat* and *rev* were RNA-binding proteins, and not DNA-binding proteins as had been expected. He left LMB in 2002, to become Chairman of the Department of Molecular Biology and Microbiology at Case Western Reserve University School of Medicine in Cleveland, Ohio.

Rob Kay

Rob Kay graduated as a Biochemist at University College, London, obtaining his PhD in 1973, with work on nuclear envelopes. He continued in this line as an EMBO postdoc, working with Werner Franke in Germany. He returned to London in 1974, to the Imperial Cancer Research Laboratories, at Mill Hill, to join a small group of young developmental biologists nurtured by John Cairns. In 1984, the group was dispersed as the lease on the laboratories expired and Rob in particular was forced to seek a new environment, less constrained by the narrow scientific

186. *Rob Kay, 1999.*

limitations set by the incoming Director of ICRF. He approached Sydney, who passed his application on to the Divisional Heads, Mark Bretscher and Peter Lawrence. Part of Mark and Peter's strategy for the Cell Biology division was to combine cell and developmental biology, on the basis that developmental instructions must be carried out in the embryo by cell biological means, and development often provides extreme examples of cell biological processes for study.

Rob was attempting to identify morphogens – signal molecules that have a key role in patterning embryos into tissues and organs – and his organism of choice was the slime mould, *Dictyostelium*. These social amoebae have a life-cycle which alternates between single feeding cells and multi-cellular fruiting bodies, and so provides many fascinating cell biological challenges, such as to find out how cells consume bacteria, move and chemotax towards particular chemicals. Rob succeeded in identifying his morphogen – an unusual chlorinated molecule called DIF[25] – and spent many years trying to understand how it functions in development. He was also one of those instrumental in establishing the International *Dictyostelium* Genome Project, with Bart Barrell, who had moved from the PNAC Division to the Sanger Centre, and Paul Dear, still in PNAC. As if in validation of the original strategy, Rob later joined with Mark Bretscher to study how *Dictyostelium* cells move.

When Rob joined the Cell Biology Division in 1984, he found an intense and exciting environment, but one also constrained by space and sometimes by funds. The corridors were already overflowing with equipment, and, to find freezer space, he was forced to scour the building, eventually finding a niche in the basement. He shared a small office with Kim Nasmyth, Mike Wilcox and Jonathan Hodgkin, graduating after some years to what was believed to be Francis Crick's old desk. This battered heirloom had drawers with a tendency to self-locking, and had been forced with a screwdriver at some time in the past, perhaps by Francis himself.

At this time, all group leaders in the Division worked actively at the bench, and, like postdocs and PhD students, were expected to report on their work once a year at the Wednesday talks of the Division. Held in the Divisional library, with people hunched on the floor, balanced on bookcases or peering round the open door, and with cakes provided by the speaker, these seminars were intense yet informal.

Graphs, photographs and autoradiographs showing key experiments would be passed round for inspection and comment. Mark and Peter, as joint Heads of Division were by tradition guaranteed a seat at the central table in the room, and could also be guaranteed to ask the traditional questions at the end of each seminar (which they seemed to take it in turns to pose): 'What is the question you are asking? Why are you doing this work?' Some years later, their shared and interchangeable purpose was cruelly lampooned in the Christmas review, where they formed the 'Gang of One-and-a-Half', but were only given one chair between them to sit on.

People worked hard, and lights could be found burning late into the night every day of the week; in fact, a second, semi-nocturnal Division existed at times, whose members came in around lunch time, warmed up by tea, reached their peak in the evening but continued to work long after midnight. This work ethic and single-mindedness did not generally result from overt pressure, but more from a mixture of fascination, ambition and a desire to live up to the past achievements of the laboratory. Happily, Rob found the atmosphere to be generally cooperative and supportive with thoughts and help freely given, again in the traditions of the lab.

John Kilmartin

John Kilmartin first arrived at LMB in 1965 as a student of Max Perutz in Structural Studies. He remembers waiting to talk to Max and being greatly awed by the 'names' walking about – Crick, Kendrew, Brenner, etc. The awe and the striking casualness of the LMB society struck him again when he arrived to start work – Max gave him Crick's desk to occupy for two months, Crick being away.

John's thesis work was on the binding of carbon dioxide to haemoglobin, and he went on to sequencing and studying the physiological effects of chemically modified haemoglobins and the mechanism of the Bohr effect.

In 1984, he transferred to the Cell Biology Division and began work on microtubule polymerisation, which led to the study of the yeast spindle and particularly the spindle pole body. He was joined by Dick McIntosh, now at Boulder, Colorado, on a sabbatical in 1984. In 1990, with Michael Rout, monoclonal antibodies were produced against three components in the spindle and spindle body and their locations established

187. John Kilmartin, 1975.

by immunofluorecent staining and confirmed by immunoelectron microscopy. Later, mass spectroscopy was used to identify most of the components and in 1997, an outline structure of the yeast spindle pole body was proposed with Esther Bullitt, Michael Rout and Chris Akey.

John was elected a Fellow of the Royal Society in 2002.

Ed Lennox

Ed Lennox was at LMB from 1977 to 1985, as head of a sub-Division of tumour biology. Much of his group's work was on developing monoclonal antibody probes, first for blood group antigens and then for antigenic sites on tumours with Karol Sikora and César Milstein's group.

Graeme Mitchison

Graeme joined Cell Biology in 1969, and was initially involved in investigating pattern formation with Michael Wilcox, and later became interested in the formation of vein patterns in plants. In 1981 he went to the Salk Institute for a year, visiting Francis Crick, resulting in papers on dream sleep – which they proposed was a method of suppressing over-excited intercell activity in the cerebral cortex – and on the distribution of long axons in the striate cortex. From 1982 to 1995 he was

188. Ed Lennox, c. 1974.

189. Graeme Mitchison, 1985.

at the Physiological Laboratory in Cambridge, and worked on stereoscopic matching and on neuronal branching patterns. He returned to LMB (Structural Studies) in 1995, and became involved with Richard Durbin in applying pattern recognition techniques to biological sequences and worked with Sarah Teichmann on genomic questions. In 2005, Graeme transferred to the Department of Applied Maths and Theoretical Physics.

Sean Munro

Sean Munro came as Hugh Pelham's research student in 1983 to work on the heat shock protein. They also showed in 1987 that proteins that permanently reside in the lumen of the endoplasmic reticulum are distinguished by the C-terminal sequence Lys-Asp-Glu-Leu (KDEL). Following this, during a postdoc visit to Harvard, working with Tom Maniatis, he isolated a cDNA encoding for murine interferon γ receptor and demonstrated its expression. He returned to LMB in 1988 and formed a group studying the Golgi apparatus – the stack of membrane-bound compartments which are involved in the targeting of proteins and vesicles to specific organelles within a cell – and particularly the mechanisms by which the specific targeting is achieved.

190. Sean Munro, 1999.

Kim Nasmyth

Kim graduated at York in biology in 1974, and began working on yeast for his PhD in the Zoology Department at Edinburgh under J.M. Mitchison, studying DNA replication in *Schizosaccharomyces pombe*. He obtained his PhD in 1977, and in 1978 went to the University of Washington, Seattle as a postdoc. After a year at the Cold Spring Harbor Laboratory, he came to LMB in 1982 and continued with work on yeast – the molecular genetics and also transcriptional regulation, largely with David Shore. In 1988, he moved to the IMP (Research Institute for Molecular

191. Kim Nasmyth, 1985.

Pathology) in Vienna, and in 1997 became its Director. He moved to Oxford with his group in 2005 when he became the Whiteley Professor of Biochemistry. Kim was elected a Fellow of the Royal Society in 1989.

Barbara Pearse

Barbara joined LMB originally in 1972 as a student in Ieuan Harris's group in the Protein and Nucleic Acid Division. In 1982 she transferred to Structural Studies and in 1984 to Cell Biology. In 1976, she discovered clathrin – the protein coat of coated vesicles. She continued work on this area, cooperating with Tony Crowther and John Finch in a structural investigation showing that the vesicle coats are formed by clathrin aggregating into hexamer/pentamer cages. With Guy Vigers, a three-dimensional reconstruction of a coat was computed in 1986 from electron micrographs of the cages in ice, and this work continued with Corinne Smith and Nikolaus Grigorieff. The structure of a domain of the AP2 adaptor, which interacts with a number of accessory proteins involved in regulating the formation of coated vesicles, was solved by X-ray diffraction with David Owen, Phil Evans, Yvonne Vallis and Harvey McMahon. Using structure-directed mutagenesis, it has been shown how clathrin binding to the complex would release the accessory proteins at the site of vesicle formation. Barbara was elected a Fellow of the Royal Society in 1988.

192. Barbara Pearse, c. 1985.

193. Hugh Pelham, 2001.

Hugh Pelham

Hugh Pelham came to LMB in 1981 and worked initially on the mechanism of the reaction to heat shock in *Drosophila*, mammalian cells and yeast. More recently he has become interested in the area of intracellular membrane traffic, using yeast genetics to identify proteins involved in membrane fusion and to investigate traffic pathways. In 1990, with Mike Lewis, the receptor for the C-terminal, residence-qualifying sequence, KDEL, for proteins in human endoplasmic reticulum was established. Hugh was joint Head of the Division from 1992, and was sole Head from 1995 until 2006. He became Deputy Director of LMB in 1996 and Director in 2006. He was elected a Fellow of the Royal Society in 1988.

Karol Sikora

Karol Sikora was a member of Ed Lennox's group working on tumour biology from 1974. In 1977 he became the head of a unit funded by the Ludwig Institute for Cancer Research housed in the LMB building until this closed in 1986. Since then he has been Professor of Clinical Oncology at the Imperial College School of Medicine at Hammersmith.

194–200. Reception for C. elegans meeting at LMB in 2003 to celebrate the award of the Nobel Prize to Sydney Brenner, Bob Horvitz and John Sulston in 2002:

194. (top left) Nichol Thomson.
195. (top right) Peter Lawrence and John White.

196. (left) John Sulston.

205

197. *(above) Peter Lawrence and John Sulston.*

198. *(left) John Sulston, Bob Waterston and Fred Sanger.*

199. *(opposite page, top) Aaron Klug and Sydney Brenner.*

200. *(opposite page, bottom) Jonathan Hodgkin and Richard Henderson.*

1. F.H.C. Crick, 1966. Codon–anticodon pairing. The wobble hypothesis. *Journal of Molecular Biology*, 19, 548–555.
2. S. Brenner, L. Barnett, E.R. Katz and F.H.C. Crick, 1967. UGA: a third nonsense triplet in the genetic code. *Nature*, 213, 449–450.
3. H.D. Robertson, S. Altman and J.D. Smith, 1972. Purification and properties of a specific *Escherichia coli* ribonuclease which cleaves a tyrosine transfer ribonucleic acid precursor. *Journal of Biological Chemistry*, 247, 5243–5251.
4. M.S. Bretscher, H.M. Goodman, J.R. Menninger and J.D. Smith, 1965. Polypeptide chain termination using synthetic polynucleotides. *Journal of Molecular Biology*, 14, 634–639.
5. A.O.W. Stretton, S. Kaplan and S. Brenner, 1966. Nonsense codons. *Cold Spring Harbor Symposia on Quantitative Biology*, 31, 173–179.
6. M.S. Bretscher, 1968. Translocation in protein synthesis: a hybrid structure model. *Nature*, 218, 675–677.
7. M.S. Bretscher, J.N. Thomson and B.M.F. Pearse, 1980. Coated pits act as molecular filters. *Proceedings of the National Academy of Sciences of the USA*, 77, 4156–4159.
8. S.C. Satchwell, H.R. Drew and A.A. Travers, 1986. Sequence periodicities in chicken nucleosome core DNA. *Journal of Molecular Biology*, 191, 659–675.
9. From the Foreword by Sydney Brenner to *The Nematode Caenorhabditis elegans*, edited by W. Wood. Cold Spring Harbor Laboratory, 1988.
10. *Ibid.*
11. *Ibid.*
12. Jonathan Hodgkin and Nichol Thomson, personal communications.
13. J.G. White, E. Southgate, J.N. Thomson and S. Brenner, 1986. The structure of the nervous system of the nematode *Caenorhabditis elegans*. *Philosophical Transactions of the Royal Society of London*, 314B, 1–340.
14. J.E. Sulston and H.R. Horvitz, 1977. Post-embryonic cell lineages of the nematode, *Caenorhabditis elegans*. *Developmental Biology*, 56, 110–156.
15. H.R. Horvitz and J.E. Sulston, 1990. Joy of the worm. *Genetics*, 126, 287–292.
16. P. Berg *et al.*, 1974. Letter: Potential biohazards of 'recombinant' DNA molecules. *Science*, 185, 303.
17. P. Berg, 2002. Asilomar and recombinant DNA. In 'Still Going Strong at Seventy Five', supplement to *The Scientist*, March, p. 5.
18. J. Sulston and G. Ferry, 2002. *The Common Thread*. Bantam Press, London.
19. *Ibid.*
20. J. Hodgkin *et al.*, 1998. *C. elegans*: sequence to biology. *Science*, 282, 2011–2046.
21. E.S. Lander *et al.*, 2001. Initial sequencing and analysis of the human genome. *Nature*, 409, 860–892.
22. Sulston and Ferry, *op. cit.*
23. A. Klug, 2001. The human genome project. *Life*, 51, 1–4.
24. F.H.C. Crick and P.A. Lawrence, 1975. Compartments and polyclones in insect development. *Science*, 189, 340–347.
25. H.R. Morris, G.W. Taylor, M.S. Masento, K.A. Jermyn and R.R. Kay, 1987. Chemical structure of the morphogen differentiation inducing factor from *Dictyostelium discoideum*. *Nature*, 328, 811–814.

Chapter Eight

Protein Chemistry (became Protein and Nucleic Acid Chemistry in 1965)

This was the Division created in the new LMB in 1962, to house Fred Sanger and his group from the Biochemistry Department. Both Fred's group and Max's Cavendish Unit were funded by the MRC, and both were under internal pressure to expand and external pressure not to – at least in their University locations. The members of the Cavendish Unit were also interested in expanding the biochemistry techniques available to them – the work in 1957 of Vernon Ingram in determining the amino acid change in haemoglobin causing sickle cell anaemia, for example, had been made possible by contact with Fred, and the joint proposal to MRC for laboratory space was the result.

Fred's intention was to continue in experimental work rather than general overseeing, and he brought few personal collaborators – in fact only Leslie Smith who had worked with him on insulin. But he did bring other senior people to develop their own groups – Ieuan Harris (plus research student Richard Perham), and Brian Hartley – as well as Richard Ambler and John Hindley. César Milstein, who had worked with Fred in Biochemistry, returned from Argentina and came to LMB in 1963.

Richard Ambler sequenced cytochrome c-551 and azurin, from Pseudomonas fluorescens and went on to Edinburgh in 1965. John Hindley came with Ieuan Harris and began work aimed at reconstituting chromatin as well as working with Ieuan on the protein of turnip yellow mosaic virus. He went on to Bristol in 1966.

Although the later name of the Division – Protein and Nucleic Acid Chemistry – survives, its main interests have now diverted towards research in immunology, cancer and biotechnology.

FRED SANGER

I think the move to the new laboratory was probably an influence in my conversion to nucleic acid sequencing. Previously I had not had much interest in nucleic acids. I used to go to Gordon Conferences on Proteins and Nucleic Acids when the two subjects were bracketed together, and would sit through the nucleic acid talks waiting to get back to proteins. However, with people like Francis Crick around, it was difficult to ignore nucleic acids or to fail to realize the importance of sequencing them. An even more seminal influence was John Smith, who was the nucleic acid expert in the new laboratory and who was extremely helpful to me, so that I could turn to him for advice in this new field.[1]

201. Fred Sanger.

RNA

The development of sequencing methods for nucleic acids required small precise molecules on which to experiment. The first ones reported were tRNAs and work began on these almost immediately in the new LMB. DNA work began a bit later, in the mid-1960s.

The existence of tRNAs was reported by the group of Zamecnik and Hoagland at Harvard in 1957, and the indications were that the molecules contained only about 60 nucleotides – a useful size to try sequencing. After a sabbatical in Zamecnik's laboratory, Leslie Smith returned to LMB to try to purify individual species, but did not get very far with this before leaving the laboratory for the USA in 1965.

In 1963, Kjeld Marcker, a Danish postdoc, joined Fred and they decided to try to inch towards sequencing a tRNA by attaching its corresponding radioactive amino acid and determining the sequence of nucleotides around the binding site – similar to the method used to look for the amino acid sequence around the active sites of enzymes. They chose methionine (convenient for labelling with ^{35}S) and its tRNA in *E. coli*. However, after paper electrophoresis, an extra spot was found, and further experiments showed that the methionine in this spot was formylated. In 1966, Kjeld with Brian Clark showed that there were, in fact, two methionine-accepting species of tRNA, only one of which could be formylated. They found that the resulting formyl-methionine was incorporated into the N-terminal

202. Kjeld Marcker, c. 1970. Courtesy of Kjeld Marcker.

203. George Brownlee, c. 1975.

position of proteins in *E. coli* and showed that it was important for the initiation of protein synthesis. Initiation via formyl-methionine was found to be common to all bacteria and, with his student Alan Smith, Kjeld showed it was present in other prokaryotic-type organelles, and a similar system in eukaryotes.

George Brownlee joined Fred as a research student in 1963. Given the choice of working on RNA or protein, he chose RNA (which Fred considered was a strong factor in pushing the attention of the whole group more in this direction). However, attempts to purify individual tRNAs from each other went very slowly and efforts were concentrated on developing rapid and simple fractionation techniques, using ribosomal RNAs which were too large to hope to sequence at this stage, but which could be purified and prepared in a radioactive form. Influenced by the group's recent experience with ^{32}P-labelled proteins and autoradiography, they decided to apply it to RNA, since every nucleotide contains a phosphorous atom.

A two-dimensional partition method was developed (electrophoresis first on cellulose acetate and then on ion exchange paper) which proved to be a great improvement over the previous methods tried. One of Fred's strongest memories is of Bart Barrell, who had joined Fred as a technician in 1964, showing him the first developed film with clear, round, separated spots on it instead of the streaky,

211

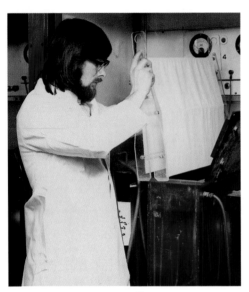

204. Bart Barrell, c. 1975.

unresolved pictures they had been getting. The composition of small polynucleotides determined the positions of the spots on the two-dimensional fingerprint, and were read off using an overlying composition/position graticule. The isomeric nature of each spot showed itself by splitting, which to some extent could be used for sequencing – an isomer with a 5′ terminating A, for example, was found to move more slowly than those with other 5′ terminators.

More sequencing data was obtained with the introduction of spleen phosphodiesterase. Starting with a ribonuclease T_1 digest (giving polynucleotides with G at the 3′ end), spleen phosphodiesterase cuts nucleotides from the 5′ end, and each of the three nucleotides gave a different shift to the spot on the following fingerprint. By these means, the sequences of at least tetranucleotides could be deduced.

The technique was applied to digests of the 5S ribosomal RNA, a newly reported, relatively small (about 100 nucleotides) candidate for sequencing, but it was not adequate for determining the complete sequence and a new fractionation system, homochromatography, was developed to cope with larger oligonucleotides.

Homochromatography was another two-dimensional separation, the first by electrophoresis, and the second by displacing the labelled polynucletides with unlabelled polynucleotides from a background 'homomixture' – a digestion product of yeast RNA. Separation of digestion products up to 25 nucleotides was now possible, and George Brownlee sequenced these by overlapping the smaller products of further digestion. Overlap of the larger products gave the overall 5S sequence which was published in 1968. (The first RNA sequence had already been published in 1965, that of tRNA[Ala] (75 nucleotides) purified by Holley and colleagues at Ithaca by counter-current fractionation, and sequenced by methods similar to those applied to proteins.)

By the late 1960s, general methods of purifying tRNAs were being developed and Fred with Bart Barrell sequenced tRNA[Phe] from *E. coli*. Other tRNAs were sequenced in the laboratory by Howard Goodman, Suzanne Cory, John Smith and others in the Molecular Genetics Division. In 1968, Jim Dahlberg established the terminal sequences of some phage RNAs, and Joan Steitz in the Molecular Genetics Division established the RNA sequence of the ribosome binding sites of the three proteins coded by the R17 phage genome.

One of the initial enticements for working on RNA was the possibility of comparing the sequence of a messenger RNA with that of the protein it was coding for,

205. Jim Dahlberg and Suzanne Cory at Cold Spring Harbor, 1970. Courtesy of Cold Spring Harbor Laboratory Archives.

and so break the code. Bacteriophage provided promising sources of coding-RNA, and in 1970 some work was done on the phage R17, whose coat protein had been sequenced. The whole genome contained over 3,000 nucleotides, and some of the larger products from digestion with ribonuclease T1 were sequenced by Peter Jeppesen using the homochromatography system. Some of the product was given to Jerry Adams, who was using acrylamide gel electrophoresis, and surprisingly he obtained an autoradiograph showing a number of sharp, well-separated bands representing fragments up to 50 nucleotides long, and one of these turned out to be the code for a region of the coat protein. The genetic code had by this time been determined by other methods, but the group's results gave good independent confirmation. Alan Coulson joined Fred at this time (1967). Bart Barrell had taken over the actual sequencing, leaving Fred free to work on developing the techniques, and Alan came to help on this side.

206. Alan Coulson, 1987.

213

DNA

The success with RNA soon prompted thought on what could be done with DNA. One problem was its size – there were no small DNA entities comparable to tRNA or 5S RNA on which to develop methods. The smallest were those of the single-stranded DNA bacteriophages with about 5,000 nucleotides. Another problem was the lack of suitable enzymes for cutting DNA in a specific way. Work on RNA had depended on ribonuclease T_1 with its ability to cut only at G residues, and the very specific restriction enzymes for cutting DNA were not discovered until 1968 and not generally used for another five years.

The first attack on DNA in the group was made in the mid-1960s by Ken Murray, who developed some two-dimensional systems for fractionating and analysing up to tetranucleotides from partial digests, but there was no way of locating them in their original chains.

By the early 1970s there were about ten people in the group working on DNA, including Gillian Air, Elizabeth Blackburn, John Donelson, Clyde Hutchison, Vic Ling, Hugh Robertson (nominally in Cell Biology), John Sedat, Maria Szekely and Ed Ziff. The methods being used were developments of those used for RNA. One of the more useful sequencing techniques was the 'wandering spot', two-dimensional chromatographic method introduced by Vic Ling in 1972, using the fact that the direction of the vector between two spots on the chromatogram differing by one nucleotide was characteristic of the type of nucleotide. The method was particularly useful for polypyrimidine stretches of DNA and runs of up to twenty nucleotides from the DNA of the phage fd were sequenced.

Fred became more interested in trying to use *E. coli* DNA polymerase I. This had already been used by Ray Wu and Dale Kaiser at Ithaca and Stanford respectively, in 1968, to determine the sequence of the twelve-nucleotide 'sticky ends' of the DNA of phage λ – the first piece of DNA to be sequenced. Fred, however, used it to introduce a ribonucleotide, largely rCTP, into a sequence otherwise consisting of deoxyribonucleotides, copied using the plus strand DNA of the phage f1 as template. This gave a means of specific cutting at these ribonucleotide sites by ribonuclease. The resulting fragments were analysed by homochromatography and several oligomers of 50 nucleotides were sequenced by 1973. (A rumoured prize of a three-week holiday for the first person to sequence 50 residues had to be divided by the ten people involved, and resulted in everyone having a weekend off.)

But these methods were slow and laborious and it was clear that to tackle the long DNA sequences of genetic materials, new ideas were needed. A new direction had been suggested by Charles Weissman and his colleagues at Zurich (collaborating with John Hindley, now at Bristol). The RNA phage Qβ contains an RNA polymerase that copies its own RNA, and they had developed pulse-labelling techniques for sequencing this RNA.

Prompted by this, Fred became interested in using DNA polymerase I and T4 polymerase to develop a more general approach to DNA sequencing and eventually the 'plus and minus' method evolved in 1974. Starting with a single-stranded length of the DNA under study (the template), a complementary copy of a short length of this (the primer) was hybridised to the template and extended using DNA polymerase I to give random lengths which ended over the region to be sequenced. These lengths were now extended by polymerase treatment in the sole presence or absence of a particular nucleotide. This resulted in eight samples ($^+/\_A$, $^+/\_C$, etc.), which were then run on an acrylamide gel, and from the eight band patterns the nucleotide sequence could be deduced. For this approach to be feasible, a fractionation system was required that would separate the larger polynucleotides exactly according to size. The use of longer acrylamide gel electrophoresis and severe denaturing conditions (8M urea and high voltage which allowed the gel to become hot) reduced complications in the patterns caused by secondary structure in the DNA, and allowed sequences up to about 50 nucleotides to be directly read off. The single stranded DNA of the phage φX174 (total length about 5,000 nucleotides) was chosen as the subject of investigation and the method was clearly simpler and quicker than other previous methods.

Over 1975–76, with Elizabeth Blackburn, Gillian Air and Clyde Hutchison, larger and larger pieces of φX DNA were sequenced. They had started with the earlier techniques and progressed to using the plus and minus method. By late 1976, virtually the complete sequence had been determined. The explanation for an apparent discrepancy between the length of DNA in the genome and the amount required to code for all the viral proteins was now evident – the phenomenon of overlapping genes had been discovered.[2] In tidying up, the group was joined by Nigel Brown, John Fiddes, Pat Slocombe and Mike Smith, and the completed provisional sequence of the φX DNA was published in 1977.

207. (left) Elizabeth Blackburn, 1973.
208. (centre) Gillian Air, 1973.
209. (right) Clyde Hutchison, 1975.

The dideoxy- method

Meanwhile, Fred and Alan Coulson were back on the development of a new method. The plus and minus was slowly improving as it was being used, but there were still problems. One of these was the limited spread in the lengths of polynucleotides from a given nuclease digestion, so that a preliminary incubation with samples taken out at various times was needed to get a wide distribution of sizes. Another problem was the wide variation in strength of different bands – some being completely missing. The possibility occurred to them of using chain-terminators. Arthur Kornberg at Stanford had shown that dideoxythymidine triphosphate (ddTTP) could be incorporated into a chain by DNA polymerase, but that after this, no further nucleotides could be added. So by including ddTTP in the incubation mixture with DNA polymerase, one could make a mixture of polynucleotides all ending in T where the ddTTP had been incorporated. Fred was given some ddTTP by Klaus Geider in Ladenburg, and the result of a single incubation was better than anything seen before. Bands of more or less equal strength were spread over a long distance on the gel. However, the other three dideoxys (dideoxynucleotide triphosphates) had never been made. Alan and Fred set about preparing them, although until then they had had no experience of nucleotide chemistry. With advice from Mike Gait and Bob Shepherd they were successful, but it did take about a year.

Fred writes:

> My main experience in synthetic organic chemistry had occurred about 30 years earlier when I was making amino acid derivatives, and particularly the DNP amino acids. This required a good deal of crystallization, which I very much enjoyed doing. The first sign of a pure compound was to come into the lab in the morning and find a flask full of beautiful crystals, though more often all one found was an oily mess at the bottom. I think the fun of preparing nice crystals was one of the factors that attracted me to chemistry when I was studying. I was therefore rather disappointed when I found that nucleotide products did not crystallize, and that to test for purity you had to run them on some chromatography system. This certainly took some of the fun out of the work but we settled down to it and it was well worth the effort. (This observation may seem rather trivial, but I think one should not underestimate the importance of 'fun' in research.)[3]

Alan Coulson remembers that Fred dropped one of the syntheses (the product of about three months' work) on the floor one day. After Fred decided to go home, Alan was able to rescue it from the floor. Fred also once said that what they did was not exactly a chemical synthesis, since they did not purify or crystallise the product, but nevertheless, their impure mixture seemed 'to do the trick'.

The dideoxy- method was published in late 1977[4] and shows readable gels of up to 120 nucleotides. A small technical improvement that made a big difference to the work was reported in 1978 – the use of thinner acrylamide gels (0.4mm instead of 1–2mm). This resulted in much narrower bands, considerably increasing the resolution, and also allowed higher voltages to be used, again reducing secondary structure and the complications arising from it in the band pattern. Runs of up to 465 nucleotides could now be resolved. The method was immediately applied to checking the φX DNA, and about 30 revisions were found to be necessary in the 5,386-nucleotide sequence. It was by far the longest sequence to be determined at the time (1978) and so far no mistakes have been reported. (Clyde Hutchison and others at Rockville, Maryland, have recently (2003) synthesised the sequence. Although there could have been two mistakes in the third positions of codons, the result was fully active!)

210. *Rodger Staden, 1975.*

By this time the group was using computers for storing and analysing the data. In the early stages, Fred was rather reluctant – it would take the pleasure out of looking at the sequences and seeing what could be made of them. However, as methods became quicker and more and more data were collected, it became clear that a computer should be used at least for storing the sequences. Initially the sequence storage was set up by Mike Smith and his brother who was in another laboratory, but when Mike left LMB, Bart Barrell persuaded Rodger Staden, who was involved in computational work for the X-ray diffraction groups in Structural Studies, to become interested in sequences. Rodger organised the storage and wrote programmes for analysing the data and eventually left X-ray work and worked full-time on sequence analysis, developing the 'Staden Software Package'.

At about the same time as the dideoxy method came out, another rapid sequencing technique was developed by Maxam and Gilbert at Harvard in 1977.[5] The method was similar in that it gave an autoradiograph from which a sequence could be read off. However, instead of mixtures of fragments all terminating at the same nucleotide, they used chemical methods on fragments labelled at their 5′ ends, to cut preferentially at each of the four nucleotides in turn. Their gels were capable of reading up to 100 nucleotides.

The method worked well and was widely used in preference to the plus and minus method and probably in preference to the dideoxy technique in the USA initially. For this work, Fred and Walter Gilbert were jointly awarded half of the Nobel Prize for Chemistry in 1980, 'for their contributions concerning the determination of base sequences in nucleic acids'. (The remaining half was awarded to Paul Berg for his fundamental biochemical studies of nucleic acids.)

211–214. Celebration of Fred Sanger's second Nobel Prize, in the canteen, 1980:

211. (opposite page, top) Fred with Sydney. Hugh Huxley, Dave Zimmern and David Secher looking on.
212. (opposite page, bottom) With Bart Barrell and others viewing the champagne.
213. (this page, top) Fred speaking.
214. (this page, bottom) General joke. Left to right: Sally (Fred's daughter), David Secher, Fred,
Sydney, Max and Joan (Fred's wife).

The dideoxy method was only applicable to single-stranded DNA, which was fine for the naturally single-stranded φX. But most DNA is double-stranded and it is often difficult to separate the strands. Various ways to overcome this were tried, but most successful was a cloning procedure worked out in 1978 by Gronenborn and Messing in Germany[6] using a single-stranded phage M13, in which a double stranded stretch of DNA is incorporated and converted into a single stranded stretch in the phage DNA. The cloning procedure was not generally applicable to the method of Maxam and Gilbert and so most laboratories switched to the cloning and dideoxy system and it continues to be the method of choice today.

With the new cloning technique, Fred's group felt prepared to tackle DNAs that were double-stranded and larger than φX. The first choice was the relatively small mitochondrial DNA – about 16,000 nucleotides in all – which codes for tRNAs and ribosomal RNAs and a few proteins. Slight differences in the genetic code of the mitochondrial DNA were noticed by Bart Barrell when work began on this in 1979 with Alan Bankier and Jacques Drouin – UGA is used as a tryptophan codon rather than a termination codon, and AUA seemed to be a methionine rather than an isoleucine codon. The sequence of a 2,771-nucleotide restriction fragment of human mitochondrial DNA was worked out in 1980 with Andrew Smith and Bruce Roe, and the complete sequence of 16,569 nucleotides in 1981, with Stephen Anderson, Maarten de Bruijn, Ian Eperon, Donald Nierlich, Peter Schreier and Ian Young. The following year, the 16,338 sequence of bovine mitochondrial DNA was published.

Since there were severe containment regulations required for the human mito-chondrial study, much of the cloning procedure was tried out first on the DNA of the bacteriophage λ. Work on this was therefore completed next, the 48,502 sequence being published in 1982, by Fred with Alan Coulson and Guofan Hong, Diana Hill and George Petersen.

Fred retired from the LMB in 1983, at the age of 65. He had been the head of the Division since 1962, and the joint head with César Milstein since 1981. César remembers his abrupt leaving. The conventional finishing date in the MRC is 30 September, and on that day Fred was doing experiments – on 1 October his laboratory was empty and he was gone.

Unlike many scientists, I decided to give up research when I reached the age of 65. This surprised my colleagues, and to some extent myself also. I had not thought about retirement until I suddenly realized that in a few years I would be 65 and would be entitled to stop work and do some of the things I had always wanted to do and had never had time for. The possibility seemed surprisingly attractive, especially as our work had reached a climax with the DNA sequencing method and I rather felt that to continue would be something of an anticlimax. The decision was I think a wise one – not only because I have greatly enjoyed the new lifestyle, but also because the aging process was not improving my performance in the laboratory and I think that if I had gone on working I would have found it frustrating and have felt guilty at occupying space that could have been available to a younger person. For more than 40 years I had had wonderful opportunities for research, and had been given the chance to fulfill some of my wildest dreams.[7]

Fred Sanger was elected a Fellow of the Royal Society in 1954, awarded a CBE in 1963, became a Companion of Honour in 1981, and was appointed to the Order of Merit in 1986. His two Nobel awards were in 1958 and 1980.

To mark his retirement, Sydney Brenner, the Director at the time, wrote to all the alumni who had been associated with Fred both at the Biochemistry Department and at LMB, asking for donations to a Fred Sanger Fund to be set up in his memory. Fred was keen that the money should be used to help pay for travel costs of young workers in both departments. Based on a precise calculation of the times that Fred had spent in them, Sydney worked out that $5/13$ should be allotted to Biochemistry and $8/13$ to LMB. The amount subscribed allows for travel grants to be allocated to two or three people per year in each laboratory.

In 1993, the laboratory for genomic studies set up jointly by the Wellcome Trust and the MRC at Hinxton, about ten miles from Cambridge, was named the Sanger Centre in Fred's honour. It was later renamed the Wellcome Trust Sanger Institute. In 1997, the Biochemistry Department in Cambridge opened its new building, and called it the Sanger Building and Fred was asked to officially open it. He recalled working in the Department in the 1940s, when the Director was away at war work, and the financial head was in prison for embezzlement – 'though the laboratory seemed to run quite well. We had state-of-the-art equipment – consisting mainly of test-tubes and pipettes'. They had also been promised a new building – 'and here it is after only 48 years!'

On Fred's retirement, Alan Coulson joined John Sulston in sequencing the worm genome (see chapter 7). Bart Barrell with other members of the group moved on to the DNA of Epstein-Barr virus and the 172,282-nucleotide sequence was published in 1984. This was followed by the 240,000-nucleotide sequence of human cytomegalovirus, which took five years and was published in 1990. He then began working on yeast and moved to the Sanger Centre with Alan Coulson and John Sulston in 1992. After ten years at the Sanger Centre working on the nematode and human genome sequences, Alan Coulson returned to LMB in 2002 and retired in 2007.

George Brownlee was involved with sequencing both RNA and DNA specimens at LMB until 1980, when he left to become Head of Chemical Pathology in the Sir William Dunn School of Pathology, Oxford. His student, Stan Fields (1977–1980), sequenced several of the segments of the RNA genome of influenza virus, collaborating with Greg Winter and Guilio Ratti.

BRIAN HARTLEY

215. *Brian Hartley, 1969. Courtesy of Jens Birktoft.*

Brian Hartley graduated from Cambridge in 1947 and in 1949 joined the Biochemistry Department at the University of Leeds. His research began on novel organo-phosphorous insecticides with Bernard Kilby, but after finding that they labelled the active site of chymotrypsin, Brian switched from killing locusts to 'The Mechanism of Action of Chymotrypsin' as a thesis topic – a problem that took another twenty years to solve. In 1952, he joined the Biochemistry Department in Cambridge, continuing work on chymotrypsin, trypsin and elastase. In 1959, he collaborated with Fred Sanger on sequencing around the reactive serines of these enzymes (one of the earliest uses of P^{32} labelling for sequence determination), and wrote one of the *Annual Reviews in Biochemistry* on Proteolytic Enzymes, in which he invented the category of 'Serine Proteases'. He then went to the laboratory of Hans Neurath in the University of Washington, Seattle for a year, and carried on working towards the complete sequence analysis of chymotrypsinogen-A. He continued this work on his return to Cambridge, and developed the Dansyl-Edman technique of amino acid sequencing with his first student Bill Gray. With Michael Fuller, Brian designed the arrangement of the third floor laboratories for the new LMB building and moved into this with the rest of the Sanger group in 1962.

The sequence of chymotrypsinogen-A was completed and published in 1964, and, with some corrections sorted out with Dorothy Kauffman in 1966, appeared very conveniently for use in the interpretation of the 2Å Fourier map of α-chymotrypsin obtained by David Blow's group in 1967. Brian also continued the study of the sequences around the active centres and disulphide bridges in serine proteinases with Larry Smillie.

In 1963, he was joined by Alan Weeds as a student to work on myosin. The substructure of myosin was at that time uncertain and in particular whether the number of chains in the molecule was two or three. In Alan's thesis work, some proteolytic fragments were sequenced, and the number of cysteine sequences was found to be inconsistent with a three-strand structure. Alan continued with myosin work, completing the sequence of the smaller light chain, but transferred to the Structural Studies Division in 1970, into Hugh Huxley's group.

In 1966, David Shotton came to work on pancreatic elastase as a PhD subject. Improvements in the method of purification led rapidly to crystallisation of the enzyme and a complete amino acid sequence analysis. A crystallographic study with Herman Watson and others in the Structural Studies Division went extremely smoothly, resulting in an interpretable 3.5Å map published in 1970 (see chapter 6), by which time David had moved to join Herman Watson in Bristol.

Brian also began work on aminoacyl tRNA synthetases in 1966, firstly on tRNA^{Met} synthetase from *E. coli* – a method of purifying the enzyme was worked out with Robert Heinrikson, and it was shown that it catalysed amino acylation of both forms of the tRNA, whether able to be formylated or not. The study was taken up as a PhD project by Chris Bruton in 1966, but there was uncertainty on the subunit structure of the enzyme until 1974 when Chris and Gordon Koch showed that it was dimeric with two very similar subunits.

216. Chris Bruton, 1975.   *217. Gordon Koch, 1973.*

Brian applied for the Chair of Biochemistry at Imperial College when it became vacant on the retirement of Sir Ernst Chain. Chain made a special trip to Cambridge to try to persuade Brian to withdraw his application, and to apply instead for the vacant Cambridge Chair to which he was an elector. His motive was in part that he hated Molecular Biology, which he stated vehemently would never be useful, and he also had other candidates for the Imperial Chair. However, Brian was attracted by the palatial seventh-floor 'penthouse' flat on top of the Department that had been built for Chain by the Woolfson Foundation, and also by a large Fermentation Pilot Plant, which Brian thought would be useful to make large quantities of super-stable enzymes from thermophiles in which he had become interested. He was appointed Head of Biochemistry at Imperial in 1974.[8]

When Brian left to take up the Imperial Chair, links with LMB were not severed. Chris Bruton followed him in 1975, but Brian continued to supervise Greg Winter, who had arrived as a student in 1973 and whose PhD subject was sequencing tryptophanyl tRNA synthetase from *B. stearothermophilus*. The result of this was published in 1977 and also a paper on the sequence homologies between this enzyme and that from *E. coli*. In 1983 the amino acid sequence of the tyrosyl-tRNA synthetase from *B. stearothermophilus* was worked out with Greg and Gordon Koch at LMB and David Barker at NIMR, the MRC institute at Mill Hill. One of Brian's students at Imperial College was Michael Neuberger, who came to LMB in 1980.

IEUAN HARRIS

218. Ieuan Harris, c. 1960s.

Ieuan Harris graduated in Chemistry from the University College in Wales in 1945, and for his PhD worked at NIMR in the laboratory of T.S. Work. He then went to the USA, firstly to Yale with J.S. Fruton and then to Berkeley in C.H. Li's laboratory, becoming interested in protein sequencing, particularly of pituitary hormones.

In 1955, he introduced the method of determining the C-terminal residues of proteins using carboxypeptidase, and with C.A. Knight in the Virus Laboratory at Berkeley applied it to tobacco mosaic virus. Only threonine was released, in an amount corresponding to a subunit of molecular weight 17,000, confirming the indications of X-ray diffraction that the virus particles were made up of a regular arrangement of relatively small subunits. (This was quite important at the time, since in some quarters X-ray diffraction results were taken with a grain of salt.) Also, the virus particles without the C-terminal threonines were infective, and gave progeny with an intact terminal threonine, confirming that the replication information of the virus did not reside in the protein. After a year at the laboratory of Linderstrøm-Lang at the Carlsberg Foundation in Copenhagen, he joined Fred Sanger's group in the Department of Biochemistry in 1955 as a member of the MRC staff, and came with that group to LMB in 1962.

Ieuan continued his interest in virus structure with one of his first students, Robin Offord, who studied the rod-shaped tobacco rattle virus. But at LMB, Ieuan became more interested in enzymes, particularly those containing cysteines with active thiol groups. These could be labelled using ^{14}C-iodoacetic acid for studying amino acid sequences in the neighbourhood of the cysteine residues. In 1963, with his student Richard Perham, the method was applied to GPDH (D-glyceraldehyde-3-phosphate dehydrogenase) from yeast and muscle and later to alcohol dehydrogenase. With Barrie Davidson, Mike Sajgo and Harry Noller, amino acid sequencing was extended to the complete GPDH enzyme from lobster (1967), with Richard Perham to the pig muscle enzyme (1968) and with Graham Jones to the yeast enzyme (1972).

The lobster GPDH sequence became important when Michael Rossman's group at Purdue took over the X-ray diffraction study of the lobster enzyme. However, although the enzyme was stable when the co-factor NAD^+ was present, it became unstable when NAD^+ was removed and in this state it could not be crystallised. This ruined the intended study of the mechanism of binding of NAD^+ to the enzyme. But, in 1966, Amelunxen in Kansas reported that the enzyme from the moderately thermophilic *Bacillus stearothermophilus* was more stable to heat. Following this up, Ieuan with Koichi Suzuki showed that the NAD^+-free enzyme was also sufficiently stable to crystallise, and this led on to a sequence and X-ray study in LMB with Gregory Biesecker, Jean-Claude Thierry, John Walker and Alan Wonacott. From the resulting map, published in 1977, it was clear that extra salt bridges made a major contribution to the thermostability of the tetrameric substructure. This work influenced Ieuan to pursue the study of other thermostable enzymes, in particular phosphofructokinase from *B. stearothermophilus*, with Phil Evans, Peter Hudson, Hans Hengartner and Edith Kolb.

Tragically, Ieuan died in 1978 aged 53 (by carbon monoxide poisoning from a faulty heater in his summer cottage in Wales), but his idea of taking advantage of the extra stability of the enzymes from thermophilic bacteria continues to be applied.

JOHN WALKER

John Walker joined LMB in 1974. He had gained his DPhil in 1969, at Oxford, working at the Sir William Dunn School of Pathology on peptide antibiotics, and had spent two years at the School of Pharmacy, University of Wisconsin, and three years in Paris. In 1974, he met Fred Sanger and Ieuan Harris at an EMBO workshop in Cambridge, and was invited to join their Division at LMB. At this time Fred was developing his DNA sequencing methods and applying them to the related bacteriophages φX174 and G4, and to DNA from human and bovine mitochondria. In parallel studies, John analysed the amino acid sequences of the corresponding proteins. In the case of G4, in addition to confirming the DNA-suggested sequence and the modified genetic code in mitochondria, the work with Denis

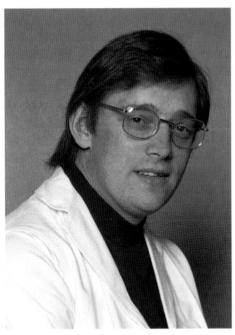
219. John Walker, 1982.

Shaw and Bart Barrell led to the discovery of triple-overlapping genes and to the discovery that the subunits I and II of cytochrome-C oxidase were coded in DNA within the mitochondrion.

During the work on mitochondria, John developed an interest in the enzyme complexes in the inner membrane of that organelle and in 1978 began a structural study of the ATP synthase from bovine heart mitochondria – a complex that generates the high-energy adenosine triphosphate (ATP) used as a fuel to drive other biological processes. He was given a clone containing the entire ATP synthase operon by Sydney Brenner, whose student Conrad Lichtenstein had produced it as part of his work on the transposon Tn5. He was joined by Mike Runswick in 1980, Nick Gay and Matti Saraste in 1981 and Ian Fearnley in 1982. The work eventually resulted in a complete sequence analysis.

In the 1960s, Efraim Racker in New York had shown that the mushroom-shaped knobs, about 100Å in diameter, seen in electron micrographs of the inner membranes of bovine heart mitochondria, were the ATP-synthesising enzyme complex. The head of the mushroom is a globular complex, known as the F_1 domain, where the catalytic sites of the complex lie. It is attached, via a slender stalk, to the hydrophobic membrane domain, F_0. F_0 transports hydrogen ions through the membrane to the catalytic domain F_1, releasing energy which is used to drive ATP synthesis from ADP and inorganic phosphate.

The F1 domain consists of nine subunits (3α, 3β, 1γ, 1δ, 1ε), with a combined molecular mass of about 371,000. Both the α and β subunits bind nucleotides and the group found that their sequences were weakly related. By comparing them with the known structure of adenylate kinase and the sequences of myosin and phosphofructokinase, other enzymes that bind ATP or ADP in catalysis, Walker and Saraste proposed that two short sequence motifs that they found in all the enzymes were involved in helping to form their nucleotide binding pockets. One of these has become established as a reliable indicator of the presence of purine nucleotide binding sites in proteins of known sequence but of unknown biochemical function. It helped the group identify the oncogene p21 as a GTPase. From the atomic structures of F_1-ATPase and other proteins, the two sequence motifs are now known to be involved in forming the phosphate binding regions of the nucleotide binding sites (the P-loop sequences).

One of the ultimate aims of the group was to determine the atomic structure of F_1-ATPase from bovine heart mitochondria by X-ray diffraction. Although crystals were grown quite early on, they were relatively poorly ordered and diffracted to only low resolution. About seven years were then spent in systematically investigating the factors influencing crystal formation, during which the order gradually improved until 1990, when suitable crystals were obtained which diffracted to 2.8Å resolution. René Lutter and Rose Todd were key collaborators at this time. Getting rid of all trace impurities was one of the important factors for growing these crystals, and another was to remove the endogenous bound nucleotides and replace them with an analogue of ATP, which had the effect of locking the complex in a unique configuration. In collaboration with Jan Pieter Abrahams and Andrew Leslie, a crystal structure was obtained in 1994.[9]

The structure was consistent with a rotary process for the mechanism of the enzyme, first proposed as a possibilty by Paul Boyer at Los Angeles in 1982, from substrate binding studies. The three α- and three β-subunits are arranged alternately like the segments of an orange around a central 90Å long α-helical section of the γ-subunit. The three β-subunits must always interact in different ways with this central α-helix, resulting in three different conformations and accounting for their different binding characters for ATP and ADP. Each goes through the same cycle of 'open', 'loose' and 'tight' states, generated by the relative rotation of the γ-subunit.

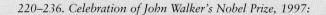

220–236. Celebration of John Walker's Nobel Prize, 1997:

220. Four Nobel Prizewinners: César, Aaron, John and Fred.

221. John with Andrew Leslie.

222. With Megan Davies.

223. With John Kilmartin.

224. With Aaron and Jennifer Cornwell.

225. John speaking by Aaron, Fred and César.

226. With Jon Karn and Hugh Pelham.

227. Gebhard Schertler and Michael Fuller.

228. Megan and Greg Winter.

229. *Fred and Mark Bretscher.*

230. *César and Margaret Brown.*

231. *Mark Skehel, Ross Jakes and Michel Goedert.*

232. *Aaron speaking.*

233. *John and Rachel Whant.*

234. *Mike Runswick with Aaron.*

235. *John with Nick Gay and Rob Kay.*

236. *With Terry Rabbitts and Ian Fearnley.*

John Walker was elected a Fellow of the Royal Society in 1995 and was awarded the Nobel Prize for Chemistry in 1997 with Paul Boyer (California) and Jens Skou (Aarhus) for the work on ATP synthase. In 1998 he was appointed Director of the MRC Dunn Nutrition Unit, and joined it in the 'Titanic' building next to the LMB when this was completed in the following year. In 1999 he was knighted.

CÉSAR MILSTEIN

César Milstein was born in Bahia Blanca, Argentina, in 1927. He graduated from Buenos Aires University and obtained a PhD in the Medical School on kinetic studies of the enzyme aldehyde dehydrogenase. In 1958, funded by the British Council, he joined the Biochemistry Department in Cambridge to work for a PhD under Malcom Dixon on the mechanism of metal activation of the enzyme phosphoglucomutase. During this work he collaborated with Fred Sanger, whose group he joined with a short-term Medical Research Council appointment. (Two weeks into his first preparation of the enzyme the news of Fred's Nobel Prize arrived and was celebrated sufficiently heartily that afterwards César, realising that he should not attempt any more work that

237. César Milstein, 2000. Courtesy of Cristina Rada.

day, went to put his enzyme prep. away, dropped it into the low temperature bath and lost it. He accepted it philosophically: 'a Nobel Prize is worth two weeks' work – even if it is in celebration of somebody else'.[10])

He returned to Argentina in 1961 for two years, during which he extended his studies of mechanisms of enzyme action to the enzymes phosphoglyceromutase and alkaline phosphatase. However, the political persecution of liberal intellectuals and scientists manifested itself as a vendetta against the director of the institute where he was working, forcing him to resign. He came back to Cambridge in 1963, and rejoined Fred Sanger in the Protein Chemistry Division of LMB. After his previous stay he 'felt it was like coming back home'.

Fred asked what he would like to do, and César suggested continuing with the phosphatase work, but Fred was not very keen and suggested two subjects, one of which was gamma globulin and antibodies. (Rodney Porter, who was awarded a Nobel Prize in 1977, had been Fred's first PhD student and, later, when he specialised in antibodies, had tried to interest Fred in them.) By chance, during his stay in Argentina, César had taken over the supervision of a student who was working on gamma globulin, and whose supervisor had left the University. So César had already become interested in the problem and jumped at Fred's suggestion and accepted it.[11] Fred also suggested iodination experiments, currently then in fashion for marking particular sites, and César was keen to look for disulphide bonds. (During the Argentinian episode, César had wondered whether antibody diversity might arise by joining a variety of small polypeptides by disulphide bridges and was later relieved that he never put the idea into print.) The iodination experiments were in themselves a complete disaster and were abandoned after a year (along with some hundreds of fingerprints), but they did show that there was an enormous, heterogeneous system involved – in fact, a background repertoire of many million different antibody molecules, sufficient to ensure cross-reaction with any antigen.

However, the disulphide work was applied to Bence-Jones protein. This had been identified as free immunoglobulin light chains secreted into the blood from myelomas – cancerous growths arising from a single plasma cell – and its great advantage was that it was monoclonal and therefore its progeny homogeneous. (A plasma cell is the antibody-producing form of the B-lymphocyte. Lymphocytes are the white blood cells responsible for immune reaction. B-lymphocytes produce antibodies and T-lymphocytes are responsible for cell-mediated immunity.) César's first paper on this was published in 1964, and in it he acknowledges the assistance of John Jarvis, who stayed with César for the rest of his research life. During the next four years César identified the number of disulphide bridges and some stretches of the amino acid sequences in the light chain proteins. With Blas Frangione, John Clegg and research students Richard Pink, Jisnuson Svasti and David Secher, the sequences of proteins from different sources were compared, and these showed that while they were invariant in the C-terminal half, the sequences in the N-terminal half were variable. More limited sequence studies on the heavy chains suggested that the fragments alongside the

238. John Jarvis, 1973.

light chains were similarly composed of constant and variant halves (C and V regions).

The mechanism by which antibodies achieved their enormous diversity of structure was a mystery at this time. Lederberg[12] had proposed that it was a consequence of a high rate of mutation confined to a few genes, but there was the difficulty of defining a mechanism that operated on only part of a gene. César with

231

Sydney Brenner (an unlikely combination probably engineered by Francis Crick) proposed in 1966[13] that this could be achieved by having on the C region of the gene a recognition site for an enzyme which cut the DNA alongside it in the V region. The cut and/or repair of this could then involve leeway or errors and so generate a large number of different sequences. However, the initial attraction of this theory was dampened when the variability in the sequence of the V regions of both the light and heavy chains was found to be confined to three small regions, with the remaining framework relatively constant.

By the early 1970s, César was convinced that antibody structure in itself would not explain the genetic basis of diversity, and began to look for some other approach to the problem. The Division was becoming more interested in nucleic acids and one of Fred Sanger's students, Peter Fellner, had earlier been interested in the messenger RNA for light chain, but at that stage their work together had not gone too far. Now, however, George Brownlee had become involved, but after several, preliminary failures it became clear that for homogeneous preparations, work with myeloma cells in tissue culture was required.

At that time, there was little tissue culture work going on in the laboratory and Abraham Karpus from the Haematology Department of the Medical School, housed in the basement, helped a great deal in the early stages of the work. The first idea was to grow individual clones of the myeloma cells, looking for spontaneous immunoglobulin mutants, with David Secher developing ways of detecting them as electrophoretic variants. The cloning technique, however, became bogged down until César persuaded a new postgraduate visitor from Australia, Dick Cotton, that he didn't really want to do protein chemistry, but rather to help in getting the tissue culture technique going efficiently, and within a week he had started to clone cells. Using his system, David stepped up his search for immunoglobulin mutants; 7,000 clones later, it was accepted that none were informative on the problem of diversity. Although there were several mutants with amino acid sequence changes arising from changes in somatic (normal body) cell genes – the first to be found – the mutants were not in the interesting variable regions that contact the antigen.

The growth of cells in tissue culture made it easy to label the RNA with P^{32} for sequence work. The mRNA for light chains was isolated using an oligo(dT)-cellulose column, a vital contribution introduced by Nick Cowan, and a cell-free system was set

239. David Secher, 1982.

232

up for its assay with Tim Harrison and Mike Mathews. The system actually produced larger precursor light chains and it was suggested that the added N-terminal sequence was a signal sequence which acted as its ticket for secretion through the cellular traffic. It was predicted that this could be a common phenomenon for secreted proteins, as indeed was found later for many other secreted or cell surface proteins. Sufficient sequence of the mRNA was obtained in 1973 to show correspondence to segments of both V and C regions, and so to show that at this stage both were encoded in one molecule.

Hybrid-cell work began at this time. César was interested in how the V and C chains came together and Dick Cotton in allelic exclusion – the fact that for genes that encode antibodies, only those from the maternal or the paternal side are expressed, but not both. Myeloma cell lines from mouse (secreting complete IgG molecules and excess light chains) and rat (secreting only light chains) were cultured together. Mutants of each cell line were chosen which were respectively deficient in the enzymes TK and HPGRT and these were grown in a medium, HAT, that required both enzymes for cell survival – only fused cells survived, forming hybrid clones. The resulting hybrid cells showed no allelic exclusion – they secreted immunoglobulin of both parental types. Good yields of molecules with mouse heavy chains and rat light chains were obtained, and non-symmetrical molecules with one light chain of each parental type. However, there were no scrambled light or heavy chains, i.e. with parentally different V and C regions.

Monoclonal antibodies

A little after the above work, César gave a talk in Basel, which was attended by Georges Köhler, who asked if he could join César's group at LMB. He had shown César how he could do four isoelectric focusing gels in one go, and César had impressed him by describing David Secher's technique of doing eight sets of twenty at a time when examining the 7,000 clones. Georges arrived in Cambridge in 1974. By this time Dick Cotton had left and the tissue culture work had been taken over by Shirley Howe.

The initial aim was to produce a myeloma cell line which produced antibodies and which one could clone and look for variants of antibody specificity. Both César and Georges were convinced that localised mutation was an essential component of the origin of antibody diversity. However, the work with David Secher had not been very successful in finding this, and the trouble with myeloma antibodies was that they tended not to bind to antigens, also neither Georges nor Shirley could grow reproducibly the most appropriate cultures – ones with antigenic specificity. So they went back to fusion, and although Georges found that fusion between myeloma cell lines worked out well in terms of tissue culture, they were stuck at the next stage, of finding the specificity of the antibody produced.

César and Georges then together had the idea of producing their own antibody-secreting cell line by cell-fusion. The first of the fused cells were from mouse spleen, as a source of B-lymphocytes (the cells producing antibodies), from a mouse immunised with sheep red blood cells – by themselves these are short-lived in culture. The second cells were from a mouse myeloma that were quite happy in tissue culture (*immortal* in the jargon). Fused cells were identified (later named *hybridomas*, see below) which secreted immunoglglogulins from both parents. Some of them secreted antibody against the red blood cells and it was possible to isolate clones that secreted a single molecular species of that antibody. The clones could be maintained in culture, the first continuous culture secreting a monoclonal antibody of predefined specificity. Their paper reporting this was submitted to *Nature*, who replied that they would accept it, but they did not regard it as of general, article-warranting interest and so it would have to be cut to 1,500 words to fit in as a letter. It was published in August 1975, and finishes with the sentence: Such cultures could be valuable for medical and industrial use.[14]

(The name *hybridoma* was coined by a visitor to César's group, Len Herzenberg from Stanford, talking to Tim Hunt over dinner at Clare – before that César had used the term *hybrid myeloma* and was not keen to change. David Secher offered to consult Charles Brink, a fellow member of his college, Caius, and Professor of Classics, who pronounced that *hybridoma* mixed Latin and Greek and so did not make etymological sense and that it would be better to stick with *hybrid myeloma*. Len, however, had publicised the new word widely and it stuck. For some time César and his group continued to use *hybrid myeloma*, but it was in vain.)

In 1984, César and Georges Köhler were awarded the Nobel Prize for their work, shared with Niels Jerne, a leading theoretician in immunology. In the same year they received a joint Lasker Award and, with the resulting interviews, it was clear that after this time they had differing memories regarding the sequence of events leading to the vital hybridoma experiment. They both agreed, however, that

240. *César and Georges Köhler, 1982. Courtesy of Celia Milstein/LMB.*

it was joint, synergistic work, resulting in the collaborative paper, and issued a statement to this effect, finishing:

> We both have a most pleasant memory of an exciting period in which a word, a comment or a passing remark made by one had a resonant effect on the other. We do not want such happy memories, which have sealed a close friendship, to be disturbed by superficial interpretations of our individual recollections. It was a collaborative work, it was a collaborative paper.[15]

After writing up the 1975 paper, Georges Köhler returned to Basel and for some months in neither laboratory was the work repeatable. In Cambridge this was due to the toxicity of a new batch of the HAT growth medium and after this was tracked down by Giovanni Galfré, all was well. However, the original aim of the work – to find mutants in the binding (variable) region – although followed up by a student, Deborah Wilde, was not successful.

With the immediate block on getting anywhere with antibody diversity, César shelved the problem for a few years to demonstrate with Giovanni Galfré the practical importance of monoclonal antibodies. They showed that hybridomas could be used for the production of standard reagents in areas of basic research and clinical diagnosis. In particular, work with Alan Williams in Oxford in 1977, using the procedure for the study of cell surfaces, impressed on César how important monoclonal antibodies would be.

241. *Pamela Hamlyn, 1975.*

In 1975, Pamela Hamlyn joined the group and worked on adapting Sanger's fast DNA sequencing methods to sequencing light chain mRNA. Her eventual success in 1981[16] involved the use of specific primers to sequence directly from mRNA, thus facilitating the sequence analysis of many immunoglobulin mRNAs without cloning. Her technical innovation made possible the rapid sequencing of the mRNA of light chains of monoclonal antibodies produced in response to a predefined antigen, and so monitor the diversity of antibodies during an immune response. The antigen chosen for much of the following investigation was the hapten, 2-phenyloxazolone (phOx – a small molecule which had been shown to have a narrow range of antibody production under the right conditions) and many subsequent members of César's group spent their time sequencing the genes of the heavy and light chains of the resulting antibodies using her method.

The initial response, seven days after immunisation, was studied with Matti Kaartinen, Gillian Griffiths and Alex Markham, and the result published in 1983 showed that there was little variation in the mRNA sequences. This primary response is from the 'naïve repertoire' of antibodies present initially – the result of joining all combinations of the current fragments: V and J for light chains and V, J and D for heavy chains, plus the diversity due to additions and deletions during the joining of the genetic fragments. The total repertoire was estimated as around 10^9, from which the antigen was selecting the few that had binding affinity, and triggering proliferation of the cells producing them. With Claudia Berek, the group showed that after another seven days, although there was an increased affinity for the antigen, most antibodies still showed similar though not identical sequences. This suggested a high degree of mutation, and the continued selection for the antibodies with best affinities. This hypermutation was located in the V-genes, and not randomly distributed but including some hot spots – sites with particularly frequent mutations. The study of this was continued particularly with Michael Neuberger and his group, and with Cristina Rada who joined César as a student in 1989.

242. *César's group, 1997. (from left) Caroline Napper, Adrian Woolfson, José Yélamos, Said Aoufouchi, César, John Jarvis, Cristina Rada*

Although César retired officially in 1994, he remained actively interested in the immunological work in the laboratory, both on the biological side, continuing the study of the mechanism of the immune response, and in the biotechnological developments from Greg Winter's group.

With the change in government in Argentina, after the Falklands war of 1982, and the news of his Nobel Prize in 1984, and memories of the publicity of his resignation in 1963, César became a local celebrity and in 1987 a meeting was held in his honour in his home town, Bahia Blanca. Several of his group and collaborators were invited, and the proceedings were televised. Because of the latter, César was asked to deliver his talk in Spanish, but since all the other speakers would speak in English, César insisted on speaking in English too. On television his talk was accompanied by a simultaneous translation, and the translator must have been impressed to give as accurate an account as possible, since Greg Winter remembers hearing even César's 'er's faithfully reproduced.

César became joint head of the Division of Protein and Nucleic Acid Chemistry in 1981 with Fred Sanger, and on Fred's retirement in 1983 he became sole head until 1987, when he was joined by Terry Rabbitts until his own retirement in 1994. He was elected a Fellow of the Royal Society in 1975. The award of the Nobel Prize was in 1984, and in 2000 the MRC organised a conference in London to celebrate the 25th anniversary of the discovery of monoclonal antibodies. He became a Companion of Honour in 1995. He died in March 2002, aged 74.

243–245. Celebrating César's Nobel Prize, 1984:

243. (right)
César and Max.

244. (below left)
Margaret Brown, César
and Jenny Brightwell.
245. (below right)
César with John Walker.

PATENT PROBLEMS AND LATER DEVELOPMENTS –
TECHNOLOGY TRANSFER

In 1975, a meeting was organised by the MRC on various safety aspects of research work – provoked by the then recent development of genetic engineering. Among others, César Milstein, who with Georges Köhler had just shown how to produce monoclonal antibodies from hybridomas, was invited to talk on his recent work. Tony Vickers, an MRC officer attending the meeting, suggested that the work should be patented and asked for a copy of the paper which had by then been submitted to *Nature*. Later, in July, he wrote to César that he had drawn the attention of the National Research and Development Council (NRDC)[17] to the preprint.

Nothing happened for about fourteen months. The general feeling in LMB at that time was that patenting was acceptable for machines that would be built by outside firms, but research results and techniques should be openly published and available, and so there was no strong pressure by César to chase things further. (César was also rather cool about NRDC, since they had not been very impressed with the machine built by Nick Cowan which automatically monitored parameters to control growth of a tissue culture in a desired fashion.) However, in 1976, Sydney Brenner visited the MRC headquarters and inquired what had happened. NRDC were contacted but had no record of receiving the manuscript and César was asked to send them a copy of the paper. They then wrote back to say, firstly that it was now too long after publication for patenting, and secondly that they thought the general method was not patentable – they would need a firm diagnostic application or industrial end product.

In 1978, two scientists from the Wistar Institute in Philadelphia applied for a patent for an anti-viral monoclonal antibody and other US firms were proposing to manufacture them. This provoked an article in *Nature* by David Dickson,[18] a staff editor, which reopened the question of whether the original technique should have been patented. In 1980, the Spinks Report was published – the conclusions of a Working Party set up to report on Biotechnology in Britain. Included in the report was the following:

> There appears to be a lack of awareness in practice of the obligations on recipients of government money and of the rights of NRDC. This must be remedied. We are concerned that a lack of appreciation of NRDC, particularly by young scientists, may continue to result in situations such as that which occurred of monoclonal antibodies where patent protection was not sought early enough and British advantage was reduced.

César was infuriated by this – he felt he had fulfilled his obligations by contacting NRDC and had informed the Working Party of this. Prime Minister Margaret Thatcher accused Jim Gowans, the Secretary of the MRC, of having wasted a marvellous patent opportunity. (Gowans had, however, only been the MRC Secretary since 1977, in 1975 the Secretary had been Sir John Gray, and the matter had not then been thought of sufficient significance to be brought to his attention.) The 'history' created by these events has unfortunately remained accepted to a large extent. Thus, in a 1993 issue of the pharmaceutical journal *Scrip Magazine*:

> It seems incredible that in the mid-1970s the two British (!) scientists who discovered how to make monoclonal antibodies decided not to patent their invention. In accordance with a long scientific tradition they felt they had no right to try to benefit commercially and personally by obtaining a patent.[19]

Although the original Köhler and Milstein method probably would have been patentable if it had been submitted immediately, the direct applications of mouse antibodies have been limited to diagnostics rather than therapy because of cross-species immune reaction. However, the above events did help to produce a more patent-conscious atmosphere in the laboratory. In 1980, David Secher with Derek Burke of the University of Warwick made a monoclonal antibody against interferon, and were concerned to follow MRC policy. They submitted their *Nature* manuscript well in advance to Head Office, and received advice from MRC and NRDC that it was not patentable. However, David began to worry that it might be patentable, and after doing some research in the University Law library on the 1977 Patent Act, he decided that it would be in the MRC's best interests to file the paper as a preliminary application. He did this – without MRC approval – paying £5 and depositing the manuscript in the Patent Office. (Later, the patent passed to Celltech, who derived quite a lot of money from it. In 1993, it was challenged by Hoffman la Roche in the USA, but this was not sustained.) The antibody is still in production over twenty years later, being used in the purification of interferon for therapeutic purposes.

As a result of the Spinks Report, Celltech, the UK's first biotechnology company, was set up in 1980 with the National Enterprise Board (NEB)[20] as its major shareholder, the aim being to keep more of the development of biotechnology in the UK, using the latest techniques licensed from the MRC. On being pressed, César became a member of its scientific advisory board, but after a year he became frustrated by the lack of interest in developing the monoclonal antibody side and resigned.

In 1982, an Industrial Relations Group was formed at MRC Headquarters, with a policy of effecting technical transfer for the maximum benefit of the UK economy. Initially, this transfer was organised via the British Technology Group (BTG),[21] but from 1985, the BTG's 'right of first refusal' to exploit research funded by Research Councils was ended by Sir Keith Joseph, the Secretary of State for Education and Science.

In line with the increased patent-awareness in LMB following the above events, David Secher was appointed Industrial Liaison Officer in LMB by Sydney in 1985, the post being taken over by Gordon Koch when David left LMB in 1987.

Greg Winter and CAT

246. Greg Winter.

After his PhD work with Brian Hartley on protein sequencing, Greg Winter changed to RNA sequencing, and in 1979 began working on the RNA of influenza virus with George Brownlee and George's student Stan Fields. From 1981 to 1985, he was involved with site-directed mutagenesis of tyrosyl-tRNA synthetase with Alan Fersht. He had become quite interested in protein engineering and had thoughts of applying it further, designing binding sites in proteins and catalytic sites in enzymes. Talking about his plans with César, he was told 'don't think about enzymes, *think antibodies*', a course he then followed very successfully.

Antibodies have a great variety of binding sites for different antigens and seemed good candidates for protein engineering. In 1985, Michael Neuberger, with Gwyn Williams, John Flanagan and Terry Rabbitts, had used protein engineering to produce a chimaeric antibody for therapeutic use – fusing a human constant region to a mouse antibody-recognition region, the CDR (complementary determining region) – which could be grown in quantity in mouse myeloma cells. Greg was more interested in the variable domains. The structures of these had been analysed by Arthur Lesk and Cyrus Chothia. Structurally, they consisted of a scaffold or framework which had been shown to be very similar in different antibodies, and a series of loops which varied extensively, but whose packing against the framework remained very similar. Greg realised that it would be possible to exchange all the loops from one antibody to another but retain the shape of the binding site – effectively transplant mouse antigen binding regions on to a human antibody, with the promise of a great reduction in immunogenicity over the chimaeric molecule when introduced into a human patient.

Unfortunately, Greg had been attacked one morning on his way to the laboratory and lost the use of his right arm because of nerve damage. It took many months to recover, and being unable to do laboratory work, he learnt how to use the Evans and Sutherland computer-graphics system and immersed himself in the antibody structure. Sydney Brenner supplied him with a gap student, Paul Dear, who was chained to an early synthesiser to make hybrid genes, and César provided a research officer, Peter Jones, who assembled nucleotides. About a year later, Peter succeeded in expressing the humanised antibody to a hapten (a small-molecule antigenic adapter), Michael Neuberger showed that it bound to the antigen and Jeff Foote showed that its level of binding was within a factor three of the normal. (Describing this at the César Memorial Meeting, Greg commented that the work on what was probably his most important paper was actually done by three other people.)

Another humanised antibody, against lysozyme, was made with César and Martine Verhoeyen in 1988. Also in 1988, Lutz Riechmann and Greg, with Michael Clark and Herman Waldmann in the Department of Pathology in Cambridge, produced the first examples of a humanised antibody, called Campath-1H, for therapeutic use – against human lymphocytes (later shown to be anti-CD59) as a possible cure for lymphoma. Waldmann showed dramatically that by using this to treat a patient with lymphoma, no mass of tumour remained after 30 days.

The technique was patented, and Celltech expected to take it over, although many other companies were also interested. The usual procedure at that time was for the MRC to pass on its antibody inventions to Celltech. However, the new LMB Director, Aaron Klug, put a stop to this, and despite being leaned on by the MRC Head Office, wound down (and effectively wound up) the LMB's relationship to Celltech, with the support 'hang in there' of the new, incoming MRC Secretary, Dai Rees.

It was felt that the field was too big for a single company to be able to exploit all the opportunities, and so three principles for licensing were drawn up. First, the product was to be for the benefit of patients; second, there was to be no enforced commercial secrecy; and third, investigators would be allowed to collaborate and publish freely while mindful of needless disclosure. A wide, non-exclusive, licensing policy was adopted by the MRC satisfying these principles and as a result of applications in the fields of transplantation, infection, cancer treatment and other clinical uses, there are now many tangible benefits to human health and the MRC has received royalties of some tens of millions of pounds per year, and some individual payments of hundreds of millions.

The next development was to produce completely human antibodies. The polymerase chain reaction was used to clone antibody gene libraries from pools of B lymphocytes. This produced a library of the entire current human antibody gene repertoire. The problem then was to pick out rarities and grow them in quantity. For this the phage display technique was used. The genes were attached to the coat protein gene of a filamentous phage, fd, and the phage grown in its appropriate bacteria. Each antibody then became displayed on the surface of a phage and a particular one could be selected by an antigen bound to a solid phase, and amplified by re-infection of bacteria. This mimics the normal immune system, where the antigen binds to the lymphocyte producing its antibody, and signals the amplification of its production. The advantage of the phage–bacterium system is that it does not lose viability and is effectively a phage + antibody factory. The antibodies in the repertoire produced in this way include some which are forbidden in the immune system, such as those against hormones, self-antigens and cancer cells.

At the stage of investigating the possibility of using phage display, Greg Winter was alarmed to hear that a large group at the Scripps Research Institute in California, allied with the US biotechnology company Stratagene, were working along the same lines. He therefore felt an urgent need for resources to continue and compete and, by the summer of 1989, the need became desperate. He discussed the issue with Geoffrey Grigg of Peptech Australia, who agreed to provide money on condition that they retained all the intellectual property rights. Greg declined this, but it was suggested that a new company be started in which Peptech would invest but not have a controlling interest. Greg was then approached by David Chiswell, who was just leaving Amersham and was keen on starting a new company around the new technology. David Chiswell had worked in the MRC Institute of Virology in Glasgow, the Department of Immunology and Microbiology at UCLA and in the Department of Tumour Virology at the ICRF in London, before becoming involved in product development and research management at Amersham International. In the autumn of 1989, Cambridge Antibody Technology (CAT) was formed with a £750,000 loan from Peptech and equity investment from private individuals and investment funds. The MRC was given a share in the equity (see below). It was set up very rapidly, 'on a handshake, and very little input from lawyers'. John McCafferty, a CAT employee, was initially housed by the MRC and showed that phage could display antibodies. The technology then took off, with most of the development work being done in Greg's group, which included Andrew Griffiths, Jim Marks, Peter Jones, Hennie Hoogenboom, Tim Clackson and Tim Bonnert in the University-LMB offshoot, the Centre for Protein Engineering. The work was patented as appropriate and licensing was exclusively granted to CAT.

Greg was given the freedom to act as a scientific entrepreneur. He was allowed to hold a stake in starting up the new company, benefited through the Awards to Inventors scheme of the MRC (see chapter 10) according to the income received by them, and allowed to continue his work and remain in the employment of the MRC. Although the MRC may have lost out a little by the non-patenting of the original monoclonal antibody discovery, the lessons learned regarding its patent ensured that there was strong patent protection for the later humanised and completely human developments. These have yielded a list of therapeutic monoclonal antibodies producing real clinical benefits and supporting a strong biotechnology industry in the UK and abroad. They have made the monoclonal antibody story one of the greatest MRC successes.

It is interesting to note that the MRC were initially very resistant to owning any equity in CAT. Aaron Klug, who was LMB-director at that time, was keen that they *should* benefit from the exploitation of the project, but David Noble at MRC headquarters maintained they could not own equity – as a Public Service Research Establishment, this was forbidden by the Treasury. Aaron was able to tell them that they already did – in the US firm Somatogen. In 1985, Somatogen had wanted, but could not afford, to fund a postdoc who was developing, with Kiyoshi Nagai, the making of synthetic haemoglobin, a product they were interested in. Instead of cash, they offered 25,000 of their shares. Aaron was keen that the project should go ahead and, not knowing that it was forbidden, suggested that the LMB Industrial Liaison Officer ask for 50,000 shares, which was agreed, and he funded the postdoc from a spare post in his Director's Division. So, the LMB was already holding shares on behalf of the MRC, and since the practice was already established, the MRC were persuaded to take 4 per cent of the CAT equity, and thus forever changed Treasury and MRC policy. Their holding was later increased to 10 per cent when Aaron became MRC representative on the CAT Board.

Greg Winter was elected a Fellow of the Royal Society in 1990. Since 1994 he has been joint Head of the PNAC Division and since 2006, Deputy Director of LMB. He was appointed CBE in 1997, and knighted in 2004 for his services to biotechnology.

All the participants in the non-patenting controversy were gathered together for a Witness Seminar organised through the Wellcome Trust in 1993.[22] César recorded his memories of the background to the discovery of monoclonal antibodies and its non-patenting in a review article written in 2000.[23]

247. *Speakers at the Milstein Memorial Meeting at LMB in 2003. Clockwise from top left: Tim Springer, Fred Sanger, George Brownlee, Jeff Foote, Herman Waldmann, Michael Neuberger, Roberto Poljak, Terry Rabbitts, Cristina Rada, Abraham Karpus, Claudio Cuello. Centre from top: participants, Greg Winter, Richard Pink.*

TERRY RABBITTS

248. Terry Rabbitts, 2000.

Terry Rabbitts joined César's group in 1973 from the Department of Genetics in Edinburgh. John Bishop, in that Department, had shown that by hybridising RNA with a large excess of DNA (Cot hybridisation), the kinetics are relatively simple, and it is possible to estimate the reiteration frequency of multiple DNA sequences from the hybridisation of the total DNA with RNA complementary to the multiple sequences. Terry went to work with John Bishop to learn how to use the Cot hybridisation method to apply to the problem of antibody diversity, having become interested in antibodies and immunology whilst doing his PhD at the National Institute for Medical Research, where Peter Medawar worked. César had also realised that hybridisation might be a way of deciding between the two main theories for the origin of antibody diversity – the germline theory, whereby all the diversity was inherited as a large number of genes present in the germ cell (the original fertilised egg), and the somatic mutation theory, favoured by César, whereby, starting from a small number of germline genes, diversity is generated by somatic (normal post-germ) cell processes. After some preliminary collaboration between the groups, César decided that it would be better if Terry could work in closer collaboration and eventually offered him a post in PNAC. Terry remembers his interview with César, meeting him in his lab coat, smoking his pipe and carrying a none-too-clean coffee mug and spending three hours talking about Terry's work. This was before the days of risk assessment – any handy spatula, maybe specially cleaned for RNA work, was fair game for César to tamp down his pipe tobacco.

In Terry's initial work, started in Bishop's lab in Edinburgh, he showed, using cDNA copies of mRNA, that the C region of Ig light chain was present as a single gene. But this raised the question about the number of V genes – because the cDNA populations were of relatively short size, the V region was not included and was not therefore assessed. In Terry's first hybridisation experiments with mRNA, César, with George Brownlee and John Jarvis, had made purified (although not completely pure) P^{32}-labelled light chain mRNA from myeloma cells. This was hybridised to genomic DNA and revealed two components, one of which hybridised to several copies (of the order of 10–100 genes) and one which hybridised to a single gene. They interpreted this as showing that there were 'several' V genes and the one C gene shown by the earlier cDNA hybridisation experiments. However, the impurity of the mRNA did not make the interpretation of the result unambiguous and they concluded that a pure probe was required in a reasonable quantity. After many approaches, and with support from César and George, but from few other LMB colleagues, one approach finally came to fruition – Terry showed that it would be possible to make a 100 per cent pure probe by bacterial cloning of cDNA into bacterial plasmids. In 1976, he showed that a cDNA copy of mRNA, made using reverse transcriptase, could be added to a plasmid and converted to a double-stranded copy of the gene, ready for protein production.[24] The method worked initially with rabbit globin cDNA cloning and subsequently for mouse L chain, and although the line of research was interrupted by the moratorium on work involving recombinant DNA, it had demonstrated a technology that has since been of pivotal use in all areas of molecular biology, biotechnology, biomedical research, protein production for structural analysis and medical use, in whole genome mapping and sequencing projects, although this has never been acknowledged by the MRC as an invention made in one of their research institutes.

Although the cDNA cloning work was to prove a key development in gene mapping and structure analysis, the cloning moratorium impeded progress. During the hiatus, Terry had to resort to other approaches to the problem of antibody gene diversity and used his older approach of making cDNA copies of mRNA, but now using semi-specific primers. In this way he showed, using a novel genomic DNA-based S1 nuclease protection assay, that the V and C genes were separate from each other in the genome and these are joined at the level of the RNA.

In part because the cloning moratorium severely impaired Terry's work on antibody diversity, and partly because of his interest in the origin of human leukaemias, he began work on human Ig genes. In the early 1980s, with Mike Hobart, he showed that the heavy chain gene was located in chromosome 14 and with David Bentley (Terry's first PhD student) and Sue Malcolm, at Queen Elizabeth College, London, he showed that the gene for the κ-light chains was in chromosome 2 and confirmed that the λ-light chain gene was in chromosome 22. These chromosomal locations had significant implications for some chromosomal translocations of malignant lymphoid tumours such as Burkitt's lymphomas in which the cells showed a translocation of genetic material from chromosome 8 to 14, and in variant cases from chromosomes 2 to 8 and from 8 to 22. The material involved in chromosome 8 was adjacent to the *c-myc* proto-oncogene and Terry with Pamela Hamlyn (later to become Pamela Rabbitts) showed that translocation moved it into the immunoglobulin gene region and with Richard Baer that this translocation allowed it to make use of the somatic mutation capabilities of the immunoglobulin system, with oncogenic results.

Like the enormous diversity of antibodies produced by the somatic mutation system in B-cells, a comparable diversity of receptors is similarly produced on the surfaces of T-cells to react with antigens on the surfaces of unwelcome cells. In 1985, the genes for T-cell receptors were shown to be on chromosomes 14 and 11 by Terry collaborating with groups at ICRF, and in France, Switzerland and Finland. In 1988, on investigating a chromosomal translocation from chromosome 11 to 14 in an acute T-cell leukaemia, with Thomas Boehm, Alan Forster and Richard Baer, a proto-oncogene was found.[25] Its predicted product was found to be a highly conserved protein, rhombotin, subsequently called LMO1, with two cysteine-rich regions, which were subsequently identified in three transcription factors, and termed LIM domains. Using a LIM-specific probe, two other LMO genes were found, one of which was near another region of chromosome 11 involved in translocations occurring in another T-cell leukaemia. This identified the LMO2 gene which has been implicated in around half of human T-cell leukaemias. Thus the LMO gene family defined a new class of oncogenes particularly relevant to T-cell tumours – these would normally give rise to transcription factors involved in developmental processes, but when activated out of context after translocation lead to tumours (embodying Terry's master gene model of the acute cancers).

Their work on identifying chromosomal translocation oncogenes led Terry's group to work on methods for generating *in vivo* models of chromosomal translocation mimics to develop a basis for understanding the biological role of these oncogenes. He developed a method called *knock-in* for mimicking translocations, and then followed this with two inducible chromosomal translocation mimics, namely the translocator and invertor models which involve *in vivo* recombination approaches. A second and major motivation for working out these methods has been to provide a setting for the pre-clinical testing of new regimes for their molecular therapeutic values, which include the use of molecules derived from the development of methods for isolation of intracellular antibodies.

Terry was joint Head of the PNAC Division from 1987 to 2002. He was elected a Fellow of the Royal Society in 1987 and Fellow of the Academy of Medical Sciences in 1998. He was awarded the Colworth Medal in 1981 and the CIBA Medal in 1993.

MICHAEL NEUBERGER

Michael Neuberger joined Brian Hartley at Imperial College in 1974 as a PhD student, trying to evolve enzymes with new specificities. He wrote up an extension of this for a research fellowship from Trinity College and spoke to people at LMB on the possibilities of working at the laboratory. He told Sydney that he was not keen on carrying on with enzymes, but was interested in antibodies and so was directed towards César. César did not seem very keen to take him on until Michael, playing what he later realised could have been a mastercard, asked César who else he should try, and César then agreed that he could join his group. He did this in 1980 after a year in Cologne with Klaus Rajewsky, learning immunology – trying, with hybridomas, to get antibody diversification going in cultures. On his return, César

247

249. César, Michael Neuberger and Greg Winter, c. 1993.

suggested possible lines of research – investigating ways of redesigning antibodies, or the regulation of antibody gene expression.

In fact, the two lines of work complemented each other. Devising ways of introducing immunoglobulin gene DNA back into lymphoid cells coupled to an identification of the DNA elements regulating antibody gene expression allowed recombinant DNA technology to be exploited for the production of genetically engineered antibodies. Recombinant antibody/enzyme chimeras were first produced in 1984 with Gareth Williams and Robert Fox[26] – the gene for a nuclease was introduced into the immunoglobulin gene (transfection) and resulted in an antibody with nuclease activity. In 1985, chimaeric antibodies (in which the antigen-binding variable portion of a mouse monoclonal antibody was linked to human constant regions) were produced. An immediate application was the production of quantities of a chimaeric human IgE antibody (the immunoglobulin class responsible for allergy) since human IgE was only available in limited supply and there was no monoclonal human IgE of known antigen specificity.

Other chimaeric human antibodies were produced in collaboration with Marianne Bruggemann (at Babraham) and Herman Waldmann (Department of Pathology), but it was clear from animal studies that such chimaeric antibodies were still immunogenic and there was a need for humanised versions. The first

CDR-grafted antibodies in which the variable portion (the Complementary-Determining Region) was also humanised were made in the following year with Greg Winter, Peter Jones, Paul Dear and Jefferson Foote.[27] However, Michael (in collaboration with Marianne Bruggemann) followed an alternative strategy, creating transgenic mice carrying segments of the human immunoglobulin gene loci such that the translocus mice would generate repertoires of human antibodies following immunisation.[28]

Studying the regulation of antibody gene synthesis allowed Michael (at the same time as the Schaffner (Zurich) and Tonegawa (MIT) laboratories) to discover that the expression of cellular genes was regulated by transcription enhancer elements. Indeed, subsequent work in collaboration with John Mason, Kerstin Meyer and Sven Pettersson revealed that immunoglobulin gene transcription was regulated not just by a single intronic enhancer but by the promoter and multiple enhancers at various positions in the gene locus.

It also became apparent from the transfection experiments that antibody gene expression was additionally regulated at the post-transcriptional level. Work performed together with Roberto Sitia in 1987 showed that if a plasma cell (whose role is to secrete antibodies into blood) was forced to synthesise the membrane form of immunoglobulin, then this membrane immunoglobulin was degraded intracellularly, not reaching the cell surface. Michael, Roberto and César wrongly attributed this failure to reach the cell surface in terms of a non-specific failure of membrane immunoglobulin to muddle its way through the extensive internal membrane network of the plasma cell. They were put on the right track by Reth in Germany, who showed that surface transport of membrane immunoglobulin needed B-cell-specific accessory molecules, laying the ground for Michael, together with Ashok Venkitaraman and Gareth Williams, to show that, for all immunoglobulin isotypes, the core antigen receptor on the B-cell surface is in fact composed of membrane immunoglobulin surrounded by a common B-cell heterodimeric sheath polypeptide, which was needed both for transporting the immunoglobulin to the surface and for transducing signals following encounter with antigen.

In 1985, Michael established a collaboration with Azim Surani at Babraham in order to use transgenic mice to find out whether the immunoglobulin enhancers were sufficient to direct tissue-specific expression *in vivo*. At the suggestion of Terry Rabbitts, Michael then approached César Milstein a year or two later, suggesting that a transgenic mice approach would also allow César to advance investigations of antibody diversification by somatic hypermutation. César agreed, but on the basis of it being a joint effort, thus marking the start of a ten-year collaboration between Michael's and César's laboratories. The experiments were initially pioneered by Melanie Sharpe, a postdoctoral fellow who joined the laboratory from Oxford, and were continued by a pair of graduate students (Cristina Rada in César's laboratory and Alex Betz in Michael's). The work allowed the intrinsic features of the antibody hypermutation process to be identified (revealing mutation hotspots, DNA strand bias, etc.) and showed that the mutator was not recruited by sequences located within the immunoglobulin variable gene target itself but rather in the transcription regulatory sequences flanking it.

Targeted somatic hypermutation had been put forward as a model to account for the generation of antibody diversity by Sydney Brenner and César Milstein in their only joint publication back in 1966.[29] This model viewed mutation as being caused by an error-prone polymerase that was recruited to the immunoglobulin locus to repair a locally created DNA strand break. Whilst they did not appreciate it at the time, one of the first indications that a simple polymerase-error type of model was unlikely to be correct came in 1998 when Cristina Rada and Michael Ehrenstein, together with César and Michael, analysed antibody gene diversification in mice deficient in the mismatch repair protein MSH2. They found an altered spectrum of antibody mutations in these mice, leading them to propose that hypermutation normally occurred in two phases, first targeting G/C pairs and then targeting A/T pairs.

Other experiments in Michael's laboratory were indicating that the other pathways of antibody gene diversification were also initiated by some sort of mischief at G/C pairs. Thus, Michael Ehrenstein, who was looking at immunoglobulin class-switch recombination (which transforms IgM antibodies into IgG/IgA or IgE) in MSH2-deficient mice, concluded that a common type of DNA lesion initiated both somatic mutation and class-switch recombination. Julian Sale, who had succeeded in developing cell-line models in which to study antibody gene diversification *in vitro*, concluded that gene conversion (which birds and rabbits use to diversify their antibody variable regions) was also likely initiated by lesions at G/C pairs. These results led Michael to put forward the DNA deamination model of antibody gene diversification in which the AID enzyme (which had been discovered in Honjo's laboratory in Japan and proposed to be an RNA editing enzyme) was envisaged as triggering all three processes of antibody gene diversification by targeted deamination of deoxycytidine to deoxyuridine residues in immunoglobulin gene DNA. Together with Svend Petersen-Mahrt, Reuben Harris, Javier Di Noia and Cristina Rada, Michael gathered evidence for this model, demonstrating a DNA-deaminating activity in AID itself, as well as showing that the pathways of antibody diversification were perturbed in a predictable way if enzymes involved in resolving the deoxyuridine lesion were removed. In collaboration with Michael Malim's laboratory in London, Reuben Harris and Michael showed that targeted DNA deamination is also used as an innate anti-retroviral strategy, accounting for some of the diversity seen in HIV sequences. Antibody gene diversification and DNA deamination continue as the major themes in Michael's current research.

Since 2002 Michael has been joint head of the PNAC Division, with Greg Winter. He was elected a Fellow of the Royal Society in 1993.

1. F. Sanger, 1988. Sequences, sequences and sequences. *Annual Review of Biochemistry*, 57, 1–28. With permission from the *Annual Review of Biochemistry*.
2. B.G. Barrell, G.M. Air and C.A. Hutchison III, 1976. *Nature*, 264, 34–41.
3. Sanger, *op. cit.*
4. F. Sanger, S. Nicklen and A.R. Coulson, 1977. DNA sequencing with chain-terminating inhibitors. *Proceedings of the National Academy of Sciences of the USA*, 74, 5463–5467.
5. A.M. Maxam and W. Gilbert, 1977. *Proceedings of the National Academy of Sciences of the USA*, 74, 560–564.
6. B. Gronenborn and J. Messing, 1978. Methylation of single-stranded DNA *in vitro* introduces new restriction endonuclease cleavage sites. *Nature*, 272, 375–377.
7. From 'Selected Papers of Frederick Sanger' – World Scientific Series in 20th Century Biology – Vol. 1, p. 343.
8. B.S. Hartley, 2003. How I became a biochemist. *IUBMB Life*, 55, 431–432.
9. J.P. Abrahams, A.G.W. Leslie, R. Lutter and John E. Walker, 1994. Structure at 2.8Å resolution of F1-ATPase from bovine heart mitochondria. *Nature*, 370, 621–628.
10. From an interview with César Milstein by David Secher at LMB in 1999.
11. *Ibid.*
12. J. Lederberg, 1959. Genes and antibodies. *Science*, 129, 1649–1653
13. S. Brenner and C. Milstein, 1966. Origin of antibody variation. *Nature*, 211, 242–243.
14. G. Köhler and C. Milstein, 1975. Continuous cultures of fused cells secreting antibody of predefined specificity. *Nature*, 256, 495–497.
15. E.M. Tansey and P.P. Catterall, 1996. Technology transfer in Britain: the case of monoclonal antibodies. *Contemporary Record*, 9, 409–444, and in *Wellcome Witnesses to Twentieth Century Medicine*, 1, April 1997. Both are transcripts of a Witness Seminar organised by the Wellcome Trust in September 1993.
16. P.H. Hamlyn, M.J. Gait and C. Milstein, 1981. Complete sequence of an immunoglobulin mRNA using specific priming and the dideoxynucleotide method of RNA sequencing. *Nucleic Acids Research*, 9, 4485–4494.
17. NRDC, the National Research and Development Corporation, had been set up after the war to exploit new inventions for the national interest following the debacle of the failure to patent penicillin. During the war, the head of the MRC and the President of the Royal Society had both opposed patenting penicillin as unethical for a life-saving drug, although the chief chemist involved, Ernst Chain, maintained that it was unethical not to protect the country against exploitation. As a result of non-patenting, the UK had to pay millions of pounds to use a method for producing penicillin on a large scale, devised in the USA in 1941. NRDC was therefore set up by the Attlee government in 1947 to commercialise British publicly-funded research. It was combined with the National Enterprise Board (NEB) in 1981 to form the British Technology Group (BTG), which was privatised in 1991 as BTG plc. The NEB was a government body set up in the UK by the Wilson government in 1975 to extend public ownership of industry, and so the aim in forming BTG was to combine the technological expertise of NRDC with the financial expertise of the NEB.

18. D. Dickson, 1979. California set to cash in on British discovery. *Nature*, 279, 663–664.
19. H. Schwartz, 1993. Talking points: American protectionism – the Schwartz view. *Scrip Magazine* (June), 6–7, quoted by David Secher in ref 15.
20. See note 17.
21. See note 17.
22. Tansey and Catterall, *op. cit.*
23. C. Milstein, 2000. With the benefit of hindsight. *Immunology Today*, 21, 359–364.
24. T.H. Rabbitts, 1976. Bacterial cloning of plasmids carrying copies of rabbit globin messenger RNA. *Nature*, 260, 221–225.
25. T. Boehm, R. Baer, I. Lavenir, A. Forster, J.J. Waters, E. Nacheva and T.H. Rabbitts, 1988. The mechanism of chromosomal translocation t(11;14) involving the T-cell receptor C(delta) locus on human chromosome 14q11 and a transcribed region of chromosome 11p15. *EMBO Journal*, 7, 385–394.
26. M.S. Neuberger, G T. Williams and R O. Fox, 1984. Recombinant antibodies possessing novel effector functions. *Nature*, 312, 604–608.
27. T. Jones, P.H. Dear, J. Foote, M.S. Neuberger and G. Winter, 1986. Replacing the complementarity-determining regions in a human antibody with those from a mouse. *Nature*, 321, 522–525.
28. M. Bruggemann, H.M. Caskey, C. Teale, H. Waldmann, G.T. Williams, M.A. Surani and M.S. Neuberger, 1989. A repertoire of monoclonal antibodies with human heavy chains from transgenic mice. *Proceedings of the National Academy of Sciences of the USA*, 86, 6709–6713.
29. Brenner and Milstein, *op. cit.*

CHAPTER NINE

Other Sections

THE MECHANICAL WORKSHOP

(Its name was changed in 1991 to Technical Instrumentation Workshop, though the name on the door is MRC Engineering Department.)

The Mechanical Workshop was headed in 1962 by Len Hayward, who had come with the Unit from the Cavendish. Len had joined the MRC Unit in 1956 as an instrument maker from the Pye company in Cambridge. (This was a large electrical and general instrument firm that ran its own technical training school, and it was from this background that many of the later LMB workshop staff were recruited. The original Pyes were the foreman of the Cambridge Scientific Instrument Company – started by Horace Darwin, son of Charles – and Horace's son, who was Rayleigh's technician at the Cavendish.[1]) Len had been accommodated in a small workshop in the basement of the Austin Wing at the Cavendish Laboratory with a few small milling machines and his personal lathe. (Len had converted this for finer work by incorporating an innovation with a left-hand thread, which made it rather confusing for other people to use.) As soon as the new space was available, Mick Fordham, a friend of Len's son, both of whom worked at Pye's, was enrolled and helped in the movement of equipment to LMB. Shortly after, Ernie Norman (from Pye), Vic Hayes (from the Cambridge Instrument Company) and Fred Walker (from Marshall's) joined, and as work built up, more feelers went out to Pye, and Mick Bitton and Dave Hart (father of Paul Hart, the current IT manager) were recruited, and in 1963, Tony Woollard to look after the running of the X-ray sets. (Tony was part of the techniques laboratory and since Len had not interviewed him, he was not that welcome in the workshop initially.) Chris Raeburn came in 1965, responding to an advertisement for an assistant for Tony, but Ken Holmes, recognising that he was an experienced toolmaker, persuaded Len to take him in that capacity. Steve Stubbings arrived in the workshop in 1972 via the stores and the electronics workshop. Steve Scotcher was initially a cleaner, but replaced Fred Walker when he retired.

250. *The original LMB workshop in 1963. The nearer three staff are, from the left, Ernie Norman, Mick Fordham and Len Hayward, the workshop head. Courtesy of Mick Fordham.*

252. *The workshop staff in 1983. From the left, Chris Raeburn, John Wasylyszyn, Terry Bailey, Steve Stubbings, Dave Hart (the workshop head), Mick Bitton, Mick Fordham, Tony Woollard and Fred Walker.*

251. The delivery of a new milling machine in 1963. Len Hayward is on the left and Mick Fordham on top. Courtesy of Cambridge Newspapers Ltd.

Although the workshop was well stocked with machinery – everyone had their own lathe – much of it was second-hand, commonly ex-war department, so when a new milling machine was delivered in 1963, it made news, and a picture of it being transferred by our loading crane into the workshop bay appeared in the *Cambridge Evening News* – with Mick Fordham standing on one end to keep it balanced upright.

X-ray generators

Much of the work at the beginning was connected to the X-ray sets, firstly re-installing the Broad rotating anode tubes that came up from the Cavendish (named after Tony Broad, their designer) and then modifying them (see chapter 6). The first modification was the idea of Ken Holmes and Bill Longley, to replace the electron gun by a design giving a smaller focus on the anode, and hence a brighter X-ray source for the same power. The next modification was to the anode. Ken Holmes and Hugh Huxley realised that more power could be put into the rotating anode by increasing its diameter, giving more circumference to disperse the heat accompanying the X-ray generation (Hugh had been worrying about X-ray intensity and focal spot heating and cooling since he began X-ray work in 1949). The diameter was set by the largest that could be accommodated in a workshop lathe – 24 inches. (Elliott's later version was 18 inches diameter, for probably the same reason.) To minimise weight, the anode was a cylindrical shell held together by spokes through which cooling water was directed towards the outer surface. X-rays were produced, but there was much trouble with internal water leaks. Hugh Huxley pointed out that with a more solid construction, the cooling water need not be piped to all the surface of the anode, but only to the main brass body. At this point Elliott's took over, and constructed a satisfactory working 18-inch anode. Three X-ray sets on this basis were installed in LMB and probably about 30 were manufactured and sold altogether before production ceased.

Densitometers
In addition to the X-ray tube work, the Flying Spot densitometer (see chapter 6) was being designed and built in the late 1960s. To cope with this and with other background work, more staff had been taken on but there was a need for more space. In 1968, therefore, the workshop was extended out towards what was then the car park, doubling its size. The major jobs after this continued to be for Structural Studies, including the various other densitometers (see chapter 6) and the Arndt/Wonacott rotation X-ray camera.

Densitometers continued to be important, both for the increasing number of X-ray films being produced, and also for measuring electron micrographs for image analysis and reconstruction purposes. A commercial instrument, the Optronics OP1000, was bought in 1972 for densitometering the X-ray films, but its step size was too big for the electron microscopy work being developed in 1973–74 by Richard Henderson and Nigel Unwin. Making photographic enlargements of the micrographs and densitometering these was not very satisfactory. At the Royal Greenwich Observatory at Herstmonceux, they had a Perkin Elmer PDS-1 with better resolution, but this proved very unreliable, and at the end of 1974 it was decided that there was a definite need for a new filmscanner. In 1975, Richard and Nigel tried to persuade Hugh Huxley to buy a PDS-1, with an available £120,000, but it was a choice between this and a new electron microscope, a Philips EM400, and the microscope won.

A 7μ scanner was being built at the Astronomy Department in Cambridge by Ed Kibblewhite, for £1 million and weighing three tons, and was intended for 12 inch by 12 inch whole star images. It wasn't ready at that time, but was later run by Mike Irwin, who had been David Blow's student at LMB. However, Richard and Nigel heard of a machine being built by Joyce-Loebl and in February 1974 visited their works at Gateshead. There was just one, used prototype, which had been used for development, with many problems and no data. In December 1974, the US company that had taken over Joyce-Loebl cancelled the project, having delivered one machine to eSystems in the USA (Perkin Elmer were already taking over the market), but they offered LMB all their remaining parts for £2,000. Richard and Mick Fordham hired a van and drove to Gateshead to collect them and found the machine had been stripped down to the castings, with hundreds of individual parts wrapped separately. They had one day to find out what was what and were given dozens of drawings to help. Back at the LMB, it was made operational, with the original lead screws and pancake motors, but it was not completely reliable. Shortly after, linear motors were fitted and, since 1977, with periodic upgrades, it has run very satisfactorily, and with a step size of 2.5μ, for a long time it was the best densitometer of its type in the world.

The confocal microscope

One of the most successful instruments with which the workshop was involved was the confocal microscope. This project was initiated by Aaron Klug in 1985. Since his involvement in optical and computing methods of processing electron microscope images, he had followed developments in optics and had come across papers on confocal microscopy, a technique involving scanning, by which the resolution of microscope images, especially in depth, could be improved by reducing or eliminating out-of-focus blurring. By chance, Aaron was given a paper on chromatin structure to review,[2] in which Brakenhoff in the Netherlands convincingly demonstrated that confocal imaging could essentially eliminate out-of-focus blur in fluorescence images of a biological specimen.

Excited by this, he told John White, who had been trying to study changes during the development of the embryo of the nematode *C. elegans* by immunofluorescence-staining of whole-mount embryos. The resulting images had been disappointingly degraded by out-of-focus flare. John began considering the application of confocal techniques for these studies, but after looking at the various instruments available, decided he could do better. He produced a design that used oscillating and rotating mirrors for scanning the beam rather than the stationary beam and scanning stage systems used by others. There were two other key innovations. A large variable pinhole was included, allowing a compromise to be struck between ideal confocal performance (infinitesimally small pinhole) and high signal levels (wide pinhole). Also an ordinary microscope eyepiece was used as the scanning lens for the laser beam – this made it possible to build the system as an external add-on to a conventional light microscope. John gave a presentation on this to the Workshop Committee, which after some suggestions accepted the project.

Mick Fordham constructed the first instrument, paying special attention to the mechanical design to make it easy to align optically. It was built in the workshop enclosed in old blackout material, which became known as the Bedouin Tent. The project was joined by Brad Amos, who had an excellent background in biological microscopy, and by Richard Durbin, John White's research student, who had outstanding programming skills. This prototype was tested on a variety of specimens with dramatic improvements in image details. The results were sent in to the *Journal of Cell Biology*, and the paper accepted with a request by one of the editors to purchase the instrument as soon as possible.[3]

A drawback of John White's patented design was that it required relatively high scan angles and the scanning beam was relayed into the microscope by refractive telescopes, which produced chromatic aberration and consequent difficulties in imaging multicoloured preparations. There was also no provision for a transmission image. Brad devised and patented an all-mirror relay system (using galvanometer mirrors) for scanning the beam and a transmission pick-up (not patentable) which allowed the formation of all types of non-confocal transmission image in register with the confocal image.

Richard Durbin wrote the powerful and elegant software for the system which made it easy to use. It was so good that it had an independent commercial life as an early image-processing package.

A second version was constructed quickly, with the inclusion of an expensive image grabber (a framestore obtained by Aaron from the Engineering Department), which allowed real time data collection and calculation and, in particular, permitted frame-averaging to be performed with a huge improvement in image quality. The result was a working instrument, much more compact than any other instrument then available and ready for commercial exploitation.[4,5] All this was done in the face of the government's then doctrinaire attitude that no 'near market' research was to be carried out in Public Sector Research Establishments, but turned over to private industry.

In spite of its obvious marketability, none of the major microscope companies was interested in taking it on commercially. As late as 1987, the main European manufacturer, Zeiss, asserted that this 'so-called confocal microscope would be too complex and delicate an instrument to be worth manufacturing'. The MRC selected a US company, Bio-Rad, mainly because of its strong marketing organisation, but manufacture and R&D were both carried out entirely in Britain, providing about 60 jobs and initially only very small changes from the prototype to the commercial instrument were required. A pre-production prototype, which had been developed within LMB at the wise insistence of John White, was shown to Bio-Rad in May 1987. Full constructional details and abundant help were supplied to them, and they were thus able to begin shipping units to purchasers in the USA

253. The Queen's Award for Technology, 1991 for the development of the confocal microscope. From the left, Brad Amos, Richard Durbin, Mick Fordham and John White.

by Christmas 1987. This was a remarkable but absolutely necessary achievement since the microscope manufacturers, particularly Zeiss, were quick to realise their mistake in neglecting confocal technology and were hurrying to produce competing models. The impact, particularly in the USA, was so great that *Science* showed a cartoon with a small child asking Father Christmas for a confocal laser-scanning microscope.

In 1991, LMB was awarded the Queen's Award for Technology, and BioRad, the Queen's Award for Export. In 1994, the Cambridge team were awarded the Royal Society's Mullard Medal in recognition of their work. (For the McRoberts Engineering Award, the microscope was in the final three, but was beaten by the Mini Metro which had a fairly unique engine.)

From 1997, Brad revised the design, substituting a Keplerian telescope for the long optical path of the original design, making the system much smaller. He also introduced many other innovations, particularly optical jigs for production purposes, the use of optical fibres and a lens system for increasing signal strength at the expense of confocal performance. This gave rise to the *Radiance* and *CellMap* series of models. With the *Radiance*, the company was able to keep a reasonable market share in the 1990s, but the competition from established microscope companies had become fierce.

In 2004, Bio-Rad sold the UK scanning laser microscope business to Zeiss, who promptly discontinued all the models and closed the factory. Over the nineteen years of the project, well over 2,000 microscope systems had been manufactured to the White/Amos design, and royalties of over a million pounds had been paid to the MRC. Unfortunately, these royalties were halved and then frozen altogether in the latter years as a result of litigation by Zeiss.

Other work

Although the aim in the workshop was always prototype development with outsourcing of all background repetitive jobs, one that got through was the making of miniaturised gel-electrophoresis devices. These had been developed in LMB, largely by Paul Matsudaira around 1984, and became very popular both here and as a hidden export (taken back to their home laboratories by many visitors). Attempts were made to farm their construction out, but the standards and tolerances were not maintained by the firms building them, and the workshop staff spent so much time modifying the results that it was more satisfactory for them to make them in the first place, though it took over much of their time. Eventually a local firm, Engineering and Design Plastics, became interested and created a new company, Cambridge Electrophoresis, to manufacture them.

Chris Raeburn's speciality has been modifying the electron microscopes as techniques needed to be developed before the manufacturers could build them in – for example, enabling low dose work to be done by Nigel Unwin on the Philips 301 and introducing CCD detectors with Wasi Faruqi as well as much work on cryo-stages.

Len Hayward, the first workshop head, died in 1974, and was succeeded by Dave Hart. In 1984 the laboratory was reviewed by a Dr Bard from the Management Services Group. The resulting Bard Review was critical about the way work was done via the workshop and Dave thought he was being unfairly blamed for the system and applied for a job advertised by Schlumberger, at a Cambridge section of the firm connected with the oil industry. His application was successful and he joined them, taking Terry Bailey with him as his deputy. Dave Hart was succeeded by Mick Bitton as workshop head until he died in 1990, then by Mick Fordham until 2000, and since then, by Roger Lucke.

THE TECHNIQUES LABORATORY – ELECTRONICS

This was the name given initially to the general service staff other than those in the mechanical workshop. It was headed by John Fasham, an electrical engineer who had taken over from Tony Broad just before the move to LMB. It included apprentice technicians Paul Phizackerley and Barry Ambrose, and Tom Allison. Paul became a PhD student of Uli Arndt in 1967 and investigated the optimum ways of collecting X-ray data by the crystal-oscillating method which was subsequently used in the Arndt/Wonacott camera. After finishing his thesis, Paul went to the USA and is now a professor at Stanford, running the X-ray beam line there. Barry also worked with Uli Arndt on image intensifiers, but left in 1967 and formed his own small component and instrument firm.

Tony Woollard was also included in this section to begin with, but became part of the general Structural Studies technical staff, outside the workshop. He had been hired in 1963, to look after the X-ray sets, although he had had no experience of these and none of vacuum systems. The Broad X-ray tubes were fitted with vacuum safety switches which ideally would switch off the sets if the vacuum deteriorated. These switches were controlled by Penning vacuum gauges, which were over sensitive to contamination and to the occasional sparks from the high voltage system inside the X-ray tube. Sometimes these troubles prevented the tubes running for any length of time and Bill Longley showed Tony that the way round this was to remove the gauge from the safety circuit, and, provided nothing catastrophic occurred, X-rays were continuously available. John Fasham was, however, shocked by this and insisted it be reconnected, and so initially there was some friction until Tony became more confident and took over completely. Arising from the work on

254. Tony Woollard with the big-wheel X-ray generator, c. 1989.

the X-ray tubes, he became the laboratory specialist in curing general vacuum system troubles.

Tony lived through the development of the X-ray tubes and their takeover by Elliotts and became an expert in knowing the symptoms of ailing sets and curing them. He was also involved with setting up new X-ray cameras as they became available. He retired in 2001.

In the early stages, after John Fasham left in 1965, the group was overseen by George Grindley, but with the growth of electronically controlled systems, there was a parallel growth in the staff dealing with them. In 1971, Alec Wynn joined LMB and became head of the electronics workshop, formed including Barry Canning, Chris Bond and Mike Thompson. Howard Andrews and David Cattermole came in 1982 and Martin Kyte in 1992. Ian Bland was also included in this section – Ian was an electron microscope service engineer from Philips who was persuaded to join LMB permanently in that capacity. Alec retired in 1989, was succeeded by Barry Canning, followed by Howard Andrews in 1997.

The remainder of the group included Bill Whybrow, who had come to LMB in 1963 as a technician with Alfred Tissières, preparing ribosomes for him before Alfred returned to Geneva in 1964. Bill then joined Brian Clark in Cell Biology and transferred to Sydney when Brian left, and then on to dealing with general LMB safety matters until he retired in 1997. Michael Fuller oversaw a subgroup that looked after the instrumental servicing side, including Tom Allison, Keith Horton and Paul Hart who came in 1982. These were absorbed into the electronics workshop after about 1984. Towards the end of the 1980s, there was a considerable growth in the number of personal computers in the laboratory and Paul assumed responsibility for looking after these, obtaining certification by Apple to fix Macs, and later building up the Information Technology Section with Marc North and Wayne Rednall. Tom

255. Bill Whybrow, 1987.

Allison, who specialised in repairing small instruments, retired in 1992, was succeeded by Harold Hopkins, followed by Geoffrey Wills in 1994.

THE LIBRARY

David Blow was responsible for setting up the library in the new LMB and was the over-librarian for the first two or three years. I took over until I retired in 1995. I was succeeded by Stephen Hunt, and in 2002 by Sean Munro. The library was located at the west end of the third floor until 2003, when it was moved to the east end of the ground floor into space vacated by the Haematology Department when that moved into the Titanic.

Joan Blows was initially in charge of day-to-day running on a part-time basis until 1966 when Elsie Cousins was appointed for this full-time. Elsie was a great sports enthusiast – organising the darts evenings, and an enthusiastic supporter of the cricket and football teams. Unhappily, Elsie died from cancer in 1976. Mary Dowsing then took over the library. When copying machines became available in the laboratory, popular journals began to disappear as soon as they were received while people made copies of the contents. To get around this, photocopies of the contents pages of these journals were pinned up so that anyone requiring a copy could tick and initial an article they would like to be copied. It was however too

256. *The original LMB library in mint condition, 1962. The space at the west end of the building on the third floor is now occupied by the laboratory T19. Photo: Ramsey & Muspratt, D16/0. Courtesy of Cambridgeshire Collection, Cambridgeshire Libraries.*

easy, and so much copying was generated that help was required to cope – the main task of Wanda Bullock when she first came to LMB in 1979 as a part-time assistant, with Edna Eusden. But the procedure was very wasteful, many of the copies were not even collected, and the arrangement was stopped (as Sydney put it – *Neurox it, not Xerox*). Wanda left the library in 1986 and moved to Reception full-time, but she returned to the library in 1988 to take over when Mary Dowsing retired. Wanda remained librarian until retiring in 2003, being succeeded by Ian Walker, with Wanda continuing as a part-time assistant.

The growth in size and number of journals soon filled the three modules of the original 1962 library and overflowing volumes were accommodated in more and higher shelving around the walls, across windows and in free-standing shelving installed in the working space. A solution to the squash appeared in 1980, when the Clinical School was built next door. The MRC was financially included in this, with the idea of combining our library in with the new Medical Library with its vast amount of space. But after second thoughts in the LMB, it was decided to keep our library for current journals and about the latest five years, and house earlier

volumes in the Medical Library. This has worked fairly well except for the irrita-
tion of looking up things that happened about five years ago and span the two
libraries. But journals continue to grow and the extra module provided for the new
library in 2000 was welcome – in spite of the growth of e-journals.

ARCHIVES

Despite the many exciting results that have come from the laboratory since the
MRC Unit was set up in 1947, and the prestigious awards to the people working
in it and the subsequent and other publicity, the setting up of an Archive Section in
LMB to collect together material to record its history has been a relatively new
development. It stems mainly from an intrinsic interest of Margaret Brown who,
as personal assistant to the Director (or Chairman) from 1965 to 1996, came into
contact with much archive-appropriate material, such as photographs, newspaper
cuttings and articles relevant to the laboratory, and began making a collection.

Margaret's retirement, in 1996, coincided with that of Aaron Klug as Director,
and the new Director, Richard Henderson, was concerned that the younger people
in the laboratory were becom-
ing less aware of its history and
the achievements of the founding members of LMB – their
many outstanding and historic
discoveries. He was keen to
retain a communal memory of
these, feeling that this could be
valuable to us in the future,
providing a cultural background from which further
research goals or an LMB
research style might evolve in a
positive way. So Margaret was
persuaded to continue part-
time, partly to continue work
with Aaron and partly to create

257. Margaret Brown at her retirement dinner, 1996.

the formal archives. Richard was also keen that we should build up a complete
database of alumni so that we could keep in contact and benefit from occasional
interaction or advice. Margaret began work on this, but shortly after, in 1998, died
of cancer.

Her part-time archive work was taken over by Kirsty Knott. Kirsty was a student of Vivien Perutz (Max's daughter) at the Cambridge College of Arts and
Technology, studying Art and Architecture, and she needed a part-time job while
recovering from injuries resulting from being run over by a car. She left in 2000,
having recovered sufficiently to take a full-time job in London.

The part-time work of Margaret and Kirsty had shown the value of an LMB Archivist, and was sufficient to persuade the MRC to allow LMB to create a full-time post. Annette Faux – who had been the librarian for ten years at the Biochemistry Department – was recruited and began work in 2001, and was more-or-less immediately involved in the organisation of the DNA50 celebrations in 2003.

The archive collection has a growing selection of photographs, books, tapes and documents of various sorts and the database of alumni is complete to date. Video-interviews have been recorded of Francis Crick (1997), John Kendrew (1997), César Milstein (1999), Aaron Klug (2001) and Hugh Huxley (2004), and audio-interviews of several other notables in the history of LMB. In addition to organising the collection, Annette has become the first call for information on the laboratory, for both external and internal inquiries.

PHOTOGRAPHY – VISUAL AIDS

258. Ken Harvey, 1965.   *259. Annette Snazle (now Lenton) and Caroline Barrell, 1965.*

From 1965, the Photography Section was headed by Ken Harvey, initially with just Caroline Barrell as an assistant. A small room on the third floor accommodated the printing facilities. Ken's predecessor had apparently been a keen student of the turf – on the darkroom walls was a collection of graphs recording racehorse performances (probably a result of our not being too far from Newmarket). In 1968, the old canteen was vacated. This occupied what is now all the visual aids area at the west end of the fourth floor, but only half of this was given initially to photography. The rest was used for model-building – wire models were still being built using

Richards Boxes, and the combined volumes of these were enormous, and had over-filled the designated model room on the first floor. The structure of tRNA was built in the fourth floor room in 1974 – a way of keeping it 'under wraps', since there was much competition in that field. (Aaron installed a padlock when Alex Rich was visiting.)

Ken was taken up in a Tiger Moth (biplane) from Marshall's to photograph one of the laboratory extensions being built, and remembers that they were warned to beware of Messerschmitts – the *Battle of Britain* film was being made at Duxford, and frequent dogfights could be seen between them and Spitfires, usually ending in a diving plane emitting clouds of smoke. The canteen balcony provided a good viewing place for these.

Annette Lenton (then Annette Snazle) came to LMB in 1966 as a 'clerical assistant' – nominally as an assistant to Audrey Martin, but her duties included helping Joan Blows in the Library, working in the Stores and on the phone switchboard and helping the computer girls plotting contours. She was initially housed in the corridor (even then there was pressure on space), but was later accommodated with the computer girls. Her artistic skill was noticed by Paul Sigler, and gradually her role developed into that of full-time illustrator. However, her base on the first floor, far from the photographers, was not very convenient and so, when the possibility of joining the expanded photography section occurred in 1968, Annette was pleased to escape from being under the prim eye of Audrey Martin and moved with Ken and Caroline to the fourth floor, producing illustrations then for the whole laboratory. Apart from a break for family-raising between 1976 and 1989, she has remained with the section.

260. Visual Aids Group, c. 1997. From the left, Shirley Wheeler, Neil Grant, Annette Lenton, Graham Lingley, Anna Marriage, Joanna Westmoreland and Brian Pashley, the head of the group.

Although the Visual Aids Department became part of the MRC Centre and provides services for all the local MRC Units, its numbers have not increased vastly – six at maximum under Ken Harvey (two illustrators and four photographers), and seven under Brian Pashley, who took over when Ken retired in 1986. There has, of course, been a considerable change in technology, from photographs and negatives to electronic methods and from slides to PowerPoint. The group took over the whole of the old canteen space in 1997. Neil Grant joined the group in 1983, Graham Lingley in 1987, Joanna Westmorland in 1992 and both Lesley McKeane and Paul Margiotta in1997.

PEPTIDE AND NUCLEIC ACID CHEMISTRY AND SYNTHESIS

When the first building extension, with thirteen extra bays, was completed in 1968, one complete floor remained empty, being reserved for new groups. One of these, the peptide chemistry group, was established in 1971 under Bob Sheppard, from the University of Liverpool. There was a general interest in LMB in how polypeptide chains folded up into proteins and it was thought that by synthesising short lengths of peptides, their folding behaviour could be studied, hopefully giving some insight into the *in vivo* mechanism.

261. Peptide and Nucleic Acid Chemistry Group, 1980. Front: Willy Hübscher, Vivienne Woolley, Brian Williams and Bob Sheppard, the head of the group. Rear: Evelyn Brown, Richard Titmas, Eric Atherton, Mike Gait, Mohinder Singh, Hans Matthes, Leo Benoiton and John Wade.

Partial synthesis was the most straightforward method to begin with – chopping off small sections from a protein and synthesising new replacements, and the first protein to be investigated in this way was the small bovine pancreatic trypsin inhibitor, BPTI. Tom Creighton had joined LMB in 1967 and had become interested in the folding problem and studying BPTI. A joint project was therefore set up to investigate the effects on folding of small changes in sequence.

Although relatively straightforward, the partial synthesis method was slow and selective in its possibilities. The solid phase method – adding blocked amino acids one at a time to a chain anchored to a polystyrene resin bead, de-blocking and adding the next, introduced by Merrifield at the Rockefeller University in 1965 – was quicker, but had its own drawbacks. Eric Atherton, who joined the peptide group in 1972, began a study of the chemistry involved with the solid phase and introduced a modified polyamide support resin to replace polystyrene and this considerably improved the solvation properties – the stability in solvents used to minimise the aggregation of the growing polypeptide and hence keep its growing end accessible. In 1976, Chris Logan helped devise a blocking group which required much milder conditions in use (for removal or neutralisation). In 1977, Reza Arshady, an experienced polymer chemist, came and devised a method of producing homogeneous preparations of the polyamide beads rather than specimens consisting largely of amorphous aggregates. In 1980, a local biochemical company, Cambridge Research Biochemicals Ltd (CRB), took over much of the routine preparations of materials being developed by the group and also used it for custom peptide synthesis. The company later became part of the Zeneca organisation, and Eric Atherton left to join it in 1985. In 1989, the laboratory was granted a Queen's Award jointly with CRB for the peptide synthesis developments.

The group was initially part of the PNAC division, and with the nucleic acid sequencing going on then, the need for oligonucleotide sequences to be synthesised was made known to them. As a result, Mike Gait arrived in 1975 – the first non-peptide chemist in the group. He came from a two-year postdoc fellowship making synthetic genes in Khorana's laboratory at MIT, and soon showed that the new polyamide supports greatly improved the synthesis of polynucleotides. From then until 1984, the group was in a leading position in this field until overtaken by the machine technology of Applied Biosystems using the chemistry of Caruthers in Colorado. In 1985, Mike Gait set up an oligonucleotide service using this chemistry.

Bob Sheppard retired from the laboratory in 1994, having set up the service system for the synthesis of polypeptides, as well as continuing and overseeing peptide research. Tony Johnson took over until 1996, when he left to join a small firm Peptide Therapeutics in Cambridge, with Martin Quibell. In 1996 Mike Gait, who had set up his own group in 1980, investigating mainly RNA-involved systems such as RNA synthesis, RNA catalysis and protein-RNA recognition, took over responsibility for all the chemistry in LMB.

Another member of this group was Dan Brown, who had joined LMB in 1981 after retiring from the Chemistry Department in Cambridge. In the early 1950s, with Alexander Todd, he had worked on the basic chemistry of nucleotides and nucleic acids, establishing some of the facts that provided a basis for Watson and Crick's establishment of the double helical structure. He had continued working on nucleic acids, including deducing the mechanism of action of hydroxylamine as a mutagen. At LMB, he has synthesised degenerate bases – pyrimidines that can emulate either cytosine or thymine and purines that can emulate adenine or guanine – and also a 'universal' base that can base-pair to any of the four normal bases. One idea was to get over the problem of not being able to predict the nucleotide sequence coding for an amino acid sequence because of the genetic code degeneracy in the third base of the codons. This sequence is required, for example, for priming in the polymerase chain reaction. However, oligonucleotides containing the degenerate bases can act as the required hybridisation probes and primers.

262. *Dan Brown, 1984.*

Dan was elected a Fellow of the Royal Society in 1982, and retired from LMB in 2000. Greg Winter's farewell speech given at his retirement is reproduced in chapter 10.

DIRECTOR'S SECTION

This was established in 1981, soon after Sydney Brenner became Director, and gathered together those working in his particular interests. This initially included Leslie Barnett, Jon Karn, Ed Lennox, John Sulston and Bill Whybrow, and gradually grew taking in David East (from 1983), Eric Atherton (1984) and Sean Heaphy, working with Jon Karn on HIV (1985). After Aaron Klug became Director in1986, the Peptide and Nucleic Acid Group was included, with Mike Gait and Bob Sheppard, Rodger Staden and Michel Goedert, and later, Colin Dingwall (1987), Richard Durbin, Tony Johnson and Bill Turnell (1990).

After Richard Henderson succeeded Aaron in 1996, although some of the scientific posts remain attached to the Director's Section, providing short-term flexibility, the people in these posts are attached to the main Divisions and effectively only non-scientific staff such as Ian Walker, the librarian and Annette Faux, the archivist, are firmly in the Director's Section. The Stores and Visual Aids Sections, though formally part of the MRC Centre, largely serve LMB.

COMPUTERS AND COMPUTING

Main computers

- EDSAC1 in Maths Laboratory, Cambridge (1949–1958) – used for the first Fourier map of a protein – myoglobin at 6Å resolution in 1957 (published in 1958).
- EDSAC2 (1958–1965) – used for haemoglobin at 5.5Å in 1959, for myoglobin at 2Å in 1959, and by Rossman and Blow for the early rotation function work.
- IBM7090 at IBM in London (1962–1964), with the advantage of FORTRAN – used in the later work of Rossmann and Blow, and by Ken Holmes for TMV calculations.
- IBM7090 at Imperial College – used instead of IBM's machine, 1964–1970.
- Titan in Maths Laboratory (1964–1973) – used for haemoglobin work in 1966. Autocode, the first higher-level language was introduced in 1965, followed later, after pressure from scientific users, by FORTRAN.
- IBM360/44 at the Institute of Theoretical Astronomy, Madingley Road (IOTA) (1968–1974) – took over all the crystallographic computing.
- IBM370/165 at Maths Laboratory (1974–1982). In 1975 a 'Remote Job Entry' card reader and line-printer output, both communicating directly with the Maths Laboratory, were installed at LMB, and the Phoenix command language was introduced.
- Vax 11/780 (1982–1987), the first of LMB's in-house main computers, introduced the VMS command system.
- Vax 8600 (1987–1991).
- Alliant from 1991 introduced the transition to Unix.
- Dec alf1 from 1994, alf2 added 1995. Alf1 + alf2 replaced with a new alf1 in August 1999, and by another in August 2003.

JANET

Our internet and email facilities are provided by our connection to JANET, the Joint Academic Network, which was created in 1984. Its internet protocol service began in 1991. SuperJANET involved the introduction of a fibre optics network which began operation in 1993, with a considerable increase in speed, and introduced the possibility of video traffic.

Control computers

Argus 400 was installed in 1963 initially to control the X-ray diffractometer, but subsequently for use in plotting and densitometry. After about ten years a PDP11/10 took over the control of the diffractometer and other PDP11s were acquired to control the Optronics film scanner and the Evans and Sutherland

Vector Graphics model display system. The PDP11 was superseded by the minia-turised version LSI11, which became the standard instrumentation machine in the laboratory.

Crystallographic computing

Max's first Fourier maps (Pattersons) had used Beevers-Lipson strips for calculating the projections (1947) and a Hollerith tabulator to calculate the three-dimensional map (1949). But in 1954, when John Kendrew's group obtained phase angles (by hand-drawn constructions) for myoglobin, and electron density maps could be calculated, the computer at the Cambridge Maths Laboratory, EDSAC1, was available.

EDSAC1 (Electronic Delay Storage Automatic Calculator) was first operational in 1949, calculating the squares of integers 1 to 99 and printing them out and tak-ing 2 minutes 35 seconds to do it. Programmes and data were read in from paper tape. It was built from 3,000 war-surplus thermionic valves (vacuum tubes) and consumed about 12kW. Apart from the scale, this part was fairly straightforward to put together, using wartime experience (and much other war surplus material).

263. Some of the valve racks of the computer EDSAC1 in the Maths Laboratory, Cambridge, which first ran in 1949 and was used by John Kendrew to calculate the first map of a protein molecule, myoglobin, in 1957. Courtesy of the Computer Laboratory, University of Cambridge.

However, the idea of memory – the storage of data and instructions – in such a machine was new. Adapting an idea thought of for use with radar in the war, delay lines of mercury were developed. These were cylinders five feet in length and capable of storing 576 ultrasonic pulses by sending them in from one end of a column of mercury with one piezo-electric crystal, and collecting them at the other end with another and recycling them with a cycle time of about 1msec. The 576 pulses were split into 32, 18-bit words. Initially a battery of sixteen delay lines was functional, with a total of 512 words of main memory. Later in its life another battery was added.

(EDSAC1 was the world's first working electronic stored-program computer to be available for serious mathematical work. It was, however, preceded by a 'baby' experimental computer at Manchester University which ran first in June 1948, and used CRT screens for storage. The first major working digital electronic computer was the Mark 1 Colossus, which began work at Bletchley Park in 1943, followed by ENIAC, built in Philadelphia, which began work in 1945, but neither of these stored programs and were effectively wired up to do particular jobs.)

Hugh Huxley had a friend in the Maths Laboratory – John Bennett – and together (towards the end of 1949) they produced the first two-dimensional Fourier synthesis program to calculate a Patterson projection. Hugh then moved away from myoglobin into muscle research and so John Kendrew, after a few months of tuition from John Bennett, began writing programs himself. EDSAC1 was a bit temperamental in its running. If it failed at night or at weekends, no technical help was available and users were left to their own initiative to try to get it going again. Often the gains in the valves had to be adjusted by turning up potentiometers, but since it was difficult to be sure which potentiometer correlated with which valve, these adjustments could well make things worse. John Kendrew remembered that particularly quirky valves were prodded with an India rubber by Eric Mutch (and no one else was allowed to do this). He recalled working with EDSAC1, if it was running, for complete weekends, being brought sandwiches by his wife Elizabeth or friends.

EDSAC1 was used for calculating the 6Å Fourier map of myoglobin from amplitudes and phases of 400 reflections calculated by hand from five derivatives. It took 70 minutes, and the density was plotted on sixteen sections printed on a teleprinter in a single digit output. EDSAC1 ran from 1947 to 1958, when EDSAC2 became operational.

EDSAC2 was used for the 2Å myoglobin map and for the 5.5Å haemoglobin map. It was again built from valves, since semi-conductors were only just appearing. The mercury storage tubes were replaced by ferrite cores, which could be magnetised either way to store 0 or 1. These were developed during the design, and provided a main memory of 1,024 words. There was also a reserved read-only store with information, such as input/output routines and useful subroutines, permanently available. From 1959, extra storage on magnetic tape appeared.

During the haemoglobin work, Michael Rossmann tried to get Max involved in the computing. Max was not very keen, but was persuaded to feed a paper tape into the reader. Immediately, there was a strong smell of burning and clouds of smoke appeared. Max said 'I told you I should not have done it'. There was a delay of about a week for repairs, which was frustrating, especially for John Kendrew who was next in the queue. It was just unfortunate that the fault occurred with Max – such things happened from time to time with the EDSACs, whoever was using them.

Valerie Coulson remembers being given a guided tour of the EDSAC facility,

in the course of which I was shown what seemed to be room after room filled with row-upon-row of banks of valves. I was also shown the whereabouts of no fewer than nine different fire extinguishers scattered about the place. After signing a form to say that I knew the locations of all the fire extinguishers, I was given a piece of paper which declared me to be a 'partially authorized user'. Then I was left to my own devices. Alas the tour had not included showing me where to feed in the paper tape or explain the system of queuing used.

The early calculations of Michael Rossman and David Blow, developing computer methods to exploit non-crystallographic symmetry and to use numerical methods to calculate phase angles, also used EDSAC2. However, they found it and its machine code limiting and were keen on changing to an IBM7090 machine and using FORTRAN. After the move to the new laboratory in 1962, they applied successfully for free time at an IBM installation in London. (IBM had been refused planning permission to establish a Cambridge base.) This led to the only strike to occur at LMB. Packs of punched cards, held together with elastic bands, were taken up by train to London by one of the computing assistants, and then by underground or taxi – specified by the MRC accounts people according to the weight of the cards, or if there were more than two boxes – to the IBM headquarters off Oxford Street in London. (Their computing room was used in the film *Dr Strangelove* for Peter Sellers to press a console handswitch and send all the tape-drives into fast reverse – very impressive.) The LMB had a pre-booked time for their run during the evening and then taxi/underground back to the station for the Cambridge train. The computer assistants were not paid overtime for this transporting, as they would have liked, but given time off *in lieu*. One day's refusal to take the cards was sufficient for Audrey Martin to persuade MRC to pay overtime – the first for MRC employees.

Valerie Coulson remembers that being able to take a taxi to IBM also had its down side, since claims could only be made for the fare and not any tip. Tipping had therefore to be paid out of the meal allowance. She tried not tipping one evening and learnt several new words as the driver expressed himself on the situation.

Tony Sainty remembered dropping some packs on a tube platform during the rush hour one evening and collected up some rather grubby, trodden-on cards in random order, and did not expect to be well received on his return to the laboratory – but it happened on the evening of one of the Nobel celebration parties and everyone at LMB was in a rosy, forgiving mood.

After the free computing time at IBM was used up, paying for the facility proved expensive, and an arrangement was made with Imperial College, who also had an IBM7090, and this was used until 1970.

In parallel with the IBM machines in London, some of the computing was still being done at the Maths Laboratory using EDSAC2 to start with and from 1964, TITAN. TITAN was a joint venture between the Maths Laboratory and Ferranti and was a modified version of a machine called ATLAS which was being developed by Ferranti. It was designed to support multiple-access for up to 64 terminals, and to connect with magnetic tapes. The first higher-level language was Autocode, though FORTRAN was later introduced under pressure from scientific users. Hilary Muirhead used this machine for much of the haemoglobin work at this time, before changing to the IBM360 at Fred Hoyle's Institute of Theoretical Astronomy (IOTA) in Madingley Road. From 1970 to 1974, most of the LMB computing was done on the IOTA machine for which LMB shared the cost.

TITAN ran until 1973 and was then superseded in the Maths Laboratory by an IBM370/165, which we began using in 1974. At this time, it was still a case of transporting punched cards to and from the computer, plus magnetic tapes for data or output. However, in 1975, we installed a 'Remote Job Entry' card reader and line-printer output communicating directly with the Maths Laboratory, and in 1976 VDU connections began to appear, superseding teletype machines, both using their home-built operating system, Phoenix.

Our first in-house large computer, a Vax11/780, was acquired in 1982 followed by the 8600 from 1987, both using VMS. In 1991, after much deliberation, the Vax was replaced by an Alliant, a parallel(26)-processer, with a transition to Unix. Unfortunately, the US makers more-or-less immediately went into a 'Chapter 11' situation (not quite bankrupt), leaving problems regarding servicing and updating. It was, however, kept going until 1994, when the first of the series of Dec-alphas, 'alf1', arrived.

Paper tape
In the late 1950s and 1960s, much of the communication to and from machines was via five- and later eight-holed paper tape, and using this is recalled with mixed feelings. Angela Mott remembers splicing them with navy blue sticky tape and also throwing them down the five-flight stairwell to disentangle the coiled mass when their centres had fallen out. They also showed one's programs zipping through the tape reader when their slot got more time because the diffractometer program had crashed – the sheer visibilty of early time-sharing.

Valerie Coulson remembers:

> the haemoglobin group used a lot of paper tape and I spent a lot of time patching and splicing, and consequently picked up the simple code and used to read through

the tape quite fast to get to where I needed to make a modification. I was sitting at my desk doing this one day (it must have been the weekend because I was alone in the room) when Bill Longley came in with some American visitors he was showing around. I didn't look up straight away as I was afraid of losing my place on the tape. Bill stood for a moment in silence and then said 'This is our automatic tape reading machine. We call it Valerie'. Early on in my time at the lab, Scott Mathews showed me a large collection of paper tapes. 'We're not going to need these any more', he said, 'so you can pack them all away in cardboard boxes, label them and store them on the top shelf.' I was puzzled. 'If we're not going to need these tapes any more, why bother to keep them?', I asked. I have always loved his reply: 'Because you're a careful worker.' There was no response to that one.

The tapes were available in different colours and, in later years, out of date ones made quite good party decorations.

THE CANTEEN

264. *The original LMB canteen in 1962. It was on the west end of the fourth floor of LMB, in space now occupied by the Visual Aids Group. Photo: Ramsey & Muspratt, D16/C. Courtesy of Cambridgeshire Collection, Cambridgeshire Libraries.*

Since there were no local alternatives, it was recognised that a canteen was a necessity for the new building in 1962. But apart from this, Max was very enthusiastic for it – to provide a place where people could chat over morning coffee, lunch and tea, and stimulate the exchange of ideas. He had noticed that laboratories often failed because their scientists never talked to each other. Max was also keen on there being no 'class distinction' – at the Cavendish, for example, there were three tea-rooms catering for the scientific, the technical and the secretarial staff, all rigidly segregated. At LMB, there was (and is) one canteen with one queue for all. It was overseen for over twenty years by Max's wife, Gisela.

(The workshop staff is the one group in LMB that has never used the canteen in a routine way – probably a hangover from the systems in the workshops where they were trained and became used to eating lunch and having coffee and tea together by their machines.)

Initially the canteen was on the west end of the fourth floor, in the space now occupied by Visual Aids, and was a great success as a meeting place between the different groups – a catalyst for joint projects. It was not served by a lift, however –

265. Gisela Perutz on her retirement from looking after the canteen.

the local planners would not allow the building to be above the general skyline, and this limited the laboratory to the height of the lift-motor housing on the fourth floor. But much higher buildings were soon allowed on the site and, when the first laboratory extension was built in 1969, a new larger canteen was included at the opposite end of the building to accommodate the increase in staff, and a lift to this floor was included. Gisela Perutz was again involved in the design and its running to begin with, but later she left this to a committee of members of the laboratory and the canteen staff as it became a more full-time job.

In the early days, the computer girls and secretaries took turns at the cash register. Valerie Coulson remembers panicking a few times when there was a rush,

> and instead of looking up the prices of individual meals or their components, I hit on the strategy of just charging everyone half a crown. It certainly helped the queue to move and nobody actually complained, although I did get a few funny looks, presumably from people who had the same thing the day before at a different price!

The lady running the canteen at the time, Mrs Tynsdale (famous for her scones) always kept her eye on one chap she didn't trust and would come dashing over: 'Watch out for X, he has a boiled egg hidden under his lettuce. Make sure you charge him for it.'

Joy Fordham came in 1967 for two weeks, while Ruth Lee, the assistant to Mrs Tynsdale, was on maternity leave. But Ruth did not return, and Joy stayed on as her replacement. From 1969, Joy and Shirley Davis took over the running of the canteen. In those days the canteen staff had an hour off for lunch and as Shirley had previously worked as a hair stylist, the staff were able to have haircuts during the break. After Shirley left, Joy continued until her retirement in 2004.

266. Joy Fordham, 1997.

In the early years, the LMB canteen was the only one on the hospital site. As more hospital buildings appeared, a canteen was built for their staff. For LMB people, this was useful for evening and weekend meals and on other days when the laboratory was officially closed, but it did not rival our canteen at other times. During the 1980s, however, 'Blossom Time', run by Arjuna, the health food store in Mill Road, appeared in the Medical School next door, and, serving mainly salads, began attracting LMB staff. To counteract this, a salad bar was installed in our canteen and proved very popular.

In 1989, however, financial problems arose. The recruitment of staff for the canteen became a problem – the salary levels that could be offered were too low to attract new staff – and the work load placed on the Administration could no longer be carried without additional help, and this could not be funded by the MRC. The then Administrator, Alasdair Douglas, had looked into the finances and discovered that the MRC had no responsibility for the canteen, and he was keen to contract-out the catering operation to a private company. Aaron, the Director, agreed that Alasdair could investigate the possibility. Proposals were received from the food service company, Compass, and from the Civil Service Catering Organization, both of which included a reduction in the number of staff. However, the Canteen Committee felt their proposals were not in the best interests of the laboratory – besides the drop in staff, the prices would have increased considerably. So it was decided instead that the Committee should take full responsibility for running the canteen. This allowed them to offer wages at the market rate, and employ external help for dealing with the accounts and paperwork for the employment of staff. These changes were implemented quite smoothly and, despite some rises in prices, custom increased. More recently, the opening times have changed, from the three sessions around morning coffee, lunch and tea, to continuously from 10.00am to 4.30pm. Following Joy's retirement, the canteen management has been taken over by the University Graduate Centre, although the Committee still retains overall responsibility.

The recognition of the LMB canteen as 'the intellectual centre of the laboratory'[6] has led to its reproduction in other institutions despite the 'wonder that any work gets done in LMB, with the temptation to enjoy the virtually unlimited opportunity for profitable conversation in its atmosphere'.[7]

267–274. Joy's retirement, 2004:

270. The canteen staff in 2004: Margaret Lilley, Rushan Topal, Darren Ruddy, Joy, Charlotte Gilby, May (surname unknown) and Sue Bischoff.

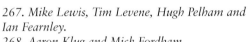

267. Mike Lewis, Tim Levene, Hugh Pelham and Ian Fearnley.
268. Aaron Klug and Mick Fordham.
269. Richard Henderson presenting Joy with a caricature leaving card.
271. Joy with Alec and Mary Wynn.
272. Joy and Doreen Burton.
273. Tony Woollard and Eileen Southgate.
274. Alan Fersht and Ken Harvey.

INSTITUTIONS

Laboratory talks

The week of talks was suggested by Francis Crick soon after the start of LMB, the idea being that everyone could hear what everyone else was doing. It was also an opportunity for airing problems and perhaps promoting solutions or collaborations. Initially, most of the researchers gave talks, but as their number has grown, a more selected collection of speakers has become necessary to keep to the time scale of four days (Wednesday being a recovery day). The format has remained fairly constant, though review-type talks occasionally have been included. It is perhaps not quite so daunting nowadays without Francis and Sydney in the front row listening, questioning and making sharp comments.

Max disliked an atmosphere of cigarette smoke and one year put up a notice banning smoking during the talks. Sydney was a fairly continuous smoker and remained outside, watching the proceedings on a CCTV relay to the canteen. Mark Bretscher was giving a talk and started by opening a small cupboard used for board cleaners etc., on the door of which he had put a notice 'Smoking now Allowed' and immediately Sydney came in to a round of applause.

275. The 1966 programme of laboratory talks.

Christmas party

The first gatherings were fairly formal, crowded occasions, held at Peterhouse, where Max was a Fellow. Later in the 1960s, they transferred to the Graduate Centre, and became rather lighter. However, since the new canteen became available in 1969, the parties have been held there.

One of the items that began almost immediately in LMB and became included with the party over the years is The Pantomime, a send-up of current laboratory topics and staff – usually, but not always, taken in good part. This began separately in the Lecture Room but was soon incorporated into the Christmas party. One of the well-remembered earlier sketches from the party in 1967, held on this occasion in the nearby Bell School of Languages, was the 'Ballet of Protein Synthesis' including John Abelson as '30S' and Paul Sigler as 'magic magnesium', both in tutus. From the late 1970s, the scriptwriters included Gerard Evan and Jim Watson from the Clinical Oncology Unit. Brad Amos too became involved at this time – Richard Henderson was so taken by Brad's imitation of Aaron in the canteen that he was persuaded to contribute, and in 1987 this developed into a discussion between 'Aaron' and Aaron on the humanisation of Greg Winter. One of the products in 1984 was a mock lessons and carols service including the 'make us British' song repeated at the 2003 DNA50 party, and a reading from the Book of Millspeak followed by a 'Ninth Nobel' carol. The canteen has been a favourite theme – in 1987 the 'Muppet Show' contained Fanny Fordham's recipe of the week with Joy played by Jude Smith, and a song in 1989 recorded the attempt by the 'Hatchet Man in Admin' to privatise it. 'This Is Your Life' in 1990 was devoted to Diana Dumpling. In 1991, 'Aladdin' included a genie with the name of Fuller, offering anything on special order ('a non-focal microscope?'), and a wicked Uncle Dai planning to turn everyone into neurobiologists under his slave Nigel Onion. 'Cinderella' in 1992 had the two ugly sisters Bretschia and Lawrentia trying unsuccessfully to prevent Cinderella from going to the lab talks, at midnight she manages to escape, but leaving some of her DNA behind, making Dandini search for the girl with the complementary strand.

276. Christmas concert, probably 1963. From the left, Ieuan Harris, Brian Hartley, Liz (surname unknown), Pat Brown (later Leberman), unknown, Bill Gray, Alan Weeds, John Clegg and probably Richard Ambler. In front is Robin Offord. (Source unknown.)

277, 278. *Christmas sketch, 1967 – the Ballet of Protein Synthesis:*

277. *Paul Sigler, as the 'magic magnesium', sparkling before John Abelson, the '30S' ribosome subunit, with Diana Singleton labelled HIS and an unknown man labelled HERS. (Photograph by John Haselgrove.)*

278. *The overall cast. From the left: Steve Martin, John Abelson, Robin Buckland, David Shotton, Graham Jones, HERS, and Paul Sigler. (Photograph by John Haselgrove.)*

Christmas raffle

This began in 1972 when the laboratory van driver and general help, Dick Tompkins, found a pound note and handed it in to the office. After a few weeks it was not claimed and Dick said to give it to charity. It was used to buy the ingredients for a cake made by Doreen Burton which was raffled. The proceeds from this were used to buy prizes for a Christmas raffle, the draw taking place in the canteen, with the Canteen Committee's approval (with mince pies made by Joy Fordham) and the raffle has become an annual event with a vast number of donated prizes. The popularity of the draw attracts a very high proportion of the laboratory staff and so provides a convenient venue for the presentation of the various trophies of the laboratory sports clubs.

Until she retired in 2000, the raffle was largely organised by Doreen, and many different charities have benefited – on the whole relatively small, local ones, often with connections with members of the staff, and the proceeds have risen from about £100 in the 1970s to over £1,000 in 2004.

279. Christmas raffle, 1972. Ross Jakes presenting a television set to a nurse on the children's ward, and Doreen Burton with the pick-up truck. Courtesy of Doreen Burton.

RECREATION

Many of the young and energetic people joining the LMB in its early days were keen sportsmen, playing cricket or football for their local teams or those connected with their previous jobs. Some continued with this, but soon sufficient numbers of interested players arrived to think about forming Laboratory teams.

Cricket was the first to be organised. Interested people included Bart Barrell, George Brownlee, Alan Coulson, Brian Clark, Ieuan Harris, Dave Hart, John Jarvis and Bill Whybrow, and the arrival of Ross Jakes in 1968 was the spur to get things going. Ross came for an interview to join Brian Hartley and was spotted by Graham Jones, who was then working in Protein Chemistry, but playing cricket for the Biochemistry team in the Laboratory League. Ross was asked if he would organise and set up a team and captain it if he came to the Laboratory. He agreed, did come and captained the team for twenty years. The cricket club was formally constituted – a committee was set up by Max Perutz, and a Chairman, Secretary and Treasurer were elected, and the team colours, yellow and green, taken from the Laboratory logo. The first Chairman was Max, followed by Fred Sanger, Ieuan Harris and John Walker. Fred was quite an interested player in the first friendly games – he was a member of the team when it visited NIMR at Mill Hill for an evening game. George Brownlee remembers another visit to London to play the MRC Head Office. He was naïvely surprised that they could raise a team, assuming the Office would only have a handful of staff, but he then learnt that there were over 300! Bart Barrell, besides playing as a slow bowler, often 'kept the score book – good training for genome annotation having to record every ball and what happened to it'.[8]

280. *The lab First Team winning the challenge cup in the University Inter-Lab League, 1970. From the left, front row: Fred Northrop, Robin Buckland, Peter Rigby, Ross Jakes (the captain), Graham Jones, Alan Coulson, Bill Whybrow and Dick Russell. Back row: Martin Hooper, Peter Macdonald, Tony Cashmore, George Brownlee, Bart Barrell and Lou Jaggard. Courtesy of Ross Jakes.*

280–285. Cricket:

281. *League Champions, 1980. From the left, front row: Brian Wright, David Walker, Ross Jakes (captain), Mike Runswick, John Walker. Back row: John Jarvis, Dave Hart, Gordon Koch, Eric Atherton, Brian Williams, Alan Coulson, Richard Titmas, and Bart Barrell. Courtesy of Dave Hart.*

282. *League Champions Cup, Runners Up, 1980. From the left: Brian Wright, Gordon Koch, unknown, Alan Coulson, Mike Runswick, John Walker, David Walker, Dave Hart, Ross Jakes, George Brownlee and Brian Williams. Courtesy of Dave Hart.*

283. Dave Hart hitting out. Courtesy of Dave Hart.

284. George Brownlee.

285. Spectator (Chris Nobbs), Player (Brian Clark) and Scorer (Bart Barrell).

Almost immediately, however, moves began to enter a team into the University Laboratory Cricket League. After some negotiation, LMB was made an honorary University Department and the team began playing in 1969, and immediately began winning trophies – the first by winning the league in 1970. In addition to the league trophies, three trophies were created for the club, to commemorate keen players and supporters who had died. The Elsie Cousins trophy was presented to the person contributing most to the club over the year, the Ieuan Harris trophy was for the best batting performance and the Rhidian Abbs trophy was for the best bowling performance. (Rhidian Abbs was a worker in the canteen who died from an aneurysm during a friendly game in 1992.) The trophies were presented annually at the Christmas Raffle Draw in the canteen. In the early days, home matches were played on the Downing sports ground, close to the LMB (where the multistorey car park now is), but since its disappearance they are mainly played on the Emmanuel ground. Other sides use other college sports grounds, and knockout finals have been played at Fenners, the University ground. Ross Jakes remained captain of the team from 1968 to 1988, and was succeeded by Mike Runswick. A record wicket partnership of 121 was scored by Lou Jaggard (one of the LMB plumbers) and Ross Jakes in 1970. It was closely approached (120) in 1974 by Ross with Dave Hart, but the record was well broken in 1989 by John Walker and a non-LMB inclusion, Will Graham, with a score of 152.

Football began around 1969 in the form of friendly matches against teams from local villages and firms and University Departments, with Robin Buckland, Alan

286–288. Football:

286. *An early team, 1971. Back row, from left: Bob (surname unknown), Eric Atherton, Brian Clark, Eric Cunliffe, unnamed, John Kendrick-Jones, Robin Ison, Rod King, Fred Walker. Front: Nigel (surname unknown), John Jarvis, Ross Jakes, Peter Rigby, Tim Morley, Dave Hart. Courtesy of Dave Hart.*

Coulson and Brian Pope as 'club officers'. Alan particularly remembers a game against Tube Investments, who were then still in Hinxton Hall, on their ground which was sited where the Sanger Centre would be built later, and in which he would be working. Home matches were often played on the Downing sports ground, but were not always allowed, particularly if it was very wet, for fear of ruining the hallowed cricket area, and matches were then played on a Coldhams Lane pitch or sometimes at Longstowe. The team wore plain Cambridge-blue shirts which lasted for many years, but which became a dull grey after being washed many times.

Enthusiasm for more competitive matches heightened with the arrival of Eric Cunliffe and Peter Rigby. Eric Cunliffe was in the Pharmacology Department housed in what is now the CPE building, and Peter Rigby had come to LMB in 1968 as a student of Brian Hartley and became the club secretary. In 1971, the team decided to apply for admission to the Cambridge Sunday Football League, and in their first game won by 10–3. They also won their second match against the ARC at Babraham 2–1 and together the games gained a headline in the *Cambridge Evening News*: 'Hospital side blast out 12-goal warning.' In the league, the games were quite competitive and lively – sufficiently so in one case that the game was abandoned and had to be replayed with a stronger official as the referee.

In addition to the league team, a second one was organised by Brian Pope to play friendly matches and a five-a-side team played in the small Howard Mallet sports centre, predecessor of the Kelsey Kerridge, near Mackay's shop. Since the first team had taken over the blue shirts, Max donated some of his lecture-fee money to pay for a second set of shirts (Celtic green and white). This second team fizzled out while Brian left LMB for two years, and its goalkeeper, Mike Squires, set up a mixed hockey team. Brian returned in 1974, and with Robin Buckland and Alan Coulson found the football league games too competitive, and so started up another team interested in playing friendlies on Sunday mornings using various college grounds as allowed. The LMB league team withdrew from the Sunday League in the late 1970s, but the friendly team continued for another twenty years. During the 1990s, these games were organised by John Dean, and home matches were played on the floodlit astroturf pitch on Coldhams Common. On his return in 1974, Brian also organised five-a-side football, as and when invited for competitions, peaking in the mid-1980s with a tournament organised by the firm Anachem at Luton, matches being played on the Luton Town football ground. Luton Town were then in football's top flight (now the premiership) – some moments to savour for the players, using the same facilities as the top footballers of the day. During the 1980s, five-a-side games were played weekly at the Kelsey Kerridge Sports Hall.

In 1977 a Christmas match was organised between teams from older and younger people in the laboratory, and this began a tradition which continued for nearly twenty years. From 1977 to 1991, the average dividing age was 31 and apart from one in 1980 and two drawn games, the older team won the rest. By the early

287. 'Pros v Beginners', 1977. Back rows, from left: John Jarvis, Eric Atherton, Brian Spooner, John Kendrick-Jones, Bill Whybrow, David Gilmore, Steve Stubbings, Brian Pope, Tito Baralle, S. Chambers, Herbert Schmitt, Rodger Staden, Mike Runswick, Jon Scholey, Robin Buckland, Dave Hart, Peter Workman and Alan Coulson. Front row: Alan Smith, David Freeman, J. Turner, Paul Wagner, Alan Forster and Mike Squire. Courtesy of Brian Pope.

288. 'Pros v Beginners', 1991. Back row: Suds MacIver, John Dean, Lutz Reichman, Stuart Ingham, Brian Pope, Mike Squire, John Kendrick-Jones, Alan Forster, Andrew Smith and Neville Barnes. Front row: Reinhard Wugner, Tony Rowe, Jamie Kendrick-Jones, John Allison, Ian Collinson, Graham Lingley, Kevin Hardwick, Oliver Nayler, Gerard Campbell, Jonathan Derry and Mark Seftan. Courtesy of Brian Pope.

1990s the younger players assumed some ascendancy as the older players grew 'more mature' and the matches ceased when Brian hung up his boots in 1996.

A darts club became popular in the later 1960s, especially by members of the workshop, and other interested people including Bart Barrell, Doreen Burton, Elsie Cousins, John Jarvis and Marie Tweed, the workshop secretary. Games were played in the University Assistants Club in Cambridge, again after negotiations to over-come not being a University Department – the team were made Associate Members of the Club. The matches became regular Friday evening social events and trophies were awarded for winning players and teams. Ted Thompson, an earlier co-worker with Fred Sanger in Biochemistry and occasional visitor to LMB, was persuaded to contribute a cup. The awards were presented by lab-notables such as Max and Audrey Martin. After the Frank Lee Centre opened, darts matches tended to be organised and played there.

289. Darts: award presentation by Audrey Martin, c. 1970.

The Frank Lee Centre for Leisure and Fitness opened on the hospital site in 1972. Members of staff of all the authorities permanently based on the site were eligible to become members – the MRC had made a loan towards its construction. Dave Hart remembers being on a committee drawn from all the participating groups to run the centre and taking a lifesaving course so that he could patrol the swimming pool on Sunday mornings when it was reserved for children.

Facilities for badminton and squash became available in the Frank Lee, and Brian Pope organised competitions for both these and took responsibility for the squash for 25 years until his retirement in 2005. In 1977, the Beckman company were persuaded to donate a tankard to be awarded to the winner of the squash contest. This was decided on a knock-out basis and among the early winners, John Gurdon, Rodger Staden and Paul Jolley appeared more than once. Brian thought that there should be another award that was not so geared to the top players, and perhaps not so male-biased. In 1983, Kay Buck, a technician working for John White and a keen badminton player, died after a fall while on holiday in Ireland. With her family's approval, it was agreed that a good way of remembering her would be to have a trophy in her name available for females to win. However, only three girls entered to play for it as a badminton trophy and so it was converted to an open trophy for the winners of a laboratory squash league – awarded to the most consistent player – and it continues to be presented as part of the Christmas Raffle Draw. For the badminton winners, a shield was designed and for some years the ladder was organised by Wanda Bullock, a keen player, and the award was also presented as part of the Christmas Raffle Draw. Wanda's long connection to the game is being recognised by the award of a Wanda Bullock Trophy in a revived Badminton Ladder organised by Justin Pachebat.

The financial sides of the various sports were initially organised separately, but rather than arranging lots of small events to raise money, it was decided at a meeting of all the club secretaries in 1982 to pool their resources and arrange joint money-raising events – ice skating in Peterborough, theatre trips to London, sweepstakes, etc. The initial title 'The MRC Sports and Social Club' did not meet with the approval of the powers that be and 'The Centre Sports and Social Club' came into being, chaired by Dave Hart. This fund was also used to support the annual Christmas party and in latter years relied heavily on Pat Edwards and her sales of the popular T-shirts and sweat-shirts, first designed in 1987 to mark the 40th anniversary of the founding of the MRC unit.

In addition to the above, there have been less physical recreations. Collections of interested people have frequently met for the production of music of various sorts. In the 1960s, a Madrigal group was begun by Ken Holmes, and included Susan and George Brownlee, Tom and Joan Steitz, Gwynne Goaman, Mary Holmes and Hilary Muirhead. Ken remembers a concert that the group contributed to and which included the Brahms clarinet trio, the clarinet being played by Bill Lipscomb, on sabbatical at LMB, with the piano played by Christopher Longuet-Higgins, Professor of Theoretical Chemistry, and cello by Naomi Butterworth. The latter is now Professor of Cello at the Trinity College of Music in London, but had then been touring with John Cleese and company with the Cambridge Footlights.

Over the years there have been several spells in which a sufficiently enthusiastic film-buff has organised a film club. The first of these was begun in the 1960s by Reuben Leberman, with films being shown in the original Lecture Room. More recently the club has revived with films being shown in the more highly technically equipped Max Perutz Lecture Theatre.

1. J. Meadow, 2005. *The Victorian Scientist*. The British Museum, London.
2. G.J. Brakenhoff, H.T.M. van der Voort, E.A. van Spronsen, W.A.M. Linnemans and N. Nanninga, 1985. Three-dimensional chromatin distribution in neuroblastoma cell nuclei shown by confocal scanning laser microscopy. *Nature*, 317, 748–749.
3. J.G. White, W.B. Amos and M. Fordham, 1987. An evaluation of confocal versus conventional imaging of biological structures by fluorescence light microscopy. *Journal of Cell Biology*, 105, 41–48.
4. W.B. Amos, J.G. White and M. Fordham, 1987. Use of confocal imaging in the study of biological structures. *Applied Optics*, 26, 3239–3243.
5. W.B. Amos and J.G. White, 2003. How the confocal laser scanning microscope entered biological research. *Biology of the Cell*, 95, 335–342.
6. H.E. Huxley, 2002. Max Perutz (1914–2002). *Nature*, 415, 851–852.
7. T.A. Steitz, 2003. In his talk at the DNA50 meeting.
8. LMB Cricket Club on http://www.srcf.ucam.org/lmbcc/content/History.html.

CHAPTER TEN

Appendices

GROWTH OF LMB

*290, 291. Aerial views of Addenbrooke's site from about the same direction, c. 1963 and 2006.
Courtesy of Cambridge University Landscape Modelling Unit, and Medical Photography Unit.*

Thirteen-bay extension

As soon as the new LMB building was occupied in 1962, thoughts turned towards growth (and have never stopped!). A general laboratory proposal for future expansion was drafted and presented to the MRC in October 1963, and in 1968, the thirteen-bay extension of the original building eastwards, towards Hills Road, was built. (As one might have guessed, when the original building was designed, possible extensions to the west were envisaged, but not to the east, so the east end had a solid wall and the west a semi-temporary one which was not completely weatherproof and after a few years needed a fair amount of rebuilding.) The extension was planned for part-immediate and part-future expansion. The basement and ground floor were immediately filled by the University, and included the Department of Haematology, and the third floor was occupied mainly by Structural Studies. The fourth floor became the new larger canteen (the old canteen was eventually completely taken over by the Visual Aids section). From 1969, the second floor housed the development groups of Peter Lawrence and Michael Wilcox in Cell Biology. The first floor remained empty(-ish) until 1972, when it was fitted out for the Developmental Biology group of John Gurdon and Ron Laskey, and the Peptide Synthesis group of Bob Sheppard. In 2001, the space on the ground floor housing the Department of Haematology was vacated by them and taken over by LMB for a new library location.

Workshop extension

In 1968 too, the mechanical workshop was effectively doubled in area to accommodate more machinery and staff. Over this was built more office space and a new 'model room'. This housed the wire models of haemoglobin, myoglobin and chymotrypsin, and accommodated the vast Richards Boxes for building the structures of new molecules from large, projected electron density contour maps.

Block 7

This was built as a side-shoot off the main building towards Long Road and completed in 1980. It was planned and built by MRC without any space allocation for LMB and initially against the wishes of LMB, but eventually someone from MRC came and 'read the riot act' to LMB as its paymaster, and the building went ahead. The levels in Block 7 were obliged to follow the numbering in the rest of the hospital site, with the lowest being level 1. The rest of LMB retains the original terminology of basement, ground floor, first floor, etc., so that one has to remember to add (or is it subtract?) 2 on going between the buildings, from level to floor.

Initially, Block 7 was intended to house the MRC Dunn Nutrition Unit from Milton Road, and the MRC Biostatistics Unit, but there was some disagreement about the Dunn's occupation and instead some smaller MRC-funded Units were installed (Neurochemical Pharmacology (NCPU, this closed in 1985 and was succeeded by the Molecular Neurobiology Unit, MNU), Mechanisms in Tumour Immunity (MITI), and Clinical Oncology and Radiotherapeutics (CORU)) and together with the LMB the overall collection was called The MRC Centre. The function of the MRC Centre became firmer under Bronwen Loder in 1983, when it took over the administration of all these and other Cambridge-based, MRC-funded Units. The single-storey prefabricated building by the side of Block 7 was constructed in 1984 to provide centralised accommodation for administrators, but these have become dispersed again in the main buildings and the prefab is now occupied by the Electronics and Information Technology Sections.

Over the years, as the separate Units in Block 7 closed (the last in 1996), the space was continuously taken over by LMB – substantially with the creation of the new Division of Neurobiology in 1993, with Nigel Unwin as Director – until it is now wholly part of LMB.

The Clinical School

Next to LMB, this was opened in 1980. The Medical Library was incorporated in it, and it was originally planned that this would also house the LMB library. The MRC had bought into the construction and running costs for this (at the level of 25 per cent of construction and 8 per cent of running costs) and for the use of lecture rooms. However, rather than lose the convenience of the library in our own building, it was decided to keep the latter for current and reasonably recent journals and only house older volumes in the Medical Library.

CPE Building

In 1989, the separate building constructed in 1970 for the University Department of Pharmacology was refurbished as the Centre of Protein Engineering, funded by the MRC, Industry and Charitable organisations, with Alan Fersht as Director. It was officially opened by Margaret Thatcher in 1990 – although she had recently been deposed as Prime Minister, she was keen to open it as it was initially one of the Interdisciplinary Research Centres promoted by her government.

The western end of the building was originally the animal house section of the Pharmacology laboratory, and then taken over as the University/MRC CBS (Centre for Biomedical Services). It was refurbished to house transgenic animals etc. in 2001.

Max Perutz Lecture Theatre

The Max Perutz Lecture Theatre, built to accommodate 188, and new reception/foyer was completed in 2002. In the original 1962 LMB building, space was reserved at the west end on the second floor for a lecture room for 70 people, and on the third floor for the library. The latter was moved to the new location on the east-end of the ground floor in 2001. The lecture room was closed around 1976 since it became too small for popular lectures and a prefabricated lecture room accommodating 100 was built in the rear car park until the lecture rooms in the clinical school became available in 1980.

292. *The Max Perutz Lecture Theatre.*

293–307. *Opening of the Max Perutz Lecture Theatre in 2002:*

293. *(top left) Robin Perutz and family by the plaque.*
294. *(top right) Gisela Perutz with César Milstein and Fred Sanger.*

295. *(far left) Arthur Lesk and Mike Gait.*
296. *(left) Murray Stewart.*

297. *Andrew McLachlan and Brian Pope.*

298. *K.J. Patel and Andrew Travers.*

299. *Cyrus Chothia and Greg Winter.*

300. *Tony North and Uli Arndt.*

301. *Andrew Griffiths and Cyrus Chothia.*

302. *John Meurig Thomas and Michael Fuller.*

303. *Gebhard Schertler and Celia Milstein.*

304. *Daniela Rhodes, Mark Bretscher and Barbara Pearse.*

305. *Nancy Lane and John Walker.*

306. *David Blow and Gerard Bricogne.*

307. *The Support Staff. From left: Howard Andrews, David Pledge, Chris Raeburn, Jenny Brightwell, Mary-Ann Starkey, Jennie Lightfoot, Wanda Bullock, Annette Faux, Sue Ellis, Rachel Whant, Michael Fuller and Paul Hart.*

In addition to the above, three other major buildings have been built with close links to LMB: the Titanic and the Hutch are both physically quite close to LMB, and the Sanger Centre on the Hinxton site, about seven miles south.

The Titanic

The Wellcome Trust/MRC building was completed in 1998 and, because of its large 'funnels' and the coincidental release of the film, promptly became known as the Titanic. It rehoused the Dunn Human Nutrition Unit, with John Walker as its newly appointed Director, and the remainder became the Cambridge Institute for Medical Research, which rehoused the Haematology Department and other University research groups from the original LMB buildings freeing space for LMB use.

The Hutch

Alongside the Titanic is the Hutchison/MRC Research Centre, opened in 2002. This new cancer research centre is the result of a collaboration between the MRC, the University and the Cancer Research Campaign (now Cancer Research UK), and the building was funded jointly by the MRC and Hutchison Whampoa Ltd. Its joint directors are Ron Laskey and Bruce Ponder.

The Sanger Centre

This was built in 1993, on what would become the Wellcome Trust Genome Campus at Hinxton. It was financed jointly by the MRC and the Wellcome Trust, initially to house the project to sequence the genome of *C. elegans* (see chapter 7), and later to include the sequence work on the human genome.

ADMINISTRATION

From 1962 until she retired in 1973, Audrey Martin was the sole listed administrator for the laboratory. Her dog 'Slippers' lay under her desk during the day. Audrey was helped by Joan Blows, and they were joined by Doreen Burton in 1968. Audrey Martin was succeeded by Frances Taylor, who carried on with the same system. Frances' retirement in 1980 coincided with the creation of the MRC Centre, and the resulting expansion and the taking over of more things locally that were previously looked after by the MRC-HQ led to the splitting of the job into two. Joan Blows carried on with the accounts section, and was succeeded by Doreen Burton in 1985, until she retired in 2000. Peter McHugh took over personnel, followed by Jennifer Cornwell in 1985. Michael Snelling was appointed to manage all administration. He was succeeded in 1985 by Lindsay Dane, and in 1988 by Alasdair

308. *Audrey Martin at her retirement in 1973 with her dog Slippers.*

Douglas with, as deputy, Jennifer Cornwell who herself succeeded to the post in 1990.

Michael Fuller took charge of the purchasing and technical service side in 1962 and was joined by John Dean as a temp in 1987. In 1988, John took over purchasing and Michael carried on with the technical services side until he retired in 1997, when he was succeeded by Paul Loveday.

In 1983, an overall senior administrator, Bronwen Loder, was seconded from the MRC-HQ and appointed as Assistant Director (Administration) of LMB, and Head of the MRC-Centre. She was succeeded in 1986 by Diana Dunstan, in 1991 by David James, and in 1996 by Megan Davies. The MRC-Centre today (2003) numbers about 108, including central service sections such as Visual Aids, Maintenance and Safety, as well as the financial and personnel sides, and a large team of cleaners.

AWARDS TO INVENTORS

The MRC set up their first Awards to Inventors scheme in 1961. A subcommittee was set up to decide whether an award should be made in respect of a particular invention and 'the level of the award, taking into account factors such as the practical value of the invention to research or healthcare, any especially innovative contribution made by the inventor, and the utility of the invention as demonstrated by its revenue earning capacity' (*MRC News*, May, 1983).

In the early days of LMB, inventors were rewarded by an *ex gratia* payment decided by this subcommittee. However, the amounts received by the inventors were often rather small compared with overall values of the inventions. In the financial climate of the later 1980s, the MRC began discussion of a new Awards to Inventors scheme to encourage Units and inventors to take a greater interest in the exploitation of their ideas by giving them a prescribed right to a share in the exploitation revenue. Aaron Klug was much involved in these discussions. Just after he became Director, in 1986, the LMB confocal microscope reached the stage of being commercialised and this prompted Aaron to argue with the MRC that they should set up the new scheme. It was introduced in 1987 and allocates, on a sliding scale, proportions of the gross income to the inventor, his or her Unit, and an MRC Commercial Fund for such things as patenting and legal expenses.

MEMORIES OF LMB AND EARLIER

Sidney Altman

Sidney Altman (see chapter 7) was at LMB from 1969 for two years in Cell Biology. The article in *Genetics* (Vol. 165, 1633–1639, 2003) is a modified version of the reminiscing talk he gave during the DNA50 celebrations in 2003.

Perspectives

Anecdotal, Historical and Critical Commentaries on Genetics

Edited by James F. Crow and William F. Dove

RNA Processing: A Postdoc in a Great Laboratory

Sidney Altman[1]

Department of Molecular, Cellular and Developmental Biology, Yale University, New Haven, Connecticut 06020

The author is Sterling Professor of Molecular, Cellular and Developmental Biology at Yale University and, in 1989, shared the Nobel Prize in Chemistry with Tom Cech for the discovery of catalytic RNA. This essay is based on a talk presented at the reunion of the Medical Research Council Laboratory of Molecular Biology (MRC-LMB) held at Cambridge, England, on April 26, 2003. Naturally, some of the local elements of that talk have been modified, and a discussion of topics and personalities has been added as extracts for the benefit of the readers of GENETICS.

—EDITORS

IN 1963, Sydney Brenner wrote a letter to Max Perutz about the future of research at the MRC-LMB. He said, "... The entry of large numbers of Americans and other biochemists into the field will ensure that all the chemical details of replication and transcription will be elucidated. ..." (cited by BRENNER 1988). He then went on to describe the new plans for developmental biology he was exploring. I was one of the North Americans to come and work out the details Sydney had mentioned in his letter. I came with a rather modest reputation in biochemistry. Along my route as a postdoctoral fellow at the MRC-LMB, there were moments of great luck and disappointment. At every moment, however, I felt so extremely privileged to be an associate of the greatest laboratory of molecular biology at that time. That experience, in itself, made my stay worthwhile, even if nothing of significance in science emerged from my activities.

As a child, I became interested in the great age of physics in the twentieth century. I read a lot about Einstein and Bohr with his amazingly productive group. It was too much to ask for, but I hoped that one day I might be part of such a group, particularly one like Bohr's. Ultimately, I did join such an amazing collection of personalities, but they were in molecular biology and were located in Cambridge at the MRC-LMB.

The atmosphere of the great physics groups and their intimate collaboration and communication can be briefly reviewed in A. Pais's books about Einstein and Bohr (PAIS 1982, 1991). Einstein had finished his major efforts and worked more or less by himself, even while in Berlin, although he was an astute and responsive listener. Bohr worked constantly with several young people around him, communicating and discussing new ideas throughout the days and weeks. Several of his associates went on to great fame.

My first contact with the group, if contact is the right word, came when browsing through an issue of *Nature* in 1961. I saw the Brenner and Francis Crick article about the nature of the genetic code (CRICK *et al.* 1961). I copied that article and read it. My fascination with that paper was in how anyone had been able to learn what the article said had been learned.

At that time, late in the spring of 1962, I was in Colorado, working and going to summer school as a physicist. Later that summer, I met George Gamow at a party for students. He was obviously the most colorful person there. Gamow was well known to anybody who studied physics, as I had up to that point. He made the first calculations on alpha particle decay and went on to a plethora of important contributions in physics, among them the theory of the Big Bang. He also played a critical role in the early days of the genetic code. After reading about the structure of DNA, Gamow recognized that there might be a relationship between the number of bases read in the linear sequence, three at a time in this case, and the order of amino acid residues in a protein (no discussion yet of mRNA) to make a protein. He made a simple calculation of the number of possibilities of amino acids you could code from a sequence of DNA (using the wrong number of amino acid residues)

[1]*Address for correspondence:* Department of Molecular, Cellular and Developmental Biology, KBT 402, P.O. Box 208103, Yale University, New Haven, CT 06520-8103. E-mail: sidney.altman@yale.edu

Genetics **165**: 1633–1639 (December 2003)

S. Altman

FIGURE 1.—Leonard S. Lerman.

and predicted what kind of sequence you would have in a protein (GAMOW 1954). These calculations were incorrect partly because of the unknown nature of the code (overlapping, non-overlapping, etc.) and the incorrect number of amino acid residues used by nature. Nevertheless, the direction of the ideas was clear and accurate and spawned several years of intense speculation and experimentation about the nature of the code.

At Gamow's suggestion, because of my partial understanding and an interest in molecular biology, I contacted the Department of Biophysics at the Medical School in Denver. Ted Puck was the Chair of that small department. When I drove down from Boulder, I visited Leonard Lerman (Figure 1). That was the end of my career as a physicist. Leonard had just returned from a sabbatical year at the MRC-LMB. He and I hit it off, and I became his student. We agreed, shortly thereafter, on a topic for a thesis. In the meantime, Leonard did tell me about his work on acridine-DNA complexes, which he had discovered, and his life at the MRC-LMB. A few years later, in Nashville, Tennessee, where Leonard had moved and I finished my thesis, I met Sydney Brenner.

Sydney gave one of the greatest lectures I have heard in science. There were no slides. It was all about the genetic code and nonsense codons. Later, I told Sydney that I would like to work at MRC-LMB, but he said there was no space available at the moment. Disappointed, I went on, very fortunately, to Matt Meselson's lab, and there I saw Sydney again after another year or two. He was visiting the Boston area. He asked me if I was still interested in the MRC-LMB, and when I said, "Yes," he indicated that there was newly available space in the lab and suggested I might want to work on the three-dimensional configuration of tRNA, probably by NMR. Any physicist, or student of physics, could operate a big NMR machine.

I arrived in Cambridge in October 1969, just after the annual lab meeting, an important occasion that I happened to miss twice during my time in Cambridge. Very soon I had a meeting with Sydney and Francis. They told me that tRNA had been recently crystallized and that I should come by with a new, *i.e.*, my own, plan for study. Two weeks, they said, and we will meet again. They did suggest some possible fluorometric studies of tRNA in solution.

What an idea! Come up with my own research plan! I looked around, read some uninteresting papers, and then went back to Sydney and Francis. I suggested that I look for acridine-induced mutants of tRNAs. Since they had recently completed a classic study of substitution mutants of tRNAs, the idea I presented was met with what I perceived as an attitude of great boredom. Nevertheless, they said, if that is what you want to do—go ahead. I distinctly felt that if they spoke to me again, it would be an accident. The conclusion I drew was that studies of tRNA mutants were finished.

Brenner and Smith and their junior colleagues had recently published papers on substitution mutants of tRNA^{Tyr}Su$_{3+}$ that demonstrated the expected change in the anticodon of the tRNA as it became an amber suppressor and then how the properties of suppression changed as other nucleotides in the sequence were altered (ABELSON *et al.* 1970; SMITH *et al.* 1970).

I did have a few experiments left over from my previous work with Matt Meselson, which I decided to complete. Let us remember that they concerned a DNA endonuclease, so I had some experience dealing with an enzyme that cut nucleic acids. I also gave a seminar on that work, which did not excite me very much. To my surprise, Fred Sanger was the only senior member of the lab who attended, with only a few in the audience. It took me a while to figure out why Fred was there (to hear about new DNA endonucleases) and the reasons for the questions he asked. He was working on sequencing DNA and looking for new enzymes to recapitulate the work on sequencing of RNA. Jon King, another inventive T4 person with whom I did some very slow work on T4 encapsulization, was also there.

I did get started on making acridine-induced mutants of tRNA. John D. Smith (Figure 2), whom I had previously not met nor even heard much about, did help me set up the genetic system, and I worked on that for my first year. In fact, I started out with su^+_{am} mutants of tRNA^{Tyr} and did succeed in making various non-suppressing mutants. These were made in *Escherichia coli* lysogenized for $\phi80su_3^+$: the cells were induced, and the tRNA genes transferred to the $\phi80$ itself and then examined more closely. Indeed, I had several mutants that made no tRNA, but some did revert to the Sup$^+$ phenotype at frequencies of about a few percent. By this time, May 1970, I was getting ready to leave the lab and look for jobs in other fields.

I should also say that I rented a sixteenth-century,

Perspectives   1635

FIGURE 2.—John D. Smith (courtesy of the MRC-LMB).

FIGURE 4.—A description of tyrosine tRNA with locations of mutations of the amber and ochre anticodons at position 35.

very small, thatched-roof cottage in Barley, a few miles from Royston (Figure 3). It had been the priest's cottage for many years and is on a map of the village dated 1545. My life there was very quiet and gave me a good chance to think about what was happening in the lab. It was made tolerable by my friendship with Jack Wilkerson and his family, Jack being one of the squires of the village and also a very good farmer, an amateur archeologist, and a historian.

I had a 1-year fellowship that was rapidly coming to a close. It was a bad time for jobs: the market in molecular biology had not yet expanded, and my search came up empty. That was a time of deep disappointment.

Sometime in May 1970, Sydney suggested to me that I had better get something published or my meager talents would be lost to science. He had one problem, not yet solved, concerning ochre-suppressing mutants of tRNA^{Tyr}. The idea was to make an ochre-suppressing

FIGURE 3.—My cottage in Barley.

tRNA mutant and sequence it to show that it had the expected anticodon. Amber-suppressing mutants had already been characterized in earlier publications by Brenner, Smith, and colleagues (Figure 4). I started the project Sydney suggested rather quickly in my spare time. Within a week or so, I had isolated the mutants, isolated the tRNAs, and started the sequencing to show that they were the correct tRNAs. This work went almost too smoothly; there were no problems. Others in the lab had previously tried this project without success. I did everything the same way they did, except that I used a new mutagen, hydroxylamine. It was the favorite mutagen of Bill McClain, another American. I had thought it was the perfect mutagen of choice from a chemical point of view, and he had a bottle full of it, ready to use. So now I had one publication.

It is worth mentioning that I had read about Sanger's two-dimensional fingerprinting of RNA before I came to the lab. I watched people do it at MRC-LMB, but I still felt it was an impossible method; it seemed that too much voodoo was involved. So when I had to start sequencing, I asked for some help from another American, Hugh Robertson, and soon learned that there was no voodoo, although it had seemed that way to an observer. The method worked brilliantly over and over again. I tried to emulate Bart Barrell, who could do about seven or eight fingerprints simultaneously, but I never quite succeeded. The most I could do was six.

A few weeks before my fellowship terminated, I decided to do one more experiment on the tRNA acridine-induced mutants I was making. I thought that the mutants I had that reverted at high frequencies were probably partial duplication mutants and that their finished product was too "damaged" to survive for very long in

S. Altman

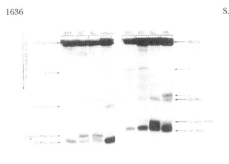

FIGURE 5.—Analysis of mature and precursor tRNAs in a polyacrylamide gel. Bands labeled X and Y are precursor tRNAs.

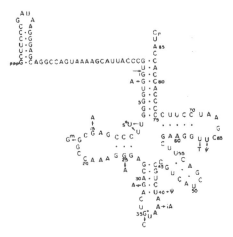

FIGURE 6.—The secondary structure of a precursor to tyrosine tRNA. The arrow between positions −1 and +1 is where RNase P cleaves this substrate. The amber anticodon is indicated at position 35, and other mutants and modified bases are also shown.

the cell. Consequently, I tried to see if I could isolate a precursor tRNA molecule in the fastest way possible. My decision was influenced by the fact that every time somebody reported such an experiment in the literature, there was always a centrifugation step to spin cells down. Even a 30-second centrifugation would be sufficient, in my mind, to destroy any unwanted transcript. I avoided such a step and added phenol directly to the cultures. The first experiment proved that I was on the right track, as I found some large molecular weight bands running above tRNA in the gel. Their size was appropriate for partial duplications (Figure 5). Soon I also included one of the older base substitution mutants and noticed that it, too, had a higher molecular weight band. My colleagues, namely, Bill McClain and Tony Cashmore, encouraged me to fingerprint these products (ALTMAN 1971). There was some skirmishing, because they wanted to see the fingerprint the moment it was developed. I think I managed to avoid that, but Tony, especially, was very excited when the fingerprint showed that I had precursor molecules.

My fellowship ended. What was I supposed to do? Francis, Sydney, and John Smith were away, but at least Sydney was accessible by mail. I wrote to Sydney explaining what I had done and asked for permission to stay, without salary, so I could work on this experiment and get the results I needed to allow me to apply for a job. Very fortunately, Sydney answered and indicated that there might be a standard, local MRC postdoc salary for 1 year. I am still grateful for this unexpected and generous hospitality.

The subsequent year found me identifying the processing enzyme that cleaved the 5′ sequence from precursor tRNAs (Figure 6). Hugh Robertson, who had extensive experience with RNases, guided me and supplied crude extracts ready to use. John Smith returned to the lab, and we worked together on mutants and other aspects of the problem.

John Smith was a venerable nucleic acids biochemist. He had worked on the nucleic acids of viruses long before coming to the MRC-LMB and was an expert on identification and characterization of nucleotides, much of it done on unlabeled material, detected by observing chromatographs under UV light. He was a quiet person but very lively in conversations about science.

We found that many previous substitution mutants of tRNAs had precursor molecules that were not cleaved properly by RNase P, our new enzyme. In addition, Bill McClain applied our knowledge to that of T4 tRNAs and, over the next few years, painted an extremely detailed picture of the genetics and biochemistry of tRNA synthesis by T4. When I went back to Yale, I followed Arthur Kornberg's dictum that every graduate student ought to purify an enzyme before he gets a Ph.D. and put a graduate student, Ben Stark, on purifying this enzyme. In the end, my MRC-LMB journey helped start the field of the enzymology of tRNA processing.

I did not realize what I had done with the precursor tRNAs. I knew it would get me a job, and it did. Sometime later that year, Gobind Khorana came through the MRC-LMB and was steered to me. It was hard for me to believe that this intellectual giant would want to hear about my work. But, of course, he was working on making a synthetic tRNA^{Tyr} gene, and he wanted everything, including the gene sequence, characterized. He went away somewhat glum, but within a year or so he succeeded in doing what he wanted.

Paul Berg also visited the lab and wanted to find out more about my work because Dale Kaiser's student, Paul

Schedl, was working on a similar project. As I recall, nobody gave him much time, but one morning he came to me and I agreed to send him my phage strains. In fact, Schedl's work became quite interesting as he had unwittingly isolated a temperature-sensitive mutant in the protein subunit of RNase P.

[I should mention that no one had isolated a radioactive, pure precursor tRNA prior to this time. Burdon and Darnell separately had looked at putative collections of mixtures of tRNA precursors in mammalian cells and had shown that crude enzymology was involved in changing their size from somewhat larger than tRNAs to that of normal tRNAs (BERNHARDT and DARNELL 1969; BURDON 1971). That was the extent of similar work at the time. Our work started the processing and detailed enzymology of E. coli tRNA. Very soon, 30S ribosomal RNA precursors were isolated in E. coli by Apirion and Schlesinger, their colleagues, and others, and it was rapidly shown that RNase III was involved in their processing. tRNA processing was also pursued in human cells by my lab, and rRNA processing in eukaryotes had several converts. The processing of mRNA also followed in quick succession (BROOKHAVEN SYMPOSIUM 1974).]

In the summer of 1970, I learned that my father had leukemia. I went home to Montreal in the early fall for about two to three weeks to be with my parents. My father was originally a penniless immigrant to Canada. He died while I was in Montreal. When I arrived back in the lab, again having missed the annual meeting, Sydney saw me as I climbed the stairs to the second floor and, as might be expected, asked why I had taken so much vacation. I still do not know if he was joking.

Later that fall, Sydney came into the then large lab room on the second floor with a blue airmail letter in his hand. "Who wants a job at Yale?" was the greeting, shouted loudly enough so that everyone heard him. It is my recollection that my hand shot up: "I do." Ultimately, I did receive an offer from Clem Markert, the Chair of the Yale department. Of course, Markert offered me a salary that was much lower than that offered by other places, and when I timidly commented on this, his typical answer was, "You can be bought?" Nevertheless, he gave me a little more money, and I took the job. (That was my first experience with Markert, an outstanding developmental biologist and a superb, courageous person who fought with the Lincoln Brigade in Spain and was a determined and brave opponent of Senator Joseph McCarthy.)

The enzymology we did on RNase P at the MRC-LMB was a solid beginning to the next phase that was carried forward at Yale: the complete purification and characterization of the enzyme, which had, as it turned out, a large catalytic RNA subunit. It is worth remembering that in those days we were still in the millicurie era. Each experiment I did to label tRNA (or precursors) or to prepare substrates for RNase P involved putting about 3 mCi in a bubbler tube for several minutes and then extracting the labeled RNA. One day in the summer of 1971, shortly before I left, I was doing an experiment with 5 mCi in an attempt to label the wild-type tRNA^{Tyr} precursor and to determine its fingerprint. In this case, without my knowledge the bubbler tube I was using developed a small hole in the water bath. A stream of highly radioactive ^{32}P was scattered all over my bench and the surrounding area when I removed the bubbler tube.

John Smith, our radioactive safety officer, was away, and Sydney muttered, "I'm too busy. Go and see Fred (Sanger)." Fred listened to me and came downstairs to the second floor. Without a word, he put on some rubber dishwashing gloves, grabbed a can of Ajax and some sponges, and knelt down to try to see how much radioactivity he could get off the floor. Not much. I objected to what he was doing because I thought I should be doing that job. Quite soon, he said that I had done enough and decided to clear the area. I stripped my clothing off, donned a lab coat, and drove home where I left the clothes in the coal shed to "cool" off. Hugh Robertson called the contaminated space Yucca Flats, and some time later that whole floor and bench area were removed.

I cannot imagine a person of Fred's reputation taking on such a modest and thankless task and refusing any help. The image of him, on his knees on the floor, trying to wash away the radioactivity I had spilled, is still fresh in my mind. There are many ways, I suppose, of exhibiting humility and greatness, and this was one of them.

I have described my history as a postdoctoral fellow at the MRC-LMB. The lab itself was such an amazing place in which to work and deserves significant comment. Mike Fuller ran the stockroom both efficiently and in a friendly fashion to ensure that we always had what we needed. The library, with a modest collection of journals, was always available and supplied with photocopies of articles on demand. There was, importantly, a collection of brilliant younger colleagues, each with his own bizarre identity. The air was bubbling with notions of both useful, practical ideas on how to go about things and theoretical notions that were interesting to discuss. The postdocs were international and vibrant. John Smith liberally dispensed his fund of knowledge, the more liberal the better you knew him. The generated ideas whizzed around the lab, many not useful, but when one was, it was recognized as such and shone brilliantly. There were also many extraordinary social and sporting functions with the postdocs and staff. I can instantly create a picture in my mind of playing football (soccer) for the MRC-LMB B team on a local village's meadow on a Sunday morning. Needless to say, while the events I have described are mostly joyful, there were moments of great disappointment during that first year, and episodes of quarrel and disagreement among the many prima donnas in the lab.

While I was at the MRC-LMB, Sydney was steadfastly

A Nobel Fellow on Every Floor

1638   S. Altman

FIGURE 7.—Several of the senior leaders in the MRC lab around 1967. Seated from left to right: Hugh Huxley, Max Perutz, Fred Sanger, Sydney Brenner; standing left to right: John Kendrew, Francis Crick (courtesy of the MRC-LMB).

plugging away on the histology of the nematode and beginning to develop a system for mutant isolation. Occasionally, I would meet with him to discuss some science; those meetings were filled with dazzling fireworks. There were rockets and flares that fizzled and burned out, and others that cast their illuminated glow on the landscape and burned brilliantly forever. His fund of knowledge was enormous, and the ideas flowed freely. Many were not practical, but some always were.

Francis was preoccupied with chromosome structure. In fact, he surprised me on a solitary Saturday afternoon when he approached me in the hall, very excitedly, and wanted to tell me about a new theory. I was, of course, flattered but dumbfounded. I understood very little about the chromosome and the theory we were discussing, and this conversation did not further my knowledge much. Fred Sanger was working on the sequencing of DNA, I believe having already given up on using the various enzymes that he had employed with proteins and RNA (see STRETTON 2002). Max Perutz was heavily involved in trying to understand the mechanism of hemoglobin action; Aaron Klug was finishing up further details of tRNA crystal structures and getting started on nucleosomes; and Cesar Milstein was busy with antibodies (Figure 7).

Sydney still had an abiding interest in tRNA suppressors, so in the summer of 1971, Larry Soll, who had recently received a Ph.D. from Stanford, came to give a talk on su_7^+. Sydney showed up after a while dressed in his usual James Dean outfit of chinos and a tee shirt with a cigarette pack stuffed inside one of the sleeves. He managed to ask some good questions and, afterwards in the hall, Larry asked, "Who was that far-out freak with the good head?" That created a round of hysterical laughter from the surrounding people. I am not sure we have heard a better definition of Sydney. In any case, John Sulston, in *The Common Thread*, writes about Sydney

as a "complex and powerful personality" (SULSTON and FERRY 2002). For those of us who know Sydney, that can be considered only the essence of a very vague description. More recently, Bargmann and Hodgkin described Sydney as "outrageously brilliant, charismatic and witty," a much more satisfying description when complementing Sulston's words (BARGMANN and HODGKIN 2002).

One has to remember that Sydney and Francis shared an office, an assignment unheard of in the United States. That fact immediately marked the lab as unusual and interesting. Sydney and Francis needed to talk to each other. We can only imagine what wonderful conversations they had. And if one of them was not around, then whoever was in the coffee room became the focus of talks.

Conversation was always a pleasure. I enjoyed tea, mornings and afternoons, and lunch every day where everything, from local British politics to matters of serious scientific interest, was discussed.

Of course, the primary and most important feature for those of us who were new in the lab was that everybody was heard. Holding a position at the lab meant, as the senior people showed every day, that you had a respectable opinion on science and that your opinion was treated the same as everybody else's. The dedication to science was paramount. Everybody paid attention. However, if what you said was incorrect or foolish, you were promptly told so. You were also expected to work, more or less alone, with no immediate help from senior people. The assumption was that everybody could do experiments well. The senior people taught by example: everybody was in the lab, working. These permanent, abiding lessons of how to do science have remained with me and, I hope, have been passed on to my students over the years.

I spent the last several months in the MRC-LMB trying to finish up my experiments. Two years had seemed like a lifetime. I had some reasonable results to work on, and I seemed to be able to convince people that the results were important.

My time at the MRC-LMB frequently seems to me to be the beginning and the end of my supposedly fabulous career as a scientist. After I left, except for a brief visit to finish a manuscript that Hugh Robertson and I were working on, I stayed away for many years because I did not want the MRC-LMB to guide my life. My scientific work gradually drifted away from tRNA mutants and focused on RNase P, which I still work on. Later, when I did come back for a few days from time to time, it was always a great pleasure to see Sydney and the others. Gradually, as Sydney and Francis left the lab, my friendship with Aaron Klug grew, and we have worked on RNA proteins jointly.

Work on RNase P is usually a 3- to 4-year period of boredom and fright. Now we are in one of the fifth years. My lab is currently concerned with RNase P in both *E. coli* and human HeLa cells. In *E. coli*, we have

306

identified small, intergenic RNAs that are substrates for RNase P, an indication that this enzyme is involved in determining gene expression in operons. In HeLa cells, we have shown that there are at least ten protein subunits of the enzyme as well as an RNA subunit. We have also shown that in transient transfection experiments, the inhibition of the expression of the protein subunits does affect some but not all the subunits if one of them is specifically targeted.

There is no doubt that Sydney and the beautiful atmosphere of the lab for doing science were my greatest inspirations. Sydney, although from some viewpoints distant, arrogant, or hard to deal with, became for me a very familiar person. The community of immigrants in South Africa in which he grew up was not terribly different from the immigrant community where I grew up in Montreal. He is a tremendous comic when he wants to be, as well as arrogant and deprecatory, with humor, when he feels that it is appropriate. His knowledge of biology is encyclopedic. I learned, as a postdoc, not to speak to him unless I had something more or less correct to say. In more recent years, I have forgotten that discipline: questions can be asked that are not totally appropriate. In fact, about 2 years ago at Yale, Sydney suggested that what I was saying about a topic he was working on was "all tryptophan," a familiar phrase to those of us who know him and probably as close as he gets to profanity in public.

Memory can be elusive. Perhaps, we may consider this essay as "all tryptophan" or, if that is not adequate or fitting, please be kind in selecting your own appropriate word.

Recently, John Heuser wrote in *Science* of the words that Sir Bernard Katz used in describing his own career. Among these were, ". . . a good mentor and a great deal of luck" (HEUSER 2003). My good fortune in the first category starts with Lee Grodzins in physics at MIT, went on to Leonard Lerman, a friend and thesis supervisor, Matt Meselson, and finally, as written here, Sydney Brenner and the amazing collection of senior personalities at the MRC-LMB. In fact, very shortly after I arrived at the MRC-LMB, I saw Sir Lawrence Bragg, who came to the lab to see a model of the new crystal structure of tRNA. The names that were to become famous were all about us every day.

All the postdocs worked very hard, knowing full well that when a word of advice was needed, it was always there, down the hall, at a door that was always open.

LITERATURE CITED

ABELSON, J. N., M. L. GEFTER, L. BARNETT, A. LANDY, R. L. RUSSELL *et al.*, 1970 Mutant tyrosine transfer ribonucleic acids. J. Mol. Biol. **47:** 15–28.

ALTMAN, S., 1971 Isolation of tyrosine tRNA precursor molecules. Nat. New Biol. **229:** 19–21.

BARGMANN, C., and J. HODGKIN, 2002 Accolade for elegans. Cell **111:** 759–762.

BERNHARDT, D., and J. E. DARNELL, 1969 tRNA synthesis in HeLa cells. J. Mol. Biol. **42:** 43–56.

BRENNER, S., 1988 Forward, pp. ix–xiii in *The Nematode Caenorhabditis elegans*, edited by W. WOOD and the COMMUNITY OF *C. ELEGANS* RESEARCHERS. Cold Spring Harbor Laboratory Press, Cold Spring Harbor, NY.

BROOKHAVEN SYMPOSIUM, 1974 *Processing of RNA*, Vol. 26. Brookhaven Symposium in Biology, Brookhaven, NY.

BURDON, R. H., 1971 Ribonucleic acid maturation in animal cells. Prog. Nucleic Acid Res. Mol. Biol. **11:** 33–79.

CRICK, F. H. C., L. BARNETT, S. BRENNER and R. J. WATTS-TOBIN, 1961 General nature of the genetic code for proteins. Nature **192:** 1227–1232.

GAMOW, G., 1954 Possible mathematical relation between deoxyribonucleic acid and proteins. Dan. Biol. Medd. **22:** 1–13.

HEUSER, J., 2003 My little spontaneous blips. Science **300:** 1248.

PAIS, A., 1982 *Subtle Is the Lord.* Oxford University Press, New York.

PAIS, A., 1991 *Niels Bohr's Times.* Oxford University Press, New York.

SMITH, J. D., L. BARNETT, S. BRENNER and R. L. RUSSELL, 1970 More mutant tyrosine transfer ribonucleic acids. J. Mol. Biol. **50:** 1–14.

STRETTON, A. O. W., 2002 The first sequence: Fred Sanger and insulin. Genetics **162:** 527–532.

SULSTON, J., and G. FERRY, 2002 *The Common Thread.* Bantam, London/New York.

Dick Dickerson

Dick Dickerson (see chapter 2) joined John Kendrew's group in the MRC Unit at the Cavendish for a year in 1959, and was involved in pushing the X-ray work on myoglobin to obtain a higher resolution (2Å) structure published in 1961. He recalled life in the hut in an article in *Protein Science* (Vol. 1, 182–186, 1992).

Protein Science (1992), *1*, 182–186. Cambridge University Press. Printed in the USA.
Copyright © 1992 The Protein Society 0961-8368/92 $5.00 + .00

RECOLLECTIONS

A little ancient history

RICHARD E. DICKERSON

Molecular Biology Institute, University of California, Los Angeles, Los Angeles, California 90024

(RECEIVED August 28, 1991; ACCEPTED August 29, 1991)

In September 1957, Peter J. Wheatley despaired of supporting a wife and two daughters on his Leeds University professorial salary of £900 per annum (then $2,500), resigned from the university, and prepared to move to Zurich to head up a new crystallographic laboratory for Monsanto. He was to take with him his graduate student John Daly, but with only 3 months left of my postdoctoral year at Leeds, I was told to find another supervisor. (John Daly was notable in my memory for two things: He brewed ginger beer in the closet of his apartment, having occasionally to endure the trauma of exploding beer bottles, and he was a tireless promoter of a series of fantasy novels that no one else had ever heard of, *The Lord of the Rings*, by an obscure British academic named Tolkien.)

Leeds University had a decent inorganic X-ray structure group for its day. It had oscillation cameras for data collection. An electronic computer was available at Manchester University, just over the Pennine Hills, and one could always go there to calculate a three-dimensional Patterson map from a new data set. After that you were on your own at Leeds, with Beevers-Lipson strips and a desk calculator. Understandably, we worked in projections. My project was a five-atom structure, dimethyl-sulfoximine, $(CH_3)_2SONH$, which to no one's surprise turned out to be tetrahedral. It was somewhat of a comedown from my nine-atom boron hydride thesis project with Bill Lipscomb at Minnesota. But my wife Lola and I thoroughly enjoyed Yorkshire, and we hated to cut short our time in England.

Fortunately, just at that juncture, Max Perutz and John Kendrew at Cambridge University began advertising worldwide for postdoctoral fellows. John's low-resolution map (6 Å) of myoglobin showed solid cylinders that everyone fully expected would turn out to be Linus Paul-

ing's α-helices. John was gearing up for a high-resolution analysis of myoglobin, while Max was working toward an initial low-resolution picture of hemoglobin. Peter Wheatley, perhaps in a fit of conscience, sent them a warm letter of recommendation on my behalf. Bill Lipscomb, my Ph.D. supervisor in Minnesota, also had recommended me, so I received a telephone call suggesting that I might like to drive up to Cambridge for an interview. (In England, one travels "up" to Cambridge, and suspended students are "sent down." The only exception to this barographic hierarchy is London: *Everyone* goes "up to London.") I visited them, and we all went (up) to London to see David Phillips, who was collaborating with Kendrew on myoglobin data collection at the Royal Institution. There was a meeting of minds, and at the end of 1957, Lola and I moved all our worldly goods, which fitted into one very small British Ford "Popular," south to Cambridge. (The next larger model, which we couldn't afford, was called the "Prefect." Ford Prefect later became famous as the adopted name of the alien hero of the *Hitchhiker's Guide to the Galaxy*, but that's another story.) I had written to Herb Gutowsky at the University of Illinois to see if they would wait one more year for their assistant professor, and if they would be happy having a protein crystallographer rather than an inorganic crystallographer. They would. I also wrote to Lipscomb for advice, and he replied, "It's a wonderful opportunity, but be careful — don't become a professional postdoc!"

Max and John's offices and wet laboratories were in a one-story corrugated prefabricated building in a courtyard of the Cavendish Physics Laboratory complex. This construction, known as "the Hut," had been built for Metallurgy during the Second World War. It was a great experience to sit in an office with fellow postdoctorals Roger Hart and Alver from Norway, with John Kendrew in the adjacent office separated only by a plasterboard partition, Sidney Brenner and Francis Crick across the corridor, and Max Perutz across from John. Eleven o'clock coffee was heralded each morning by Francis

Reprint requests to: Richard E. Dickerson, Molecular Biology Institute, University of California, Los Angeles, Los Angeles, California 90024.

182

308

Crick's unmistakable laugh ringing down the corridor. When he left for an extended visit of his own to the U.S., he was sorely missed.

At one end of the long building was the densitometer room, where several young women spent their days feeding precession films through a Joyce-Loebl double-beam microdensitometer and measuring peak heights by hand with a millimeter scale. At the other end was the sole wet lab, occupied by people such as Seymour Benzer and Leslie Barnett. Figure 1 shows part of the structure group outside the Hut in 1958. The universal suit and tie among men did not reflect any "dressing up" for a photograph; these were standard laboratory wear at the time. The French popular science journal *La Recherche* once paid Max a left-handed compliment by describing him as, "a person who gives the appearance of wearing clothing chiefly to keep warm." In England in 1958 this was no small matter!

The Hut still is to be seen in the Cavendish courtyard, a melancholy relic that stands open to the weather and is used only as a bicycle shed. No one there apparently realizes today that the Hut is an historical treasure, and should be bronzed. Once while I was there in 1959, two Russian visitors came to visit Perutz. As he hosted them in his office in the Hut, they exclaimed in puzzlement, "But where is your Institute?" It is typical of Max that he

took pleasure in telling them with a smile, "This is my Institute." Several years later (1962) he got his Institute, on the Addinbrooks Hospital site on Hills Road. But it just wasn't the same thing.

Fortunately, there was room for the rotating anodes and other X-ray data collecting equipment in the basement of the adjacent New Cavendish Building. Cambridge, unlike Leeds, actually had a computer of its own: EDSAC II, a marvel with 2,000 words of fast access core storage, plus magnetic drum and tape. People there told me how tedious the old EDSAC had been, and how much of an improvement the current machine was. There were three categories of customer: "Users," "Partially Authorized Users," and "Fully Authorized Users." Users could perform calculations only during the day, or under the watchful eye of one of the higher grades. Fully Authorized Users were competent to turn on EDSAC II at the beginning of the day, and turn it off at night when the last job was finished. I ultimately rose to the rank of Partially Authorized User: I wasn't allowed to power up the computer, but could work as late as I liked at night, shutting down the machine at the end by throwing off a set of wall switches in carefully prescribed order.

I elected to work with John Kendrew on the high-resolution structure analysis of myoglobin. When I arrived, the plan had been to work at 2.5-Å resolution, but every-

Fig. 1. Part of the myoglobin/hemoglobin structure team outside the Hut in 1958, with the brick New Cavendish Laboratory and the chimneys of Old Cavendish behind. From left to right: Larry Steinrauf and Dick Dickerson (postdoctorals), Hilary Muirhead (graduate student), Michael Rossmann (postdoctoral), Philip ? (face obscured), Anne Cullis (research assistant), Bror Strandberg (postdoctoral), ? Wiebenga and unknown (technicians), and Max Perutz (white coat). In front: Leslie Barnett and Mary Pinkerton (research assistants).

one worried whether the cylinders of the 6-Å map would resolve themselves into α-helices at 2.5 Å. The largest circle of data that could be collected on a 5-inch-square precession film cassette with our 90-mm film distance was 2.0 Å, so we decided in laboratory discussions to go for the limit and to jump to 2.0 Å in one step. We were still worried, however. At 2.0 Å resolution, would an α-helix be a solid rod, a hollow "garden hose," or a hollow tube with spiral pattern around the outside? No one was really sure. Roger Hart was an electron microscopist, and had come from London to Cambridge after the tragic and premature death of Rosalind Franklin, with whom he had been a postdoc. Alver and I were small-molecule crystallographers and shared the odd distinction of being the only people in the laboratory who had ever solved an X-ray structure at the atomic level, Perutz and Kendrew included. But soon our ranks were swelled by the arrival of Michael Rossmann, to work with Perutz. Michael had moved from J. Monteith Robertson's crystal structure group in Glasgow, to a postdoctoral position with Bill Lipscomb in Minnesota, and we had overlapped for the last few months of my doctoral work there.

Michael shared an office with David Blow, and the two became our computing experts. I don't recall whether Michael ever achieved Fully Authorized User status on EDSAC II, but his least-squares and rotation-translation programs became so complex that the Computing Center developed the practice of using one of them for morning computer checks; they put the EDSAC to a more strenuous test than did their own diagnostic routines! EDSAC II was a thermodynamic monster, with a panel in the rear containing an array of 4-foot-long pull-out vacuum tube racks, each with a large handle. A twist of its handle and a pull would bring one rack sliding out, with vacuum tubes arranged in double rank like soldiers. The wiring diagrams for EDSAC II were in pencil on a large bundle of mechanical drawings. Whenever a change in wiring was made, the old diagram would be erased and the new circuit pencilled in. There may have been proper ink diagrams somewhere, but I never saw them.

Input/output on the EDSAC II left something to be desired: standard British telegraph tape readers and punches. The reading was mechanical rather than optical. Little fingers in the tape reader pushed against the tape, looking for holes. We developed the sloppy habit of editing minor tape glitches with patches of Scotch tape, but this gave the Computing Center fits. The patch eventually would be pushed off the computer tape, and the adhesive would gum up the tape reader. The Computing Center periodically fulminated against such a practice ("Any input tape found to be patched manually will be confiscated!") but could not stop it completely. The 2-Å myoglobin data set consisted of nearly 10,000 reflections from native myoglobin and each of three heavy atom derivatives. We wrestled with the problem of how to sort and merge 40,000 data points, in a computer with only

2,000 words of rapid-access memory. Finally we decided to cut the four original data tapes into strips of a common h and k, sort them by thumbtacking them onto a grid on a large piece of bulletin board, and then merge them manually by running the strips through a tape reader and punching out a new one-piece data tape. Figure 2 illustrates this process.

The three derivatives were parachlormercuribenzene sulfonate (PCMBS), mercury diammine, and gold chloride. The two mercurials were freshly prepared, but the gold chloride came from a cache of heavy atom diffusion trials that had been set up 2 years earlier by Gerhard Bodo and Howard Dintzis. Several hundred 2-cc vials of crystals were stored in a laboratory cupboard, along with Bodo's and Dintzis' log books. Bror and I tested endless numbers of these on the precession camera, looking for those that gave usable intensity changes. Under gold chloride, Bodo or Dintzis had written, "Two weeks: No changes," and "Twelve weeks: No changes." But after 2 years, I found beautiful intensity changes in one single vial with gold chloride-soaked myoglobin crystals. This became our third isomorphous derivative, but one with unexpectedly tragic consequences.

I found crystal mounting to be a tedious and fiendishly difficult process. The myoglobin crystals in general were too large to fit into the 1-mm-diameter glass capillaries, and had to be cut into quarters under the microscope with a sharp razor blade. A fragment then had to be maneuvered into the capillary, a plug of mother liquor added at each end, and the ends sealed with hot wax. I broke one capillary after another trying to learn how to do it. It looked so easy when Kendrew had shown me how. One of my office mates, Roger Hart, was surveying hemoglobin derivatives for Perutz, like Strandberg and I with myoglobin. Roger's hands were crippled by polio, and he became a challenge—if Roger could learn to mount crystals, then by God I could too. I finally mastered the technique. Later I discovered that Roger didn't mount his crystals at all—Max came in evenings to mount a batch for him!

Max and John were utterly different in personality. Kendrew came in two or three mornings a week to discuss the progress of the research, and to give help where help was needed. He was a great mentor for someone who wanted to learn how to be an independent investigator. At other times he was busy as a science advisor to the British government (on the Polaris missile system as I recall), as an administrator of Peterhouse (college), and on other affairs. In contrast, Max was never so happy as when in the laboratory at the bench, doing science. One learned by talking with John, but by watching Max.

The tragedy of gold chloride occurred one black Monday morning when I came into the laboratory ready to mount more crystals for data collection and found that I had failed to screw down the cap of the 2-cc vial tightly the previous Friday. The tube with the precious crystals

Fig. 2. Bror Strandberg (left) and Dick Dickerson (right) returning from the EDSAC II computing center carrying the paper tape sorting board for the myoglobin 2-Å data set. Individual strips of tape contained intensities from minimum to maximum l, and were sorted manually on h and k by thumbtacking them to the proper square on a grid drawn on the sorting board (high tech!). Tape strips for native myoglobin and the various heavy atom derivatives were tacked together and later were read through a tape reader again to produce one long master data tape.

was completely dry, and an efflorescence of dried salt covered the outside of the tube. I was stunned. I walked into Kendrew's office, explained briefly what had happened, and tendered my resignation.

Kendrew didn't shout at me and didn't laugh at me, which would have been even worse. Instead, he said calmly that of course I wasn't going to resign over a thing like that; we would just have to see where we were with the gold derivative. As feared, there were no more vials of crystals in gold chloride, and the project obviously could not wait 2 years for more gold to diffuse in. So we went with what we had already collected. Hence to be accurate, the 2-Å resolution structure analysis of sperm whale myoglobin was not carried out with three isomorphous derivatives, but with 2.75.

Space forbids saying much about how the data were collected, derivatives refined, and phases analyzed. The final calculation of the three-dimensional electron density map on EDSAC II was an all-night party. Dave Phillips and some of his group came up (sorry, down) from London for the event. (One heavy atom data set had been collected at the Royal Institution.) It took literally all night to calculate the map. John was sufficiently worried about machine errors that he then repeated the entire Fourier synthesis calculation on a defense computer to which he had access at a military base. We plotted the map sections on Plexiglas sheets, stacked the sheets over a light box, and threw a cocktail party at dusk on the Peterhouse lawn to celebrate. I vividly remember Sir Lawrence Bragg, director of the Royal Institution and the man who had brought Perutz and Kendrew to Cambridge, taking the elbow of guests at the party and propelling them to the light box, pointing at an α-helix that ran obliquely through the map sections, and saying excitedly: "Look! See, it's hollow!" Hollow it was indeed, and striped with a barber pole pattern that was clearly resolvable into a $-NH-C_\alpha-CO-$ polypeptide backbone. As a genuinely unexpected dividend, at 2.0 Å you could even use the carbonyl groups to figure out which way the backbone chain ran. A small thing today, perhaps; but in 1958 who knew what to expect? It had never been done before.

The map was calculated in August 1959. I literally threw the maps on Kendrew's desk and ran for the boat train to Southampton. Bror Strandberg stayed 3 months longer and helped interpret the map in detail. Herman Watson joined the group and carried on the interpretation.

One interesting postscript: J.D. Bernal of Birkbeck College once remarked that you would never be able to interpret the three-dimensional Patterson map of a protein unless you built a model big enough to walk through.

R.E. Dickerson

That was nearly true of the Fourier map of myoglobin. Kendrew built a "wire forest" model by sinking 4-foot steel rods into a 6-foot-square plywood base on a 1-inch grid, and then color-coding electron density with small spring clips: white for the highest density — yellow — orange — red — green — blue — black. He then invented what today are called "Kendrew models" — accurate skeletal wire atoms and groups held together by locking couplings — and built the myoglobin molecule into the forest of wires. When the International Union of Crystallography held its Congress in Cambridge in the summer of 1960, Kendrew's huge myoglobin model was one of the showpieces. But the saying about a prophet being without honor in his own country was true. The room in which the model was constructed was owned by Electrical Engineering, and John was told in no uncertain terms that he would have to get his junk out of that room before the Fall term commenced! Part of the wire forest model is preserved today in the Science Museum in South Kensington in London.

Max Perutz and John Kendrew were awarded the Nobel Prize in Chemistry in 1962 for their hemoglobin/myoglobin analyses, and Francis Crick, Jim Watson, and Maurice Wilkins shared the Nobel Prize in Medicine that same year for their DNA structure. Did we consciously think we were working on Nobel Prize projects in 1958? Not really. We were aware that we were breaking new ground, and that the results would be considered important, but it was not clear how important. Max and John worked hard because they were passionately interested in the answers. Hemoglobin was, and still is, Max Perutz' life (along with skiing, the structure of ice, and a few other diversions). There is an old cartoon of a young boy at a children's party, in suit and tie with party hat and streamers, saying self-consciously to another child, "I hate this kind of thing, but I want a happy childhood to look back on." I regard myself as having had a very happy scientific childhood: enjoyable at the time, and even more pleasurable in retrospect as the field moves on. It was true in 1958, and still is true today that, to paraphrase an Arabic saying about Grenada quoted by Washington Irving: "Allah gives to those whom he loves, the means of living in Cambridge."

Michael Levitt

Michael Levitt came as a research student in 1968–71, with Bob Diamond as supervisor. His thesis subject was 'The Conformation Analysis of Proteins', but he was involved in several other subjects in this and other, subsequent stays at LMB (see chapter 6). His review of 'The Birth of Computational Structural Biology' was published in *Nature Structural Biology* (Vol. 8, 392–393, 2001). By permission from Macmillan Publishers Ltd.

history

The birth of computational structural biology

Michael Levitt

Like Sydney Altman[1], I too was initially rejected by the renowned Medical Research Council (MRC) Laboratory of Molecular Biology in Cambridge, England. The year was 1967 and I was then in my final year of a B.Sc. degree in Physics at Kings College in London. Enthralled by John Kendrew's BBC 1964 television series "The Thread of Life", I wanted desperately to do my Ph.D. at the MRC in Cambridge. Alas there was no room for any new postgraduate students in 1967!

After some negotiations, I was accepted for the following year. More importantly, John Kendrew said that I should spend the intervening period at the Weizmann Institute in Israel with Shneior Lifson. Kendrew had just heard of Lifson's initial ideas[2] on the consistent force field (CFF), which was an attempt to simulate the properties of any molecular system from a simple potential energy function. He believed that these methods should be applied to protein and nucleic acid macromolecules. I arrived in Israel in October, 1967 and set to work programming the consistent force field under the supervision of Lifson and his Ph.D. student Arieh Warshel. At that time, computing at the Weizmann Institute was amongst the best in the world; in 1963 computer engineers there had built their own machine, appropriately known as the Golem, after the Jewish folklore automaton.

In a few short months we had a program called CFF that allowed us to calculate the energy, forces (energy first derivatives with respect to atomic positions) and curvature (energy second derivatives with respect to atomic positions) of any molecular system. Warshel went on to use the program to calculate structural, thermodynamic and spectroscopic properties of small organic molecules[3], while I followed Kendrew's dictum and applied these same programs to proteins. This led to the first energy minimization of an entire protein structure (in fact we did two, myoglobin and lysozyme) in a process that became known as energy refinement[4].

I began my Ph.D. at the MRC in Cambridge in September, 1968 and was immediately immersed in the annual tra-

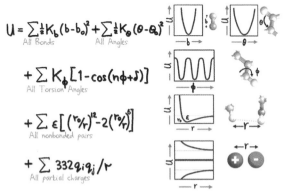

$$U = \sum_{All\ Bonds} \tfrac{1}{2} K_b (b-b_0)^2 + \sum_{All\ Angles} \tfrac{1}{2} K_\theta (\theta-\theta_0)^2$$

$$+ \sum_{All\ Torsion\ Angles} K_\phi [1-\cos(n\phi+\delta)]$$

$$+ \sum_{All\ nonbonded\ pairs} \epsilon \left[\left(\tfrac{r_0}{r}\right)^{12} - 2\left(\tfrac{r_0}{r}\right)^6 \right]$$

$$+ \sum_{All\ partial\ charges} 332 q_i q_j / r$$

Fig. 1 The total potential energy of any molecule is the sum of simple allowing for bond stretching, bond angle bending, bond twisting, van der Waals interactions and electrostatics. Many properties of a biomolecules can be simulated with such an empirical energy function.

dition of Lab Talks. These talks by members of the three divisions at the Laboratory of Molecular Biology at that time (Structural Studies Division under Kendrew, the Cell Biology Division under Sydney Brenner and Francis Crick, and Protein and Nucleic Acid Chemistry Division under Fred Sanger) were a treat for newcomers to the Lab. The 'Molecule of the Year' was tRNA, which had been predicted to exist by Francis Crick 10 years before[5] and was now the subject of intense structural and genetic interest. I decided to try to build a model of tRNA and started off playing with CPK space-filling models at home. Transfer RNA has almost 2,000 atoms and a space-filling model weighs over 100 pounds. My most vivid memory is lowering the tRNA CPK model from the first floor window of our terrace cottage in Newnham, while my somewhat pregnant wife was having a hard time controlling her laughter. The model, which was then rebuilt from brass components, towered over me as I measured all atomic positions with a plumb line (a pointed metal weight hanging from a string onto graph paper) so that the model could be energy refined. Modeling tRNA led me to

interact closely with both Crick and Aaron Klug and so I was exposed to the wonders of molecular and structural biology.

The model was published in 1969 (ref. 6) and I settled down to work on my thesis entitled "Conformation Analysis of Proteins"[7]. This was entirely devoted to computational biology and included chapters entitled "Energy Parameters from Proteins", "Interpreting Problematic Regions of Electron Density Maps Using Convergent Energy Refinement", "Energy Refinement of Enzyme/Substrate Complexes: Lysozyme and Hexa-N-Acetyl-glucosamine" and "Energy Refinement of Tertiary Structure Changes Caused by Oxygenation of Horse Haemoglobin".

Work on nucleic acids was not neglected and at that time it seemed that RNA folding would be easier to tackle than protein folding[8]. Computational work on protein folding began in 1973 during my postdoctoral research with Shneior Lifson back at the Weizmann Institute. Arieh Warshel had returned from his postdoc at Harvard and we started to work together again on both protein folding and enzyme reactions. Each project led to novel simulations[9,10] that became the basis for a great

nature structural biology • volume 8 number 5 • may 2001

history

deal of future work, with much still to be done a quarter of a century later.

I returned to a staff position at the MRC in Cambridge in October, 1974 and Warshel joined me there as a visitor. Warshel focused his attention on quantum mechanics in biology and published a model of the initial steps in the visual process, based on a molecular dynamics simulation[11]. Meanwhile I worked with Cyrus Chothia on the classification and analysis of protein architecture[12] and with Tony Jack, who passed away in 1978, on the refinement of large structures by simultaneous minimization of the molecular energy and crystallographic R-factor[13]. Both papers were to lead to significant future science: Chothia went on to develop the first web database, SCOP[14] and Axel Brünger based his wonderfully useful X-PLOR program[15] on Jack's work with me.

While Warshel and I were travelling around the world, our computer program, CFF, had wings of its own. Arieh Warshel took the program with him on his postdoctoral visit to Martin Karplus' lab at Harvard in 1969. In 1971, Bruce Gelin, who was just released from the US army, began working with Warshel and started writing a new version of the code. This rewrite was essential as I had learned my programming from an IBM FORTRAN II manual, whereas Bruce Gelin was much better trained. I can still recall my excitement when I saw his version of the program — many of the variable names were those I had invented but the code was so much more elegant!

Bruce Gelin's code led to his pioneering work with Andy McCammon and Martin Karplus on the simulation of protein dynamics[16]. This work, published in 1977, marks the start of the next phase of computational structural biology in that it signaled the linking of computational chemistry with biology. Work in the field was becoming much more widespread; the original program that I wrote with Arieh Warshel went on through Bruce

Gelin's rewrite to form the basis of the next generation of programs including CHARMM (Chemistry at HARvard Molecular Mechanics) from Karplus' group at Harvard, AMBER from Peter Kollmann's group at UCSF and Discover from Arnold Hagler's company, Biosym.

Looking back to that period, it is much easier to appreciate who were the key contributors. Shneior Lifson, who passed away on 22 January, 2001, really started it all by defining the form of the empirical potential energy function still in use today (Fig. 1). In particular, he was the first to realize that the hydrogen bond could be described by simple electrostatic interaction of partial charges. With Warshel, he also set up a consistent procedure for deriving the energy parameters.

Sequence analysis, which forms such a key part of modern computational biology, was born in that same 1969–1977 period. In 1969, analysis of tRNA sequences revealed a correlated base change[6] (two bases not in a helical stem change together to maintain function, thereby indicating a possible interaction); in 1971, Needleman and Wunsch applied the computer science method of dynamic programming to sequence alignment[17]; and in 1977, Sanger and coworkers started genome-scale DNA sequencing with the φX-174 bacteriophage sequence[18].

I still remember with much chagrin that day in 1976 when Bart Barrell approached me to help analyze the φX DNA sequence only to be rebuffed; I felt that structure was just so much more interesting than sequence. Having confessed what may be the greatest misjudgment of my career, I would like to conclude with a few words about the future of computational biology.

Computers were made for biology: biology would never have advanced as it did without the dramatic increase in computer power and availability. One day we would like to be able to simulate complicated biological processes, perhaps even going from the genomic sequence to a full simulation of the organism's phenotype.

In thinking about how to do this, it is interesting to compare Nature with simulated biology. Some things that are very difficult in Nature are trivial for computers: consider how much cellular machinery is needed to transcribe DNA sequence to RNA sequence — in the computer all one needs to do is change 'T' to 'U'. Translating RNA sequence to protein sequence is even more difficult in the cell, but in a computer one just applies the genetic code table. Other things that appear very easy for Nature are almost impossibly hard for computers: once synthesized a protein sequence spontaneously folds into the native structure, whereas simulating even a part of this process is still well beyond our computational capabilities. Computational structural biology will remain very challenging well into the 21st century.

Michael Levitt is in the Department of Structural Biology, Stanford University, Stanford, Calfornia 94305-5400, USA. email: michael.levitt@stanford.edu

1. Altman, S. *Nature Structural Biology* **7**, 827–828 (2000).
2. Bixon, M. & Lifson, S. *Tetrahedron* **23**, 769–784 (1967).
3. Lifson, S. & Warshel, A. *J. Chem. Phys.* **49**, 5116–5129 (1968)
4. Levitt, M. & Lifson, S. *J. Mol. Biol.* **46**, 269–279 (1969).
5. Crick, F.H.C. *Symp. Soc. Exp. Biol.* **12**, 138–163 (1958).
6. Levitt, M. *Nature* **224**, 759–763 (1969).
7. Levitt, M. Ph. D. Thesis *Conformation analysis of proteins* (Cambridge University, Cambridge, UK; 1971); *http://csb.stanford.edu/levitt/Levitt_Thesis_1971/ Levitt_Thesis_1971.html*.
8. Levitt, M. In *Polymerization in Biological Systems* Ciba Foundation Symposium **7**, 146–171 (Eds Wolstenholme, G.E.W. & O'Connor, M., Elsevier, Amsterdam; 1972).
9. Levitt, M. & Warshel, A. *Nature* **253**, 694–698 (1975).
10. Warshel, A. & Levitt, M. *J. Mol. Biol.* **103**, 227–249 (1976).
11. Warshel, A. *Nature* **260**, 679–683 (1976).
12. Levitt, M. & Chothia, C. *Nature* **261**, 552–558 (1976).
13. Jack, A. & Levitt, M. *Acta Crystallogr. A* **34**, 931–935 (1978).
14. Murzin, A.G, Brenner, S.E., Hubbard, T. & Chothia C. *J. Mol. Biol.* **247**, 536–540 (1995).
15. Brünger, A.T., Karplus, M. & Petsko G.A. *Acta Crystallogr. A* **45**, 50–61 (1989).
16. McCammon, J.A., Gelin, B.R. & Karplus, M. *Nature* **267**, 585–590 (1977).
17. Needleman, S.B. & Wunsch, C.D. *J. Mol. Biol.* **48**, 443–453 (1970)
18. Sanger,F. *et al. Nature* **265**, 687–695 (1977).

Anand Sarabhai

Anand Sarabhai came to the MRC Unit at the Cavendish in 1959 as a PhD student of Sydney Brenner, his thesis aim being to show the co-linearity of the gene and its polypeptide chain (see chapter 7). He stayed on in LMB until 1967. His memories of life at the MRC were published in the *Journal of Biosciences* (Vol. 28, 665–669, 2003).

Perspectives

After DNA at the MRC

ANAND SARABHAI

The Retreat, Shahibag, Ahmedabad 380 004, India

(Email, sarabhaianand@hotmail.com)

1. Introduction

In 1959, when I went to Cambridge and first saw the MRC Laboratory of Molecular Biology, it was housed in a modest building buried inside the majesty of the famous Cavendish Laboratory. You could easily walk by without noticing it, thinking it was some kind of prefab workshop for physicists (figure 1). You would be partially right in that it was jam-packed with physicists; but what they were doing was not so much physics as laying the conceptual framework of life itself. The scientists you might run into were an extraordinary lot. There was Max Perutz, the founder-director of the laboratory, invariably in a neat tweed jacket; John Kendrew, the deputy director, with a shock of white hair; and of course Francis Crick, with his booming laugh, tall and patrician, sharing a small office with Sydney Brenner who was always bursting with ideas. The many post-docs, students and sundry visitors made up the rest.

February 28, 1953, when I was almost fifteen years old, was when the structure of DNA was discovered. 1953 was also the year in which Tenzing and Hillary climbed Mount Everest, Joseph Stalin died, Queen Elizabeth II was crowned the Queen of England and so on. Somehow I remember this year as one filled with both important and trivial events. Jim Watson's famous book *"The Double Helix"* describes the competition with Linus Pauling, the most famous of all chemists, for solving the DNA structure. It so happens that February 28 was also Pauling's birthday. The MRC Laboratory thus generated a birthday gift, welcome or otherwise. But more than that it helped set in place a conceptual framework to explore and explain the most fundamental aspects of life, the mechanisms of reproduction and inheritance.

When I was asked to write a short piece on the laboratory to mark the occasion of the 50th anniversary of the discovery of the structure of DNA, I hesitated. Accounts like this often are anecdotal and not interesting except for the person who is reciting the anecdote. On the other hand, there was something special about the MRC Lab in those days, not to mention the fact that it played an unrivalled role in ushering in the molecular biology revolution. I was privileged to be both an onlooker and a participant in some of the science that went on there in the early 1960s. What I can try to do is to give a flavour of what it was like to be in this incredible lab.

When asked whether there were simple guidelines to organize research so that it would be highly creative Max Perutz is said to have commented (according to Anthony Tucker): "No politics, no committees, no reports, no referees, no interviews – just gifted, highly motivated people picked by a few men of good judgement". Max ran the lab in this spirit and spent most of his time on haemoglobin crystallography. Likewise John Kendrew, on myoglobin. At the other end from crystallography was molecular genetics with Francis Crick and Sydney Brenner at the helm. In spite of the excitement and fast pace of science, a great deal of attention was paid to detail. Max as Director read all the papers which went for publication even if they were not in his field. In one instance he queried the common usage for sucrose density gradients and pointed out that the opposite of a steep gradient was not a shallow gradient. The opposite of shallow was deep and the opposite of steep was gentle. Francis Crick once commented that what I was saying was possible but not plausible. I remember going post-haste to the first dictionary I could lay my hands on to understand the difference between these two very similar words. As Francis Crick wrote in *The Scientist* "It was a blissful period, because the problems were important, only a few people (most of them friends) were working on them and thanks to the Medical Research Council's support, we didn't have to write grant requests and could study whatever we liked". Work and play co-existed. Francis and Odile Crick had a beautiful tall house on Portugal Place where the most lively parties were held. The artists, poets, philosophers,

315

666   *Anand Sarabhai*

historians and scientists who were invited made the parties memorable. Crick considered the chapels, a part of the history of the Cambridge colleges, as an unfortunate mistake of the past. Consequently, he refused to accept a fellowship in any college. Things changed when Churchill College was established with a promise not to build a chapel. Francis accepted a fellowship there. Such were the people and the philosophies which guided the MRC Laboratory and resulted in so many Nobel Prizes to Crick, Watson, Perutz, Kendrew, Klug, Milstein, Brenner, Sulston and others.

If you peered into the laboratory you could see a maze of equipment and glassware, all seemingly enjoying the chaos and crowding that was so obvious. Some of the

visuals were quite comic, such as a rigged-up glass assemblage to grow large quantities of bacteriophage, called the Fraser Machine (figure 2).

One day I was struck by the sight of Francis Crick staring intently at some molecular structures and squinting in a special way. He told me that seeing a 3-D structure stereoscopically required practice and invited me to try it out. Try as I might, I just could not make my eyes squint in the required manner. The overriding impression for me was that the school of the time-tested British genius of "making do" was in action and that string and tape and chewing gum would be handy if required for an experiment.

If you ventured as I did in 1959, you felt a huge sense of energy and purpose with conversations and arguments

Figure 1. The old MRC prefab building (photograph taken in 2003).

J. Biosci. | Vol. 28 | No. 6 | December 2003

Figure 2. Apparatus for growing phage on a large scale. F, Fraser apparatus; H, electric fire; A, air line connected to sinter of F; T, air trap filled with cottonwool.

galore. Francis and Sydney's office was just to the right as you entered the main door. It was tiny and the size of the book piles were huge, making one wonder whether they held up the roof. The blackboard was a visual treat and changed its appearance constantly (figure 3a), as many times during the day as new theories speculations and facts began to emerge. It conveyed a sense of energy reminiscent of a Cy Twombly painting (figure 3b).

The main experimental laboratory was largish, about 30 feet by 25 feet. I was given a bench top about 3 feet in length. I had walked over from the Biochemistry Department across the road to ask Francis and Sydney if they would accept me for a Ph. D Program. At Biochemistry the Professor and staff often wore a coat and tie. When I arrived at the MRC, Francis Crick was in blue jeans and a black sweater and Sydney was also in informal clothes. Without ado, I was told to address them by their first names, not Drs Crick and Brenner as would be the case at Biochemistry. The crystallographers at MRC, Perutz and Kendrew, were busy with deciphering the molecular structures of haemoglobin and myoglobin. Fred Sanger, who had just completed the chemical structure of insulin, was housed in Biochemistry and Sydney was collaborating with him on using the new protein fingerprinting technique to analyse bacteriophage head protein.

The original Watson-Crick DNA model stood in one of the small rooms in the prefab building. It was a reminder

of how many new things needed to be explored. The little office of Francis and Sydney reverberated frequently with fascinating arguments and an ever changing blackboard. One of the key postulates of the "Sequence hypothesis" was that the linear sequence of bases in DNA of a Gene Coded for a linear sequence of amino acids for the protein product of that gene, i.e. that the gene and 'its' protein were topologically co-linear.

Gene	A	B	C	D	A	B	C	D
Protein	A	B	C	D	B	A	D	C
			Co-linear				Not co-linear	

If A, B, C and D represent point mutations in a gene resulting in amino acid substitutions in the corresponding protein then there are, roughly speaking, two alternatives as shown above. The alternatives indicate what the main approaches to the problem were as pursued in a number of laboratories, the MRC at Cambridge, Charles Yanofsky at Stanford, George Streisinger at the University of Oregon and Cyrus Levinthal at Columbia University. The experiments consisted of creating point mutants and mapping

Anand Sarabhai

Figure 3. (a) Blackboard Reunion: Francis Crick and Sydney Brenner, 1986. Courtesy of MRC Laboratory of Molecular Biology. (b) Painting "Ohne Titel (Roma)" 1969.

them to create a genetic map. The protein product of the gene was fingerprinted to locate the amino acid substitution. Everyone believed that the gene and the protein would be co-linear but still this had to be proved. There was a sense of competition between the groups as to who would get the proof of co-linearity first. The books by Judson (1996) and Morange (1998) should be consulted in order to place this problem in context and for an appreciation of the discoveries that led to coding being, in a sense, the problem in molecular biology in the early 1960s. Whitehouse (1973) gives an excellent account of the experiments that led up to the deciphering of the genetic code. Both

Crick (1988) and Brenner (2001) have provided first-person accounts.

My thesis problem was to show the co-linearity of the gene and its polypeptide chain using mutants of bacteriophage T4 that Sydney had isolated. He had selected mutants that were resistant to osmotic shock. It was conjectured that they would have an altered amino acid sequence of the head protein. In retrospect it was an ingenious but risky assumption; it did not work out. I had a lucky break when I met Dick Epstein, the discoverer of nonsense mutants (amber mutants) of T4 in Geneva. The mutants were so named by Dick after the mother of Bernstein, a Caltech graduate student; Bernstein is the German for amber. These mutants (it was believed) did not make a full polypeptide in a normal cell but did so in a suppressor-positive cell. What was not known was whether the amber mutations kept terminating and releasing the synthesized peptide or simply got jammed at the amber site.

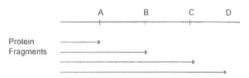

I told Dick that I could test this in Cambridge quickly. What I found was that the amber mutants kept terminating and releasing the polypeptide, so that you got large amount of fragments of polypeptide of lengths dictated by the position of the amber mutations in the gene. This broke open the co-linearity problem (Sarabhai *et al* 1964).

The Yanofsky group succeeded at the same time by using point mutations and altered amino acid substitutions (Yanofsky *et al* 1964). We published our papers at the same time. For a graduate student, to take on a fundamental problem like this may have been foolhardy. But I enjoyed the race. Many visiting scientists from around the world would come by for a few days to give a talk or just to visit, some to get converted to doing biology. I remember the visit of Don Glaser while he was on his way back to Berkley after winning the Nobel Prize for Physics in 1960 for his invention of the bubble chamber. He came to find out what he could do in biology. After his return to California he got so deeply involved that he went on to establish the Cetus Corporation one of the first Biotechnology Companies. Meanwhile the MRC was in high gear on other projects: Sydney on messenger RNA, Francis and Sydney proving that the code was a triplet by using the most elegant genetics. I went on to define the properties of inter-cistronic space, the space between the stop signal of a previous gene and the start signal of the next gene in a constructed operon.

The blackboard kept on changing but now in a grand new multistory laboratory.

References

Brenner S 2001 *My Life in Science* (Biomed Central Ltd.)

Crick F 1988 *What Mad Pursuit* (Baisc Books)

Judson H F 1996 *The eighth day of creation* (Expanded edition) (New York: Cold Spring Harbor Laboratory)

Morange M 1998 *A history of molecular biology* (Oxford: Oxford University Press)

Sarabhai A, Stretton A O W, Brenner S and Bolle A 1964 Co-linearity of the gene with the polypeptide chain; *Nature (London)* **201** 13–17

Sarabhai A and Brenner S 1967 A Mutant which reinitiates the polypeptide chain after termination; *J. Mol. Biol.* **27** 145–162

Whitehouse H L K 1973 *Towards an understanding of the mechanism of heredity* (3rd edition) (Edwin Arnold)

Yanofsky C, Carlton B C, Guest J R, Helinski D R and Henning U 1964 On the colinearity of gene structure and protein structure; *Proc. Natl. Acad. Sci. USA* **51** 266–272

Mitsuhiro Yanagida

Mitsuhiro Yanagida joined Aaron Klug's group in 1968 for a year to learn optical diffraction techniques for analysing electron micrographs of polyheads produced by mutants of T4 phage. He wrote up his memories of the visit in *Nature* (Vol. 429, 135, 2004). By permission from Macmillan Publishers Ltd.

essay **turning points**

Heads and tails

How a visit to the home of structural biology inspired a young scientist.

Mitsuhiro Yanagida

I first visited Cambridge in June 1968 to attend the International Symposium on Interactions Between Subunits of Biological Macromolecules. It was an excellent meeting, with talks by prominent researchers — I was particularly pleased to hear Francis Crick, who often led the discussions. A mere eight months before this meeting, I had joined Eduard Kellenberger's group at the Institute of Molecular Biology in the University of Geneva, Switzerland. Eduard saved me from being a graduate student in University of Tokyo — the riots in Japanese universities erupted soon after I joined him, and many of my generation were unable to continue their studies.

My work involved using phage morphogenesis as a model for more complex biological structures. My first project was to use an optical diffractometer to analyse the images of electron micrographs showing the tubular 'polyheads' produced in bacteria that were infected with phage T4 mutants. The polyhead was an ideal structure to study with the diffraction analyses of electron micrographs, a technique developed by Aaron Klug in the Laboratory of Molecular Biology (LMB), Cambridge. Although electron microscopy had a theoretical resolution at the atomic level, actual micrographs of biological specimens rarely achieved this because of deformation, damage, noise and the superimposition of images at different focal planes. However, if the biological particles consisted of regularly repeated structures, diffraction analysis could be a powerful tool for obtaining information from the average lattice structure. Another technique, optical filtration, also enabled selection for the side image of helical structures. I inherited the polyhead project from another student, who had left to become an activist on the independence of Jura. In retrospect, social unrest was responsible for two lucky events in my early scientific career.

I obtained a large number of diffraction patterns from polyhead electron micrographs. It seemed clear to me that the polyhead was not the precursor of the normal T4 head shell, as its lattice structure was polymorphic; the polyhead was therefore probably an abnormal assembly. I gave a short talk on these findings at a specialist workshop organized by Aaron after the main symposium. He told me that David DeRosier had found the same things in his laboratory, but that my micrographs might be good enough for further analysis by the optical-filtration method. Although Aaron had already pioneered the

computational Fourier reconstruction for the three-dimensional phage tail structure from electron micrographs, he was still interested in studying the head-related structures by manual diffraction methods.

Aaron and Eduard decided to submit an application for a short-term European Molecular Biology Organization (EMBO) fellowship, which would enable me to work at the LMB for a few months, and I arrived there on a cold, rainy day in December 1968. The laboratory had been established in 1962 by the UK Medical Research Council, following the pioneering work in Cambridge of the previous decade — which included the discovery of the structure of DNA by Watson and Crick. Many of the staff (Max Perutz, Crick and Fred Sanger) were already Nobel laureates and others would soon follow.

On the first day, I was nervous and afraid that I might not understand what Aaron would talk about. From his famous papers on the X-ray crystal analysis of tobacco mosaic virus (initially working with Rosalind Franklin), the quasi-equivalent bonding in the icosahedral virus shell (with Don Caspar) and helical diffraction theory (with Crick), I was convinced that he was a theoretical physicist. I was concerned that with my poor knowledge of diffraction theory, I might be asked to return to Geneva immediately.

To my great surprise, Aaron was interested in experimental details and interpretations, and spent most of the time talking about how to get a clue or a starting point for determining the assembly mechanism of T4 head proteins. I was relieved to find myself discussing ideas with him. He was an extremely good physics teacher, and a fantastic experimentalist. He had the amazing ability to analyse details of various images by eye, and

was able to uncover so many things from raw data. Aaron also spoke of his broad interests in science — beside those of the principal projects of his group. It is no wonder that he was later successful in elucidating the structures of transfer RNA, the nucleosome and the zinc-finger transcription factor, among others. I did not realize at the time, but he had already completed the studies for which he would get a Nobel Prize. Through Aaron's ability and interest, I understood for the first time the depth and strength of structural molecular biology at the LMB. My stay was over all too soon, but by then we had produced several very beautiful filtered images of polyheads.

By merely breathing the air of the LMB, something ultimately changed in my mind and flesh. Everywhere, the spirit of freedom in scientific thinking prevailed — in the seminar room, cafeteria and even the corridors. People there simply exchanged scientific ideas on equal terms. The LMB looked to me like a paradise for the élite scientists who worked there. A second short visit to Cambridge later strengthened this feeling.

I began to have an increasing affinity for British ideas on philosophy, science and life. In my short time working with Aaron at the LMB, I was inspired to make a career as a scientist. However, it took six more years and my own tiny research group in Kyoto University to determine how the three distinct subunits were arranged to form the normal T4 head shell. After that peak of excitement, and a brief intermission with the visualization of single DNA molecules in solution, I encountered the fission-yeast chromosome — which was to be my playground for next 25 years.

Mitsuhiro Yanagida is at the Graduate School of Biostudies, Kyoto University, Yoshida-Honmachi, Kyoto 606-8501, Japan.

The enthusiasm of Nobel prizewinner Aaron Klug added to the unique atmosphere at Cambridge.

NATURE | VOL 429 | 13 MAY 2004 | www.nature.com/nature

135

APPENDICES

Nikolai Kiselev

Nikolai was a visitor to Aaron Klug's group from the Soviet Academy of Sciences Institute of Crystallography in Moscow, initially in 1966–67. During that visit he worked with Aaron and David DeRosier on optical diffraction and filtering on electron micrographs of helical tubes of catalase and virus proteins, but since then he has made many return trips concerned with other topics.

He recorded his memories of his first visit to LMB in the article from which these extracts are taken, written in 1969 for the Academy journal, *Himiya I Zhizn* (Chemistry and Life) (No. 7, 65–73 and No. 8, 61–69).

The organization of the working day in the LMB is rather curious. As in other scientific British institutions, an important role is played by systematic breaks for coffee, lunch and tea. At 11 am, all life ceases in the laboratory: everyone is sitting in the canteen drinking coffee. At about 1 pm, comes another break for lunch. All meet for a third time in the canteen at 4 pm to drink strong tea with milk. However, during these breaks food is not the only concern, for exchanges on all kinds of topics are very lively. This is a well established tradition, and a number of scientists have told me that they would be quite unable to get on with their work without the accustomed cup of tea in the company of colleagues. It had seemed to me at first that such frequent breaks hampered work, but later I got used to them, and after some months began to enjoy them. These breaks establish a definite rhythm for the working day which undoubtedly heightens efficiency and is good for one's health.

The inception of the LMB was due to such eminent scientists as J. Bernal and Sir Lawrence Bragg. Today, those working there are Max Perutz, John Kendrew, Francis Crick, Sydney Brenner, Hugh Huxley, Aaron Klug, David Blow and other 'stars' of modern molecular biology. To conclude my notes I shall try to say something about some of them.

For Soviet readers, one of the most interesting among Cambridge scientists is Francis Crick. Readers of 'Chemistry and Life' have already learnt much about him from Watson's book, *The Double Helix*. The image of the man created by Watson is in many respects a true one. For instance, Crick does talk a great deal on a large variety of subjects. It may be that this brings some relief to his brain from overstrain which is so often prematurely experienced by many talented scientists, and is helpful to the inception of new ideas, some of which bear the stamp of genius.

On my first meeting Crick, I was somehow reminded of portraits of nineteenth century soldiers. This impression may have been partly due to the way in which at the time Crick brushed his not too abundant hair towards his temples. He is tall and broad-shouldered. He dresses inconspicuously: at the laboratory: throughout the winter he wore a red sweater, and in summer a coloured sports shirt.

321

Crick's future biographers will probably see his personality as complex and contra-dictory. On the one hand it is well known that Crick dislikes official honours and on one occasion declined some honorary title. On the other hand he unceremoniously dominates everyone in social conversation. According to 'Who's Who' he particu-larly enjoys talking to attractive women. If in the laboratory you hear his voice sounding louder and more animated than usual, you can be sure that he is talking to a woman. Ladies say that they find Crick very good company.

Francis Crick has become a legendary figure in Cambridge, and not only in Cambridge. Interest in his personality does not wane. It is not for nothing that Perutz jokingly foretold during one of his interviews, that in the year 2000, the quantity of genetic information would be measured in megacricks.

Perutz is not only an eminent scientist but also an excellent organizer. On becoming the director of LMB, he succeeded in ordering things so that he can give up no more than 10% of his time to administrative matters, devoting the rest to research work. Yet his administrative staff is not large: the director's personal secretary, an account-ant (she is also the cashier), an assistant in charge of supplies, and perhaps two or three others. And this for one hundred and sixty working scientists!

Perutz carries on his research practically single handed (leaving out of account the special group in charge of the X-ray diffractometer). He can be seen in the labora-tory both late at night and on non-working days. When I asked him why he so over-burdened himself, he explained that there was no one to whom he could entrust his work. At one time he had an excellent co-worker, but she left on getting married. And those who came after her made mistakes, and Perutz gave them up.

One last trait to characterize Perutz as director. At first I addressed him as 'Dr Perutz', but at the second or third time he interrupted me saying: 'Please Nicholas, everyone here calls me Max'.

In spite of a far from robust health and unsportsmanlike figure, Max's favourite recreation is mountain skiing. At one time he even trained a team of skiers. He also likes gardening, though this takes second place with him after skis. In the fellows gar-den of Peterhouse, of which he is a fellow, Perutz showed me, with the pride of a true garden lover, red 'Arabian Night' dahlias. They reminded me very much of the dahlias growing in the front gardens of our villages near Moscow. At Peterhouse, Perutz also showed me some of the rooms and the dining hall panelled in age-darkened wood, its walls hung with portraits of scholars who had been fellows in the 15th–17th centuries. He told me that as early as 1948, Kendrew had X-rayed them and discovered the original paintings under the later layers of paint. The paintings were later restored. This seems to have been the first utilization of X-rays in art restoration.

On one occasion the members of LMB discussed in all seriousness who in the laboratory was a genius. The agreed that there were three of them: Francis Crick, Sydney Brenner and Aaron Klug. [Klug] is indeed one of the most intelligent men endowed with a great insight whom I have ever met. However, his most attractive quality is a talent for having pupils. In Cambridge, it is not customary to assist young scientists. Klug also follows this rule, but does it rather subtly, determining with remarkable nicety the right moment for lending a hand. At the beginning of the work he usually has a long talk with the scientific worker and discusses with him the plan of research and the methods. As a rule, he sets only practicable tasks. After this, the young scientist is left to fend for himself. Of course this does not mean that he cannot come to Klug with some problems. The latter will always give him the necessary explanations, at the same time writing down something like a résumé of what he is saying and drawing diagrams. Even such men as Crick himself come to him with problems. And when the work begins to show results, Klug confidently helps to determine the most important line of future research, actively participating in it and taking home the results for working them over.

Surprisingly contrasted to Klug is another outstanding scientific worker in LMB – Hugh Huxley. This is a prematurely grey-haired man, always dapper, even in a dirty overall stained with the blood of frogs (he studies their muscles). Klug I have never seen in an overall, and by the nature of his work he is more of a theorist. As for Huxley, he is a wonderful experimentalist, truly of Rutherford's school, the basic rule of which, to carry out an experiment by all possible means with minimum expenditure, he evidently adopted already at the time when he was working at the Cavendish Laboratory. The settings on which he carries on his X-ray research on muscles are striking by their apparently primitive character – no stands with lamps, no colourings or polishing.

Huxley has almost no pupils. He works from morning till late at night doing everything himself. In the old Cavendish Laboratory, such men were called 'hermits'.

My notes on Cambridge are coming to an end. Much about what I have written has now altered, some of it imperceptibly, and some very considerably. The old LMB building where I worked remained as it was for only six years. In 1968 an extension was built on to it, doubling its working surface. One by one, scientists formed within its walls leave LMB, while others come in their place. Who knows. Perhaps there will be among them some new Watson and Crick, Perutz and Kendrew, Klug and Huxley?

Nicholas Kiselev

Jim Paulson

Jim was at LMB from 1977 to 1981 as a postdoc with Aaron Klug, and, now at the University of Wisconsin, he recalled memories of Cambridge in an email to me (JTF) in 2005:

My first visit to Cambridge was actually in September 1975 when I attended Aaron's course (EMBO sponsored, I believe) on image reconstruction from electron micrographs. I had previously met Aaron when he came to give a seminar in Princeton (early in 1975, I think). When he left Princeton, I had the privilege of driving him to John F. Kennedy Airport in New York, giving me the opportunity to talk to him along the way.

At the Cambridge course I met a number of people whom I would later see a great deal of when I returned to the MRC as a postdoc. These included Bill Earnshaw (whom I actually knew previously from Cold Spring Harbor Phage meetings), Jim Deatherage, Tony Crowther, Nigel Unwin and Linda Amos among others. The course was wonderful. We were housed in Peterhouse. I had a room in a new, high-rise dormitory which was reached from the old part of the college by walking through a garden or orchard behind the Fitzwilliam Museum. I remember thinking what a wonderful place Cambridge was, as I breathed in the cold crisp air and looked up at the beautiful blue sky while crossing the garden to go to breakfast on those September mornings. Later, when I came back as a postdoc in October 1977, I didn't see any blue sky for about the first two months!

At Peterhouse, we ate our meals at the high table. The menus in French disguised the fact that the cuisine was rather heavy on potato dishes – sometimes three different ones at a single meal. But it was all a great experience.

The porter closed the gates of Peterhouse at 10 p.m., I think, but David DeRosier showed the course participants how to get in after hours. This was accomplished by walking down a footpath from Fen Causeway toward the University Centre, on the west side of the college. There was a certain point at which one could skirt the end of a ditch and slip through a gap in the hedge to reach the college garden.

I wasn't as well prepared for the course as I should have been, but I got enough out of it to apply what I had learned to my thesis project – the structure of the gp22 cores in T4 phage polyheads. I stayed on in Cambridge for an additional five weeks to do this, under the tutelage of Linda Amos. I had brought with me my best micrographs of phage polyheads, which I learned to scan and digitize on a drum densitometer that Richard Henderson had used for the work on purple membrane protein. As I remember, the data was stored on magnetic tape and delivered to the computer center at the New Museums Site to do the Fast Fourier Transforms. When I left Cambridge, I had to buy a new backpack in order to carry all the computer printouts. In the end, I only got one 'bit' of data from those five weeks of work, but it was an important one. I determined that the polyhead core in elongated pro-heads contained an even number of helices. Since the dimensions of the core strongly indicated either 5 or 6 helices, this bit of information showed that it must be six. I found this to be very interesting because it meant that the symmetry of the core could not match the phage head surface (five-fold symmetry), but it might match the phage tail (three-fold or six-fold symmetry), and I had previously found mutations in the core protein which affected the positioning of the tail. This led to the idea that the initiation of head assembly would involve a connector, perhaps with 15-fold symmetry, that joined the shell and core of the pro-head and later became the site of tail attachment.

While working at the MRC during those five weeks, I lived at the Lensfield Hotel, a bed and breakfast in Lensfield Road near the Chemistry Department. I rented a bicycle and pedaled out to Hills Road, to the lab every day. I worked fairly long hours, and often ate my evening meal at the New Addenbrooke's Hospital Staff Canteen, where I became familiar with the traditional English fare such as shepherd's pie, bangers and mash, toad-in-the-hole, welsh rarebit, and, of course, baked beans on toast.

I arrived back at the MRC in early October 1977. I couldn't do any lab work at first as Linda Sperling was still finishing her PhD thesis and I was to get her space after she left. So for the first few months I had desk space on the first floor. This was fine, because I wasn't sure what to do. I had proposed to the Jane Coffin Childs Fund a systematic study of chromatin fiber fragments by EM, but by that time Fritz Thoma had already done it better than I would have been able to do, so I was looking for another project.

After a few months Linda left and I got her lab bench space in room 305, a very interesting place to work. I remember being told which benches had been used by Uli Laemmli, Roger Kornberg and others. A wooden box on the top shelf, we were told, contained the original TMV gels used by Klug and Franklin in the 1950s.

I sat back-to-back with Len Lutter. It was a real pleasure to be around Len, whose honesty, genuine concern for people, and love of fun I really appreciated, especially in difficult times. I remember a great deal of excitement in the lab when Len first tried running the high resolution DNA gels on nucleosome core particle DNA. The distribution of DNA sizes, centered on about 146 basepairs, was clear to see. Even Aaron was excited about it. As I remember, this was very important to him because the size of the DNA was thought to influence the unit cell in the nucleosome crystals.

I didn't have much interaction with the top guys in the lab except for Aaron. I was rather intimidated by Perutz, Brenner, Sanger and so forth. Perutz stepped down as head of the lab about the time I started, and Sydney Brenner took over. I was impressed by the way Brenner put his faith in the young scientists. I remember him saying that the role of the administrators, like him, was to give the young people what they needed to do their research and then get out of the way.

I had little or no personal interaction with Sanger, but it was clear that he was a man with a nice, dry sense of humor. I recall how he spoke at the lab talks, saying 'Well after we sequenced ϕX174, we wondered what more there was to do, and somebody said there's still a lot of DNA out there. So we looked in the refrigerator and we had some λ-DNA, so …' At the time, sequencing λ phage DNA was considered an extremely audacious step, and everyone (as I remember) reacted to the boldness of it, and Sanger's very understated way of telling it, by laughing with amazement.

Francis Crick left for San Diego the summer before I came, but he used to come back for a certain amount of time each year (and no more, for tax reasons I was told). The only time I met him was over lunch with Len Lutter in the canteen. Len introduced me as having worked with Ili Laemmli. When Crick started to say something about Laemmli's EM pictures of histone-depleted chromosomes, Len interrupted him and pointed out 'those were Jim's pictures'. I was definitely very grateful to Len for sticking up for me.

Perhaps the most memorable moment during my time at the MRC was the one where I found myself standing just inches away from Prince Philip, completely by accident. This occurred because I happened to look up an article I needed at the Medical School Library on the day it was being officially opened. I noticed that the plaque on the wall in the stairwell was covered with a cloth that hadn't been there before. Then I remembered hearing somewhere that it was the day of the opening ceremony. Turning onto the second flight of stairs, I noticed a huge TV camera at the top, aimed at the covered plaque. As I left the library several minutes later, after finding my article, I was surprised to see that there was now a man at the TV camera, and I stopped to watch what he was doing. Just at that moment, Prince Philip and another man came up the stairs, stood on either side of the landing, looked up at the camera, and pulled the cover off from the plaque. They then continued on up the stairs, passing right by me. Philip, like me, was also curious about the camera and also stopped to look at it and see what the cameraman was doing. I found myself inches away from him, looking at the back of his neck! I remember thinking, this is the most immaculately groomed back of any person's neck that I have ever seen! I'm sure he didn't notice me at all, or merely took me (in the grubby clothes of the late 1970s American postdoc) to be the cameraman's assistant.

Andrås Fodor

Andrås was a visitor from Hungary in 1977, working in Sydney's group and involved in looking for nematode mutants with Muriel Wigby.

Happy Birthday

In my year when I was in the lab, Sydney was 50 years old. According to my silly and old fashioned continental way I wanted to congratulate him, but fortunately Muriel warned me.

'Don't do that András!' she said, 'Sydney is not happy at all. He thinks that the age 50 means that he is not young any more.' She added: 'A 50 year old man is really very old isn't he?'

I did not reply, because Sydney was everything but not 'old man'. I could not reply anyway because Sydney had entered the room. When he saluted us by a 'good morning' and not by 'hello', we all knew that he was in a very bad mood. Muriel, Marleen and I were in the lab, and naturally Sydney. It was real British weather outside. We were silent and we worked hard. Muriel and I were at our microscopes scoring for nematodes, just behind us Sydney worked alone with his bacteria. He refused any help and did not say a single word. Marleen was busy also with her nematodes at the other corner of the lab. According to the usual timetable, the dear Naresh Sing came over from John Sulston's lab at exactly 10-o-clock and called his wife as usual, talking to her in Hindi. We learnt the magic words 'Acha! Acha' (Yes, Yes), because Naresh has been the best husband in the world. This day however, we were really afraid that after one of the 'acha's something dramatic would happen. But nothing happened. Naresh left the lab and we worked hard in silence. It was a quarter to eleven when, again according to the 'timetable', two of our women colleagues came to see Marleen as usual. They did not know of Sydney's birthday and just started to chat, first very quietly, but more loudly later on. One of the ladies had a very tasteful Cambridge dialect, so it was really impossible not to pay attention to what she was saying.

The intensity of the women's voices together with a kind of tension was definitely increasing. Finally a new voice arose – the refrigerator started to give an unpleasant noise. At that moment Sydney missed something in his experiment and dropped his pipette into the basket shouting 'SHUT UP'.

Everybody was startled by him, my heart almost stopped working when he came out from the corner through the lab with severe and weighted steps. He reached the refrigerator and surprisingly kicked at its door with a spectacular movement, like a soccer star. The refrigerator stopped giving the unpleasant noise, and everyone started to laugh loudly. The tension was over and Sydney started to smile. Everybody went back to work, and Sydney started to talk to us, made jokes, and what is more, the sun started to shine outside. And this was the day I found the *let-2(el370)* mutant. A wonderful day!

The Visitor

Sydney was very upset when he had to interrupt his experiment because of some administrative reason, including welcoming guests who came for just a short time. In these cases he used to say: 'Well, now I have to smile'. Then he would glance below the table 'Where is my smile'.

One day a really respected professor came from one of the eastern bloc countries. He was a very good scientist, and Sydney respected him very much. When Professor E. came to the lab, Sydney was busy with his experiments, so when our guest entered the lab, Sydney said hello to him and also that he would be free within a few minutes.

When he had finished his work, he went to Professor E. who was waiting for him, standing by the door of the lab. When shaking hands, the distinguished guest said:

'Professor Brenner! I am absolutely surprised that you are doing your experiments yourself.'

Sydney startled him when he replied, still keeping each others' hands.

'Professor E., I am absolutely surprised that you, who come from a country where the working people rule the power, are surprised. Why? Who should make my experiments?'

'I believed' Professor E. said 'that your assistant or your postdoc, or graduate students would be in charge of doing your experiments.'

'No' Sydney replied, 'they are running their own experiments.'

Next to the nematode genetics, this was probably the most important thing that I learnt in the MRC from Sydney Brenner.

Fusion

The library (tearoom, coffee room) was the place where everyone in the Cell Biology Division spent a few minutes after lunch, or between two experiments. Sydney was very talkative and it was really an excellent experience to talk to him when he was talking about science or about some everyday events. When Sydney was in such a bright mood, Gianni or Riccardo would come to me saying: 'Let's go to the tearoom! There is a Sydney show going on there.'

In the majority of cases the topic was science. Sometimes there were severe debates. Sydney was sometimes very sarcastic, but he was never sarcastic to young people. He always had time to listen to young people's ideas, and commented on them seriously and constructively. But he changed his mood when a respected senior scientist was his partner in the debate.

Once a respected scientist came to the lab and was talking about an idea that had just come to him during the coffee room conversation. To be honest, the idea was not very bright. Probably he had not thought over what he was saying; he suggested solving a certain problem using the cell fusion technique, but this problem obviously could not be approached by this method.

Sydney was listening to him, his chair standing on its two back legs and with his hands over his head. When our colleague had finished his short talk, Sydney said very slowly, looking at him:

'I think this idea is absolute garbage. I prefer fusion of a very different kind, you know; next to soft music and red light ... This is the fusion that I like'.

Ron Morris

Ron joined Aaron's chromatin group from 1974 to 1976. He studied largely the chromatin of the mould *Aspergillus*, but also with Ron Laskey on nucleosome assembly. The following extracts are from a letter to Aaron in 1987:

The year I spent in Cambridge was perhaps the best year of my life and was tremendously important in helping me to do better science. It was also a year of significant accomplishment for the [*chromatin*] group, i.e., the crystallization of the chromatin core, and for me personally.

Just before I joined the lab I had shown (for the first time) that fungi have histones, so it was reasonable for me to join the chromatin group. I came just after the octomeric structure of the core histones had been demonstrated, and the air was charged with excitement. However, Roger [*Kornberg*] was gone and Marcus [*Noll*] was about to go. Jean Thomas came to lab meetings only from time to time. A new fellow, Len Lutter, had just arrived, but the chromatin group seemed small and fragile, so much so that Francis asked me – to my horror – to represent the group at the lab talks, which were about six weeks after my arrival. I was fortunately able to get some data that convincingly showed that, although the nucleosome repeat in *Aspergillus* was much shorter than the repeat in mammalian liver, the size of the DNA associated with the nucleosome core was identical. [Ron continued the study of the nucleosome repeat lengths in other tissues, but carried on a second project with Ron Laskey.] We were able to show that apparently authentic nucleosomes could be assembled on SV40 DNA under physiological conditions, using frog egg extracts. Ron continued this work to isolate nucleoplasmin. We spent so much time together on this project that we were called 'the two Ronnies', after the comedians.

I don't have any significant physical memorabilia of my stay at the laboratory, and all my photographs are of my family; but I do have a great many fond mental images, for example Francis playing what seemed to be conjurer's tricks with pieces of ribbon and beer cans, trying to work out the topology of twist, wind and writhe as applied to nucleosomes to solve the paradox of nucleosome dimensions and DNA turns. I have a wonderful remembrance of Ron and I showing you [Aaron] a pentagonal structure from a nucleosome reconstitution experiment that you worked out a model for, and when to our embarrassment it turned out to be an artifact, of your kindly, but I also think honestly, saying that working out the model was worthwhile in any case. I remember with chagrin you and Francis coming to dinner one night, when my tenant in the States rang up saying that the other tenant was trying to break into her appartment to kill her. That was the same night that my wife, on Ron Laskey's urging, showed her pentagonal prints to you, the result of which was to send Francis into a topological frenzy. Odile said she had to sedate him to get him to sleep. The next morning he told me he had solved the structure in the bath tub. The day after that he asked for a Xerox of the pattern and showed me how to do a Fourier analysis of it. I never could get Francis to talk about my experiments after that. He always wanted to talk about the pentagons. Fortunately that was near the end of the year, so no great harm was done.

Bob Sweet

Bob was part of David Blow's group in 1972, working on the complex of trypsin and soybean trypsin inhibitor. He remembers he was one of several American post-docs at that time, including Philip Pulsinelli, Lynn Ten Eyck, Arthur Arnone, and Christine and Tonie Wright, who were to be found in LMB at night and on week-ends.

Memories of Postdoc Days at the MRC, early 1970s
A strong memory is of what I call the Aaron Klug effect. The effect appeared during seminars at the MRC, and usually only when the speaker was a visitor, probably a young American.

About a third the way into the talk, when the speaker was beginning to pick up speed, Aaron would interrupt to ask a question. Almost always the question was a simple thing: what pH did he use, was the symmetry such-and-such? The speaker, however, realizing the identity of his interrogator and knowing that this person might very likely know more about his topic than he did, would believe that the question being asked was actually a very hard question. The fact that it sounded like a simple one was simply because he, the speaker, would make up in his mind the question he imagined Aaron to be asking, and would answer that one.

This, of course, would confuse Aaron because he didn't get an answer that seemed to be in context. So, frowning and struggling to choose just the right words, he would ask the same question in a slightly different way. The speaker, astonished that his first answer had had no impact and hearing again what sounded like the same simple question, he now imagined it must have incredibly subtle implications for his entire research effort, and would invent yet another even more difficult question. Since surely this must be the one being asked, he would try to answer that.

Ultimately the whole thing, which sometimes would take several minutes and would have the rest of the audience yawning, was often resolved by someone like Tony Crowther, Jo Butler or Francis Crick. One of them either would tell the speaker that the question was what it sounded like or would nudge Aaron to whisper the answer. Then the seminar could continue, with the speaker somewhat the worse for wear and occasionally none the wiser as to what really had happened.

Leigh Anderson

Leigh was a PhD student of Max and in his haemoglobin group from 1971 to 1975. The following are extracts from a letter to Margaret Brown in 1987. He recalls one haemoglobin mutant in particular, Hb-Hirose:

Hirose was the 'mutant' that John Vincent Augustine Desmond Kilmartin crystallized after his famous 'purification' procedure and submitted for crystallographic analysis by yours truly. The structure was a very clean one since John had crystallized the normal 50% of the material rather than the mutant (which got thrown away). As penance, he showed me how to do tryptic peptide maps, which seemed fair at the time.

There are of course many amusing memories from those years, though I expect they will best be told by others. I remember the mirth when Gerry Rubin spilled 800 millicuries of P^{32} on the centrifuge room floor; when John (the same) Kilmartin pulled all the plants out of the canteen planter on the occasion of the annual cabaret; when John and I founded the short-lived Cambridge 5-liter Erlenmeyer Ensemble (the Erlenmeyer is often underrated and universally misunderstood, as a musical instrument): and particularly a party I shall always remember in John's back garden. That event marks the most boisterous and the most inebriated I have ever seen molecular biologists. Judd Fermi became trapped in the loo, and we burned reprints on a bonfire in hopes of them getting read in heaven. I don't believe they were. Finally, I remember having dinner regularly at the hospital canteen at 1.00 in the morning and then waiting patiently for the man who tended the railroad crossing on the way to Shelford to wake up and raise it at 4.00. And the almost ungovernable temptation to kill all the undergraduates using the Maths Lab machine to print out Mickey Mouse calendars at 2.00 am, while they giggled over 'error B37' and refused to bathe more than monthly.

But most particularly I remember having the feeling that we were working at Molecular Biology Central, that there were no limitations of any consequence placed upon us and that anything could be accomplished between 7.30 at night and 5.00 in the morning. And that nothing of any importance got done before 10.00 in the morning, that coffee lasted 'til lunch, lunch until close to tea, and tea until the Frank Lee opened. Then it seemed that Science Club would begin to assemble, Guinness would flow, and the Hard Core begin to mumble about what would be attempted that night in the lab. I'm sure it wasn't this way all of the time, but it remains much more vividly in the memory than the boring slog of all the things that didn't work or weren't tried because of inadequate adrenalin levels.

I would love to read George Pieczenik's thoughts about all this because, as I remember it, he along with Ed Ziff, Hugh Robertson and Bart Barrell, sort of established the tone for our generation in the lab. Some rather strange and romantic ideas were held at that time, about the value of science and baked beans on toast. And it was cheaper to take a student flight to Paris (on a really dangerous old Comet) than to take a train to the Lake District.

During the Pax Merutz, we all were allowed to live with the profound misconception that the lab required no administration whatsoever. The inventory behind Stores was infinite. Nothing was a big problem. I would still trade any ten Harvard MBAs for one Miss Martin, Miss Taylor or Miss Brown. They always made it look so easy.

So I guess it was a great time. From what I've seen since, it was a rare occurrence and one for which I remain profoundly thankful. God bless the MRC and that peculiar University. And in the end I'm not sure anyone knows how it happened. Max said he didn't, and who else would?

EMAIL FROM TOM STEITZ TO RICHARD HENDERSON ON THE DEATH OF MAX

Friday, 8 February 2002

Dear Richard,

It was with deep sadness that I received your message, transmitted to me in New Zealand by Peggy, reporting the death of Max Perutz. I have wanted to write to someone to express my profound sense of loss, but have not known to whom to write. So I write to you. Max has been my private, secret scientific hero ever since I heard him give the Dunham Lectures at Harvard Medical School in the spring of 1963 when I was a first year graduate student at Harvard. At that time I was trying to decide what direction my new research career should take, and those three lectures convinced me beyond any doubt that I wanted to study protein structure and function using X-ray crystallography.

I remember the lecture hall in which the Dunham Lectures were given as being enormous and completely filled by well over 1,000 in the audience; Max appeared rather small at the front. Probably the moment that no one who was in that room will ever forget came when Max showed us the first stereo slide that any of us had every seen. The lecture hall had the shape of a large gym with a very high ceiling and the screen was likewise simply enormous. We had all been given stereo glasses and watched with great anticipation as the two stereo images were being adjusted on the large screen. Suddenly, they were adjusted and the picture of the skeletal model of myoglobin jumped into three dimensions for everyone in the room at the same time. The whole audience simultaneously let out a loud 'Oh'. There in front of us was the modest sized Max Perutz, who appeared to be standing under an enormous myoglobin molecule, two or three times the size of Max, that had popped out from the screen. We were all entranced as Max, with his pointer stick uplifted, described the intricacies of a protein structure that none of us had ever seen before; and Max was just as excited as we were. Unforgettable.

Max, of course, did not simply describe structure, but clearly put forward the biological problems to be addressed by these structures, particularly the still emerging structures of hemoglobin, oxy and deoxy. To me the future of understanding enzyme mechanisms in structural terms seemed completely clear from Max's lectures, and I quickly found my way to Lipscomb's laboratory to work on the crystal structure of carboxypeptidase and its substrate complexes.

Max continued to be an inspiring example for me when I went to the LMB in late 1967, starting with his 'Please call me Max' after I addressed him as 'Dr. Perutz'. Rightly or wrongly, I have always credited the collegial, interactive style of LMB to Max – the fantastic canteen (not the food) that allowed me to meet everyone in the whole building in the first two weeks and participate in a new, exciting scientific conversation three times a day. Most impressive to me, particularly now as I struggle to get through my largely administrative day, was Max's ability to run the finest molecular biology laboratory in the world and yet spend every afternoon taking X-ray photographs of hemoglobin crystals. We all learned not to interrupt Max in the laboratory, but I also quickly learned to adjust my exposure times of chymotrypsin crystals to match those of Max's so that they could be developed simultaneously. This gave me three minutes of development and a couple of minutes of fixing time to talk to Max.

Max was excited by the success of others and always included the youngsters in his celebrations. When Dorothy Crowfoot Hodgkin, Guy Dodson and colleagues solved the structure of insulin in the late 60s, Max decided to mount a Cambridge expedition to Oxford in order to help celebrate this great event. He obtained the lab van, which he drove accompanied by a small group of us to Oxford. He brought with him a large bottle of champagne that he had received some six or seven years earlier upon the occasion of his receiving the Nobel Prize in chemistry. The half dozen or so Cambridge celebrants arrived at the party hosted by David Phillips, and some of us (me) looked forward to sampling Max's champagne. Since Max did not drink wine himself and was not familiar with the methods of wine storage, he had not kept his bottle on its side. Thus, the cork had dried out and the champagne was vinegar.

Max wasn't always right, but he always took the time and effort to share his insights with me. When I suggested a non-symmetric arrangement of hexokinase subunits based on a native Patterson map, he was skeptical. He also encouraged Joan and myself to accept the Princeton offers of faculty positions rather than those from Yale because he felt the Princeton biochemistry faculty members were better than Yale's, which they indeed were in 1970. We, however, were drawn by New England, the greater diversity of biology provided by the presence of Yale Medical School and another hero, Fred Richards, and accepted Yale's offers.

After leaving Cambridge my interactions with Max were less frequent but always memorable. In 1972, Joan and I attended the fourth and last of Max's and Walter Hoppe's Austrian protein crystallography ski meetings in Alpbach, Austria. It turned out to be too warm for a ski meeting, but I remember Max's excitement in informing all of us that the gentian were already blooming and his encouraging us to see them for ourselves. On one day of the meeting, Max asked Joan and myself to join him in a climb to the top of a local peak. We, of course, were thrilled. Off Joan and I went with Max, who excitedly described the latest results of John Kilmartin. It was 'des-His', 'des-arg', 'Bohr proton', 'oxy', 'deoxy', 'hemoglobin' all the way to the top of the peak. On the top Max and I (Joan remained a little below to 'take in the view') lingered only briefly. He described his goal as a youth to climb all of the Austrian peaks above 3,000 meters. I asked whether he had been successful and he admitted that he had not. Unusual for Max, but I guess science and World War II got in the way.

My next encounter with Max dramatically showed that not all Nobel Prize winning laboratory directors are alike. Joan and I decided to split the location of our first sabbatical from Yale between the Max Planck Institute for Biophysichalische Chemie in Goetingen, West Germany, and the LMB. In Germany, we joined the laboratory of Klaus Weber, a friend from our Harvard days. Klaus's lab was one floor below that of Herr Doctor Professor Director Manfred Eigen, whose lab had just begun to study aspects of an RNA phage, Q=DF. We were never introduced to the director (whom I have yet to meet) in spite of the fact that Joan's work on R17 in the Watson lab made her a far greater expert on RNA viruses than anyone in Eigen's lab. There was no encouragement of or format for inter-lab interactions and no chance to meet any of the abteilung directors since they refused to eat in the general dining hall with the rest of the laboratory workers.

Moving to Cambridge in the spring of 1977 was a breath of fresh air. Upon my first entry into the LMB canteen, Max came up to me and said, 'Let's have lunch together. Tell me what you have been doing.' What a difference!

When my lab had its first success in phasing the X-ray diffraction intensities from the 50 S ribosomal subunit crystals and produced an electron density map at 9Å resolution that showed the right handed turn of RNA helices in early 1998, my first impulse was to write to Max to share my excitement at this new insight into macromolecular structure, just as he had shared his excitement in the Dunham Lectures 35 years earlier. Max, of course, wrote back an encouraging letter.

The last time I saw Max was in March of 2001 when I was in Cambridge to assist in a review of the LMB by a panel gathered together by MRC headquarters. Max had asked to talk to me, and we met in his office where he told me of the latest results on the role of Gln rich tracks in the formation of amyloid plaques, consistent with his recent earlier hypothesis that these sequences could more easily form cross-beta structures. Max had proposed that these structures could possibly explain the formation of amyloid plaques by the prion protein in Alzheimer's disease, a proposal he made many years after his retirement. As I had been teaching his proposals in my proteins and nucleic acids graduate course for several years, I was most interested in its possible clinical relevance, which he described.

I shall miss these infrequent, but inspiring interactions with Max. We shall all miss Max.

Richard, I shall also send a hard copy of this. Perhaps, you will have a 'Max' file to which this could be added.

Best regards,

Tom

KEITH MOFFAT'S LETTER

This was in reply to a query from Richard Henderson in Edinburgh in 1966 on LMB and Cambridge. Keith was already at LMB, a student of Max Perutz from 1965 to 1969. Richard and Keith had met as undergraduates in physics at Edinburgh, Keith graduating in 1965 and Richard in 1966.

7.5.66

Dear Richard

I'm sorry I haven't replied to your letter sooner – life has been pretty hectic lately (as indeed it always is around here!)

Colleges are not so important to a research student as to an undergraduate, the former's life revolving mainly round one's supervisor and work. Nevertheless they differ in their attitude towards research students and this can make a great deal of difference. Some seem to regard them mainly as an extra source of income, to be tapped as much as possible, giving as little as possible in return, while others go to great lengths to integrate them into the life of the College. To be more specific: King's College, of which I am a member, takes a great interest in their research students without seeking to limit their activities in any way; the opportunities for contact with Fellows are there in abundance, to be taken up or not as desired. No rooms are at present available in College for research students owing to an extensive rebuilding scheme. I live in a flat with two others. No eating-in requirements are imposed; some Colleges demand that research students eat-in at least, say, three evenings a week, which some find tiresome. The Fellows include the best representation of molecular biologists in Cambridge: Sanger, Huxley, Brenner, Stretton, Freedman. The biological side is strong, but not the physical, mathematics excepted. King's is also very rich and prestigious in Cambridge circles. Peterhouse, of which Max and John Kendrew are Fellows, is small, has, I believe, rooms for first year research students and has a reputation for the best College food in Cambridge. The sporting record is very poor – if that counts for anything! Corpus Christi has a truly magnificent post-graduate hostel called Leckhampton, ultra-smooth, full of interesting people, and much sought after. No molecular biologists but plenty of chemists, an enlightened attitude towards research students – recommended. I see a lot of it as a number of my friends live there, including two Edinburgh chemistry graduates from my year, Gavin Currie and Ian Stenhouse. It's a bit out of town but the setting more than makes up for the comparative isolation – a gigantic garden with swimming pool, rose garden, Henry Moore statue, squash courts and playing fields – the lot. Churchill, a new College, is probably the one which integrates research students most into College life, with a joint common room, bar, and, I believe, rooms in College for most 1st year research students. It too is a bit isolated – but the lab itself is so far out that a bit further doesn't really matter. Molecular Biologists there include Francis Crick, Herman Watson and Richard Watts-Tobin. Gonville and Caius is also said to be quite reasonable but I've no first-hand knowledge of it. One other unusual College is Darwin, a purely post-graduate College, very small but expanding fast. The Fellows and students – including my roommate of last year at Edinburgh, Julian Paren – are on an equal footing – none of the High Table nonsense. As a result, the food is superb, ridiculously cheap, and the social life on a higher plane altogether. This may change as the College expands – now 20-odd students as against Kings, say, 450 (90 research) but seems likely to be much the same for a few years yet. If you have a yen to build your own traditions instead of mauling those left by centuries of predecessors, Darwin is worth consideration. It is true, though, that the traditional College system is one of the distinguishing features of Cambridge life – which Darwin does not provide. It has one Molecular Biologist, Ieuan Harris. The rest I know little about. Trinity and St John's are vast, tending, I'm told, to the impersonal in their dealings with research students. One fairly safe bet for admission is Pembroke – the Master is a Watsonian and the College has a fairly Scottish bias. For my money, I'd put King's and Corpus at the top, depending on whether one wants freedom or complete attention, followed by Peterhouse and Churchill (tradition and modernity), with Darwin if the unusual appeals. The rest are much of a muchness – but avoid Selwyn, Sidney Sussex, Downing and Magdalene.

The above should give you some idea of what goes on. The Molecular Biologists in a College are not a prime consideration, as one sees a lot of them at the Lab. anyway.

Workwise – the lab is first-rate, a fabulous place to work, making the Physics Dept. at Edinburgh seem like a (whisper it gently) quiet backwater. I understand you may be working with David Blow on chymotrypsin – he's one of the best and most pleasant people there. Frankly, it doesn't matter – just to work in the Lab. is enough. I've been going to Biochemistry Part I, Organic Chemistry Part I (both + practicals), Part II Crystallography, Electronic Structure of Molecules, some Biochemistry Pt II lectures, and for kicks, Dirac himself on Quantum Mechanics. The first 3 are the most important, although the organic was a bit of a time-waster. The Biochemistry is useful as background but mostly irrelevant – nevertheless a good idea. Frankly I'm a bit choked with lectures, I much prefer getting on with research in the Lab itself – after all one can always do a crash reading program if some particular subject is necessary. The background can only really be acquired after years of experience. In molecular biology one must be jack of all trades and master of half of them – a fair task. Physics, I still reckon, is the best single preparation. I'm out of paper now – if there is any further help I can give, I'll be glad to. All the best in your finals – they're not worried here about your results.

Sincerely

Keith Moffat

STRUCTURE OF GLOBLGLOBIN – JERRY DONOHUE

Jerry Donohue wrote this paper lampooning the current work in the MRC Unit when he was visiting it in 1953. It was submitted, unsuccessfully, to the erratically appearing *Journal of Irreproducible Results*.

Not Sent Unit before 1150-54

THE STRUCTURE OF GLOBLGLOBIN

33

We wish to report the first complete structure determination of any protein. As is well known, proteins are very interesting substances, and because of their wide occurence they are sometime rather important. It will be remembered that they are giant molecules containing hundreds, sometimes even thousands, of atoms. Work on the structure of globlglobin has been underway in this laboratory for the past twentythree years, eight months and two weeks, except for a short lacuna four years ago caused by the epidemic of fowlpest. The elucidation of the detailed structure of globlglobin may well be of interest since it is now known that it is an important constituent of not only the tears of the Sahara crocidile from which it was first isolated, but is also, for example, found in the lateral extensor muscle of the tail of the Manx cat, the eyelid membrane of the snowy owl, and in the lining of the appendix of the great marsh tit. It is from this last source that most of our material was isolated. We wish to thank the Southwestern East Anglian Bird Watchers Association for their invaluable aid in maintaining a constant supply of tits. It has also been recently discovered that globlglobin is directly responsible for the reddish colouration of certain eyeballs; we are indebted to our colleague Dr. F. Bonamie, who is an expert in these matters, for this observation.

The only previous work on globlglobin is that of Sorey and co-workers, whose brilliant and painstaking researches were able to establish unequivocally beyond any doubt that it was not possible with the data at hand to come to any definite conclusions concerning the size and shape of the molecules, or their position in the unit cell.

-2-

We have discovered that avian globlglobin crystallizes
in a variety of forms which differ only in cell dimensions, space
group, and number of molecules in the asymmetric unit. This as yet
unexplained phenomenon was of no use to us. The form chosen as
most suitable for exhaustive examination was triclinic, with a = 735 ,
b = 75 A, c = 74 A, α = 103°, β = 91°, and γ = 1°37'. The space
group is P1, and there are three molecules in the cell, if we assume
that the molecular weight is best represented by an average of the
values 169,325 and 21,768 as given by the ultracentifuge and osmotic
pressure respectively. Moreover, the published data concerning the
density are inadequate.

The crystals were prepared with the aid of Dr. O.N. Bearish,
who was of great assistance with the washing up. The first attempts
yielded small specimens only, but eventually crystals were obtained
which could be measured with ease by use of the Standard British Yard.
Complete intensity data were rapidly collected over a period of
seven years with an improved Weissenberg camera, the alterations in
which had best not be described. A new type of X-ray tube with a
spinning cathode enabled the exposure times to be reduced to the order
of 10^{-3} microseconds. We have found that these short times entirely
eliminate errors due to fluctuations in the power supply. Systematic
absences observed are: (hk0) absent if k = 2n+7, and (h0l) absent if
h = 3n+17. It is therefore obvious that each molecule consists of
three identical halves.

All recent work points to the fact that the w-helix is the
basic structure for proteins. We have accordingly adopted it in
the present study, since globlglobin shows the familiar strong reflec-

-3-

tion at 0.063 A, as predicted for the w-helix by all earlier workers.
One difficulty is, however, that globlglobin is known to contain no
end groups, whereas the light scattering data clearly show that the
molecule is 120 A long.   We were therefore led to formulate what we
call the paper chain model, which consists of interpenetrating rings
of w-helices.   This model is schematically illustrated in Fig.1.
The axis of the paper chains must coincide with the a axis of the
unit cell in order to account (within 200%) for the measured
pleochroism.

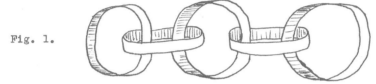

Fig. 1.

        Excellent agreement between the observed and calculated
intensities of the reflections (100) and (200) could be obtained with
this model.   The calculation of the intensities of these meridional
reflections is given by the trivial standard expression.   In order
to test additional reflections, we have, in collaboration with Mr.
I.M.A. Crock, evaluated the form factor for a paper chain.   For
reflections not on the meridian, and if the usual approximations are
made, it is found that

$$F = \sum_i \int_0^{\pi} \sum_{\zeta} f_i(0)\ \Gamma_{(x_i)} \int_{\pi}^{\frac{\pi}{2}} B_m(\gamma_i) \int_{-e}^{+e} J_n(z_i)\ dz\ d\eta\ d\zeta$$

using an obvious notation.   We may therefore expect reflections at
values of $5\sin\gamma/\pi\lambda$ given by the formula $p/T + q/E$, where T and E
are, respectively, the sets of Tschebycheff polynomials and Eulerian
numbers, and p and q are relatively prime perfect squares.   This

-4-

useful expression predicts that large values of F will be found approximately 18° from a line bisecting the angle between the meridia and c✝, as is observed on the photographs. This point is more easily grasped by referring to Fig.1, where it is easily seen that most of atoms lie on surfaces which, in reciprocal space, lead inexorably to the above condition.✝

A comparison between observed and calculated intensities for a few selected planes is made in Table 1. It is seen that the

Table 1.

(hkl)	Iobsd.	$I_{calcd.}$
100	2[a]	350
200	110	17[b]
300	c	415
001	12[d]	1738
002	36	37[e]
36.7.23	3495.73	3495.73

(a) This reflection is probably subject to extinction.

(b) The discrepancy here is not serious, and may be explained by an abnormality in the background.

(c) Not observed because of the experimental arrangement.

(d) Part of this reflection is cut off by the beam stop. The actual intensity is therefore probably much greater.

(e) Agreement could probably be improved in this case by taking into account the scattering of the hydrogen.

agreement is satisfactory, the average discrepancy, R, being 54% significantly less than for a random structure. Preliminary considerations tend to indicate that the agreement could be

---

✝ Since the above was written, Mr. Crock has made a more rigorous proof of these relations. He has shown that large values of F will be expected to uniformly distributed in the a✝ b✝ plane, instead of 18° from the bisector. We do not consider this to be a significant discrepancy. In a private communication, Prof. V. Cobbler informs us that he is attempting its explanation. We are awaiting his results with keen interest.

-5-

improved by modifying the structure so that each paper chain bends back and joins itself to form, together with additional such units, what we call the paper chain paper chain. We intend to explore this hypothesis more fully in a latter publication. In this regard, it has been emphasized to us by our colleague, Dr. S. Holmes, that it is not necessarily uncanonical to anticipate a certain degree of factitious teleology in these procedures, providing that the neo-stochastic approach is avoided. We wish to thank him for his unwonted clarity.

At this stage it was discovered that additional data could be obtained from peroxygloblglobin prepared by extracting transversely cut sections of wild rabbits. The entire laboratory staff gave most generously of their time to assist in the splitting of hares. With this additional data, we proceeded to a Fourier analysis of the three principal zones. Although none of these contain centers of symmetry, the statistical distribution of the first two orders in each tends to indicate that a pseudo centre is present. Following J. D. Lenin, who foresaw all, we assume that the intensities fall naturally into groups which are logically called constellations. Some confirmation of this is found in the observation that the reflexion (390) is quite diffuse, corresponding to the nebula in Andromeda. We have made a Fourier analysis of the various constellations of the (hk0) zone, but, instead of randomly permuting the phases, we have permuted the values for the intensities with a _fixed_ set of signs. This procedure allows many more interesting variations than mere sign permutation. In order to achieve a truly random set of numbers, we chose to use for this purpose the number of lines in the successive sonnets of Shakespeare,

-6-

taking them in the order in which they were written; we wish to
thank the Bacon Society for advice on this point.   The final
electron density is shown in Fig. 2.   It is seen that there is
striking agreement with the paper chain hypothesis.   Additional
projections are being evaluated by Mr. E. Fouls, who is using a

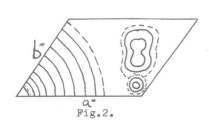

Fig.2.

cunning method of calculation in which
the sine waves are superimposed, by
appropriate vibrations, on the surface
of a trayful of jelly at the moment
it sets.   This method is very rapid,
and has the advantage that the unwanted results are edible.

Our proposed structure accounts for the observed rapidity
with which owls blink.   Simple entropy considerations of the
twisting of paper chains give 14 blinks per minute, in exact agreement with the values of 3 to 25 (average, 14) reported in the
current issue of Nature.   It is also interesting that, although
globlglobin has yet to be demonstrated as an important factor in
hereditary mechanisms, the intertwining of the chains is very
similar, and, indeed, identical, with the published microphotographs
of neurospora.

It has not escaped our notice that the paper chain
structure provides a possible method of impulse transfer in the
adrenal cortex.

We wish to thank kindly all of our colleagues for their
interminable discussion of various points related to the punctuation
of the manuscript.   One of us was aided by a grant from the
Ministry of Fish.   J. Briekopf.   Inst. of Astrobotany.

FAREWELL SPEECH TO DAN BROWN BY GREG WINTER

(27 June 2000, in Level 5 Seminar Room at about 5.30 pm)

Dan McGillivray Brown is a Scotsman: he went to Glasgow University and he has an accent to prove it. Like many other foreigners it was to the free land of England that he came to make his fortune. It was in England that he failed to make a fortune but instead he did embark on a brilliant scientific career. (DB added, 'the first is certainly true').

He came to Cambridge in the late 1940s, and got his PhD in 1952. Dan is a blast from the past with the looks of an Ancient Mariner. But do you all realize just how far he goes back? If we think of molecular biology as a recently evolved science, in evolutionary terms Dan does not belong to the age of Neanderthal man, not to the age of the missing link of humans and monkeys, nor even to that of the Dinosaurs, but to the age of that thing that started to crawl out of the primeval soup of chemicals, barely recognizable as a life form. (DB starts to walk out but is stayed.) You see Dan was one of the key figures in the elucidation of the chemical structure of nucleic acids. It was from information of the chemical structure of nucleic acid (and base ratios and some X-ray diffraction studies) that the double helix model of DNA emerged, and molecular biology was founded.

Dan was obviously a troublesome chap from the beginning. Some of his first papers related to a correction to an earlier paper of his own supervisor, Dr AR Todd, on the incorrect identification of some 2' ribonucleoside triphosphates. Unlike some modern corrections that I have seen, this retraction was clear and unequivocal, and with some pointers to the value of a technique that would come to lie at the heart of molecular biology. I quote 'the failure ... was in part due to too much reliance on the validity of the synthetic routes employed; it emphasizes the value of X-ray data in the characterization...'.

Dan's work in due course led on to the proof that the covalent structure of RNA involved 5' and 3' linkage of sugar to phosphate (rather than 5' and 2' linkages). However, in the best tradition of the free English, it was the supervisor who got the credit. From Dan's collected papers I see that shortly after this, Dr AR Todd of the Chemical Laboratory became Sir Alexander Todd, then Nobel Laureate, and subsequently Lord Todd. I think Dan was elevated many years later to Vice Provost of King's.

In the Chemical Laboratory, Dan continued his studies on nucleic acids, including the mechanisms of action of hydroxylamine as a mutagen, and in 1982 took early retirement, and it is said 'doubtless under lavish terms'. He then became something called 'an attached worker at the MRC LMB, and has hung about here ever since.

However his hanging about was rather active. He continued his programme of research with David Loakes on the development of nucleotide analogues. Most of you are familiar with this, so I will say no more. However this work was specially commended by the visiting committee in our QQR, who knowing of his earlier work with Todd were amazed that he was still alive, and still active 50 years on. David Loakes tells me that Dan was even seen to synthesize some nucleotide analogues in the last couple of months.

Many of us here and elsewhere are very grateful for his selfless insights into their problems. In 1988, Geoffrey Grigg came here to work with me, and in the brief spaces between meals, was thinking about a method for sequencing methylated cytosines in DNA. It was to Dan Brown that he turned. Dan told him to use bisulphite, as the chemistry was very well known; in fact the method as developed by Grigg has been used extensively to determine which genes are active, and I understand that the entire human genome is to be systematically checked by this method at the Sanger Centre. (DB adds, 'It will take a hell of a lot of bisulphite'.) This is only one of his many contributions to science, unsung but cumulatively very important.

Dan has been the 'Chemist in Residence' and is shortly to become 'Chemist Out of Residence'. I am sorry that he has chosen to go; I can assure you he was not pushed, at least by Richard, me or anyone in the MRC. (I cannot speak for his wife.) We hope that he will keep in contact with us, and that he will, from time to time, be willing to give advice. Dan, many thanks, and good luck in your retirement; I hope it is long and happy.

Chronology

DIRECTORS/CHAIRMEN

Max Perutz 1962–1979
Sydney Brenner 1979–1986
Aaron Klug 1986–1996
Richard Henderson 1996–2006
Hugh Pelham 2006–

		Divisional Heads			
	Deputy Director/ Assist. Director- Admin	Structural Studies	Molecular Genetics/ Cell Biology	Protein and Nucleic Acid Chemistry	Neurobiology
1962	Kendrew/–	Kendrew	Crick	Sanger	
1963	"	"	Crick/Brenner	"	
1975	–/–	Perutz (acting)	"	"	
1977	Huxley/–	Huxley/Klug	Brenner	"	
1979	"	"	Gurdon	"	
1981	"	"	"	Sanger/Milstein	
1983	Huxley/B. Loder	"	Brenner (acting)	Milstein	
1984	"	"	Lawrence/Bretscher	"	
1986	Huxley/D. Dunstan	Huxley/Henderson	"	"	
1987	Milstein/D. Dunstan	Unwin/Henderson	Bretscher	Milstein/Rabbitts	
1991	Milstein/D. James	"	"	"	
1992	"	"	Bretscher/Pelham		
1993	"	"	"	Rabbitts	Unwin
1994	"	Crowther/Henderson	"	Rabbitts/Winter	"
1995	Henderson/D. James	"	Pelham	"	"
1996	Pelham/M. Davies	"	"	"	"
2000	"	Crowther/Nagai	"	"	"
2002	"	"	"	Winter/Neuberger	"
2003	"	"	"	"	Unwin/Goedert
2005	"	Nagai/Ramakrishnan	"	"	"
2006	Winter/M. Davies	"	"	"	"
2007	"	"	Bienz/Freeman	"	"

TIMELINE

1934	First X-ray diffraction photographs from an ordered protein crystal (pepsin) taken by JD Bernal and Dorothy Crowfoot (Hodgkin) at the Cavendish in Cambridge.
1936	Max Perutz joined Bernal's group at the Cavendish.
1938	W.L. (Sir Lawrence) Bragg became Cavendish Professor.
1939–41	Max interned in Canada.
1943–44	Max involved in Pykrete work and then returned to Cambridge.
1946	John Kendrew (1946–75) joined Max as a research student, with Charles Taylor as nominal supervisor.
1947	MRC support granted for 'MRC Research Unit for the Study of the Molecular Structure of Biological Systems'.
1948	Hugh Huxley (1948–52 and 1962–87) joined John Kendrew as a research student.
1949	Francis Crick (1949–77) joined the Unit and became a research student of Max.
	Tony Broad employed to build a rotating anode X-ray tube.
1951	Pauling's α-helix paper published.
	Fred Sanger and Hans Tuppy published the sequence of the B-chain of insulin.
	Jim Watson arrived in Cambridge.
1952	Helical Diffraction paper by Cochran, Crick and Vand published Broad X-ray tube running.
	Michael Fuller and Vernon Ingram (1952–58) joined the Unit.
1953	Watson and Crick solved the DNA structure.
	Max Perutz's X-ray diffraction photographs from crystals of mercury-haemoglobin demonstrated that the isomorphous replacement method could be used to solve protein structures.
	Sequence of A-chain of insulin published by Fred Sanger and Ted Thompson in the Biochemistry Department.
	At MIT, Hugh Huxley and Jean Hanson proposed Sliding Filament model for muscle contraction.
	Bragg retired from the Cavendish, replaced by Neville Mott.
	Rosalind Franklin moved from King's College to Birkbeck College, London.
1954	Projection of haemoglobin structure published by Max with David Green and Vernon Ingram.
	David Blow (1954–57 and 1959–77) joined Max as a research student.
	Max and Fred Sanger both elected Fellows of the Royal Society.
	Aaron Klug began work at Birkbeck College, London.
	Rita Fishpool (1954–95) began working for Vernon Ingram.

1955 Complete sequence of insulin with disulphide bond locations published by Fred Sanger with A.P. Ryle, Leslie Smith and Ruth Kitai.
Alex Rich visited Francis for six months and paper published on structure of collagen.
Ieuan Harris joined Fred Sanger's group.
Don Caspar joined Francis and Jim Watson for a year, working on virus structure.
Ken Holmes and John Finch joined Rosalind Franklin at Birkbeck as research students.

1956 Adaptor Hypothesis formally presented by Francis.
Eileen Southgate (1956–93) began working in Max's group.
Len Hayward (1956–74) joined the Unit as an instrument maker.

1957 6Å map of myoglobin obtained by Kendrew's group – the first map of a protein structure.
Sydney Brenner (1957–86) and Leslie Barnett (1957–92) joined the Unit.
Seymour Benzer, Mahlon Hoagland and George Streisinger came as visitors for the year.
Tony Stretton (1957–71) joined Vernon Ingram as a research student.

1958 Fred Sanger awarded Nobel Prize in Chemistry for insulin work.
Sequence Hypothesis and Central Dogma published by Francis.
Rosalind Franklin died.
Michael Rossmann (1958–64) joined Max's group.
Hilary Muirhead (1958–64) joined Max as a research student.
Vernon Ingram departed for MIT.
Journal of Molecular Biology founded with John Kendrew as editor.

1959 5.5Å map of haemoglobin obtained by Max with Michael Rossmann, Ann Cullis, Hilary Muirhead, George Will and Tony North.
Atomic resolution (2Å) map of myoglobin obtained by John Kendrew with Dick Dickerson and Bror Strandberg.
Brenner and Horne published their negative stain method for electron microscopy.
Dick Dickerson and Bror Strandberg joined the myoglobin group for a year and David Davies for six months.
Herman Watson (1959–68) joined the myoglobin group.
David Blow (1959–77) returned to LMB to begin work on chymotrypsin.
Anand Sarabhai (1959–64) began with Sydney Brenner as a research student.
Francis Crick elected a Fellow of the Royal Society.

1960 Hugh Huxley and John Kendrew both elected Fellows of the Royal Society.
Allen Edmundson (1960–64) joined the myoglobin group.

Ed O'Brien (1960–64) joined Francis Crick as (his first) research student.

1961   Proof of the triplet nature of the genetic code published by Francis Crick, Sydney Brenner, Leslie Barnett and Richard Watts-Tobin.
Theory of Mutagenesis paper published by Sydney Brenner, Leslie Barnett, Francis Crick and Alice Orgel.
Mark Bretscher joined Sydney Brenner as a research student.
Hans Boye (1961–64) joined Francis Crick as (his last) research student
Bob Shulman (1960–66) joined the molecular genetics group.
Lubert Stryer (1961–64) joined the myoglobin group.

1962   The new LMB building occupied from February with Max Perutz as Chairman and John Kendrew his deputy.
The Structural Studies Divisional head was John Kendrew and included his and Max's groups, David Blow and Michael Rossmann from the Cavendish and, from London, Hugh Huxley from University College and Aaron Klug with John Finch and Ken Holmes (1955–68) from Birkbeck College.
The Molecular Genetics Divisional head was Francis Crick and included his and Sydney's groups, Alex Schedlovsky (1961–63), Alfred Tissieres (1962–65), Jon Beckwith (1962–65) and John Smith (1962–86).
The Protein Chemistry Divisional head was Fred Sanger from Biochemistry and included his collaborator Leslie Smith (1953–65) and colleagues Ieuan Harris (1955–78) with student Richard Perham (1961–65), Brian Hartley (1952–74), Richard Ambler (1960–65) and John Hindley (1962–66).
In May, LMB officially opened by the Queen.
In October, Nobel Prizes in Chemistry awarded to Max Perutz and John Kendrew and in Physiology or Medicine to Francis Crick and Jim Watson.
Alan Weeds (1962–2005) joined Brian Hartley as a research student.
Benno Schoenborn joined the myoglobin group for one year.
Dale Kaiser (1962–66) joined Aaron Klug's group.

1963   EMBO founded with Max as Chairman.
Uli Arndt (1963–2006) joined the Structural Studies Division from the Royal Institution.
Bob Diamond (1963–85) joined the Structural Studies Division.
Brian Matthews (1963–66) came as a postdoc to David Blow's group.
César Milstein (1963–2002) and Kjeld Marcker (1963–69) joined the Protein Chemistry Division.
George Brownlee (1963–80) joined Fred Sanger as a research student.
Leo Sachs visited the Molecular Genetics Division for a year.

Tony Woollard (1963–2001) appointed to look after X-ray sets.

1964   Amino acid sequence of chymotrysinogen-A published by Brian Hartley.

Michael Rossmann left LMB for Purdue.

Steve Harrison joined Aaron's group for one year.

Joyce Baldwin (1964–2004) joined Max's group.

Jo Butler joined Ieuan Harris as a research student.

Tony Crowther and Paul Sigler (1964–67) both joined David Blow as his first PhD students.

Brian Clark (1964–75), Howard Goodman (1964–68) and Nichol Thomson (1964–89) joined the Molecular Genetics Division.

Bart Barrell (1964–93) and Ken Murray (1964–67) joined Fred Sanger.

1965   Division of Protein Chemistry renamed Protein and Nucleic Acid Chemistry (PNAC).

Andrew Travers joined John Smith as a research student.

John Abelson (1965–68) came as a postdoc to the Molecular Genetics Division.

John Kilmartin, Keith Moffat (1965–69) and Jonathan Greer (1965–70) joined Max as research students.

David DeRosier (1965–69) joined Aaron Klug's group for four years.

Ken Harvey (1965–86) appointed head of Photography Section.

1966   Francis Crick proposed Wobble hypothesis.

Richard Henderson joined David Blow's group.

Hilary Muirhead (1966–69) rejoined Max's group.

Gary Borisy (1966–69) joined the Structural Studies Division.

Suzanne Cory (1966–71) joined Brian Clark as a PhD student.

Jim Dahlberg (1966–68) joined Fred Sanger as a postdoc.

1967   Chymotrypsin structure determined by David Blow with Brian Matthews, Paul Sigler and Richard Henderson.

The first mutant of *C. elegans* produced by Sydney Brenner.

Alan Coulson (1967–93) joined Fred Sanger.

Joan Steitz (1967–70) joined Mark Bretscher as a postdoc.

Tom Steitz (1967–70) joined David Blow as a postdoc.

Andrew McLachlan (1967–2000) joined the Structural Studies Division.

Peter Moore (1967–69) joined the muscle group.

Jeff Roberts came as a postdoc to the Molecular Genetics Division for a year.

1968   2.8Å map of horse oxyhaemoglobin obtained by Max with Hilary Muirhead, Joyce Cox (Baldwin), Gwynne Goaman, Scott Mathews, Ed McGandy and Larry Webb.

3D-reconstruction of structure from electron micrographs introduced by David DeRosier and Aaron Klug.

The first LMB nucleic acid sequence, 5S RNA (120 nucleotides) determined by Fred Sanger with George Brownlee and Bart Barrell.

Ken Holmes left LMB for Heidelberg.

Herman Watson moved to Bristol.

Linda Amos joined Aaron Klug's group.

Michael Levitt (1968–71) came as a research student of Bob Diamond (returned in 1974).

Harvey Lodish joined the Molecular Genetics Division for a year.

Jerry Adams (1968–71) joined Fred Sanger as a postdoc.

Nigel Unwin joined LMB.

13-bay and the workshop and first floor extensions built.

1969   Sid Altman joined John Smith's group for 18 months during which RNAseP was discovered.

Daniela Rhodes joined Aaron Klug's group and Jonathan King came for a year.

Alan Fersht (1969–78) joined Structural Studies to bring Physical Chemistry to LMB.

Wasi Faruqi joined the Structural Studies Division.

Peter Lawrence, John Sulston (1969–93), Mary Osborn (1969–72) and Graeme Mitchison (1969–81) joined The Molecular Genetics Division.

David Hirsh (1969–71) joined the Molecular Genetics Division to work on suppression of UGA.

Alan Weeds transferred to Hugh Huxley's group.

1970   Division of Molecular Genetics renamed Cell Biology.

2.8Å map of horse deoxyhaemoglobin determined by Max with Bill Bolton.

Michael Wilcox (1970–92) joined the Cell Biology Division.

David Secher (1970–87) began with César Milstein as a PhD student.

Uli Laemmli and Jake Maizel joined Aaron's group for a year.

Cyrus Chothia and John Kendrick-Jones joined the Structural Studies Division.

1971   'SDS Gel' electrophoresis procedure published by Uli Laemmli.

First X-ray diffraction picture using a synchrotron source (DESI) obtained by Ken Holmes with Gerd Rosenbaum and Jean Witz, using a specimen of insect flight muscle.

Dan Branton joined Aaron's group for a year.

Jim Spudich came for a year as a postdoc with Hugh Huxley.

Judd Fermi (1971–97) joined Max's group.

John White (1971–94) joined Sydney's group.

Gerry Rubin (1971–74) joined Andrew Travers as a research student.

Jonathan Hodgkin (1971–2000) joined Sydney as a research student.

Elizabeth Blackburn (1971–75) joined Fred Sanger's group.
Tony Stretton left LMB for Madison, Wisconsin.
Bob Sheppard (1971–94) arrived and the Peptide Chemistry group was set up.
Electronics workshop established with Alec Wynn as head.

1972   Mark Bretscher proposed that cell membranes have an asymmetric lipid bilayer structure, spanned by specific membrane proteins.
Peptide signal sequence for protein secretion discovered by César Milstein with George Brownlee, Tim Harrison and Mike Matthews.
John Gurdon and Ron Laskey and their *Xenopus* group moved to the Cell Biology Division from Oxford.
Terry Horsnell joined Structural Studies.
Anne Bloomer (1972–2003) and Roger Kornberg (1972–75) joined Aaron Klug's group.
Barbara Pearse joined Ieuan Harris's group in PNAC as a visiting student.
Bob Waterston (1972–74 and 1975–76) came to Cell Biology as a postdoc.

1973   Murray Stewart joined the Structural Studies Division.
Greg Winter joined Brian Hartley as a research student.
Tom Maniatis (1973–74) visited Fred Sanger's group.
Terry Rabbitts joined PNAC.
Audrey Martin retired as Administrative Secretary and Frances Taylor took over.

1974   3Å map of tRNA structure published by Aaron Klug with Jon Robertus, Jane Ladner, John Finch, Daniela Rhodes, Ray Brown and Brian Clark.
The nucleosome subunit structure for chromatin proposed by Roger Kornberg.
Michael Levitt (1974–79, 1986–87) returned to the Structural Studies Division.
Ed Lennox (1974–85) joined the Cell Biology Division, heading a sub-Division of Tumour Biology.
Bob Horvitz (1974–78) joined the nematode group.
Brian Hartley appointed to Biochemistry Chair at Imperial College.
John Walker (1974–98) joined the PNAC Division.
Georges Köhler joined César Milstein's group for a year.
Dave Hart became workshop head on the death of Len Hayward.

1975   Monoclonal Antibody methodology invented by Georges Köhler and César Milstein.
The plus and minus method of sequencing DNA published by Fred Sanger and Alan Coulson.

3-D map of purple membrane at 7Å determined by Richard Henderson and Nigel Unwin.

John Kendrew left LMB to become Director (1975–82) of the new EMBL in Heidelberg.

Brian Clark left LMB for Aarhus.

Mike Gait joined the Peptide Chemistry group.

Clyde Hutchison joined Fred Sanger for a year.

1976   Peter Lawrence and Gines Morata discovered that homeotic genes define compartments in insects.

Barbara Pearse discovered clathrin – the coat of coated vesicles.

The structure of the ventral nerve cord of C. elegans was determined by John White, Eileen Southgate, Nichol Thomson and Sydney Brenner.

The sequence of nucleation and growth of TMV (tobacco mosaic virus) was established by Aaron Klug with Jo Butler, Tony Durham and Dave Zimmern.

A 5Å map of the TMV protein disk was determined by John Champness, Anne Bloomer, Gerard Bricogne, Jo Butler and Aaron Klug.

Kiyoshi Nagai joined Max's group for eighteen months.

Jon Karn (1976–2002) joined the Cell Biology Division.

Andrew Wyllie (1976–77) joined the John Gurdon group.

The Phillips Report was published.

1977   Di-deoxy- method of sequencing DNA published by Fred Sanger with Steve Nicklen and Alan Coulson.

The post-embryonic cell lineages of C. elegans determined by John Sulston and Bob Horvitz.

Myosin gene identified in C. elegans by Sandy Macleod with Bob Waterston, Rita Fishpool and Sydney Brenner.

Hugh Huxley became Deputy Chairman of LMB.

David Blow left LMB for Imperial College.

Francis Crick left LMB for Salk Institute.

1978   Sequence of single-stranded DNA of phage φX174 (5,386 nucleotides) determined by Fred Sanger with Alan Coulson, Ted Friedmann, Gillian Air, Bart Barrell, Nigel Brown, John Fiddes, Clyde Hutchison, Pat Slocombe and Michael Smith.

Phil Evans joined the Structural Studies Division.

Judith Kimble (1978–82) joined the Cell Biology Division as a postdoc.

Doug Melton joined John Gurdon as a research student.

Ieuan Harris died aged 53.

1979   Max Perutz retired as Chairman of LMB, and was succeeded by Sydney Brenner as Director.

1980   Fred Sanger awarded a second Nobel Prize in Chemistry. (Joint award with Walter Gilbert and Paul Berg.) Michael Neuberger joined the PNAC Division.

Tim Richmond (1980–85) joined Aaron Klug's chromatin group as a postdoc.

George Brownlee left LMB to be E.P. Abraham Professor of Clinical Pathology at Oxford.

Block 7 and the Clinical School built.

1981   Sequence of double-stranded mitochondrial DNA (16,569 bps) published by Steve Anderson, Alan Bankier, Bart Barrell, Maarten de Bruijn, Alan Coulson, Jacques Drouin, Ian Eperon, Don Nierlich, Bruce Roe, Fred Sanger, P. Schreier, Andrew Smith, Rodger Staden and Ian Young.

Hugh Pelham joined the Cell Biology Division and Mariann Bienz (1981–86) came as a postdoc.

Dan Brown (1981–2000) joined the Peptide Chemistry group.

Kiyoshi Nagai rejoined the Structural Studies Division.

Brad Amos joined the Structural Studies Division (unofficially).

1982   Aaron Klug awarded Nobel Prize in Chemistry.

Kim Nasmyth (1982–88) joined the Cell Biology Division.

Cynthia Kenyon (1982–86) joined Director's Section.

Barbara Pearse transferred from the PNAC Division to the Structural Studies Division.

CellTech founded. David Secher and Ed Lennox later took (permanent) leave of absence to set it up.

1983   Fred Sanger retired.

John Gurdon, Ron Laskey and their group moved to the Zoology Department in Cambridge.

Sean Munro joined Hugh Pelham as a research student.

Dick McIntosh visited the Structural Studies Division for a year.

Bronwen Loder appointed as Assistant Director (Administration).

1984   César Milstein and Georges Köhler (with Niels Jerne) awarded Nobel Prize in Physiology or Medicine.

Structure of the nucleosome core at 7Å resolution determined by Tim Richmond, John Finch, Barbara Rushton, Daniela Rhodes and Aaron Klug.

172,282 bp sequence of Epstein-Barr virus DNA published by Richard Baer, Alan Bankier, Mark Biggin, Prescott Deininger, Paul Farrell, Toby Gibson, Graham Hatfull, Graham Hudson, Sandra Satchwell, Carl Seguin, P.S. Tuffnell and Bart Barrell.

Barbara Pearse and John Kilmartin transferred from the Structural Studies Division to the Cell Biology Division.

Rob Kay joined the Cell Biology Division.

	Dave Hart resigned and Mick Bitton took over as workshop head.
1985	The zinc finger DNA-binding motif proposed by Aaron Klug with Jonathan Miller and Andrew McLachlan.
	Chimaeric Antibody engineered by Michael Neuberger, Gareth Williams, John Flanagan and Terry Rabbitts.
1986	Humanised Antibody produced by Peter Jones, Paul Dear, Jeff Foote, Michael Neuberger and Greg Winter.
	Structure of the Nervous System of *C. elegans* published by John White, Eileen Southgate, Nichol Thomson and Sydney Brenner.
	Sydney Brenner resigned as Director of LMB and was succeeded by Aaron Klug.
	John Smith retired from LMB.
	Diana Dunstan replaced Bronwen Loder as the senior administrator.
	Brian Pashley became head of Visual Aids on Ken Harvey's retirement.
1987	KDEL signal for retention in the endoplasmic reticulum discovered by Sean Munro and Hugh Pelham.
	Bio-Rad began producing the MRC confocal microscope.
	Hugh Huxley left LMB for Brandeis University, Massachusetts.
	Nigel Unwin returned to LMB after spending eight years at Stanford.
	Clyde Hutchison joined Fred Sanger for a second year.
1988	The core protein of the paired helical filament of Alzheimer disease identified as the microtubule-associated protein tau, by Michel Goedert, Claude Wischik, Tony Crowther, John Walker and Aaron Klug.
	Andrew Leslie and David Neuhaus joined LMB.
	Kim Nasmyth moved to the newly opened IMP (Research Institute for Molecular Pathology) in Vienna.
1989	Transgenic mice generating human antibodies created by Michael Neuberger and Marianne Brüggeman.
	CAT (Cambridge Antibody Technology) formed.
	CPE laboratory refurbished from the 1970 University Pharmacology building.
	Alec Wynn retired and Barry Canning became head of the electronics workshop.
1990	A 3.5Å map of purple membrane published by Richard Henderson, Joyce Baldwin, Tom Ceska, Fritz Zemlin, Erich Beckmann and Ken Downing.
	Completely human antibody variable domains selected from phage-display library by John McCafferty, Andrew Griffiths, Greg Winter and David Chiswell.
	Mario de Bono joined Jonathan Hodgkin as a research student.
	Mick Fordham became workshop head on the death of Mick Bitton.
1991	Mariann Bienz rejoined the Cell Biology Division.

	LMB awarded the Queen's Award for Technology for the confocal microscope.
	David James appointed senior administrator.
1992	Matthew Freeman joined Cell Biology.
	Venki Ramakrishnan joined Aaron Klug's group for a year on sabbatical leave from Utah.
	Michael Wilcox died.
1993	John Sulston, Richard Durbin, Alan Coulson and Bart Barrell moved to Sanger Centre.
	Sanger Centre (now the Wellcome Trust Sanger Institute) opened by Fred.
1994	2.8Å map of F_1-ATPase obtained by Jan Pieter Abrahams, Andrew Leslie, René Lutter and John Walker.
	Genetic evidence that rhomboid is involved in regulating EGF receptor signalling obtained by Matthew Freeman.
	John White left LMB for Wisconsin.
1995	Graeme Mitchison (1995–2005) rejoined LMB – Structural Studies.
1996	Aaron Klug retired as LMB Director, succeeded by Richard Henderson.
	Megan Davies appointed senior administrator.
1997	John Walker awarded Nobel Prize in Chemistry (with Paul Boyer and Jens Skou) and appointed Director of Dunn Human Nutrition Unit
	Alpha-synuclein identified as the major component of the filamentous lesions characterizing Parkinson's Disease by Maria Spillantini, Ross Jakes and Michel Goedert collaborating with a group in Pennsylvania.
	The fold of the core protein of hepatitis B virus determined by Bettina Böttcher, Sam Wynne and Tony Crowther using electron cryomicroscopy.
	John Kendrew died aged 80.
	Barry Canning retired and Howard Andrews became head of the electronics workshop.
1998	Jonathan Hodgkin elucidated the sex determination pathway in *C. elegans*.
	Venki Ramakrishnan joined Structural Studies.
2000	Structure of 30S ribosomal subunit determined by Brian Wimberly, Ditlev Brodersen, William Clemons Jr, Robert Morgan-Warren, Andrew Carter, Clemens Vonrhein, Thomas Hartsch and Venki Ramakrishnan.
	Rhomboid shown to trigger EGF receptor signalling in signal producing cell by Jonathan Wasserman, Sinisa Urban and Matthew Freeman, and that the rhomboid family of genes is widespread across evolution.
	Jonathan Hodgkin left LMB for the Genetics Chair in Oxford.

	Roger Lucke became workshop head on the retirement of Mick Fordham.
	Library relocated to ground floor.
2001	Human genome sequence published by consortium including Sanger Centre group.
2002	Sydney Brenner, Bob Horvitz and John Sulston awarded Nobel Prize in Physiology or Medicine.
	First gene required for locomotion discovered by Mark Bretscher.
	Jon Karn left LMB for Case Western School of Medicine, Cleveland, Ohio.
	Alan Coulson returned to LMB – PNAC.
	Max Perutz Lecture Theatre and new reception/foyer completed.
	Max Perutz (aged 87) and César Milstein (aged 74) died.
2003	John Smith died aged 78.
2004	Francis Crick (aged 88) and David Blow (aged 72) died.
2005	Refined structure of acetylcholine receptor at 4Å resolution determined by Nigel Unwin from electron cryomicroscopy data.
	Graeme Mitchison transferred to the Department of Applied Mathematics and Theoretical Physics.
2006	Richard Henderson retired as LMB Director, succeeded by Hugh Pelham.
	Uli Arndt (aged 81) and Vernon Ingram (aged 82) died.

List of Photographs

The copyright of all photographs is recorded with the legends. If none is stated, the copyright is MRC Laboratory of Molecular Biology, Cambridge, England. Every effort has been made to trace all picture sources, but in cases where this has not been possible, we apologise for any omission.

1. Lawrence Bragg, c. 1915.   2
2. J.D. Bernal, 1932.   4
3. Max Perutz in Pennsylvania, 1950.   6
4. Max Perutz on the Jungfraujoch, 1938.   8
5. John Kendrew at Pasadena, 1953.   9
6. Cavendish staff, 1952.   13
7. Myoglobin model built in 1957.   18
8. John Kendrew with the 'forest of rods' building structure of myoglobin, 1958.   19
9. Atomic model of myoglobin. *Les Prix Nobel*, 1962.   20
10. 5.5Å model of haemoglobin.   20
11. Pasadena Conference on the Structure of Proteins, 1953.   21
12. David Blow, c. 1967.   22
13. Michael Rossmann and Tony North, Cold Spring Harbor, 1971.   24
14. Crick and Watson in Cambridge, 1953.   28
15. Maurice Wilkins, c. 1960.   33
16. Rosalind Franklin, July 1950.   34
17. Crick and Watson, 1953.   38
18. DNA figure from *Nature*, 25 April 1953.   39
19. Jim Watson at Cold Spring Harbor, 1953.   39
20–51. DNA50 meeting in Cambridge:
20. Plaque outside Austin Wing.   41
21. Lecture room of the meeting.   41
22. Aaron Klug.   42
23. John Sulston.   42
24. Cynthia Kenyon.   43
25. Lord Sainsbury with Jim Watson unveiling a plaque outside The Eagle.   43
26. The Eagle plaque.   44

27. Joan Steitz.   44
28. Michael Rossmann and Venki Ramakrishnan.   45
29. Richard Durbin.   45
30. Sydney Brenner, Fred Sanger and Aaron Klug.   46
31. Allen Edmundson.   46
32. Jon Widom, Tom Ceska and Soraya de Chadarevian.   47
33. Angelika Daser and Celia Milstein.   47
34. David Secher.   48
35. Dan Brown and Henry Epstein.   48
36. Tim Richmond.   49
37. Sydney Brenner and Mary Osbourn.   49
38. Sydney Brenner.   50
39. Richard Perham and Hugh Huxley.   50
40. Suzanne Cory.   50
41. Elizabeth Blackburn.   50
42. Mark Bretscher.   51
43. Gerry Rubin.   51
44. Tom Steitz.   51
45. Sidney Altman.   51
46. Daniela Rhodes.   51
47. Brian Matthews.   52
48. Richard Henderson.   52
49. Hugh Huxley.   52
50. Michael Rossmann.   52
51. Tim Richmond and Don Abrahams.   52
52. Don Caspar at Cold Spring Harbor, 1962.   53
53. Vernon Ingram at Cold Spring Harbor, 1969.   55
54. Sydney Brenner, c. mid-1970s.   56
55. The hut, c. 1960.   63
56. The greenhouse, c. 1960.   63
57. Max Perutz and MRC unit staff outside the hut, 1958.   64
58. Fred Sanger, 1969.   65
59. Arthur Page, John Finch and Ken Holmes at Birkbeck, 1957.   70
60. The brand-new LMB in 1962.   72
61. The Governing Board, 1967.   72
62. Michael Fuller, c. 1970.   73
63. The Queen and Max Perutz at the LMB opening in 1962.   75
64. John Kendrew showing the atomic model of myoglobin to the Queen   75
    and onlookers, 1962.
65. Nobel Prizewinners, 1962.   76
66–69. Nobel celebration at LMB, 1962:
66. Sydney Brenner and Francis Crick.   77
67. Max Perutz and others.   77

68. Max Perutz.   77
69. John Kendrew.   77
70. Max and diffractometer, 1980.   81
71. Ferranti Argus 400, teleprinter and tape reader, 1966.   81
72. Max, at his retirement, with Sydney, 1979.   84
73. EMBO workshop in honour of Max, 1980.   86
74. Max with Margaret and Denis Thatcher, c. 1980.   86
75. Hugh Huxley, 1987.   89
76. Peter Moore.   89
77. Jim Spudich at Cold Spring Harbor, 1972.   90
78. John Haselgrove, c. 1970.   90
79. The Big Wheel, c. 1965.   91
80. Uli Arndt and three-circle diffractometer, 1956.   97
81. Uli with Microsource X-ray generator, 1997.   99
82. Chymotrypsin group, c. 1965.   102
83. Flying Spot densitometer, 1967.   104

84–86. Chymotrypsin group punting, 1969:
84. Richard Henderson.   106
85. Penny Henderson, Tom and Joan Steitz.   106
86. David Blow, Betty Wulff Birktoft, Jude Smith, Jane (surname unknown)
    and Prakash Cashmore.   106
87. Alan Wonacott, 1975.   107
88. Tony Jack, 1975.   108
89. Alan Fersht, 1971.   110
90. Gerard Bricogne, 1975.   110

91–98. Chymotrypsin reunion, 1997:
91. Participant group photograph.   111
92. Paul Sigler, Brian Matthews and Richard Henderson with David Blow.   112
93. David Blow, Tom Steitz and Richard Henderson.   112
94. Uli Arndt, Brian Matthews and Ken Holmes.   112
95. Cyrus Chothia.   112
96. Ken Harvey and Angela Mott.   112
97. Gwynne Goaman and Hilary Muirhead.   112
98. Michael Rossmann.   112
99. Aaron Klug, 1982.   113
100. Group at International Union of Crystallography Meeting,   114
    Madrid, 1956.
101. Ken Holmes, 1967.   115
102. Reuben Leberman, 1965.   116
103. Hugh Huxley and David DeRosier at Cold Spring Harbor, 1971.   118
104. Daniela Rhodes, 1973.   124
105. John Robertus, 1973.   125
106. John Finch, Aaron Klug and Brian Clark with tRNA model, 1975.   125

107. Roger Kornberg at Cold Spring Harbor, 1977.   128
108. Len Lutter, 1975.   129
109. Tim Richmond, 1980.   130
110. Louise Fairall, 2000.   131
111. Michel Goedert, 1997.   133
112. Alfred Tissières and Uli Laemmli at Cold Spring Harbor, 1977.   134
113. Jake Maizel.   134
114–134. Aaron Klug's 70th Birthday Meeting, 1996:
114. Speakers.   135
115. Don Caspar, Roger Kornberg and David DeRosier.   136
116. Kiyoshi Nagai and Mitsuhiro Yanagida.   136
117. Don Caspar and Tim Baker.   136
118. Moira Cockell and Hans Christian Thøgersen.   136
119. Rafael Giraldo-Suarez, Hillary Nelson and Gabriel Varani.   136
120. Lu Duo, Steven Brenner, Murray Stewart and Nigel Unwin.   136
121. Bill Scott.   136
122. Jonathan King and Cyrus Chothia.   136
123. Bill Turnell and Anne Bloomer.   137
124. Jake Kendrick-Jones and Jo Butler.   137
125. Michel Goedert and Maria Spillantini.   137
126. Uli Arndt and Nikolai Kiselev.   137
127. Rodger Staden and Len Lutter.   137
128. Bob Diamond and Reuben Leberman.   137
129. John Kilmartin and Brian Clark.   137
130. Mair Churchill and Andrew Leslie.   137
131. Tony Durham and Jo Butler.   138
132. Jo Butler and Joyce Baldwin.   138
133. Steve Lippard, Wes Sundquist and Aaron.   138
134. Joyce Baldwin, David DeRosier and Tony Crowther.   138
135. Linda Amos, 1975.   138
136. Anne Bloomer and David Phillips at Cold Spring Harbor, 1971.   139
137. Jo Butler, 1987.   140
138. Tony Crowther, 1987.   141
139. Kiyoshi Nagai and Daniela Rhodes, 1989.   143
140. Brad Amos, 1992.   144
141. Joyce Baldwin and Steve Harrison at Cold Spring Harbor, 1971.   145
142. Chris Calladine.   146
143. Cyrus Chothia.   147
144. Bob Diamond, 1987.   147
145. Phil Evans and Paul McLaughlin, 1993.   149
146. Wasi Faruqi, 1999.   149
147. Judd Fermi, 1994.   150
148. Richard Henderson at Cold Spring Harbor, 1971.   151

149. Terry Horsnell and Jude Smith, 1993.   152
150. Jake Kendrick-Jones, 1975.   153
151. Andrew Leslie, 1999.   154
152. Mike Levitt, 1975.   155
153. Jade Li.   155
154. Andrew McLachlan, 1987.   156
155. Aaron Klug, David Neuhaus and John Ionides, 1995.   159
156. Venki Ramakrishnan.   160
157. Clarence Schutt, 1984.   160
158. Murray Stewart, 2005.   160
159. Nigel Unwin and Leon Lagnado, 1995.   161
160. Alan Weeds, 1987.   162
161. Francis and Sydney, Joint Divisional Heads, 1975.   167
162. Francis' all-purpose reply card, 1963.   169
163. Sidney Altman.   172
164. Mark Bretscher, 1973.   173
165. John Smith, c. 1980.   175
166. Tony Stretton, c. 1960.   177
167. Eileen Southgate and Rita Fishpool, c. 1960.   178
168. Eileen Southgate, c. 1987.   178
169. Leslie Barnett, c. 1973.   179
170. Andrew Travers, c. 1960s.   181
171. Brian Clark, c. 1969.   182
172. Nichol Thomson, c. 1975.   184
173. Mick Fordham, Richard Durbin and John White with prototype   186
     confocal microscope.
174. Bob Waterston, c. 1972.   187
175. John Sulston, c. 1985.   187
176. Judy Kimble, 1982.   188
177. Bob Horvitz, 1976.   188
178. Francis and Sydney, 1986.   191
179. Peter Lawrence, 1987.   194
180. Michael Wilcox, c. 1970.   195
181. John Gurdon, 1982.   196
182. Mariann Bienz, 1983.   197
183. Matthew Freeman, 1992.   198
184. Jonathan Hodgkin, 1983.   198
185. Jon Karn, 2000.   199
186. Rob Kay, 1999.   200
187. John Kilmartin, 1975.   201
188. Ed Lennox, c. 1974.   202
189. Graeme Mitchison, 1985.   202
190. Sean Munro, 1999.   203

191. Kim Nasmyth, 1985.   203
192. Barbara Pearse, c. 1985.   204
193. Hugh Pelham, 2001.   204
194–200. Reception for *C. elegans* meeting, 2003:
194. Nichol Thomson.   205
195. Peter Lawrence and John White.   205
196. John Sulston.   205
197. Peter Lawrence and John Sulston.   206
198. John Sulston, Bob Waterston and Fred Sanger.   206
199. Aaron Klug and Sydney Brenner.   206
200. Jonathan Hodgkin and Richard Henderson.   206
201. Fred Sanger.   210
202. Kjeld Marcker, c. 1970.   211
203. George Brownlee, c. 1975.   211
204. Bart Barrell, c. 1975.   212
205. Jim Dahlberg and Suzanne Cory at Cold Spring Harbor, 1970.   213
206. Alan Coulson, 1987.   213
207. Elizabeth Blackburn, 1973.   215
208. Gillian Air, 1973.   215
209. Clyde Hutchison, 1975.   215
210. Rodger Staden, 1975.   217
211–214. Celebration of Fred Sanger's second Nobel Prize, 1980:
211. Fred with Sydney.   219
212. Viewing the champagne.   219
213. Fred speaking.   219
214. General joke.   219
215. Brian Hartley, 1969.   222
216. Chris Bruton, 1975.   223
217. Gordon Koch, 1973.   223
218. Ieuan Harris, c. 1960s.   224
219. John Walker, 1982.   226
220–236. Celebration of John Walker's Nobel Prize, 1997:
220. Four Nobel Prizewinners.   227
221. John with Andrew Leslie.   228
222. With Megan Davies.   228
223. With John Kilmartin.   228
224. With Aaron and Jennifer Cornwell.   228
225. John speaking by Aaron, Fred and César.   228
226. With Jon Karn and Hugh Pelham.   228
227. Gebhard Schertler and Michael Fuller.   228
228. Megan and Greg Winter.   228
229. Fred and Mark Bretscher.   229
230. César and Margaret Brown.   229

231. Mark Skehel, Ross Jakes and Michel Goedert.   229
232. Aaron speaking.   229
233. John and Rachel Whant.   229
234. Mike Runswick with Aaron.   229
235. John with Nick Gay and Rob Kay.   229
236. With Terry Rabbitts and Ian Fearnley.   229
237. César Milstein, 2000.   230
238. John Jarvis, 1973.   231
239. David Secher, 1982.   232
240. César and Georges Köhler, 1982.   234
241. Pamela Hamlyn, 1975.   235
242. César's group, 1997.   236
243–245. Celebrating César's Nobel Prize, 1984:
243. César and Max.   237
244. Margaret Brown, César and Jenny Brightwell.   237
245. César and John Walker.   237
246. Greg Winter.   240
247. Milstein Memorial Meeting, 2003.   244
248. Terry Rabbitts, 2000.   245
249. César, Michael Neuberger and Greg Winter, c. 1993.   248
250. The original LMB workshop, 1963.   254
251. Delivery of new milling machine, 1963.   255
252. Workshop staff, 1983.   254
253. Queen's Award for Technology, 1991 for confocal   259
    microscope development.
254. Tony Woollard with big-wheel X-ray generator, c. 1989.   261
255. Bill Whybrow, 1987.   262
256. Original LMB library in 1962.   263
257. Margaret Brown's retirement, 1996.   264
258. Ken Harvey, 1965.   265
259. Annette Lenton (Snazle) and Caroline Barrell, 1965.   265
260. Visual Aids Group, c. 1997.   266
261. Peptide and Nucleic Acid Chemistry Group, 1980.   267
262. Dan Brown, 1984.   269
263. Some of the valve racks of EDSAC1.   271
264. Original LMB canteen, 1962.   275
265. Gisela Perutz on her retirement from looking after the canteen. 276
266. Joy Fordham, 1997.   277
267–274. Joy's retirement, 2004:
267. Mike Lewis, Tim Levene, Hugh Pelham and Ian Fearnley.   279
268. Aaron Klug and Mick Fordham.   279
269. Richard Henderson presenting Joy with a caricature leaving card. 279

270. The canteen staff in 2004: Margaret Lilley, Rushan Topal, Darren   278
     Ruddy, Joy, Charlotte Gilby, May (surname unknown) and Sue Bischoff.
271. Joy with Alec and Mary Wynn.   279
272. Joy and Doreen Burton.   279
273. Tony Woollard and Eileen Southgate.   279
274. Alan Fersht and Ken Harvey.   279
275. The 1966 programme of laboratory talks.   280
276. Christmas concert, probably 1963.   281
277, 278. Christmas sketch, 1967 – the Ballet of Protein Synthesis:
277. Paul Sigler, sparkling.   282
278. The overall cast.   282
279. Christmas raffle, c. 1970.   283
280–285. Cricket:
280. First Team, 1970.   284
281. League Champions, 1980.   285
282. League Champions Cup, Runners Up, 1980.   285
283. Dave Hart hitting out.   286
284. George Brownlee.   286
285. Spectator (Chris Nobbs), Player (Brian Clark) and Scorer (Bart Barrell).   286
286–288. Football:
286. Early team, c. 1970.   287
287. 'Pros v Beginners', 1977.   289
288. 'Pros v Beginners', 1991.   289
289. Darts: award presentation by Audrey Martin, c. 1970.   290
290, 291. Aerial views of Addenbrooke's site from about the   293
     same direction, c. 1963 and 2006.
292. The Max Perutz Lecture Theatre.   296
293–307. Opening of the Max Perutz Lecture Theatre, 2002:
293. Robin Perutz and family by the plaque.   296
294. Gisela Perutz with César Milstein and Fred Sanger.   296
295. Arthur Lesk and Mike Gait.   296
296. Murray Stewart.   296
297. Andrew McLachlan and Brian Pope.   297
298. K.J. Patel and Andrew Travers.   298
299. Cyrus Chothia and Greg Winter.   297
300. Tony North and Uli Arndt.   297
301. Andrew Griffiths and Cyrus Chothia.   297
302. John Meurig Thomas and Michael Fuller.   297
303. Gebhard Schertler and Celia Milstein.   297
304. Daniela Rhodes, Mark Bretscher and Barbara Pearse.   297
305. Nancy Lane and John Walker.   298
306. David Blow and Gerard Bricogne.   298
307. The Support Staff.   298
308. Audrey Martin at her retirement, 1973.   299

Index of Photographs

Abelson, John 282
Abrahams, Don 52
Air, Gillian 215
Allison, John 289
Altman, Sidney 51, 172
Amos, Brad 144, 259
Amos, Linda 138
Andrews, Howard 298
Aoufouchi, Said 236
Arndt, Uli 97, 99, 111, 112, 137, 297
Atherton, Eric 267, 285, 287, 289

Bailey, Terry 254
Baker, Tim 135, 136
Baldwin, Joyce 111, 138, 145
Baralle, Tito 289
Barnes, Neville 289
Barnett, Leslie 64, 77, 179
Barrell, Bart 212, 219, 284, 285, 286
Barrell, Caroline 265
Barrett, Alan 111
Benoiton, Leo 267
Bernal, J.D. 4
Bienz, Mariann 197
Big Wheel 91, 261
Birktoft, Betty Wulff 106
Birktoft, Jens 106, 111, 112
Bischoff, Sue 278
Bitton, Mick 254
Blackburn, Elizabeth 50, 215
Bloomer, Anne 137, 139
Blow, David 22, 102, 106, 111, 112, 298
Blow, Mavis 75, 111
Bragg, Lawrence 2
Brenner, Steven 136
Brenner, Sydney 46, 49, 50, 56, 72, 77, 206
Bretscher, Mark 51, 173, 229, 297
Bricogne, Gerard 110, 298
Brightwell, Jenny 111, 237, 298
Broad, Tony 111
Brown, Dan 48, 269
Brown, Evelyn 267
Brown, Jim 111
Brown, Katie 111
Brown, Margaret 229, 237, 264
Brown, Pat (Pat Leberman) 281
Brownlee, George 211, 244, 284, 285, 286
Bruton, Chris 223
Buckland, Robin 282, 284, 289

Bullock, Tim 111
Bullock, Wanda 298
Burton, Doreen 279, 283
Butler, Bill 111
Butler, Carla 111
Butler, Jo 137, 138, 139, 140

Calladine, Chris 146
Campbell, Gerard 289
canteen in 1962 275
canteen staff in 2004 278
Cashmore, Prakash 106
Cashmore, Tony 284
Caspar, Don 53, 114, 136
Ceska, Tom 47
Chadarevian, Soraya de 47
Chambers, S. 289
Chang-Ming, Hua 111
Chothia, Cyrus 111, 112, 136, 147, 297
Churchill, Mair 137
Clark, Brian 125, 137, 182, 286, 287
Clegg, John 281
Cockell, Moira 136
Collard, Jill (Jill Dawes) 102
Collinson, Ian 289
confocal microscope prototype 186
    Queen's Award for Technology 259
Cornwell, Jennifer 228
Cory, Suzanne 50, 213
Coulson, Alan 213, 284, 285, 289
Crick, Francis 13, 21, 28, 38, 72, 76, 77, 114
Crick, Odile 114
Crowther, Tony 111, 138, 141
Cuello, Claudio 244
Cullis, Ann 64, 114
Cunliffe, Eric 287

Dahlberg, Jim 213
Daser, Angelika 47
Davies, Megan 228
Dean, John 289
DeRosier, David 118, 135, 136, 138
Derry, Jonathan 289
Diamond, Ann 111
Diamond, Bob 111, 112, 137, 148
Dickerson, Dick 64
DNA diagram 39
Duo, Lu 136

Durbin, Richard 45, 186, 259
Durham, Tony 138

Edmundson, Allen 46, 116
EDSAC1 271
Ellis, Sue 298
Epstein, Henry 48
Evans, Phil 111, 149

Fairall, Louise 131
Faruqi, Wasi 111, 149
Fastrez, Jacques 111
Faux, Annette 298
Fearnley, Ian 229, 279
Fermi, Judd 150
Ferranti Argus 400 81
Fersht, Alan 110, 279
Finch, John 70, 125
Fishpool, Rita 178
Flying Spot Densitometer 104
Foote, Jeff 244
Fordham, Joy 277
Fordham, Mick 186, 254, 255, 259, 279
Forster, Alan 289
Franklin, Rosalind 34, 114
Freeman, David 289
Freeman, Matthew 198
Fuller, Michael 73, 228, 297, 298

Gait, Mike 267, 296
Gay, Nick 229
Gilby, Charlotte 278
Gilmore, David 289
Giraldo-Suarez, Rafael 136
Goaman, Gwynne (Gwynne Johnson) 111, 112
Goedert, Michel 133, 137, 229
Gossling, Tim 111
Grant, Neil 266
Gray, Bill 281
Green, David 77
Green, Michael 111
Greenhouse, the 63
Griffiths, Andrew 297
Gurdon, John 196

haemoglobin 20
Hamlyn, Pamela (Pamela Rabbitts) 235
Hardwick, Kevin 289
Harris, Ieuan 224, 281
Harrison, Steve 135, 145
Hart, Dave 254, 285, 286, 287, 289
Hart, Paul 298
Hartley, Brian 111, 222
Harvey, Ken 111, 112, 265, 279
Haselgrove, John 90, 282

Hayward, Len 254, 255
Henderson, Penny 106
Henderson, Richard 52, 106, 111, 112, 151, 206, 279
Hess, George 111
Hess, Sue 111
Himsworth, Charlotte 75
Himsworth, Harold 75
Hodgkin, Dorothy 86
Hodgkin, Jonathan 198, 206
Holmes, Ken 70, 111, 112, 115, 116, 135
Hooper, Martin 284
Horsnell, Terry 152
Horvitz, Bob 188
Hübsche, Willy 267
Hut, the 63, 64
Hutchison, Clyde 215
Huxley, Hugh 13, 21, 50, 52, 72, 89, 118, 219

Ingham, Stuart 289
Ingram, Vernon 55
Ionides, John 159
Ison, Robin 287

Jack, Tony 108
Jakes, Ross 111, 229, 283, 284, 285, 287
Jaggard, Lou 284
Janin, Joel 111
Jarvis, John 231, 236, 285, 287, 289
Jeffrey, Barbara (Barbara Harris) 111
Jones, Graham 282, 284
Jubb, Janet 111

Karn, Jon 199, 228
Karpus, Abraham 244
Kay, Rob 200, 229
Kendrew, John 9, 13, 19, 21, 72, 75, 76, 77, 114
Kendrick-Jones, Jake 137, 153
Kendrick-Jones, Jamie 289
Kenyon, Cynthia 43
Kilmartin, John 137, 201, 228
Kimble, Judy 188
King, Jonathan 136
King, Rod 287
Kiselev, Nikolai 137
Klug, Aaron 13, 42, 46, 113, 114, 125, 159, 206, 279
Koch, Gordon 223, 285
Köhler, Georges 234
Kornberg, Roger 128, 135, 136
Kossiakoff, Sue 111
Kossiakoff, Tony 111

Laemmli, Uli 134, 135

Lagnado, Leon 161
Lane, Nancy 298
Lawrence, Peter 194, 205, 206
Leberman, Reuben 116, 137, 281
Lennox, Ed 202
Lenton, Annette 265, 266
Lesk, Arthur 296
Leslie, Andrew 137, 154, 228
Levene, Tim 279
Levitt, Michael 135, 155
Lewis, Mike 279
Li, Jade 111, 155
library in 1962 263
Lightfoot, Jennie 298
Lilley, Margaret 278
Lingley, Graham 266, 289
Lippard, Steve 138
LMB, brand-new 72
Longley, Bill 116
Lutter, Len 129, 137

Macdonald, Peter 284
MacIver, Suds 289
Maizel, Jake 134
Mallet, Frank 111
Mallett, Gill 111
Marcker, Kjeld 211
Marriage, Anna 266
Martin, Audrey 290, 299
Martin, Steve 282
Masters, Pat (Pat Hutchings) 111
Matthes, Hans 267
Matthews, Brian 52, 102, 111, 112
Matthews, Kristine 111
Matthews, Helen 111
McCoy, Airlie 111
McLachlan, Andrew 111, 156, 297
McLaughlin, Paul 149
Milstein, Celia 47, 297
Milstein, César 47, 230, 296
    César's group 236
Mitchison, Graeme 202
Mondragon, Alfonso 135
Moody, Peter 111
Moore, Peter 89
Morley, Tim 287
Mott, Angela 111, 112
Muirhead, Hilary 64, 111, 112
Munro, Sean 203
myoglobin 18, 20

Nagai, Kiyoshi 136, 143
Napper, Caroline 236
Nasmyth, Kim 203
Nayler, Oliver 289
Nelson, Hillary 135, 136

Neuberger, Michael 244, 248
Neuhaus, David 159
Nobbs, Chris 286
North, Tony 24, 297
Northrop, Fred 284
Norman, Ernie 254
Nyborg, Jens 111

Offord, Robin 281
Osbourn, Mary 49

Page, Arthur 70
Pashley, Brian 266
Patel, K.J. 297
Pearse, Barbara 204, 297
Pelham, Hugh 204, 228, 279
Perham, Richard 50
Perutz, Gisela 75, 276, 296
Perutz, Max 6, 8, 21, 64, 72, 76, 77
Perutz, Robin 296
Phillips, David 139
Pink, Richard 244
Pinkerton, Mary 64
Pledge, David 298
Poljak, Roberto 244
Pope, Brian 289, 297

Queen, the 75

Rabbitts, Terry 229, 244, 245
Rada, Cristina 236, 244
Raeburn, Chris 254, 298
Ramakrishnan, Venki 45, 160
Reichman, Lutz 289
Rhodes, Daniela 51, 124, 143, 297
Richmond, Tim 49, 52, 130, 135
Rigby, Peter 284, 287
Robertus, Jon 125
Rodgers, Phil 111
Rossmann, Michael 111, 112
Rowe, Tony 289
Rubin, Gerry 51
Ruddy, Darren 278
Runswick, Mike 229, 285, 289
Russell, Dick 284

Sainsbury, Lord 43
Sanger, Fred 46, 65, 72, 206, 210, 218, 219,
    296
Sanger, Joan 219
Sanger, Sally 219
Schertler, Gebhard 228, 297
Schmitt, Herbert 289
Scholey, Jon 289
Schutt, Clarence 160
Scott, Bill 136

Secher, David 48, 219, 232
Seftan, Mark 289
Shawcross, Lord 75
Sheppard, Bob 267
Shotton, David 282
Sigler, Jo 111
Sigler, Paul 102, 111, 112, 282
Simpson, Sue 102, 111
Singh, Mohinder 267
Singleton, Diana, (Diana Watson) 102, 111, 282
Skehel, Mark 229
Smith, Alan 289
Smith, Andrew 289
Smith, John 175
Smith, Jude (Jude Short) 106, 111, 152
Snazle, Annette (Annette Lenton) 265
Southgate, Eileen 178, 279
Spillantini, Maria 137
Spooner, Brian 289
Springer, Tim 244
Spudich, Jim 90
Squire, Mike 289
Staden, Rodger 217, 289
Starkey, Mary-Ann 298
Steinrauf, Larry 64
Steitz, Joan 44, 106
Steitz, Tom 51, 111, 112
Stewart, Murray 136, 160, 296
Strandberg, Bror 64
Stretton, Tony 177
Stroud, Bob 111
Stubbings, Steve 254, 289
Sulston, John 42, 187, 205, 206
Sundquist, Wes 138

Thatcher, Denis 86
Thatcher, Margaret 86
Thøgersen, Hans Christian 136
Thomas, John Meurig 297
Thomson, Nichol 184, 205
Tissières, Alfred 134
Titmas, Richard 267, 285
Topal, Rushan 278
Travers, Andrew 181, 297
Trentham, David 111

Turnell, Bill 137
Turner, J. 289

Unwin, Nigel 136, 161

Varani, Gabriel 136

Wade, John 267
Wagner, Paul 289
Waldmann, Herman 244
Walker, David 285
Walker, Fred 254, 287
Walker, John 226, 237, 285, 298
Wallace, Hilary 111
Wasylyszyn, John 254
Waterston, Bob 187, 206
Watson, Ian 111
Watson, Jim 13, 21, 39, 43, 76
Weeds, Alan 162, 281
Westmorland, Joanna 266
Whant, Rachel 229, 298
Wheeler, Shirley 266
White, John 186, 205, 259
Whybrow, Bill 262, 284, 289
Wickham, John 111
Wickham, Sue 102, 111
Widom, Jon 47
Wilcox, Michael 195
Wilkins, Maurice 33, 76
Williams, Brian 267, 285
Winter, Greg 228, 240, 244, 248, 297
Wonacott, Alan 107
Woolfson, Adrian 236
Woollard, Tony 254, 261, 279
Woolley, Vivien 267
Workman, Peter 289
Wright, Brian 285
Wright, Tonie 111
Wugner, Reinhard 289
Wynn, Alec 279
Wynn, Mary 279

Yanagida, Mitsuhiro 136
Yélamos, José 236

Zimmern, Dave 219

Index

Abbs, Rhidian, cricket trophy 287
Abelson, John
    suppression of amber mutants by altered
        tRNA 170
    ballet of protein synthesis 281
Abrahams, Don, drug development work on
      haemoglobin 83
Abrahams, Jan Pieter 154, 227
acetylcholine receptor structure 162
Adair G., supplying haemoglobin crystals to
    Perutz 6
Adams, Jerry, RNA sequencing 213
Agard, David, purple membrane 151
Air, Gillian, DNA sequencing 214–5
α-helix published by Pauling, check by Perutz
    16
Albertson, Donna 185–6
Allison, Tom 260
Altman, Sidney
    tRNA precursor, RNAse P 171
    Nobel Prize 172
    reminiscences of LMB 301
Altschuh, Daniele 139
Alzheimer's Disease 133
amber mutant stop-codon UAG 170
Ambrose, Barry 260
Amos, Brad 143
    scanning diffractometer 144
    confocal microscope development 258
    Christmas plays 281
Amos, Linda 138
    rotational symmetry of images 119
    3-D reconstruction of spherical viruses
        121
Anderson, Leigh
    memories of LMB 330
Anderson, Philip 186
Anderson, Stephen 220
Andrews, Howard 261
antibodies
    chimaeric 240
    monoclonal 233
archives 264
Argus, first LMB 'large' computer 81, 101
Arndt-Wonacott rotation X-ray camera 99
Arndt, Uli 81, 92, 96, 105, 140
    FAST – automatic X-ray television
      diffractometer 99
    four-circle diffractometer 98

linear diffractometer 97
Arnone, Arthur 82
Arnott, Struther 154
Arshady, Reza 268
Ashburner, Michael 193
Asilomar Committee 189
Astbury, W.T., working at Royal Institution 4
Atherton, Eric 268, 269
ATP synthase 226
Austin Wing of Cavendish Laboratory,
      housing the MRC Unit until 1957 61
Awards to Inventors 300

Babu, Padmanabhan 186
Baer, Richard 247
Bailey, Terry 260
Baker, Tim 120
Baldwin, Joyce 88, 144
    bacteriorhodopsin structure 144
    processing 2.8Å haemoglobin data 81
Bamberg, Jim 162
Banaszak, Len 87, 88
Bankier, Alan 220
Barcroft, Joseph 9
Bard Review 260
Barker, David 224
Barnett, Lesley 170, 179, 186, 199, 269
    mutagenesis 58, 171
    genetic code 58
Barrell, Caroline 265
Barrell, Bart 200, 226
    joining Fred Sanger 211
    mitochondrial DNA 220
    cricket 284
    darts 290
Barrington Leigh, John 98, 115
Beckwith, Jon, ochre mutants 170
Beevers-Lipson strips 15, 271
Bence-Jones protein 231
Bentley, David 193, 246
Bentley, Graham 130
Benzer, Seymour 57
Berek, Claudia 236
Berger, Jack, optical diffraction 117
Bernal, J.D.
    early life 3
    lecturer in Mineralogy department,
      Cambridge 4
    move to Birkbeck College, London 7

transfer to Cavendish Laboratory in 1931
7
Bernal's laboratory 68
Rosalind Franklin transferred from King's
38
Beroukhim, Rameen 162
Betz, Alex 249
Bienz, Mariann 197
Biesecker, Gregory, GPDH work 225
Bilder 147
Birkbeck College 7, 68
Birktoft, Jens, in David Blow's group 103–5
Bishop, John 245
Bitton, Mick 253
Blackburn, Elizabeth 190, 214–5
Bland, Ian 261
Blake, Colin 87
Block 7 294
Bloomer, Anne 139
    C-reactive protein 140
    Fourier maps of TMV protein 123, 139
Blow, David 61, 100, 141
    joined MRC Unit 21
    returned from US, beginning chymotrypsin
        work 23
    rotation function work 23
    structure of α-chymotrypsin 102
    move to Imperial College 109
    setting up of British Crystallographic
        Association 109
    librarian 23, 262
    using EDSAC 273
Blows, Joan
    accounts office 299
    librarian 262
Bodo, Gerhard 18
Boehm, Thomas 247
Bolton, Bill 82
Bond, Chris 92, 94, 261
Bonnert, Tim 242
Borisy, Gary 119
Böttcher, Bettina 142
Boutle, Stan, TV X-ray detector 99
Boyer, Paul 227
Boyes-Watson, Joy 15
Bragg W.H. (Sir William), physics professor in
        Adelaide 1
Bragg W.L. (Sir Lawrence)
    early life and coming to the Cavendish 1
    retirement from Cavendish chair in 1953
        62
Brenner, Sydney 140, 182–4, 226, 232, 238
    early life 56
    negative staining 57
    Theory of Mutagenesis paper 58
    genetic engineering moratorium 189

Director of LMB 190
Nobel prize 189
Bretscher, Mark 140, 172
    cell membrane work 174
    chain initiation 174
    coated vesicles 174
    translocation of tRNA on ribosome 173
Bricogne, Gerard
    joined David Blow's group 110
    TMV protein 123, 139
Brink, Charles 234
Brisson, Allain 162
British Crystallographic Association 109
British Technology Group (BTG) 239
Broad, Tony 91, 256
Broomhead, June 37
Brower, Danny 196
Brown, Dan 268
Brown, Don 131
Brown, Margaret, archives 264
Brown, Nigel, DNA sequencing 215
Brown, Ray, crystallisation of tRNA 124
Brownlee, George 232, 240, 245
    RNA sequencing 211
    5S ribosomal RNA sequencing 212
    cricket 284
Bruggemann, Marianne 248
Bruton, Chris, tRNA^{Met} synthetase 106, 223
Buck, Kay, trophy 291
Buckland, Robin 287
Bullit, Esther 201
Bullock, Wanda
    librarian 263
    badminton 291
Burke, Derek 239
Burton, Doreen 283
    accounts 299
    darts 290
Buss, Folma 154
Butler, Jo 126, 139, 140
    joining Aaron Klug's group 116
    assembly of TMV 121–2

Calladine, Chris 145
Campath-1H 241
Canning, Barry 261
canteen 275
Capaldi, Rod 152
Carlisle, Harry 54, 114
Carroll, Joe 155
Carroll, Lewis 92
Caspar, Don
    virus structure 53, 120
    quasi-equivalence theory 117
CAT, set up 135, 242
    MRC buy equity in 243

Cattermole, David 261
Cavendish Laboratory
    Bernal transferred as lecturer 4
    Bragg becomes Professor 7
    Perutz joins Bernal's group 5
C. elegans
    search for mutants 184
    nerve cell locations 187
    pattern of growth – programmed cell
        death 189
    genome map 191–2
    genome sequencing 193
Celltech 135, 239, 241
Ceska, Tom, purple membrane 144, 151
Chain, Sir Ernst 223
Chalfie, Martin 185, 186
Champness, John 99
    TMV protein 123, 139
Chapman, Linda 132
Chargaff, Erwin, visit to Cavendish 36
Cheetham, Graham 140
Chibnall, Charles 65
chimaeric antibody 240
Chiswell, David 242
Choo, Yen 132
Chothia, Cyrus 105, 147, 240
Churchill, Mair, zinc finger 132
Christmas party, play and raffle 280
chymotrypsin 5, 23, 101
    structure 102
Clackson, Tim 242
Clark, Brian 182
    initiator tRNA 210
    tRNA structure 123–6
    cricket 284
Clark, Michael 241
clathrin, protein in coated vesicles 174, 204
Claxton, Dave 74
Clegg, John 231
coated vesicles 174, 204
Coates, Bill 96
Cochran, Bill 30
codon table, final member added 170
Cohen, Carolyn 153
Collard, Jill 102
computers, computing 270
confocal microscope 257
Cornwell, Jennifer 299
Cory, Suzanne 168
    speaker at DNA50 meeting 168
    student with Brian Clark 182
    sequencing tRNA 212
Cotton, Dick, postdoc with César Milstein
    232–3
Coulter, Charles 87

Coulson, Alan 134
    genome sequencing 191
    joined Fred Sanger 213
    λ phage DNA sequencing 220
    cricket 284
    football 288
Coulson, Valerie 102, 273
    paper tape 274
    canteen 276
Cousins, Elsie
    librarian 262
    cricket trophy 287
    darts 290
Cowan, Nick 232, 238
Cox, Joyce, *see* Baldwin, Joyce
CPE 295
Creighton, Tom 268
Crick, Francis 123, 168
    early life 27
    helical diffraction publication, *Cochran,
        Crick and Vand*, 1952 30
    SEB paper (1957) including Sequence
        Hypothesis and Central Dogma 60
    student at MRC Unit from 1949 16
    tRNA proposed 58
    laboratory talks 280
Crowfoot Dorothy, *see* Hodgkin, Dorothy
Crowther, Tony 141
    non-crystallographic symmetry – fast
        rotation function 141
    Flying Spot densitometer 98, 105
    rotational symmetry of images 119
    3-D reconstruction of spherical viruses
        121
    Alzheimer's PHFs 133
    hepatitis B virus core structure 142
Cullis, Ann 20, 25, 157
Cunliffe, Eric 288

Dahlberg, Jim 174
    sequencing RNA 212
Dane, Lindsay 299
Danish inch 104
Darwin, Charles 27
Davidson, Barrie 225
Davidson, Edna 15
Davies, David 18, 19, 56
Davies, Megan 300
Dean, John 288, 300
Dear, Paul 200, 241, 249
Deatherage, Jim 152
De Bruijn, Maarten 220
Delbrück, Max 31
DeRobertis, Eddy 196
DeRosier, David
    weight of TYMV 117

optical diffraction and filtering 118
postdoc in Aaron Klug's group 118
3-D reconstruction from electron
    micrographs 120
Dewan, John, tRNA cleavage 126
Diamond, Bob 82, 147
    elastase structure refined 88
    myoglobin structure refined 88
Dickerson, Dick 18
    memories of Hut 307
Dickson, David 234
Dictyosteleum 200
Dideoxy-method for DNA sequencing 216
    modification for double stranded DNA
    220
Dingwall, Colin 196, 269
Di Noia, Javier 250
Dintzis, Howard 18
Director's Section 269
Dixon, Malcom 230
DNA
    Gosling and Wilkin's X-ray photographs
    33
    Franklin's X-ray work 35
    first, incorrect model by Watson and Crick
    35
    correct model of structure by Watson and
    Crick and publication in 1953 38
Doctor, Bhupendra 123
Donohue, Jerry 38
    structure of globlglobin 337
Donelson, John, DNA sequencing 214
DORIS, X-rays from the storage ring used by
    Hugh Huxley's group 93
Douglas, Alasdair 277
Downing, Ken 144, 152
Dowsing, Mary 262
Drew, Horace 146
Drouin, Jacques 220
Duncumb, Peter 99
Dunn, David 176
Dunstan, Diana 300
Durbin, Richard 269
    confocal microscope 258
    genome sequencing 192
Durham, Tony, assembly of TMV 121

Earnshaw, Bill 142
East, David 269
Edmundson, Allen 19, 87
EDSAC1 18, 271
EDSAC2 18, 157, 272
Edwards, Pat 291
Ehrenberg and Spear X-ray tube 12
Ehrenstein, Michael 250
Eisenberg, David 157

elastase, structure solved 88
Ellar, David 155
EMBO, EMBL 85, 87
Engelman, Don 151
Ennis, Peter 161
Eperon, Ian 220
Epstein, Henry
    mutant study of *C. elegans* 186
Epstein-Barr DNA sequence 221
Eusden, Edna 263
Evans, Phil 204
    phosphofructokinase 148, 225
    snurps 158

Fairall, Louise, zinc finger 131, 143
Fan, David 171
Fankuchen, Isidor, at Cavendish 5
Faruqi, Wasi 149
    densitometer 99
    development of position sensitive
    electronic detectors 92, 94
Fasham, John 260
Faux, Annette, archivist 265, 269
Fearnley, Ian 226
Fell, Honor 29
Fellner, Peter 232
Fermi, Judd 150
    refining haemoglobin structure 82
    drug development work on haemoglobin
    83
Fersht, Alan
    joining David Blow's group 110
    site directed mutagenesis 240
    Director of CPE 110
Fiddes, John, DNA sequencing 215
Fields, Stan 221, 240
Finch, John 83, 132, 142
    student of Rosalind Franklin 69
    joined LMB 114
    LMB librarian 262
Fishpool, Rita 55, 177
Flanagan, John, chimaeric antibody 240
Flying Spot densitometer 104
Fodor, Andräs, memories of LMB 326
Foote, Jeff 241, 249
Fordham, Joy 197
    canteen 277
Fordham, Mick 253, 255, 258
Forster, Alan 247
Fox, Robert 248
Fraenkel-Conrat, Heinz 54, 121
Frangione, Blas 231
Frank Lee Centre 290
Franklin, Rosalind 114
    early life and joining King's Unit 33

X-ray pictures of A- and B- forms of DNA
    35
move to Birkbeck, 1953 69
joined by students Finch and Holmes 1955
    69
poliovirus work 70
death in 1958 39, 71
Freedman, Roger 171
Freeman, Ray 159
Freeman, Matthew 198
Fresco, Jacques, tRNA 124
Fruton, J.S. 224
Fujiyoshi, Yoshinori 162
Fuller, Michael 73, 262

Gabriel, André 93
Gait, Mike 199, 216, 268
    oligonucleotide synthesis 268
Galfré, Giovanni 235
gap junction channels 161
Gay, Nick 276
Gefter, Malcom 171
Geider, Klaus 216
genetic code, triplet nature – 1961 58
genetic engineering, moratorium on
    experiments 189
Genome Research Limited 193
genome sequencing
    C. elegans 191
    human 193–4
Gergyo, K. 186
Gilbert, Peter 116
    6Å map of TMV protein 122
Gilmore, David, TV X-ray detector 99
Glaeser, Bob, purple membrane 151
Glauser, Stanley 157
Goaman, Gwynne, in haemoglobin group 80
Goedert, Michel, PHF protein 133, 142, 269
Gold, Larry 171
Goldberg, Eddie 142
Goldman, Yale 154
Goldsmith-Heidner, Betsy 82
Gooch, John 162
Goodman, Howard
    suppression of amber mutants by altered
        tRNA 170
    sequencing tRNA 212
Gosling, Raymond 33
Gossling, Tim 152
    programming Argus 141
    Flying Spot densitometer 99, 105
Gowans, Sir James 238
Graham, Jim 139
Grant, Neil 267
Gray, Bill 222
Gray, Sir John 239

Green, David 17
Green, Sheila 195
Greer, Jonathan, processing 3.5Å
    deoxyhaemoglobin data 82, 158
Griffiths, Andrew 242
Griffiths, Gillian 236
Griffiths, John 36
Grigg, Geoffrey 242
Grigorieff, Niko 144, 204
Grindley, George 261
Grungerg-Manago, Marianne 56
Gurdon, John
    Xenopus laevis group 196
    ice skating 197
    squash 291

Hagawa, H. 186
Hall, Laurie 158
Hamlyn, Pamela
    sequencing mRNA for light chains 235
    translocation of c-myc 246
Hanson, Jean 14
Harris, Ieuan 140, 224–5
    cricket 284
    cricket trophy 287
Harris, Reuben 250
Harrison, Steve
    with Aaron Klug's group 116
    Tony Jack 108
Harrison, Tim 233
Hart, Dave
    scanning diffractometer 119
    workshop 253, 260
    cricket 284
Hart, Paul 262
Hart, Roger 18, 122
Hartley, Brian 104–5, 140, 222–4
    chymotrypsingen-A sequence 222
    tRNA synthetase 106
    elastase sequence 88, 223
    move to Imperial 223
Hartree, D.R. 113
Harvey, Ken 265
Haselgrove, John, joined Hugh Huxley's
    group 92, 94
Haselkorn, Bob 117
Haurowitz F.
    suggesting haemoglobin to Perutz 6
    teaching course 31
Hayes, Vic 253
Hayward, Len
    joined MRC Unit 253
    scanning diffractometer 119
    head of LMB workshop 74, 260
Heaphy, Sean 269
Heinrikson, Robert 106, 223

Henderson, Richard 151, 264
  joining David Blow's group 105
  glucose preservation for EM 151
  purple membrane structure – cytochrome-
    C oxidase vesicle crystals – rhodopsin
    151
Hendrix, Jules 94
Hengartner, Hans 225
Herman, Bob 186
Herzenberg, Len 234
Hewitt, John 82
Hill, A.V. 29
Hill, Diana 220
Himsworth, Sir Harold 12, 66, 67
Hindley, John 127, 214
Hingerty, Brian, tRNA cleavage 126
Hinxton Hall, site for Sanger Centre 193
Hirsh, David, mechanism of UGA suppression
  171
Hoagland, Mahlon 57, 59
Hobart, Mike 246
Hodgkin, Dorothy 5, 17, 68
Hodgkin, Jonathan 198
Holmes, Ken
  student of Rosalind Franklin 69
  joined LMB 114
  modifying X-ray generators 91, 256
  TMV work at LMB 115
  tRNA 123
  move to Heidelberg 92, 115, 123
homochromotography introduced for RNA
  sequencing 212
Hong, Guofan 220
Hoogenboom, Hennie 242
Hopkins, F. Gowland 5, 65
Hopkins, Harold 262
Horne, Bob 14, 57
Horsnell, Terry 152
Horton, Keith 262
Horvitz, Bob
  mutant work on C. elegans 186
  pattern of growth – programmed cell
    death 189
  Nobel Prize 189
Hovmoller, Sven 139
Howe, Shirley 233
Huber, Robert 105
Hudson, Graham 186
Hudson, Peter, structure of
  phosphofructokinase 225
Hughes, Arthur 29
human antibodies selected 242
humanised antibody 241
  wide licensing policy adopted by MRC
  241
Hunt, Stephen 262

Huntington's disease 83
Hut, The, MRC Unit moves in, 1957 62
Hutch, The 299
Hutchinson, Arthur
  encouraging Astbury and Bernal to go to
    Royal Institution 3
  smuggling crystals to Bragg 2
  creation of Cambridge lectureship for
    Bernal 4
Hutchison, Clyde 214–5, 217
Huxley, Hugh 68, 88, 117, 139
  student at MRC Unit, start of muscle
    research 12
  programming EDSAC1 272
  work with Jean Hanson at MIT, Sliding
    Filament Model 14
  negative staining 14, 57
  X-ray tube modifications 91, 256
  storage ring DORIS X-rays used at
    Hamburg 93
  left LMB 94

ice skating on fens 197
Ingram, Vernon 17
  joined Unit in 1952 55
  showing the mutation Hb→HbS results in
    one amino acid change 56
insulin sequencing 66
Irving, Malcom 154, 257
Irwin, Mike 107
Ish-Horovitz, David, student with Brian Clark
  182

Jack, Tony
  refinement of tRNA structure 108, 126
  TMV protein 108, 122
Jacob, François 59
Jacobs, Grant, zinc fingers 132
Jaggard, Lou 287
Jakes, Ross
  work with Michel Goedert 133
  cricket 284–7
James, R.W. 113
JANET 270
Janin, Joel, postdoc with David Blow 105
Jarvis, John 231, 245
  cricket 284
  darts 290
Jeffrey, Barbara 101
Jepperson, Peter, RNA sequencing 213
Jerne, Niels 234
Johnson, Tony 83, 268, 269
Jolley, Paul 291
Jones, Graham
  sequencing GPDHs 225
  cricket 284

Jones, Peter 241, 242, 249
Josephs, Bob 119
Joyce-Loebl densitometer for X-ray films 22
    for electron micrographs 257
Jubb, Janet 152

Kaartinen, Matti 236
Kaiser, Dale 214
Kalckar, Hermann 31
Kaplan, Sam, stop-codons for amber and
    ochre mutants 170
Karn, Jon 156, 191, 199, 268
Karpus, Abraham 232
Katz, Gene 170
Kauffman, Dorothy 222
Kay, Rob 199–201
Keilin, David, suggesting MRC grant for
    Cavendish group 11
Kellet, George 82
Kendrew, John 67, 272
    contact with Bernal 9
    pre-Cavendish life 9
    student at MRC Unit 10
    structure of myoglobin 17–19
    director of EMBL 87
    founder member of EMBO 87
Kendrick-Jones, Jake 95, 153
Kenyon, Cynthia 186
Kilby, Bernard 222
Kilmartin, John 143, 201–2
    cooperativity in haemoglobin 82
Kimble, Judith 188
King, Jonathan 119, 120
King's colloquium in 1951 33, 35
Kiselev, Nikolay, memories of LMB 321
Kitai, Ruth 66
Klug, Aaron 68, 241, 257
    at Birkbeck College, work with Rosalind
        Franklin 69, 114
    at Cape Town 113
    at Cavendish Laboratory 113
    at Colloid Science Department with
        F.J.W Roughton 113
    research at LMB 117
    Awards to Inventors scheme 135
Knight, C.A. 224
Knott, Kirsty, archives 264
Koch, Gordon
    structure of tyrosyl-tRNA synthetase 224
    tRNA^{Met} synthetase 223
    Industrial Liaison Officer 239
Köhler, Georges
    monoclonal antibodies produced with
        César 233
    Nobel Prize 234

Kolb, Edith 225
Korn, Larry 196
Kornberg, Arthur 216
Kornberg, Roger 169
    chromatin structure 127
    nucleosome structure proposed 128
Krebs, Hans 68
Kreisel, George 29
Kress, Marcus 93, 94
Kyte, Martin 261

laboratory talks 280
Ladner, Bob
    CO- and met-haemoglobins structurally
        equivalent 82
    elastase refinement 88
Ladner, Jane, tRNA crystallisation 124
Lamond, Angus 181
Landy, Art, suppression of amber mutants by
    altered tRNA 170
Laemmli, Uli
    polyhead work 119
    SDS gel development 133
λ phage DNA sequencing 220
Langmore, John 160
Laskey, Ron, *Xenopus laevis* group 196
Lawrence, Peter
    pattern formation – development 193–4
Leberman, Reuben 70
    at LMB 115, 141
    move to Heidelberg 116
Lehmann, Hermann, work with Max on
    abnormal haemoglobins 82
Lennox, Ed 202, 268
Lenton, Annette 266
Lerman, Leonard 171
Lesk, Arthur 240
Leslie, Andrew 142, 154, 227
Levitt, Michael 124, 169
    PhD work 155
    refining tRNA structure 126
    refining protein structure 108
    memories of LMB 312
Lewit, Anita 130
Li, Jade, crystalline toxin inclusions in
    B. thuringiensis 155
Lifson, Shneior 155
Linck, Richard 139
Ling, Vic, DNA sequencing 214
Lingley, Graham 267
linking number 129, 169
Lipscomb, Bill 157
LMB
    the new laboratory 71
    move from the Cavendish 74

Loder, Bronwyn
  first Administrative Director 190
  MRC Centre 299
Lodish, Harvey 171
Logan, Chris 268
Lomonossoff, George, DNA structure, local
    variations 126
Long, Jim 99
Longley, Bill 261, 275
  joined LMB 71, 114
  modifying X-ray generators 91, 256
Lonsdale, Kathleen 23
Longuet-Higgins, Christopher 156
Loveday, Paul 300
Lucke, Roger 260
Luisi, Ben 147
Luria, Salvador 31
Lutter, Len, large scale nucleosome core
    production 129
Lutter, René 227
Luzzati, Vittorio 127

Maaloe, Ole 31
Macleod, Sandy 199
Maizel, Jake, SDS gel development 133
Mallett, Frank 152
  work on X-ray diffractometer 81
  densitometer 98, 105, 149
Maniatis, Tom 203
Marcker, Kjeld 123, 174, 210
Margiotta, Paul 267
Mark Hermann, suggesting that Perutz go to
    Bernal's laboratory 5
Markham, Alex 236
Markham, Roy 32
  photographic superposition 119
  work with John Smith 175–9
Marks, Jim 242
Martin, Audrey 266, 290
  secretary of new LMB 74
  accounts 299
Martin, Steve 171
Mason, John 249
Massey, Harrie 28
Mathews, Scott 80
Matsudaira, Paul, mini gel device 260
Matthews, Brian 100, 101, 102, 105
Matthews, Mike 233
Max Perutz Fund 84
Maxam and Gilbert 217
McCafferty, John 242
McGandy, Ed 80
McHugh, Peter 299
McIntosh, Dick 201
McKeane, Lesley 267

McLachlan, Andrew 156, 199
  zinc finger 131
McMahon, Harvey 204
Medewar, Peter 245
Mellanby, Sir Edward, Secretary of MRC
    1933–49 11, 29
Mellema, Jan 119, 121, 139
Melton, Doug 196
messenger RNA 59
Meyer, Kerstin 249
Milch, Jim 93
Miller, Jonathan, zinc finger 131
Milligan, Ron 161
Milstein, César 220, 230–7, 238, 247
  came to Biochemistry Department in 1958
    230
  began antibody work at LMB 230
  monoclonal antibodies produced with
    Köhler 233
  Nobel Prize 234
Miyazawa, Atsuo 162
Mirzabekov, Andrei, tRNA 124
Mitchell, Joseph, combined site for MRC and
    Radiotherapeutics Department 67, 68
Mitchison, Graeme 195, 202–3
Moffat, Keith, letter to Richard Henderson
    335
Molteno Institute 176
Mondragon, Alfonso 139
Monoclonal antibodies 233
  criticism of non-patenting 238
Monod, Jacques 59
Moore, Peter
  joined Hugh Huxley's group 89
  reconstruction computation 89, 121
Moras, Dino 139
Morata, Gines 195
Morris, Ron, memories of LMB 328
Morris, Shirley 123
Mott, Angela 102
  paper tape 274
Mott, Neville, Bragg's successor as Cavendish
    Professor 62
Muirhead, Hilary 88
  research student of Max 157
  thesis project 80
  processing 2.8Å haemoglobin data 81,
    158
Müller, A. 96
Müller, Hermann 31
Munro, Sean 203
  LMB librarian 262
Munro, Mary 170
Murray, Ken, DNA sequencing 214
Mutagenesis Theory paper 58
Mutants in rII region of T4 58

myoglobin
structure 17–19

Nagai, Kiyoshi 158, 243
SWI5 159
Nakaseko, Yukinobu, SWI5 159
National Enterprise Board (NEB) 239
Naysmyth, Kim 203
Negative staining
noticed by Hugh Huxley in 1956 14
method developed by Brenner and Horne 57
Nelson, Hillary, structure of bent polynucleotide 126
nematode worm, proposal by S. Brenner to study control mechanisms in development – differentiation 183
Nermut, Milan 119
Neuberger, Michael 224, 236, 247–50
chimaeric antibody 240
humanised antibody 241
Neuhaus, David 158
NMR introduced to LMB 158
oestrogen receptor 132, 143
SWI5 132
Neurath, Hans 222
new building, negotiations for 66
setting up Divisions 73
officially opened by the Queen, 1962 75
Nierlich, Donald 220
NMR 158
Nobel Prize
Watson and Crick, 1962 39, 76
Sanger, 1958 66
Perutz and Kendrew, 1962 76
Klug, 1982 135
Altman, 1989 172
Brenner, Sulston and Horvitz, 2002 191
Sanger, 1980 217
Walker, 1997 230
Milstein and Köhler, 1984 234
Nobbs, Chris 87
Noble, David 243
Noll, Markus, nuclease digestion of chromatin 128
Noller, Harry 225
Norman, Ernie 105, 253
North, Marc 262
North, Tony 20
Northrop, John Howard 6
NRDC 238
nucleic acid synthesis 268

ochre mutants 170
oestrogen receptor (human) 132

Offord, Robin 76, 140, 225
Ogilvie, Bridget, funding from Wellcome Trust for genome sequencing 192
optical diffraction and filtering 117
Orgel, Alice 58, 171
Oubridge, Chris 158
Owen, David 204

Paradies, Hasko, tRNA crystals 123
Parrish, Bob 15
Pashley, Brian 267
Pauling, Linus, α-helix 16, 55
DNA model 36
Pauling, Peter 36, 147
Paulson, Jim, memories of LMB 324
Peacock, Jack 74
Pearse, Barbara 142
clathrin 204
coated vesicles 174, 204
Pelham, Hugh 204–5
Perham, Richard 140, 225
Perry, Sam 153
Perutz, Gisela, canteen 276
Perutz, M.F.
wartime internment 8
marrying Gisela 8
Nobel Prize 76, 85
work at LMB 80
founder member of EMBO 85
polyglutamine polymers, Huntington's Disease 83
cricket committee 284
Perutz, Vivien 264
Peterson, George 220
Petersen-Mahrt, Svend 250
Pettersson, Sven 249
phage display used to select human antibodies 242
phase problem in X-ray diffraction 14
solved by Perutz 16
Phillips, David 87, 97
Phillips report 109
φX174 single stranded DNA sequence
by plus-and-minus 215
dideoxy- 217
Phizackerley, Paul 105
techniques laboratory 260
student of Uli Arndt 99
Pink, Richard 231
Pinkerton, Mary 25
Piper, Peter, student of Brian Clark 182
Pirie, N.W. 65
'Plus-and-minus' method for DNA sequencing 215
polyglutamine polymers 83

Pope, Brian 162
    football 288
    badminton, squash 290
Pope, W.J. 2
Porter, Rodney 230
position sensitive electronic detectors
        developed in 1971 by Hugh Huxley,
        Wasi Faruqi, Chris Bond and John
        Haselgrove 94
Price, Stephen 158
Priess, Jim 185
Princess Margaret 197
Prunell, Ariel 129
purple membrane 151
Pyke G., originator of Pykrete, Perutz's
        wartime project 8

quasi-equivalence theory 117
Quibell, Martin 268

Rabbitts, Pamela, *see* Hamlyn, Pamela
Rabbitts, Terry 245–7
    chimaeric antibody 240
    pure mRNA probe made by bacterial
        cloning 246
Racker, Efraim 226
Rada, Cristina
    student of César Milstein 236
    transgenic mice work 249–50
Raeburn, Chris 95, 253, 260
Rajewski, Klaus 247
Ramakrishnan, Venki 159
Randall, John 32
    employment of Rosalind Franklin 33
    agreement with Bragg 35
Ratti, Guilio 221
recreation 284
Rednall, Wayne 262
Reedy, Mike, joined Hugh Huxley's group
        89
Rees, Dai 241
Reid, Brian, structure of tyrosyl-tRNA
        synthetase 107
Reth, Michael 249
Rhodes, Daniela 142, 159
    joined tRNA group 124
    oestrogen receptor 132
    300Å chromatin filament 142
ribosome structure 159
Rich, Alex 56, 125
Richards Box 103
Richmond, Tim, 7Å map of nucleosome core
        130
Riechmann, Lutz 241
Rigby, Peter 288
Riggs, Austin 17

Riley, Dennis 5, 96
RNA sequencing 210
    5S ribosomal RNA 212
    R17 phage RNA 213
    tRNAs 212
Roberts, Andrew 186
Robertson, Hugh, DNA sequencing 214
Robertson, J. Monteath 23
Robertson, Robert 74
Robertus, Jon, structure of tRNA 124
Rockefeller Foundation, grant for Perutz 7
Roe, Bruce, mitochondrial DNA sequencing
        220
Roeder, Bob 131
Rosenbaum, Gerd 92
Rossmann, Michael 19, 62
    joining haemoglobin group 25
    rotation function work 23
    left LMB 101
    purple membrane 151
    using EDSAC 273
Rout, Michael 201
Rubin, Gerry 187
Runswick, Mike 226
Russel, Dick 171
Ryle, A.P. 66

Sajgo, Michael 225
Sale, Julian 250
Salvato, Maria 186
Sambrook, Joe 171
Sanger, Fred 55, 123
    early life 64
    insulin work – first Nobel Prize 66
    RNA sequencing 210
    DNA sequencing 214
    second Nobel Prize 217
    opening Sanger Centre at Hinxton 193
    opening Sanger Building in Biochemistry
        221
    cricket 284
Sanger Centre 193
Sarabhai, Anand 170
    memories of MRC 315
Saraste, Matti 226
Satchwell, Sandra 181
Schaeffer, Fred 70
Schertler, Gebhard 145, 152
Schoenborn, Benno 87
Schreier, Peter 220
Schrödinger, Erwin, *What is Life* 29
Schutt, Clarence 160
Schwabe, John, oestrogen receptor structure
        132, 143
Schwerdt, Carlton 70
Schwerdt, Patsy 70

Scotcher, Steve 253
Scott, Bill, ribozyme structure 126
Secher, David 232, 234, 239
    joined César Milstein 231
    patenting interferon antibody 239
Sedat, John, DNA sequencing 214
Sharpe, Melanie 249
Shaw, Denis 226
Sheldon, Robert 186
Sheppard, Bob 216, 268
    peptide chemistry 267
Shore, David 203
Shore, Vi 18
Short, Jude (Jude Smith) 111, 130
Shotton, David, structure of elastase 88, 223
Shulman, Bob 171
Sigler, Paul 266
    joined David Blow's group 101, 103
    borrowing Frank Mallett 149
    ballet of protein synthesis 281
Sikora, Karol 205
Simmons, Bob 94
Simpson, Sue 102
Singleton, Diana 102
Sitia, Roberto 249
Skou, Jens 230
Sliding Filament Model for muscle
    contraction proposed by Huxley and
    Hanson 14
Slocombe, Pat, DNA sequencing 215
Smillie, Larry 222
Smith, Alan 211
Smith, Andrew, sequencing mitochondrial
    DNA 220
Smith, Corinne 204
Smith, John 122, 175, 210
    tRNA work at LMB 170, 212
Smith, Jude, joined David Blow's group 111,
    130
Smith, Kenneth M. 175
Smith, Leslie 210
Smith, Mike, DNA sequencing 215, 217
Smith, Richard 195
Snazle, Annette (Annette Lenton) 266
Snelling, Michael 299
Soddy, Frederick 27, 119
solenoid structure of chromatin proposed
    128
Somatogen 243
Southgate, Eileen 177, 185
Spillantini, Maria 133
Spinks Report 238
suppression of amber and ochre mutants 170
Sperling, Linda, X-ray scattering from
    chromatin 130

Spudich, Jim
    tropomyosin-troponin complex study with
        Susan Watt 90
    actin filament bundles, structural study
        with Linda Amos 90
Squires, Mike 288
Staden, Rodger 157, 269
    programming for sequence work 217
    for genome work 191
    squash 291
Stauffer, Kathrin 162
Stein, Penny 154
Steinrauf, Larry 20
Steitz, Joan, postdoc with Mark Bretscher
    172, 212
Steitz, Tom
    postdoc in David Blow's group 105
    memories of Max Perutz 332
Stent, Gunther 31
Stewart, Murray 95, 156, 160
Stockell, Anne 157
Stowell. Michael 162
Strandberg, Bror 18
Stratagene 242
Strauss, Nick 160
Stretton, Tony 140, 170, 177
    T4 polyheads 117
Stroud, Bob 105
Struhl, Gary 195
Stryer, Lubert 87
Stubbins, Steve 253
Sulston, John 134, 186, 187–9, 192, 268
    cell lineage of *C. elegans* 188
    move to Sanger Centre 193
    Nobel Prize 189
Sundquist, Wes, telomeric ends of
    chromosomes 127
SuperJANET 270
Suzuki, Koichi 225
Suzuki, Masashi 83
Svasti, Jisnuson 231
Sweet, Bob
    postdoc in David Blow's group 105
    memories of LMB 330
Szekely, Maria, DNA sequencing 214
Szent-Gyorgyi, Andrew 153

Takano, Tsuni 88
Tardieu, Annette 130
Taylor, A. 96
Taylor, Frances 299
Taylor, Ken 139
technology transfer 238
Teichmann, Sarah 203
TenEyck, Lynn 82

Thatcher, Margaret 238
  opening CPE 295
Theory of Mutagenesis paper, 1961 58
Thierry, Jean-Claude 225
13-bay extension 294
Thomas, David, TV X-ray detector 99
Thomas, Jean 128
Tompkins, Dick 283
Thomson, Sir George 21
Thompson, Mike 261
Thompson, Ted 290
Thomson, Nichol 174, 184–5, 186
Tissières, Alfred 176
TITAN 274
Titanic, The 298
TMV
  assembly 121
  protein structure 122
Todd, Alexander 67
Todd, Rose 227
Tompkins, Dick 120
Toyoshima, Chikashi 162
transgenic mice in antibody work 249
translocation 246
Travers, Andrew 180–2
  local structure of DNA, work with Horace Drew 181
  nucleosome positioning 181
Tregear, Richard 115
Trentham, David 154
Trinick, John 154
Tuppy, Hans 66
Turnell, Bill 126, 140, 269
tRNA
  proposed by Crick in 1954 58
  structure 123
tRNA synthetase 106
Tweed, Marie, darts 290
Twinn, Keith 98

Unger, Vinzenz 145
Unwin, Nigel, purple membrane – ribosome arrays – gap junction channels – acetylcholine receptor 161

Vallis, Yvonne 204
Vand, Vladimir 30
Varani, Gabriele 159
Veigel, Claudia 154
Venkitaraman, Ashok 249
Verhoeyen, Martine 241
Vickers, Tony 238
Vigers, Guy 142
virus structure, proposal of icosahedral symmetry by Crick and Watson in 1956 54

Von Sengbusch, Peter 115
Voordouw, Gerrit 186

Waldmann, Herman 241, 248
Walker, Fred 253
Walker, Ian, librarian 269
Walker, John 156, 225–7
  thermostable GPDH work 225
  PHF protein 133
  mitochondrial proteins – ATP synthase 226
  Nobel Prize 230
  cricket 284
Wallace, Bonnie 156
Ward, Sam 185
Waterston, Bob 187
  mapping and sequencing genome of C. elegans 192
  mutant work 186
Watson, Herman 87, 88
Watson, Jim 75
  early life 30
  joined MRC Unit 1951 32
  virus substructure 54
  genome funding 192
Watt, Susan 90
Watts-Tobin, Richard 58, 171
Weaver, Warren, first use of term 'molecular biology' 7, 12
Weeds, Alan 95, 162
Weeks, John 181
Weissmann, Charles 214
Wellcome Trust, funding for genome sequencing 192
Westmorland, Joanna 267
White, John 185
  development of confocal microscope 257
  nerve cells and connections in C. elegans 185
White, Rob 196
Whybrow, Bill 262, 268
  cricket 284
Wickham, Sue 102
Widom, Jon, X-ray scattering from chromatin 130
Wigby, Muriel 180
  mutant search in C. elegans 184
Wilcox, Michael
  pattern formation – development 195
Wilde, Deborah 235
Wilkins, Maurice
  at Naples 31
  beginning DNA work 33
Williams, Alan 235
Williams, Gareth 248, 249
Williams, Gwyn, chimaeric antibody 240

Williams, R.J.P. 82
Williams, Robley 54, 121
Willis, Terry 98
Wills, Geoffrey 262
Windle, Alan 83
Winter, Greg 221, 223, 240–2, 249
Wischik, Claude, Alzheimer's Disease PHFs
    133, 142
Witz, Jean 92, 116
wobble hypothesis 168
Wonacott, Alan 154
    rotation camera 99
    thermostable GPDH work 107, 225
Woollard, Tony 253, 261
workshop
    mechanical 253
    instruments, electronics 260
Wright, Christine and Tonie, postdocs in
    David Blow's group 105
writhe, link and twist, applied to DNA
    structure 129
Wu, Ray 214
Wüthrich, Kurt 159

Wyllie, Andrew 196
Wynn, Alec 261
Wynne, Sam, hepatitis virus B core structure
    142, 155

Xenopus laevis group of John Gurdon and
    Ron Laskey 196
X-ray generator design 90, 256

Yanagida, Mitsuhiro, polyhead work 119
Yeast spindle pole body 201
Young, Frank 140
    objection to new Institute of Molecular
    Biology 67
Young, Ian 220

Zamecnik, Paul 59
Zampighi, Guido 161
Zhang, Youshang 115
Ziff, Ed, DNA sequencing 214
Zimmern, Dave, nucleation of TMV 122
zinc finger domain proposed 131
Zubay, Geoffrey 14, 117